THE BIBLE IN THEOLOGY AND PREACHING

Books by Donald K. McKim

The Authority and Interpretation of the Bible: An Historical Approach
(with Jack B. Rogers)
The Authoritative Word: Essays on the Nature of Scripture, editor
Readings in Calvin's Theology, editor
How Karl Barth Changed My Mind, editor
A Guide to Contemporary Hermeneutics, editor
Ramism in William Perkins's Theology
Theological Turning Points
Major Themes in the Reformed Tradition, editor
Encyclopedia of the Reformed Faith, editor
Kerygma: The Bible and Theology

THE
BIBLE
IN
THEOLOGY
&
PREACHING

DONALD K. McKIM

Abingdon Press
Nashville

THE BIBLE IN THEOLOGY AND PREACHING

Foreword to the revised edition and sermons

This book is printed on recycled, acid-free paper.

Library of Congress Cataloging-in-Publication Data
McKim, Donald K.
   The Bible in theology and preaching: / Donald K. Mckim.
     p. cm.
   Rev. ed. of: What Christians believe about the Bible. c1985.
   ISBN 0-687-44611-2 (pbk.: alk. paper)
   1. Bible—Criticism, interpretation, etc.—History—20th century.
  2. Bible—Sermons. I. McKim, Donald K.   What Christians believe
about the Bible. II. Title.
BS500.M35   1993
220.1—dc20   93-30549
                                                CIP

94 95 96 97 98 99 00 01 02 03 — 10 9 8 7 6 5 4 3 2 1

MANUFACTURED IN THE UNITED STATES OF AMERICA

To Jack B. Rogers

Incomparable colleague

Superb scholar

Foremost of friends

with whom I first studied the doctrine of Scripture

Dedicated with gratitude, appreciation, and affection

CONTENTS

SERMON CONTRIBUTORS

William Sloane Coffin, Former Pastor of the Riverside Church, New York City.

James Borland, Professor of New Testament and Theology, Liberty University, and Associate Pastor, Thomas Road Baptist Church, Lynchburg, Virginia.

Roger Nicole, Professor of Theology, Reformed Theological Seminary, Maitland, Florida.

Jack B. Rogers, Vice-President for Southern California and Professor of Theology, Presbyterian Seminary of the West, Pasadena, California.

Elizabeth Achtemeier, Adjunct Professor of Bible and Homiletics, Union Theological Seminary, Richmond, Virginia.

Gail R. O'Day, Associate Professor of Biblical Preaching, Candler School of Theology, Emory University, Atlanta, Georgia.

Robert Neville, Dean and Professor of Philosophy, Religion, and Theology, Boston University, Boston, Massachusetts.

Marjorie Suchocki, Ingraham Professor of Theology, School of Theology at Claremont, Claremont, California.

Stanley Hauerwas, Professor of Theological Ethics, The Divinity School, Duke University, Durham, North Carolina.

Justo González, Director of the Hispanic Summer Program, The Fund for Theological Education, and Editor, *Apuntes,* Decatur, Georgia.

Stephen Breck Reid, Professor of Old Testament, Austin Theological Seminary, Austin, Texas.

Kosuke Koyama, John D. Rockefeller, Jr., Professor of Ecumenics and World Christianity, Union Theological Seminary, New York.

Choan-Seng Song, Professor of Theology and Asian Culture, Pacific School of Religion, Berkeley, California.

Gail A. Ricciuti, Co-pastor, Downtown United Presbyterian Church, Rochester, New York.

Jacquelyn Carr-Hamilton, Assistant Professor of Religion, Virginia Polytechnic Institute and State University, Blacksburg, Virginia.

PREFACE TO THE FIRST EDITION

THIS BOOK HAS GROWN OUT OF A LONG-STANDING INTEREST IN THE DOCTRINE OF Scripture. In teaching theology at the University of Dubuque Theological Seminary, however, I found there was no one volume that explained the basics of the various contemporary views about the nature of the Bible. As I considered this, an unpublished paper by Jack Rogers and Gary Watts, "Six Theological Models of the Early 1980s: Their Theological Methods with Special Reference to Their Use of Scripture," helped to clarify a method of approaching this topic and outlined certain trajectories of thought. Thus the idea for the book was born. I am grateful to Ronald E. Pitkin, who, when he was Executive Editor of Academic and Reference Books, presented my proposal to the Academic Books Editorial Committee of Thomas Nelson Publishers. Paul Franklyn, as my editor, has been most supportive throughout the project.

My family endured several months of my sustained writing, and I express my appreciation to them. LindaJo, Stephen, and Karl have been very supportive. Also, they gave up their own time on the home computer so I could use it to write.

This book is dedicated to Jack Rogers. He has been a model to me in countless ways. He has shown me how faith, scholarship, and caring can all go together. He has demonstrated how a Christian scholar can be continually a person of faith seeking further understanding.

Donald K. McKim
University of Dubuque Theological Seminary
Easter 1985

FOREWORD TO THE
REVISED EDITION

I AM GRATEFUL FOR THE OPPORTUNITY TO HAVE THIS BOOK REVISED, ENLARGED, AND reissued. Since the volume appeared in 1985, discussions about the nature of Scripture have continued. New voices have been heard and new approaches, particularly to hermeneutics and biblical interpretation, have been proposed. Since that time it has become increasingly clear that views about the nature of Scripture need inevitable expression in the task of biblical interpretation and proclamation through preaching. Thus it is a pleasure for me to add sermons for this new edition from those who represent the various theological positions sketched out in this volume.

The body of the presentations from the first edition remain intact. Rather than extensive revisions, I have chosen to add an afterword to take into account other proposed typologies or ways of understanding how theologians regard the nature and function of Scripture. As I indicate, there are a variety of approaches even to undertanding the variety of approaches to Scripture! Additional chapters have been added for black and Asian theologies as well as material on womanist theology. Further bibliographical references have been supplied for other chapters as well.

The chapters here are helpful to both preachers and students of theology because of the writings and writers they examine as well as for assessing more recent theological movements not fully explored in other works on this topic. The chapters tend to focus primarily on historical/systematic writers and do not explicate views of biblical scholars. Nor does this book deal extensively with matters of biblical interpretation or hermeneutics (for which, see my edited volume *A Guide to Contemporary Hermeneutics* [Grand Rapids: Eerdmans, 1986]). Instead the question has been: How do these theological movements perceive the nature of Scripture? If the readers can place themselves in one or more of these movements, the preacher will begin to understand the authority of Scripture during the preaching event.

I believe the trajectories indicated here are clear enough to portray basic views so readers can form their own judgments now as they continue to read works on Scripture. I have found the present categories to be helpful and understandable in oral presentations both in seminary and congregational settings.

Those who provided sermons for this edition have been most gracious. I believe their overall theological views are congruent with the chapters to which their sermons correspond. A value of the sermons is to show how in preaching a particular perspective may be expressed. Not all of the sermons relate specifically to the nature of Scripture, but they do all involve the interpretation of Scripture where convictions about the nature of the Bible will certainly be expressed in practice. The addition of the sermons brings an important extra dimension to this work and will, I hope, expand and enhance its usefulness for a number of readers.

I also thank my editor, Paul Franklyn. In a strange providence, he was editor of the original volume when it was published by Thomas Nelson Publishers and now has served in the same capacity again with Abingdon Press. His perceptive ideas and support are most heartily appreciated.

My original dedication to my teacher, colleague, and friend, Jack Rogers, still stands. The years have only deepened its meaning.

As always, my wife, LindaJo, and sons, Stephen and Karl, have brought me joy, and I thank them for their ongoing love.

So with gratitude for the opportunity of this update, and hopes that this volume will continue to be useful in mapping out the panorama of views on the horizon today, I invite you to turn again to what Christians believe about the Bible.

—Donald K. McKim
February 1993

INTRODUCTION

MANY THEOLOGICAL OPTIONS ARE AVAILABLE TODAY. NUMEROUS THEOLOGICAL positions are found within Christian churches. Each has its own style and approach as well as its distinctive perspective that sets it apart from others.

Many different views about the Bible are present today as well. The different theologies have their own ways of understanding the nature of Scripture and its appropriate interpretation. What a Christian theology says about the Bible will significantly affect its concerns and the rest of its approach in general.

This book is written to sort out the varieties of beliefs about the Bible. What follows tries to show the basic views of major contemporary theologies about Scripture. The first two chapters deal with significant ecclesiastical traditions, while the remaining ones cover important theological positions.

For each position, a caption or "bumper sticker" is given. This blurb tries to capture the essence of that theology's views about Scripture. These are not the only slogans that could be used, but they seem appropriate in the light of the way Scripture is viewed in each instance.

Theological doctrines, to be well understood, need to be set in contexts. Each chapter presents an initial description of the theology at hand. Then attention is given to backgrounds, with concentration on important historical, philosophical, or cultural contexts from which the theology arose. This sheds light on the position and its major beliefs. It also helps to explain why Scripture is viewed as it is.

Since the doctrine of Scripture is closely connected with other theological issues and methods of doing theology, these are considered when they are particularly relevant. Since each position has its own history and development, the categories through which they view Scripture differ. In a broad way, one can say what each theology believes about topics such as revelation or the authority or inspiration of the Bible. But these categories may not be specifically developed in themselves. Thus the special focus of each position must be seen. Some views elaborate one aspect of the nature of Scripture, such as "inspiration," to a more detailed degree. Others may generally assume such a concept and work in very different arenas. So each position must be examined in itself.

The following expositions cannot be exhaustive treatments. In some cases, representative figures are chosen and citations made from a number of different works. At other times, one major figure is targeted and that person's work made the central concern. This is the case with neo-orthodox and existential theologies, where the works of Barth and Tillich are used. Other theologians could have been chosen as well. Separate chapters survey South American, African-American, and Asian-American theologies, while feminist and womanist theologies are considered within the same chapter.

It is hoped that this volume will introduce in a neutral fashion these basic beliefs about the Bible and the theological movements themselves. The chapters can be read separately or together to achieve either a specific look or a general overview of what Christians believe about the Bible.

PART ONE
ECCLESIASTICAL TRADITIONS

I

ROMAN CATHOLICISM

Classic and Contemporary

THE ISSUE OF SCRIPTURE IN ROMAN CATHOLICISM TOUCHES ON A VARIETY OF theological topics. Related to the Roman Catholic understanding of the Bible are Catholic views of authority, tradition, the church, and papal infallibility. The church's views have developed explicitness through the centuries. Chiefly, the official positions of the church about the Bible are found in the pronouncements of popes and church councils.[1] Among these are the statements from the Council of Florence (1442), the decrees of the Council of Trent (1546), the decrees of Vatican Council I (1870), and particularly the *Dogmatic Constitution on Divine Revelation (Dei Verbum)* of Vatican Council II (1965). Important papal biblical encyclicals are *Providentissimus Deus* by Leo XIII (1893), *Spiritus Paraclitus* by Benedict XV (1920), and *Divino afflante Spiritu* by Pius XII (1943).[2] Responses and instructions by the Pontifical Biblical Commission and the Holy Office have also been issued since 1905. Not all of these documents are accorded the same weight of authority in Catholic tradition. The decrees of the last three ecumenical councils (Trent, Vatican I, and Vatican II) are of highest import. Anathemas are attached to some canons of the Council of Trent and Vatican I, making them of more juridical force than other statements by councils. Vatican II did not pronounce new dogmatic definitions or issue sanctions against those who reject its teachings.[3]

While official Catholic teachings are contained in the type of documents mentioned, these do not set forth a comprehensive and systematic doctrine of Scripture. The theologians of the church are those charged with synthesizing data and producing a full dogmatic treatment. As long as theologians and individual Catholics do not move against the established doctrines of the church, they may proceed as they deem best in their systematic work. The ecclesiastical magisterium, the body that formulates official Catholic doctrine, usually plays a supervisory, judicial role and intervenes only when a serious crisis, error, or controversy arises. Thus, in a sense, "one cannot fairly set forth *the* Catholic teaching concerning Scripture. The church leaves its members free to follow any theological theories within the bounds of orthodoxy. Orthodoxy itself provides not so much a doctrine as a set of negative norms which serve as guidelines for theological speculation."[4]

This position is possible because "except for several brief but important statements issued by Trent and Vatican I, the Roman Catholic Church has not issued any infallible or irreformable pronouncements in regard to the Bible. With these exceptions, official Catholic teachings on Scripture may be regarded as fallible and therefore subject to challenge."[5]

In order to gain perspective on how these views developed as well as to see what the church's teachings are and how they are interpreted, it is necessary to survey certain background dimensions.

BACKGROUNDS

Sources of Authority

In the year A.D. 434, the theologian Vincent of Lérins wrote his *Commonitory* to attack the predestination teachings of Augustine and his successors. Vincent claimed they were innovations and deviated from the tradition of orthodoxy. In this work, Vincent described the authority of the church's tradition when he wrote that it consisted of what had been believed "everywhere, always, by all."[6] One century later in the treatise *On the Christian Faith* attributed to Boethius, the principle enunciated by Vincent was affirmed: "The catholic church, then, spread throughout the world, is known by three particular marks: whatever is believed and taught in it has the authority of the Scriptures, or of universal tradition, or at least of its own and proper usage."[7]

In these statements, the requirement of "universality" meant that in order for a doctrine to be recognized as a teaching of the church, it must be recognized by all the churches (catholic, universally). This distinguished the teaching from the private theory or viewpoints of individuals or single theologians, for it was the catholic church that was "the repository of truth, the dispenser of grace, the guarantee of salvation, the matrix of acceptable worship."[8]

The authoritative status of the church had been supported in its earliest period by several sources of authority. Christians believed that final authority for salvation and the life of faith rested in God, who embodied this authority in Jesus Christ. The authority of God in Christ was fundamental as Christ exercised Lordship over the church.

With the spread of Christianity, the church recognized that the authority of Christ was exercised through apostles and in the Christian community. Apostolic authority was not inherent in apostles themselves, but was authorized by God. With the death of the apostles, however, questions about the locus of apostolic authority became important. How would God continue to exercise authority in the post-apostolic church? Two possibilities arose. First, God could work through the apostolic writings that could be added to the church's use of the Old Testament as a "canon" of Scripture. Second, God could work through the ongoing activity of the church. Pastors and teachers could be seen as having special authority on the basis of the apostolic message they preached and taught.[9]

A related issue had to do with how the church could respond to the variety of interpretations of the faith that arose. Some of these appeared to endanger the essence of the faith. Early "heresies" such as Judaizing Christianity, Gnosticism, Marcionism, Montanism, and Monarchianism made it crucial for the church to understand where the locus of its authority rested.[10]

In the early centuries, the church came to recognize several sources as the bases of its authority.

1. Canon. With the death of the apostles, the church knew it no longer had the personal reminiscences of the apostles from which to draw. Apostolic teachings, however, were preserved and passed on to following generations through traditions. The original Christian gospel was the message of Christ spoken and transmitted by apostolic witnesses. The term to describe this "handing over" or "delivery" refers both to the process of its communication (Gr. *paradidomai*) and its content (Gr. *paradosis*).[11] The content of this body of Christian teaching was called "tradition."[12]

Until well into the second century, the Christian church looked to the Old Testament for its "canon," or collection of sacred, authoritative writings.[13] Traditionally the date of the fixing of the Old Testament canon has been connected with the so-called Council or Synod of Jamnia, ca. A.D. 90–100.[14] These writings were the Christian Bible. They were read from the Christian perspective of faith.[15] From them, "the apostles of the first century and the apologists of the second century drew their basic texts as they proclaimed and defended the gospel; the reading of them was sufficient to convince educated pagans of the truth of Christianity."[16]

During the early decades of the church, apostolic writings were produced that eventually became the New Testament Scriptures.[17] "Lists" of books appeared to designate bodies of authoritative writings for Christians.[18] In the second and third centuries, the process of ascertaining authoritative writings intensified until the first official document, which delineated the present New Testament canon, was written. This was the Thirty-ninth Festal Letter of Bishop Athanasius at Easter in A.D. 367. It listed the twenty-seven books of the New Testament, which became the church's official New Testament canon. The Synod of Hippo in 393 and the Third Synod of Carthage in 397 followed and ratified the list of Athanasius.[19] Thus the church turned to its Scriptures as a source of Christian instruction and understanding in the early centuries.

2. Creeds. A second source of authority for the early church rested in the creeds that emerged in Christian communities. Within the first Christian generation, brief summaries of the apostles' preaching developed.[20] When new converts came into the Christian faith, there was a need to instruct them in Christian beliefs. These summary statements served that purpose and were used in the context of baptisms and public professions of faith.[21] In the second century, Irenaeus referred to these summary statements as "the rule [canon] of truth."[22] Tertullian, in the third century, regularly referred to the "rule of faith," or *regula fidei.* [23]

The rise of various Christian teachings, some later called "heresies," also made it imperative for the church to have authoritative statements of its beliefs. Fixed, traditional formulas of faith became "a key to what the church thought the Scriptures came to, where it was, so to speak, that their weight fell, what was their drift."[24]

Gradually, creeds developed as confessions of this faith. At times when differing opinions on theological issues or biblical interpretation arose, the church met in councils to discuss the issue of faith. The first such council was the council of Nicea in A.D. 325, from which emerged the Nicene Creed.[25] The Apostles' Creed, with its origins in the Old Roman Symbol of the second century, gradually became the most widely used confessional statement of the Western Church and took its final form in the ninth century.[26] These two creeds, along with the Athanasian Creed from the end of the fourth century, were the first three ecumenical creeds of the church. They provided statements of Christian beliefs for the instruction of believers and witnessed to the church's faith in the face of varieties of theological positions.

3. Church Leadership. Along with the canon of Scripture and the creeds and confessions, the church recognized apostolic tradition as continuing through the leaders of the churches. The first-century "offices" of the church as found in the New Testament continued. These included apostles, prophets, teachers, *episcopoi* (bishops; overseers), deacons, presbyters, and evangelists.[27] From this time there developed "an idea of 'succession to the apostles,' which has been interpreted as succession in doctrine, or as succession in office, or both."[28]

With the rise of the variant opinions in the second century, particularly Gnosticism, the faithful transmission of apostolic teaching became crucial. The church believed that the Holy Spirit would ultimately protect the truth of the gospel. But to recognize how the Spirit protected the gospel, the church linked its reliable transmission to the "seats" or "sees" (Lat. *sed*) of bishops. The origin of sees was attributed to the apostles. The teachings from these episcopal sees "became important for the councils, which endeavored to set forth authoritative interpretations of 'the faith . . . delivered to the saints' (Jude 3)."[29]

Through these three channels of authority—canon, creed, and church leadership—the early church carried out its mission in the world. The interplay among these three was to have significant consequences for the subsequent history and development of the Roman Catholic Church. Because of these interactions, Catholic views on Scripture cannot be isolated from other theological doctrines.

Development of the Papacy

The see at Rome came to gain special significance as a seat of authority. Roman bishops were mostly aloof from early doctrinal controversies in the Eastern churches. However, by the middle of the third century, "they seem to have assumed special responsibility for preserving and interpreting the faith of 'antiquity' because of the prerogative of the See of Peter (*cathedra Petri*)."[30] Rome became in many ways the preeminent see, and the bishop of Rome the preeminent bishop.[31] Thus the papacy began to develop.

The position of the pope in the Roman Catholic Church and throughout Christendom in the coming centuries is a long and complex story.[32] It was "characteristic of the papacy, as it had already been much earlier of the episcopacy, that it was not only a practical system of ecclesiastical governance subject to adjustment and compromise, but also a doctrine that was to be believed, taught, and confessed by the church on the basis of the word of God."[33] Crucial to the doctrine of the papacy was the belief that, as Pope Innocent I expressed it, from Rome "the other churches, like waters proceeding from their natal source . . . [like] pure streams from an uncorrupt head, should take up what they ought to enjoin."[34] By the sixth century the Formula of Pope Hormisdas (515) stated that in Rome "the catholic religion has always been preserved immaculate."[35]

Roman Catholic understandings of the primacy of the bishop of Rome (the pope) and his special position rest on the interpretation of New Testament texts related to the apostle Peter and the "Petrine function." Chief among these is Matthew 16:18, in which Jesus said to Peter: "And I tell you, you are Peter [Gr. *Petros*], and on this rock [Gr. *petra*] I will build my church, and the gates of Hades will not prevail against it." As interpreted by Pope Gregory I in one of his letters:

> To all who know the Gospel it is obvious that by the voice of the Lord the care of the entire church was committed to the holy apostle and prince of all the apostles, Peter. . . . Behold, he received the keys of the kingdom of heaven, the power to bind and loose was given to him, and the care and principality of the entire church was committed to him. . . . Am I defending my own cause in this matter? Am I vindicating some special injury of my own? Is it not rather the cause of the Almighty God, the cause of the universal church? . . . Certainly, in honor of Peter, the prince of the apostles, [the title "universal"] was offered to the Roman pontiff by the venerable Council of Chalcedon.[36]

Other important texts have been John 21:17 and Luke 22:31-32. Peter is seen as the "rock" on which the church is to be founded (Matt. 16:18). It is for Peter that Jesus prays so his faith will not fail (Luke 22:32). Peter has been given power and authority in receiving the "keys of the kingdom" (Matt. 16:19) so that he with others has the task of "binding and loosing" (Matt. 18:18) as well as "strengthening the believers" (Acts 15:32).

The primacy of Peter and the growing powers of the bishop of Rome as pope are expressed in numerous theological statements, such as that of Ambrose Autpert, who said Peter was "the bearer of the person of the church."[37] For Isidore of Seville, the pope as supreme pontiff was "the chief of priests . . . the highest priest," for he appointed all other priests in the church and had all ecclesiastical offices at his disposal.[38] For Hincar, archbishop of Reims in the ninth century, the "solicitude for all the churches has been committed to the holy Roman church, in Peter, the prince of the apostles."[39]

During the early Middle Ages (600–1050), churches of the West recognized the "vicar of St. Peter" with honor, but Eastern churches rarely consulted him.[40] During the High Middle Ages (1050–1500), the papacy became the central focus of Western Christendom. Struggles between papal power and secular rulers had been a feature of Western society until Pope Gregory VII (1073–1085) declared the papacy free from secular rulers. His Gregorian reforms, summarized in twenty-seven *dicta* (*Dictatus Papae*, 1075), announced among other things that the pope had the power to depose emperors.[41]

In 1198, Innocent III became pope (1198–1216). His pontificate is often considered "the apogee of the medieval papacy, the culmination of the hierocratic tendencies for which Gregory VII had fought."[42] Of the papal office, Innocent wrote:

> To [the pope] is said in the person of the prophet: "I have set you over nations and over kingdoms, to root up and to pull down and to waste and to destroy and to build and to

plant." [Jer. 1:10] To me also is said in the person of the apostle: "I will give to you the keys of the kingdom of heaven. . . . " Thus, others were called to a part of the care, but Peter alone assumed the plenitude of power. You see then who is the vicar of Jesus Christ, successor of Peter, anointed of the Lord, a God of Pharaoh, set between God and man, *lower than God but higher than man,* who judges all and is judged by no one.[43]

In the following centuries, the medieval papacy went through a series of crises, including attempts at reforms by the conciliar movement, a great schism, and "Babylonian Captivity" with rival popes in three locations vying for power.[44] By the opening of the sixteenth century, demands for institutional and doctrinal reform in the church were being heard.[45] In the face of the Protestant Reformation, the Roman Catholic Church responded at the Council of Trent (1545–1563) by further defining its faith and instituting ecclesiastical changes through the power of the papacy.

SCRIPTURE IN ROMAN CATHOLIC THEOLOGY

Canon and Inspiration

The term *canon* means a rule or standard by which something is judged. By accepting a canon of biblical writings, "the Catholic Church implicitly declares that these writings have special authority for and in the church."[46] As noted above, by the fourth century the church had settled the books of the Christian canon. In the history of the Catholic Church, the Council of Hippo in 393 (Canon 38) officially listed the church's canonical writings. This same canon was endorsed by the Third Council of Carthage in 397 (Canon 47) and was repeated by the Fourth Council of Carthage in 419 (Canon 29).[47] Several popes in the fifth century and the Council of Florence in the fifteenth century further reasserted it, and the Council of Trent reinforced it by imposing "anathema" on those who denied the canonical Scriptures.[48] In 1870 the First Vatican Council stated, as Trent said, that the books "contained in the ancient Latin edition of the Vulgate" are held by the church "to be sacred and canonical."[49]

Perhaps the usual interpretation of the significance of the canon is that "in drawing up the canon, the church vouches for the fact that these books *and no others* are sacred, inspired, and divinely authoritative." But Avery Dulles goes on to note, "canonization also can be interpreted to mean that these books, *and perhaps others,* are sacred, inspired, and divinely authoritative. In the latter case, the church would leave open the possibility of adding to its canon."[50] While he finds it "very unlikely that the list will be changed in the future," he also states that "to the best of my knowledge, the canon never has been defined in an exclusive sense. Thus it seems possible, at least in theory, that a new book could be added."[51]

At the time of the Protestant Reformation, the Reformers followed the Hebrew Bible and its thirty-nine books of the Old Testament as constituting the Protestant canon of Scripture. The Hebrew Scriptures omit seven books (and parts of two others) that are retained in the forty-six books of the Latin Vulgate, which forms the Catholic Old Testament.[52] The Vulgate, translated in the fourth century by Jerome, is cited in Catholic pronouncements as the Bible containing the approved canon. Yet the Vulgate has not been viewed as an inspired text in and of itself. It is rather a "substantially reliable translation, free from doctrinal error."[53] The Council of Trent, while approving the Vulgate translation, also called for a critical edition of the Vulgate text.

It has been the Catholic understanding since the time of the early church that the Scriptures are inspired by God.[54] However, it was not until the First Vatican Council issued the decrees of its third session on April 24, 1870, that an assertion was made by an official Catholic body on the nature of scriptural inspiration. Earlier documents had spoken of Scripture's inspiration. The Decree of the Council of Florence (1442) professed

one and the same God as the author of the Old and New Testament, that is, of the Law and the Prophets and the Gospel, since the saints of both Testaments have spoken with the inspiration of the same Holy Spirit, whose books . . . it accepts and venerates.[55]

But Vatican I went on to add that

the Church holds [these books] to be sacred and canonical, not because, having been carefully composed by mere human industry, they were afterwards approved by her authority, nor merely because they contain revelation with no admixture of error, but because, having been written by the inspiration of the Holy Spirit, they have God for their author and have been delivered as such to the Church herself.[56]

This statement of Vatican I spoke positively of inspiration in that by "the inspiration of the Holy Spirit" (*Spiritu Sancto inspirante*) the Scriptures are documents that have "God for their author." At the Council of Trent (also quoted by Vatican I), the statement on Scripture said that church belief

is contained in the written books and unwritten traditions which have come down to us, having been received by the apostles from the mouth of Christ Himself, or from the apostles themselves by the dictation of the Holy Spirit [*Spiritu Sancto dictante*], and have been transmitted as it were from hand to hand.[57]

While Trent's statement on inspiration used the image of "dictation" to describe the inspiration of Scripture, Vatican I spoke only of God as the "author" of Scripture.[58] A further description of the mode of inspiration was provided in the papal encyclical letter *Providentissimus Deus,* issued by Pope Leo XIII on November 18, 1893. Leo's view of biblical inspiration was that

by supernatural power, [God] so moved and impelled them to write—He so assisted them when writing—that the things which He ordered, and those only, they, first, rightly understood, then willed faithfully to write down, and finally expressed in apt words and with infallible truth. Otherwise, it could not be said that He was the Author of the entire Scripture.[59]

For Leo, this view of the inspiration of Scripture also entailed Scripture's inerrancy, its depiction of truth on the matters with which it dealt. As Leo wrote:

For all the books which the Church receives as sacred and canonical are written wholly and entirely, with all their parts, at the dictation of the Holy Spirit; and so far is it from being possible that any error can coexist with inspiration, that inspiration not only is essentially incompatible with error, but excludes and rejects it as absolutely and necessarily as it is impossible that God Himself, the supreme Truth, can utter that which is not true.[60]

For Leo, "the formula of divine authorship was understood in a literary sense: author-writer *simpliciter.*"[61] By the laws of logic, if God is the "author" of Scripture and God is perfect, without error, humans as the "writers" of Scripture would also share in this perfection of "inerrancy" when writing.

The formulations of Vatican II are contained in the *Dei Verbum* ("Dogmatic Constitution on Divine Revelation"). The main features of Vatican I's teachings on inspiration were reiterated with the statement: "To compose the sacred books, God chose certain men who, all the while he employed them in this task, made full use of their powers and faculties so that, though he acts in them and by them, it was as true authors that they consigned to writing whatever he wanted written, and no more."[62]

Dulles has noted that Vatican II's statement affirmed that "the human writers were not mere secretaries but true authors, thus by implication repudiating certain 'dictation' theories."[63] Contemporary Catholic theologians, he observes, generally

> reject the idea that by inspiration, God directly infused words or ideas into the minds of the biblical writers. Inspiration does not relieve its recipients of the necessity of applying their own powers to the research and composition from which books result. It assures only that those powers are so effectively assisted that the resulting books will serve as God intends for the guidance of the church.[64]

In the light of the Vatican II insistence on the human writers as true authors, Dulles as a contemporary Catholic theologian suggests that a rethinking of the sense in which God is the "author" of Scripture should be made. His full statement is illuminating:

> The term *auctor* in Latin (or *archēgos* in Greek) does not necessarily mean *literary author,* but rather *originator.* Thus it is possible to say that God is author of the Bible in the sense that God initiates and controls the process whereby it is written, even though he does not dictate or miraculously infuse the ideas and words. In this view God would be, in the first instance, the author of the people of Israel and of their faith, and of the development of that faith through Jesus Christ. Inasmuch as God personally involves himself in salvation history, God could be called the author, indirectly, of the documents whereby the people of God express their faith in a divinely guided and reliable fashion.
>
> Thus conceived, biblical inspiration results in a body of traditional literature which represents the faith of the people of God at various stages of development. In a special way, it expresses the faith of the prophetic and apostolic leaders who helped to shape the faith of Israel and of the church. A sufficient deposit of that inspired literature has survived to allow the church of subsequent centuries to constantly test its own teaching and piety against that of the recipients of the Jewish and Christian revelation.[65]

Other contemporary Catholic theologians besides Dulles, such as Raymond E. Brown and Bruce Vawter, have noted that the Vatican II document stated that "the books of Scripture, firmly, faithfully and without error, teach that truth which God, for the sake of our salvation, wished to see confided to the sacred Scriptures."[66] The significance of this from their perspective is that the term *inerrancy,* which had been present in the earliest (1962) draft of the document, "eventually disappeared from the text of the conciliar discussion if not from the discussions themselves."[67] Vawter wrote:

> "Without error" is predicated of the Scripture specifically in respect to the truth that God willed to be present there for the sake of our salvation. The Bible is no longer seen as automatically inerrant in virtue of its being the work of an inspired writer. A certain truth only is ascribed to it, and that only as it is the vehicle of a divine salvific intention.[68]

As Raymond Brown explains this, "it is not as if some parts of Scripture teach without error 'truth for the sake of salvation,' and other parts do not. Everything in Scripture is inerrant to the extent to which it conforms to the salvific purpose of God."[69] In this way, contemporary Catholic theologians can uphold the classical teachings of the church on issues of canon and inspiration while at the same time being open, receptive, and in many cases frontrunners of current biblical scholarship.[70]

Scripture and Tradition

Roman Catholic statements about Scripture and its nature are always made—whether by individual theologians or ecclesiastical councils—within the context of the church. The issue of the authority of Scripture and its right interpretation is an issue that in Catholic theology is related to wider questions of the relation of Scripture and tradition, the nature of the church, and specifically the primacy and functioning of the pope. In the late Middle Ages, various reform movements within the Roman Catholic Church raised the issue of where ultimate authority in the church was to be found. Focused most sharply, this was the question of how scriptural authority functioned in relation to the authority of the traditions of the church. Two opposing currents of thought developed. Both were "concerned with the authority of Tradition, but Tradition conceived in two radically differing fashions."[71]

One stream, following the lead of Thomas Bradwardine (1290–1349) of Oxford, stressed the "exclusive and final authority of Holy Scripture."[72] Bradwardine argued for "the sufficiency of Holy Scripture as understood by the Fathers and doctors of the Church. In the case of disagreement between these interpreters, Holy Scripture has the final authority."[73] The tradition of the church is the means by which the faith or truth contained in Holy Scripture is received. Implicit in this postion was "a sharp distinction between the word of God in 'Scripture alone,' which was the only authority deserving of total credence, and the word of 'all the saints except for Christ,' whether popes or church fathers or even apostles, apart from Scripture."[74]

The second stream, following the views of William of Occam (1285?–1347), argued that "there are many catholic truths that neither are contained explicitly in Sacred Scripture nor can be inferred solely from its contents."[75] For Occam there were ultimately two sources from which doctrines may be derived. One source is Scripture, which contains the truth of God. The second is through the approval of the pope, who does not invent but rather "formulates what truth is in a particular respect since truth is eternal."[76] Thus in this stream authority is given to both scriptural and extra-scriptural revelation. Ecclesiastical traditions, including canon law, were seen to have an authority equal to that of Scripture.[77]

Up to the Reformation period, both traditions viewed the authority of Scripture as the primary source for Christian faith. Neither rejected the authority of the church nor treated Scripture in isolation from the Catholic Church. The question between the two views was

> whether the church, in exercising this doctrinal authority, had the right to promulgate as apostolic doctrines even some beliefs that could not find explicit warrant in what was "written in the Bible" or in what was "deduced from this alone by an obvious conclusion," but that were rather purported to have "come down to us through the successive transmission of the apostles and others, as equivalent to the canonical Scripture" in authority and apostolic authenticity.[78]

The tension between the two views had major consequences throughout the period of the Reformation. At stake ultimately was whether church tradition provided only an authoritative interpretation of Scripture or whether it also had the authority to expand the scriptural revelation. The Protestant Reformers with their stress on *sola Scriptura* argued for the primacy of Scripture over the church and rejected traditions not explicity biblically grounded. The Roman Catholic Church claimed that "the very Scripture whose 'sole' authority was being pitted against that of the church depended for its authentication on the church."[79] Because the church was the authenticating body, no truth for Catholic faith could ultimately lie completely "outside" Scripture. Going back to Augustine's dictum: "For my part, I should not believe the gospel except as moved by the authority of the catholic church," it could be argued as Gabriel Biel (d. 1495) did: "The truth that holy mother church defines or accepts as catholic is to be believed with the same veneration as if it were expressed in Holy Writ."[80] Without the authority of the church and its tradition, even the Scriptures could not be trusted.

At the Fourth Session of the Council of Trent (April 8, 1546), the Catholic Church clarified its views in the light of the challenge of the Protestant Reformers. Trent decreed that the source (Lat. *fons*) of

> all salutary truth and moral disciples [is] the gospel promised before by the prophets in the holy Scriptures, promulgated by the very mouth of our Lord Jesus Christ the Son of God, then to be preached by his Apostles to every creature [and that] this truth and discipline is contained in written books and unwritten traditions which were received by the Apostles from the mouth of Christ himself or by the Apostles themselves under the inspiration of the Holy Spirit [*Spiritu Sancto dictante*].[81]

Interpreting Trent, George H. Tavard has written that the source of all truth and Christian behavior is the gospel of Christ, which comes through the power of the Holy Spirit. The Spirit uses

> two sets of vessels: Holy Scripture and traditions. In as far as they convey the same Gospel of Christ, in as far as they channel the original impetus whereby the Spirit moved the Apostles, both Scriptures and traditions are entitled to the same adhesion of faith. For faith reaches Christ and the Spirit whatever the medium used to contact us. . . . The touchstone of a Scripture as of a tradition is the Gospel, "kept in the Catholic Church in a continuous succession."[82]

ROMAN CATHOLICISM

The question of how Scripture and tradition are interpreted becomes one of major concluding interest. During the late thirteenth and early fourteenth centuries in a controversy over poverty, the term *infallibility* came to be associated with the papal *magisterium* or teaching authority.[83] Guido Terreni, a Carmelite theologian of the fourteenth century, was one of the first to speak explicitly of the "infallible" truth of the Roman pontiff, speaking on matters of faith. He wrote that "in the determination of the things that pertain to faith the pope is directed [*dirigatur*] by the Holy Spirit and the Holy Spirit speaks in him." Guido claimed on the basis of biblical and patristic statements about the indefectibility of the church that "the immutable and invariable authority of the catholic church . . . resides universally, after Christ, solely in the supreme pontiff and not in any private person." This meant to him that "the lord pope, to whose authority it belongs to determine and declare the propositions that belong to the faith, cannot [*non possit*] err."[84] Thus the term *infallibility* (Lat. *infallibilitas*) took on a highly technical meaning.[85]

Controversy about this view of the pope's authority continued in the Catholic Church for four centuries. Conciliarists, those who sought to locate the church's teaching authority in church councils, resisted attributing this authority to the pope. On July 18, 1870, Vatican I Council gave formal definition to the dogma of papal infallibility. The canon declared that

> the Roman Pontiff, when he speaks *ex cathedra*—that is, when in the discharge of the office of Shepherd and teacher of all Christians, he defines in virtue of his supreme Apostolic authority a doctrine of faith or morals to be held by the universal Church—enjoys, through the divine assistance promised to him in Blessed Peter, that infallibility with which the divine Redeemer willed to equip his Church when it defines a doctrine of faith or morals; and therefore such definitions of the Roman Pontiff are irreformable of themselves, not however from the consent of the Church.[86]

Catholic theologians have explicated the specific meanings of this dogma of infallibility that were implicit in the Vatican I teaching.[87] Briefly, some of the important aspects are:

1. The pope must act as universal pastor and teacher. His goal must be to "define" (to impose on believers a precisely formulated truth in the name of fidelity to divine revelation) a truth contained either explicitly or implicitly in divine revelation.[88] The pope thus must be acting in his capacity as pastor and teacher of the church.

2. The pope must employ his supreme apostolic authority. The pope must invoke the full force of the doctrinal authority of his office for what he says.

3. Papal infallibility refers to a personal act of one pope. Since "the definitions of the Roman pontiff are irreformable because of their very nature and not because of the consent of the Church" (*ex sese, non autem ex consensu ecclesiae*—DS 3074), there is no external procedure of the church a pope must follow before his utterance can be infallible. His act must be a free act and must flow from his understanding. Due to this, the basic rule for interpreting infallible papal statements is to discover "the mind of the pontiff."

4. The pope must intend to define for the whole church. An intent to teach the faithful what is a universal, binding obligation must be present.

27

5. The pope's intention to define must be manifest. As the Code of Canon Law puts it: "Nothing is to be considered as dogmatically declared or defined unless that intention is manifest." This has the effect of establishing that the other conditions must be clear to the church if its members are to be bound by the pope's infallible definition.[89]

These are conditions implicit in the pope's speaking *ex cathedra* (from the chair of Peter) on matters of faith and morals. Among the further properties of infallible statements are that they agree with Scripture and tradition, with the present faith of the church, and with the universal episcopate and that sufficient investigation be made to ascertain that "his definition in fact conforms with the Christian revelation."[90] As *Lumen gentium* of Vatican II stated, the pope "strikes painstakingly and by appropriate means to inquire into that revelation and to give apt expression to its contents" (Art. 25).[91]

Only two papal pronouncements have been generally recognized as having been promulgated by papal infallibility. These are the dogma of the Immaculate Conception (1854) and the Assumption of the Blessed Virgin (1950).[92] In recent times, the concept of papal infallibility has been questioned by Catholics like Hans Küng and has led to his debates with other theologians, most notably Karl Rahner.[93]

Scripture and Tradition Today

The teachings of Vatican II specifically tried to avoid the implication that the tradition of the Roman Catholic Church contained any truth that is not also found revealed in Holy Scripture. The implication of the *Dogmatic Constitution on Divine Revelation* is that Scripture and tradition are a single source for divine doctrine. Article 9 says: "Sacred Tradition and sacred Scripture, then, are bound closely together, and communicate one with the other. For both of them, flowing out from the same divine well-spring come together in some fashion to form one thing, and move towards the same goal."[94]

Scripture is called "the speech of God" (Art. 9) and the "written Word of God" (Art. 24). Tradition is never called the Word of God, but "transmits in its entirety the Word of God" (Art. 9).

This does not mean that Scripture is all that is needed and that tradition is superfluous. According to Vatican II, it is tradition that helps assure the correct interpretation of Scripture: "Thus it comes about that the Church does not draw her certainty about all revealed truths from the holy Scriptures alone. Hence, both Scripture and Tradition must be accepted and honored with equal feelings of devotion and reverence" (Art. 9). Specifically, it is by tradition that "the full canon of sacred books is known to the Church" (Art. 8). This recognition of the place of Scripture in the church shows how Scripture and tradition coinhere.[95]

II

PROTESTANTISM

Lutheran, Reformed, and Anabaptist

THE PROTESTANT REFORMATION PRODUCED A NUMBER OF FAR-REACHING RELIGIOUS changes throughout Europe during the sixteenth century. The Protestant movement was anticipated by earlier movements for church reform reaching back to the fourteenth century. The Waldensians and Hussites (followers of John Hus, 1373–1415) in central Europe and the Lollards (followers of John Wycliffe, ca. 1329–1384) in England attacked the hierarchical and legal structures of the Roman Catholic Church. In particular, the strongest criticism was made against the papacy for what was perceived as its worldliness, corruption, and abuses of the Christian gospel. By the beginning of the sixteenth century, further social, economic, political, and intellectual factors combined with the theological leadership of prominent Reformers to launch a reformation of the church that lasted until the mid-seventeenth century in Europe.[1]

BACKGROUNDS

The Protestant Reformation began in Germany in 1517. Martin Luther (1483–1546), an Augustinian monk who was a professor of biblical theology at Wittenburg University, launched an attack against the Roman Catholic practice of selling indulgences. Luther questioned the church's authority to forgive the temporal punishment due to sin when a person bought an indulgence because the guilt of that sin was already forgiven by God. This occasioned an immediate controversy with Johann Tetzel (ca. 1465–1519), who was selling indulgences in a neighboring town for the purpose of raising money to rebuild St. Peter's Cathedral in Rome.

On October 31, 1517, Luther issued Ninety-five Theses for debate among theologians.[2] In them he questioned a number of theological points, particularly that any penance or works prescribed by the church can produce forgiveness. Instead, Luther argued that it was through the merits of Jesus Christ alone that divine forgiveness comes and "the true treasure of the church is the most holy Gospel of the glory and grace of God."[3] Luther's study of the works of Augustine had led him to reject the emphases in late medieval theology on the necessity of "good works" for salvation.[4] His study of the biblical texts, the writings of the early church theologians, and other historical studies done by Renaissance humanists such as Lorenzo Valla (ca. 1406–1457) led Luther to question the claims of the Roman Catholic pope to be the proper supreme authority for the church.[5] Instead, for Luther the supreme authority for the Christian and the church was Jesus Christ as Christ is known through the Holy Scriptures. This led Luther to rediscover what he believed to be the teaching of New

Testament Christianity: that salvation comes by the grace of God through faith in Jesus Christ and not by performing works of righteousness. This emphasis was captured by Luther's watchwords for the Protestant Reformation: *sola fide* (faith alone), *sola gratia* (grace alone), and *sola Scriptura* (Scripture alone).[6]

One of the first to be influenced by Luther's teachings was Ulrich Zwingli (1484–1531) of Zurich. Zwingli was ordained a Roman Catholic priest and served two parishes until he was called to be the people's (or preaching) priest at the Zurich Great Church in 1518. Zwingli had been trained as a Christian humanist and as such had turned to the Bible as the foundational document of the Christian faith.[7] By 1516 he had diligently studied the Greek New Testament published by Erasmus (1466?–1536) and caused tremendous excitement in Zurich when early in 1519 he announced his intention to preach continuous exegetical sermons, beginning with the Gospel of Matthew.[8] Zwingli led the Reformation in Zurich and was actively involved in giving theological leadership through drafting church confessions (e.g., the Ten Theses of Berne, 1528) and conversing with other theologians, especially Luther on the Lord's Supper and with the Anabaptists. He also dealt with various domestic and diplomatic problems as well. Zwingli was killed in the battle of Kappel while serving as a chaplain for the troops of Zurich as they fought with other Swiss cantons.[9]

Zwingli may be said to have begun the "Reformed" as contrasted to the "Lutheran" and "Anabaptist" traditions of the Reformation. But it was from John Calvin (1509–1564) of Geneva that the Reformed tradition took its most definite shape. The theology of Calvin spread from Geneva and became a powerful force in the Protestant Reformation, particularly in Switzerland, western Germany, France, the Netherlands, and Scotland. To a lesser degree, Calvinism was prominent as well in England, eastern Germany, Hungary, and Poland.[10]

Like Zwingli, Calvin was trained as a Christian humanist. His earliest published work was a *Commentary on Seneca's 'De Clementia'* (1532), through which he became adept at interpreting an ancient text with the tools of the Renaissance humanists.[11] His major theological work was his *Institutes of the Christian Religion,* which expanded from six chapters in the first edition (1536) to eighty chapters in the 1559 edition.[12] Calvin also wrote biblical commentaries on nearly every book of the Bible as well as polemical pieces, theological tracts, and thousands of personal letters and sermons.[13] His legacy, like Luther's in Lutheran churches, continues in Reformed churches throughout the world.

LUTHERAN AND REFORMED CONFESSIONS

Both Lutheran and Reformed churches since the sixteenth century have been *confessional* churches. That is, these churches have looked to various confessions or declarations of faith as their norms or sources for doctrine. The confessions define what the churches believe.

In the Lutheran tradition, the confessions of the churches are found in *The Book of Concord.*[14] This work is sometimes called *The Confessions of the Evangelical Lutheran Church* (German) or *Concordia* (Latin) and contains those documents most generally accepted as "symbols" (from the Greek *sumbolos* and the Latin *symbolus,* meaning "sign" or "mark") or confessions of the churches. *The Book of Concord* was published in 1580 and today includes the three ancient creeds of the Christian church (Apostles', Nicene, and Athanasian); Luther's *Large and Small Catechisms* (1529);

the Augsburg Confession (1530), written by Philip Melanchthon (1497–1560), Luther's colleague and successor as the leader of the emerging Lutheranism; the Apology of the Augsburg Confession (1531), written by Melanchthon against the Roman Catholics who rejected the Augsburg Confession; the Smalcald Articles (1537), written by Luther as a summary of Christian doctrine; the Treatise on the Power and Primacy of the Pope (1537), written by Melanchthon to supplement the Smalcald Articles; and the Formula of Concord (1577), written by a number of theologians to settle numerous doctrinal controversies that affected Lutheranism after Luther's death in 1546. The Formula of Concord is composed of an Epitome and a Solid Declaration, each containing twelve articles.

Churches in the Reformed tradition, on the other hand, have not consolidated their confessional standards into any one book as the Lutherans have done. Instead, as the Reformation became indigenous throughout Europe, Reformed churches in various nations, cities, and local communities often drafted their own doctrinal statements. Thus among the many confessions of the Reformed tradition there are those named from the areas of their origination: The Ten Theses of Berne (1528); the First Confession of Basel (1534); the Geneva Confession (1536); the French Confession of Faith (1559); the Scots Confession (1560); and the Second Helvetic Confession (1566) among many confessional statements.[15] Of particular significance for American churches in the Presbyterian branch of the Reformed tradition has been the Westminster Confession of Faith (1647), written in England by English and Scottish Calvinists during the time of the English Civil War. In the twentieth century, two important Reformed Statements of Faith have been written. The Theological Declaration of Barmen (1934) was written by Karl Barth (1886–1968), and was the German Confessing Church's confession in the face of the threats of Nazism and Adolf Hitler. The Confession of 1967 was written as part of *The Book of Confessions* of the United Presbyterian Church in the United States of America (now the Presbyterian Church [USA]) and represents a statement of some aspects of the Reformed faith in contemporary times.[16]

SCRIPTURE IN THE LUTHERAN AND REFORMED CONFESSIONS

The basic beliefs about the Bible of the Lutheran and Reformed traditions can be found through their confessional statements.[17]

Similarities and Differences. These two confessional traditions adopt similar stances regarding the Bible. Usually their views are set in contrast to the Roman Catholic positions, since the Protestant churches emerged out of the conflict with the Roman Catholic Church. Yet, despite their basic similarities, there are three major ways in which the sixteenth- and seventeenth-century Lutheran and Reformed Confessions differ in their approach to Scripture.

Frequently in the Reformed Confessions of this period, a list of canonical books that record the documents of Scripture is found at or near the beginning of the Confession. These books of Scripture are described as "the Word of God," which is given to the church by "the inspiration of the Holy Spirit." Lutheran Confessions, however, give no such listings of the canon.[18]

The second and third differences are that Lutheran Confessions present no doctrine of the inspiration of Scripture nor do they make any mention of a special activity of the Holy Spirit in how the process of the canonization of biblical books took place. It has been suggested that the reason for these omissions from Lutheran documents may be that "the interest of Lutheran theology was not in a book as such but in the redemptive content" of the Bible.[19] The thrust of Lutheran Confessions is toward hearing the gospel of Jesus Christ. It is the inspiration of the hearer, not primarily of the book (the Bible) that is primary. Since an explicit doctrine of Scripture is not found here, "the implicit doctrine of Scripture must be gleaned from the actual use of Scripture (in confessional documents) and from the expressed attitude to other sources of knowledge that might lay claim to being norms of church doctrine."[20] From the Reformed point of view, such omissions mean that the doctrine of the inspiration of the Bible must be developed from theological sources outside the Confessions. From the Lutheran perspective, however, the omission of an explicit statement of the inspiration of Scripture put the focus where it should rightly be: not in the giving of a canon on Scripture but in the giving of saving faith to those who believe the gospel of Jesus Christ.

Both the Lutheran and Reformed Confessions speak of the relation of the confessions to Scripture. Both traditions agree that the authority of Scripture stands supreme over all human confessions of faith. The Reformed French Confession of 1559 confessed the Apostles', Nicene, and Athanasian Creeds "because they are in accordance with the Word of God."[21] The Scots Confession of 1560 in its Preface urged its Confession to be judged to see "if any man will note in our confession any chapter or sentence contrary to God's Holy Word."[22] On the Lutheran side, the Epitome of the Formula of Concord said: "We believe, teach, and confess that the prophetic and apostolic writings of the Old and New Testaments are the only rule and norm according to which all doctrines and teachers alike must be appraised and judged."[23]

Canon and Authority. On the issue of the canon, the question between the Protestants and Roman Catholics was this: Did the church create the canon or did the canon create the church? Roman Catholic theologian John Eck wrote that "Scripture is not authentic without the authority of the church." To this the Protestants compared the church with the Samaritan woman of whom it is said in John 4:39 that "many of that city believed in Christ because of her saying." But then in 4:42 they say to her: "It is no longer because of what you said that we believe, for we have heard for ourselves, and we know that this is truly the Savior of the world." The Protestants claimed that the church bears witness to its Savior and through its witness men and women are introduced to the Christ of Scripture.[24] Similarly, John Calvin argued on the basis of Ephesians 2:20, where Paul wrote that the church is "built upon the foundation of the apostles and prophets, Christ Jesus himself as the cornerstone," that the message of God through the prophets and apostles existed *before* the church itself was called into being. The church is founded on the gospel message.[25]

For both Lutheran and Reformed traditions, the Confessions are clear that the ultimate authority in the church belongs to Jesus Christ. But the church knows Christ through the Scriptures of the Old and New Testaments. Thus the Scriptures are authoritative for the church. In this the Protestants were standing against Roman Catholic insistence that the tradition of the church should be received on a par with Scripture as a source of authority. For the Protestants, Scripture alone (*sola Scriptura*) is the source of authority for the church. As the Geneva Confession of 1536 put it: "We affirm and desire to follow Scripture alone as rule of faith and religion, without mixing with it any other thing which might be devised by the opinion of men apart from the Word of God."[26] The Formula of Concord calls Scripture "the only rule and norm."[27]

Lutheran Confessions

The main emphasis throughout the Lutheran Confessions is on the authority of Scripture. In the Augsburg Confession, Scripture is appealed to but is not made an article of faith in itself. The Preface states that the Confession seeks to be "a confession of our pastors' and preachers' teaching and of our own faith, setting forth how and in what manner, on the basis of the Holy Scriptures, these things are preached, taught, communicated and embraced in our lands, principalities, dominions, cities and territories."[28]

The second part of the Confession deals with "matters in dispute." Here the doctrine is brought forth similarly when the Confession states: "From the above it is manifest that nothing is taught in our churches concerning articles of faith that is contrary to the Holy Scriptures or what is common to the Christian Church."[29] In the conclusion, the Confession again stresses its appeal to Scripture as *the* authority. It reemphasizes that it "introduces nothing, either in doctrine or in ceremonies, that is contrary to Holy Scripture."[30]

Melanchthon's Apology of the Augsburg Confession makes frequent appeals to Scripture throughout its articles. In it Melanchthon claims he will show readers what the opponents have said and how they "have condemned several articles in opposition to the clear Scripture of the Holy Spirit." He is confident he can show his opponents have not "disproved our contentions from the Holy Scriptures."[31]

In the Smalcald Articles, Luther dealt in Part II in a section on the Mass and Purgatory with the Roman Catholic citation of passages from Augustine and the early Church Fathers, who are "said to have written about purgatory." Luther questioned this interpretation and then declared: "It will not do to make articles of faith out of the Holy Fathers' words or works. Otherwise what they ate, how they dressed, and what kind of houses they live in would have to become articles of faith—as has happened in the case of relics. This means that the Word of God shall establish articles and no one else, not even an angel (Gal. 1:8)."[32]

Luther made the same appeal in the "Treatise on the Power and Primacy of the Pope" when he sought to refute the claims of the papacy by referring in the first article to "The Testimony of the Scriptures." Throughout his Catechisms Luther made frequent reference to the Word of God, though he did not present a doctrine of Scripture in itself.

The Formula of Concord is the Lutheran document that deals most fully with Scripture. Its Epitome begins with the statement that Scripture is "the only rule and norm according to which all doctrines and teachers alike must be appraised and judged." All "other writings, ancient and modern teachers, whatever their names should not be put on a par with Holy Scripture." These writings are subordinate to Scripture and are valued only insofar as they witness to the doctrine of the prophets and apostles. After listing the documents Lutherans accept as being faithful witnesses and expositions of the Christian faith, the Formula declares Scripture as the "only judge, rule, and norm according to which all doctrines should and must be understood and judged as good and evil, right or wrong."[33] Thus "the Scriptures contain the *credenda*, the things to be believed; the Symbols the *credita*, the things that are believed."[34] This same principle is affirmed in Part II, "The Solid Declaration," where allegiance is pledged to "the prophetic and apostolic writings of the Old Testament as the pure and clear fountain of Israel, which is the only true norm according to which all teachers and teachings are to be judged and evaluated."[35]

In the Lutheran Confessions, then, strong emphasis is placed on the role of Scripture as the supreme authority from which doctrine is derived and by which all teaching and belief are to be judged and tested.

Reformed Confessions

As noted, the Reformed Confessions make their understanding of the nature of Scripture more explicit than do Lutheran standards. Among the numerous Reformed documents, the following emphases from certain Confessions stand out.[36]

Zwingli's Sixty-seven Articles (1523) declared that the basis of Zwingli's doctrine was "the Scripture which is called *theopneustos* ('inspired by God')." Although he affirmed Scripture's inspiration, Zwingli did not propound a theory about *how* the Scriptures were inspired. His emphasis throughout was on the message of the gospel that is transmitted *through* the Scriptures and calls people to faith in Jesus Christ (Art. XV).[37]

The emphasis on the purpose of Scripture for salvation was also struck by the First Helvetic Confession (1536). Here the purpose or *scopus* of Scripture was related to humans' understanding that "God is kind and gracious" and that God has "publicly demonstrated and exhibited His kindness to the whole human race through Christ His Son" (Art. 5). Knowledge of God comes through "holy, divine Biblical Scripture inspired by the Holy Spirit and delivered to the world by the prophets and apostles" (Art. 1). This Scripture is called "the Word of God."[38]

The French Confession of 1559 spoke of a revelation of God "in his works, in their creation, as well as in their preservation and control." Yet this source of knowledge of God does not stand alone, for the Confession goes on immediately to add that God is revealed "in his Word, which was in the beginning revealed through oracles, and which was afterward committed in writing in the books which we call the Holy Scriptures" (Art. II). This Scripture is not validated as canon by church councils but "by the testimony and inward illumination of the Holy Spirit" (Art. IV). The Holy Spirit is active both in guiding the acceptance of biblical books as God's Word (Art. IV) and in enlightening people in faith to believe the Christian gospel (Art. XXI).[39]

In the Scots Confession (1560), the Scriptures are said to be "the written Word of God" (Ch. XVIII) with their "authority to be from God" (Ch. XIX) for the purpose of instructing and perfecting the people of God. The Spirit of God is the proper interpreter of Scripture. In controversial issues, Scripture should be interpreted by other passages of Scripture (Art. XVIII). Biblical interpretation should seek always the "plain text of Scripture" and should be carried out by "the rule of love" (Art. XVIII).[40]

The Second Helvetic Confession (1566), composed by Heinrich Bullinger (1504–1575), dealt substantially with the doctrine of Scripture. No list of canonical Scriptures was provided, but the books of "both Testaments" were designated "the true Word of God" and as having "sufficient authority of themselves" (Ch. I). In the Scriptures, the "universal Church of Christ has the most complete expression of all that pertains to a saving faith, and also to the framing of a life acceptable to God." Thus Scripture's purpose is both theological and ethical. It is God through the Holy Spirit who illumines humans to be believers through the ministry of the preached Word. God may use means other than the preaching of the Word to produce faith. But this Confession cites Scripture to show that no "inner light" apart from preaching should be sought since Scripture commands that the preaching be done. Both the preached Word and the written Word were sufficient for the church, and "no other Word of God is to be invented nor is to be expected from heaven" (Ch. I). The Confession strongly asserts that "the preaching of the Word of God *is* the Word of God."[41]

Sixteenth-century Reformed Confessions acknowledged the authority of Holy Scripture as the written Word of God. They occupied a middle ground between the position of the Roman Catholics, who sought a blend of Scripture and tradition, and various Anabaptist groups who stressed the illumination of the Spirit as the only source of religious authority. Scripture is said to be inspired, but no formal description of how inspiration was accomplished is offered. The Confessions speak of the Scriptures carrying the evidence of their divine origins "in themselves" (Gr. *autopiston*). Scripture is thus self-authenticating as the Word of God. The Holy Spirit serves several functions in relation to the Word of God in Scripture. The Spirit *inspired* the biblical writers. The Spirit *illuminates* those who hear the Word to come to faith in Jesus Christ. The Spirit *interprets* Scripture in the present day in the church. Scripture's purpose in these Confessions is to bring people to faith and to instruct them for living a life acceptable to God. The Confessions see Scripture as infallible in achieving its purpose of proclaiming salvation in Christ. Scripture is not cited as a source for authoritative teachings for science or other worldly matters. The written and the preached Word are the means God uses to make the gospel known to the world.[42]

The foundations of the sixteenth-century Reformed Confessions on Scripture were built upon through the next centuries. The Westminster Confession of Faith (1647), produced in England during the English Civil War, devoted its first chapter in ten sections to discussing the authority and interpretation of the Bible.[43] Westminster affirmed, as had its predecessors, that the written Word of God receives its authority from God. How humans accept this authority is indicated when the Confession said that "our full persuasion and assurance of the infallible truth, and divine authority thereof, is from the inward work of the Holy Spirit, bearing witness by and with the Word in our hearts" (Ch. I, sec. 5). According to Westminster, the content of Scripture is "the whole counsel of God concerning all things necessary for His own glory, man's salvation, faith and life" (Ch. I, sec. 6). Scripture was clear about matters of salvation. It was so clear that "not only the learned but the unlearned, in a due use of the ordinary means, may attain unto a sufficient understanding of them" (Ch. I, sec. 7). The Confession acknowledged that "in all controversies of religion the Church is finally to appeal unto them [the Scriptures]" (Ch. I, sec. 8). But it urged the use of scholarship in these matters and the careful study of Scripture in its original languages. Thus in the Westminster Confession, Scripture can be approached on two levels—on the level of scholarship and on the level of spiritual need. In all cases though, Scripture interprets Scripture (Ch. 1, sec. 9) and "the Supreme Judge by whom all controversies of religion are to be determined . . . can be no other but the Holy Spirit speaking in the Scripture."[44]

Two other contemporary Reformed Confessions with their emphases may also be cited.

In 1934, against the backdrop of the rise of Adolf Hitler and Nazism in Germany, Reformed Christians (with some Lutherans and members of the United Church) produced "The Theological Declaration of Barmen." Article I of this Declaration states that "Jesus Christ, as it is attested for us in Holy Scripture is the one Word of God which we have to hear and which we have to trust and obey in life and death."[45] This stand clearly rejected any notions that a person without the revelation of Christ known through Scripture could perceive the purposes and plans of God in nature or history. In the context of the times, this was a powerful rejection of the propaganda of Hitler and the Nazis.[46]

In 1967 the United Presbyterian Church in the United States of America (now the Presbyterian Church [USA]) adopted "The Confession of 1967."[47] Consistent with sixteenth-century Reformation Confessions, the Scriptures are "the word of God written." They are said to be "not a witness among others, but the witness without parallel" to "the one sufficient revelation of God," who is "Jesus Christ, the Word of God incarnate." To Christ "the Holy Spirit bears unique and authoritative witness through the Holy Scriptures." The Confession of 1967 also recognizes that "the Scripture, given under the guidance of the Holy Spirit," is nevertheless human words written by humans who shared the "views of life, history, and the cosmos which were then current." Thus the church, says this Confession, "has an obligation to approach the Scriptures with literary and historical understanding" (see 9.27–9.30). In this way, the Confession affirms both the gospel of the Scripture and Scripture's human cultural context.[48]

THE ANABAPTIST MOVEMENT

As the Reformation movement developed, a third stream in addition to the Lutheran and Reformed movements was formed. This was the so-called left wing of the Reformation or "radical Reformation."[49] From the perspective of the sociology of religion, Ernst Troeltsch distinguished between the "churches" and the "sects" of the Reformation era and the "sects" divided between "Anabaptism" and "mysticism."[50] Others have variously pointed to Anabaptists, Spiritualists, and Protestant Rationalists,[51] or Anabaptist, Spiritualists, Enthusiasts, and anti-Trinitarians.[52] Others opt for seeing Anabaptism as "one general phenomenon, albeit with a great many different manifestations."[53]

Anabaptists wanted "reformation as re-formation."[54] While Luther's doctrines appealed to people of all classes, "many of these were not content to move slowly as he, and fundamental differences soon appeared. Some sought to substantiate social, political, and economic views by reference to the Scripture."[55] Varieties of biblical interpretation arose. Some, such as Thomas Muenster and the "Zwickau prophets," envisioned a new society based on beliefs in continuing revelations by the Spirit. They were confident God would intervene in history, destroy evil, and establish the millennium on earth. Others, turning to Scripture, desired a complete separation of church and state with the faithful living in strict obedience to biblical commands. Still others questioned the received doctrines of the churches and called for a religion based on ethics instead of dogmatics.[56]

PROTESTANTISM

Backgrounds

The backgrounds of the Anabaptist movement can be traced to the dispute between Zwingli and Conrad Grebel (1498–1526), which resulted from an adult baptism. In January 1525, Grebel baptized George Blaurock (1480?–1529) in the home of Felix Manz (d. 1527) in Zurich. This led to the designation "Anabaptist," derived from the Greek term for "baptizing again."[57]

Grebel, like Zwingli, had been trained in humanism and was a friend of Zwingli's in Zurich. Zwingli had instructed him in the Reformation faith. Initially Grebel and his friends split with Zwingli over the issue of baptism. But the deeper issue was soteriology (salvation). Zwingli recounted that the future Anabaptist leaders came to him wishing to form "a church in which there would be only those who knew themselves without sin,"[58] which meant the nature of Christian commitment was of fundamental concern. For the Anabaptists, "to be a Christian meant a voluntary and deliberate decision, which expressed itself in reception of adult Baptism and separation from the 'ungodly.' "[59]

The baptism administered by Grebel was a violation of the criminal code of Zurich. Those involved, instead of fleeing, decided to defy the authorities. After a religious disputation on January 17, 1525, in which Zwingli and the Zurich city council ruled that Anabaptists must conform or be exiled, the offenders were arrested and those who did not recant were imprisoned and later expelled from the Zurich territory. But they spread their message. Persecutions followed throughout Europe; yet Anabaptism spread into southern Germany, Upper Austria, Moravia, Hungary, the Low Countries, and elsewhere. Among the major leaders of the movement were Jacob Hutler, Balthasar Hubmaier (1485–1528), Hans Denck (d. 1527), David Joris (1501–1556), Menno Simons (1496–1561), Pilgrim Marpeck (d. 1556), Melchior Hofman (d. 1543), and the mystically inclined Sebastian Franck (1499–1543).[60]

The first major attempt to bring all Anabaptists together came in a gathering at Schleitheim. The *Brüderliche Vereinigung,* or Schleitheim Confession of Faith, was the result. The seven articles of this Confession "more succinctly than any other document sum up the distinctive convictions of Evangelical Anabaptism"[61] The Confession dealt with baptism, excommunication, communion, separation, the ministry, the sword, and the oath.[62] It presented alternatives to the positions of the Lutherans and Reformed on major issues. In particular, it designated infant baptism as "the highest and chief abomination of the pope" as well as of the Protestant churches.[63] For Anabaptists, "inward baptism" by the Holy Spirit had to precede "outward baptism" with water.

H. Bender has argued for three main views as the bases of Anabaptist thought. These were "first, a new understanding of the nature of Christianity as discipleship; secondly, a new conception of the church as the brotherhood of believers; and thirdly, a new ethics of love and defencelessness."[64] Some analysts have stressed the central concept of the church for the Anabaptist movement. They have identified this as a concern for "primitivism"— that is, the view that an ideal state existed in the early church that can be established again in the present.[65] Others present the concept of "discipleship" as the key idea. They cite the "motto" of Hans Denck: "No one can truly know [Christ] unless he follows [*nachfolge*] Him in his life."[66] While Anabaptists were not "perfectionists," they did expect their followers "to obey the commands of God and lead lives of holiness."[67]

Scripture in the Anabaptist Tradition

It is sometimes said that the Anabaptists devalued Scripture and put in its place a sole reliance on the Holy Spirit. While it is true that the Anabapists emphasized the work of the Holy Spirit, they did at the same time rigorously uphold their view of the Bible. For Anabaptists, this meant that Scripture was supremely authoritative. It was this concern for the authority of Scripture, as interpreted by the Swiss Brethren, that led them to separate from Zwingli and flee Zurich. In their concern to be biblical Christians, the Anabaptists were concerned to "carry through consistently the demands of the New Testament, and especially of the Sermon on the Mount, as they understood them."[68] This is seen too in their responses to the charges made against them by appealing to biblical texts. Yet as Reventlow has noted:

> the reference to Scripture was made in direct association with reference to the Spirit. Among the authentic Anabaptists the two cannot be separated (and in this respect the old identification with Spiritualists has proved inaccurate), but in such a way that the "inner word" provides the legitimation for reference to the outward word.[69]

It is here that the relation of Scripture and the Spirit is found. For the Anabaptists, "God's Spirit, which the Anabaptists believed themselves to possess, is the ultimate authority which first gives authority to the written Word of the Bible."[70] In their stress on the "outer" and "inner" Word, the Anabaptists were saying that "a biblical text without the penetration and testing of personal appropriation is a dead letter."[71] When Hans Denck, perhaps the first Anabaptist to use the inner/outer word pairs, drew up a list of contradictory Scripture passages, he did so not to show that Scripture should not be authoritative. Rather he wanted to point out that "in order to reconcile seemingly contradictory understandings, there must be a deeper personal penetration of what the texts are all about."[72]

In many respects, the Anabaptists shared large areas of agreement with Lutheran and Reformed Christians, not only on doctrines—such as the message of salvation by grace and exalting the authority of God—but also with regard to their understanding of the Bible. Among points of agreement between the Anabaptists and other Protestants were: (1) The Bible holds a place of authority in the church. (2) The Bible is meant to be understood. Scripture is understandable. (3) The Bible has some parts that are difficult to understand. (4) Special techniques for understanding are necessary to interpret these parts. (5) Scripture interpretation should be undertaken in freedom from the structure of church authorities who restrict intepretations. (6) The Bible should be obeyed.[73]

If these areas of broad, general agreement about Scripture had been the only perspectives of the Anabaptists, they could have perhaps worked well with the other Reformation Protestants. But disagreements were to be found too. Among these may be listed:[74] (1) The extent to which the Bible's authority was applicable, particularly to public life. This surfaced in the theological disagreements over church and state, the use of oaths, and so forth. (2) The sharp distinction between the Old and New Testaments. For Anabaptists, the Old Testament was "promise"; Jesus was "fulfillment." The Old Testament was "shadow"; the New was "reality." This was a basic principle of interpretation for the Anabaptists. To a large part this was behind, for example, Calvin's rejection of the theology of the Schleitheim Confession. With each article, "the critical issue is the hermeneutical one."[75] (3) The pre-understanding of the Anabaptists that Jesus must be followed was a crucial condition placed upon the understanding of Scripture. As has been said for Menno Simons:

> the prerequisites of understanding are seen to lie in the attitude of the one who comes to the Scriptures. Very briefly this attitude must be marked by obedience . . . a willingness to be instructed both by the Spirit and by the brethren and a personal application in seeing the truths as they apply to everyday life. . . . Wrongdoing . . . blinds people so that they do not understand.[76]

(4) That anyone who has made the commitment to obedience and has the Spirit of God can read Scripture with understanding. This belief led to a basic mistrust of the tools of biblical scholarship to come to ultimate meanings. Instead, Anabaptists often looked to the community of faith as the locus for biblical interpretation. For "the text can be properly understood only when disciples are gathered together to discover what the Word has to say to their needs and concerns."[77] From the Anabaptist perspective, "this process is designed to save Christians from the tyranny of the specialized knowledge and equipment of the scholar, as well as from the tyranny of individualist interpretation and of the visionary."[78]

For many Anabaptists, "the Word of God was broader than the Bible, although the Bible is always viewed as the chief medium for the sharing of God's Word" with humanity.[79] The Word of God can also come directly to the heart through no intermediary. This direct act of God can be the source of one's "blessedness" or "salvation." As Hans Denck wrote in 1528:

> I hold Holy Scripture above all human treasures, but not so high as the Word of God, which is living, powerful and eternal . . . for it is as God himself is, Spirit and not letter. . . . Therefore salvation, too, is not tied to Scripture, however useful and good Scripture may be to that end. The reason is that it is not possible for Scripture to make an evil heart better, though it may become better informed. But a pious heart, that is, a heart with a true ray of divine zeal, is improved by all things. . . . Thus a man chosen by God may find salvation through preaching and Scripture.[80]

The predominant emphasis in Anabaptist writers is that the Bible is written by people of faith with the purpose of inspiring faith in others. This led them to a "hermeneutics of obedience" or "hermeneutics of discipleship," which was based on certain theological assumptions.[81] In most instances they looked directly to the literal interpretation of a biblical text.[82] But they also recognized that Scripture functioned on another level: that of the Spirit. It was only as the Spirit was operative, particularly in the gathered Christian community (church), that the true meaning of the Scripture could be found. In their desire for biblical fidelity, they sought not complicated theories of interpretation but an emphasis on Scripture's basic authority for all life. As Melchior Hofmann put it: "Therefore I warn all lovers of truth that they do not give themselves over to lofty arguments which are too hard for them, but that they hold themselves solely to the straightforward words of God in all simplicity."[83]

PART TWO
THEOLOGICAL POSITIONS

III

LIBERAL THEOLOGY

Scripture as Experience

ON THE DAY AFTER THE DEATH OF FRIEDRICH DANIEL ERNST SCHLEIERMACHER (1768–1834), his colleague in the theological faculty of the University of Berlin told his students: "From him a new period in the history of the Church will one day take its origin."[1] In retrospect, one hundred years later Karl Barth applied to Schleiermacher what he said of Frederick the Great: "He did not found a school but an era."[2] Schleiermacher is often called "the father of Protestant Liberalism."[3] But his influence extended beyond the liberal movement even to those who reacted against liberalism itself.[4]

Protestant liberalism became the dominant theology in Europe during the nineteenth century and maintained this position until challenged by the emerging neo-orthodoxy of Barth and Brunner in the 1930s.[5] In America, while it continues in modified forms as a theological force today, "it was during the first thirty-five years of this century that liberalism achieved its most pervasive influence among the leading thinkers of the day."[6]

During the last quarter of the nineteenth century, liberalism gained a foothold in America as it challenged the dominant Protestant orthodoxy. It gradually replaced the modified Calvinism of Jonathan Edwards, Samuel Hopkins, Nathaniel Emmons, Timothy Dwight, Nathaniel W. Taylor, and Edward A. Park under the name "the new theology."[7] Through this rubric its adherents saw themselves as seeking a reconstruction of orthodox Christianity in a way that was congruent with the advances of the sciences, especially the natural sciences.[8] In America, the "Fundmentalist-Modernist" controversy highlighted the tensions on the theological scene and dramatized the differences between those holding to orthodox doctrine and those seeking to "modernize" Christian theology. The liberal argument was that "the world . . . has changed radically since the early creeds of Christendom were formulated; this makes the creeds sound archaic and unreal to the modern man. We have to rethink Christianity in thought forms which the modern world can comprehend."[9]

BACKGROUNDS

European Development

The theological impetus for the emergence of liberal theology came with Schleiermacher's reorientation of Christian theology.[10] Schleiermacher was one of the first theologians to respond to the critical philosophy of Immanuel Kant.[11] For Schleiermacher, religion is not a matter of belief or of practical action. As he said, "Piety cannot be an instinct craving or a mess of metaphysical and ethical crumbs."[12] Instead, true religion is a feeling or intuition. It is an affection. To find one's true religion one's own consciousness must be examined.[13] Religion is a "sense and taste for the Infinite, and of all temporal things in and through the Eternal."[14] One's religion is thus based on one's experience, on a "feeling of utter dependence" on the ground of nature—God.[15] This sense of the immediate certainty of God thus replaces the traditional arguments for God's existence. Theology's task, according to Schleiermacher, is to explicate the specific content of this divine consciousness.[16]

Schleiermacher's reorientation of Christian theology provided a way to establish religion's independence from philosophy and science. Since it was based on one's own experience, it carried its own proof and was not dependent on the arguments of philosophers or the findings of science. By shifting the focus of religious authority away from the traditional source, the Bible, to an individual's religious experience, one is not held hostage to the findings of "the scientific study of the Bible" or biblical criticism. Critical biblical studies for Schleiermacher could be a positive help, since they aided in understanding the Bible more fully.[17]

A second significant figure in the emergence of theological liberalism was Albrecht Ritschl (1822–89).[18] Ritschl elevated ethics to a place equal in importance to religion. For Ritschl, the Christian faith is an ellipse with two foci. One is the redemption accomplished by Jesus Christ. The second is the kingdom of God. The kingdom is defined as "the moral organization of humanity through love-prompted action."[19] Christ and the kingdom are inseparable. Redemption in Christ (justification) takes shape historically and communally. Thus the church as the community of believers is crucial for Christian existence. Religion for Ritschl was based on value judgments and was sharply distinct from science that is based on facts.[20] There was no need for conflict between Christian faith and science as long as each kept to its own realm. Biblical criticism was a welcomed tool in order to establish the facts on which the Christian religion is based. But biblical criticism cannot go on to make the value judgments on which Christian faith ultimately rests.

The major popularizer of Ritschl's views was Adolf von Harnack (1851–1930).[21] Harnack was a historian of Christian dogma whose lectures, published as *What Is Christianity?* (1901), did much to publicize and popularize the emerging liberal theology. Harnack used historical and critical tools in his quest to isolate "the real religion of Jesus." He wished to focus particularly on "the essence of Christianity," which he defined as meaning "one thing and one thing only: Eternal life in the midst of time, by the strength and under the eyes of God."[22] Harnack's simplified view of Christianity reduced it to three essentials:

> If . . . we take a general view of Jesus' teaching, we shall see that it may be grouped under three heads. They are each of such a nature as to contain the whole, and hence it can be exhibited in its entirety under any one of them.
> *Firstly, the kingdom of God and its coming.*
> *Secondly, God the Father and the infinite value of the human soul.*
> *Thirdly, the higher righteousness and the commandment of love.*[23]

To Harnack, the story of the development of Christian doctrines in the early centuries was the story of the "acute Hellenization" of Christianity—a Hellenization that was detrimental in that it obscured the simple teachings of Jesus himself.

American Backgrounds

At the beginning of the twentieth century, theologians in the tradition of Schleier-macher, Ritschl, and Harnack believed that orthodox theology needed reconstruction in light of the modern world. In the midst of new intellectual, social, moral, scientific, philosophical, and religious climates, liberal theology arose as an attempt to give a new mode of expression to the Christian faith.

One historian of this period has analyzed three types of influences that were significant in the development of liberal Protestant thought.[24] These factors centered on what led to an emphasis on continuity rather than discontinuity in the world; those focused on the autonomy of human reason and experience instead of on an authoritative divine revelation; and those forces that stressed the dynamic rather than the static nature of the world and human life.[25]

In brief, these influences can be summarized as follows.

Continuity. Whereas the older orthodoxy had stressed the many sharp contrasts in reality, particularly between the natural and the supernatural, new forces turned the emphases toward the continuities of life and thought. One such force was science. Mechanical causation was seen as the law of the universe and "miracles" in the traditional sense were severely questioned. The theory of evolution and other developmental theories emphasized the unitary process of which nature and human existence emerged and continued to exist. Positively, this prepared a way for an emphasis on the immanence of God.

In a similar way, the philosophies of the Enlightenment served to reject traditional sharp distinctions between reason and revelation. They also emphasized the inherent goodness of humanity and the possibility of its perfectability. Philosophical trends—such as pantheism; the absolute idealism associated with Hegel, who taught that reality consisted of the divine Spirit unfolding itself in history through a dialectical process; and Romanticism, which stressed the presence of God in nature and in human beings—also contributed to the motif of "continuity."

The rise of the study of comparative religious fanned the hopes of discovering a universal religion that would unite all peoples. Movements stressing God's immediate presence in religious experience, such as Pietism in Germany, the Wesleyan movement in England, and American revivalism, were also prominent in this period. Against the emphasis of seventeenth-century scholastic orthodoxy and eighteenth-century rationalism on the remoteness of God, these experiential movements stressed God's presence in the inner life.

The results of this emphasis on continuity were widespread, for this theme "reduces the distinction between animals and men, men and God, nature and God, Christianity and other religious, nature and grace, the saved and the lost, justification and sanctification, Christianity and culture, the church and the world, the sacred and secular, the individual and society, life here and hereafter, heaven and hell, the natural and supernatural, the human and divine natures of Christ, etc."[26]

As a leading liberal theologian put it, continuity was "the major positive principle of the liberal mind."[27]

Autonomy. In distinction from orthodoxy, with its stress on religious knowledge that comes through divine revelation given by God and stands above the reason and experience of humans, liberalism emphasized religious knowledge based on reason and experience. The emphasis in liberal thought was on the autonomy of human reason. In this sense "the principle of autonomy means that liberal theologians rejected any arbitrary appeal to external authority and insisted that all religious affirmations must be grounded in, or at least subject to confirmation by, the data of religious experience or the conclusions of reason."[28]

In science, discoveries increasingly contradicted biblical statements about history and "scientific" matters. The empirical method, which stressed the place of observation and experimentation, lessened the emphasis on authority and also led theologians to try to interpret experience objectively. Theology itself became an empirical science. A scientific world view that stressed the mechanistic nature of the universe—that it operated as Newton said through fixed, inexorable laws—made this world seem to be a machine with no human or God-given values built into it. Reactions against mechanism surfaced in various philosophies in which attempts were made to distinguish the external, law-bound world from the internal, spiritual world of faith.[29]

A related influence in the stress on human autonomy was the rise of the historical-critical method in biblical studies. Literary and historical research opened new avenues for biblical interpretation and the understanding of how the Scriptures were formed. For many this development necessitated an alternative view of the authority and relevance of the Bible from the inherited traditions of orthodoxy. The shift for the locus of authority from the "external" Scriptures to the "internal" religious experience represents a reaction to the way in which the Scriptures were understood in the light of the modern biblical research of the period.[30]

Dynamism. In traditional orthodoxy, religious truth consisted of a variety of propositions or doctrines that were to be believed. The world was believed to have been created at a definite time and humans were created originally in the form in which they exist now. The categories were static by nature. In the nineteenth century, an alternative view arose. Reality was perceived as developmental or evolutional. As one writer put it, since the eighteenth century, the "one conception that all sorts and conditions of thinkers have accepted is that, whatever else the world may be, it is not a static and finished thing, but is itself, as a whole and in each of its parts, in a process of change and growth."[31]

The philosophies of the Enlightenment era fostered views of social progress as guided by the use of reason and the spread of science. Individuals and societies were seen as being able to ascend to perfection. This evolutionary view produced a climate of optimism. This "combination of evolution and immanence goes a long way toward providing the basic context out of which liberalism came and in which it grew."[32]

Literary developments in the Romantic movement stressed the view that the world is vital and growing. History, according to philosophers such as Hegel, is the arena in which human thought, social institutions, and the world itself are in a process of "becoming." In biblical studies, the religious ideas of the Hebrews were seen as having developed over a long time. The Bible itself was viewed as containing a religion that was marked by many stages, theologies, and even ethical stances so that the Scriptures were perceived as "a record of the progressive discovery of God in human experience, not as a static body of theological dogmas all equally inspired and all of equal religious value."[33] In the light of this growing perception of dynamism as the basic category or reality, traditional views and orthodoxies were challenged and reconstructed. In this context, Protestant liberal theology emerged.

Leading Figures

In an attempt to formulate Christian theology and to bridge the gap between ancient doctrines and contemporary cultures, the central task of liberal theologians was to make it possible for a person "to be both an intelligent modern and a serious Christian."[34] Thus liberalism "can best be understood in terms of its effort to harmonize Christ and culture under the conditions set by the late nineteenth and early twentieth centuries."[35] Yet the varieties of approach among liberals differed.

Henry P. Van Dusen pointed to two basic types of liberalism. One is *evangelical liberalism,* composed of people standing within the Christian tradition who accepted the tradition as the way by which Christianity is best understood. Their intentions were to reconstruct the Christian faith in continuity with Christian orthodoxy in a way that was appropriate to the modern world. The norm of religious truth for these liberal theologians was Jesus Christ. The need was to reinterpret traditional doctrines while maintaining the meaning of the religious experiences to which these doctrines origi- nally witnessed. In Fosdick's words, there are "abiding experiences and changing categories."[36] Among the theologians who fit this pattern were William Adams Brown (1865–1943), Harry Emerson Fosdick (1878–1969), Walter Rauschenbusch (1861– 1918), A. C. Knudson (1873–1953), and Eugene W. Lyman (1872–1948).

A second type of liberal theology may be called *modernistic liberalism.* The term *modernistic* here refers to a determination to be oriented in outlook by twentieth- century thought. The empirical sciences often provided these theologians with their most promising source for a method that could establish theology in a place of respectibility in the modern world. Since "modernists" had abandoned traditional beliefs in God's revelation in Scripture, the Bible itself did not function as their norm, nor did Christ or the Christian tradition. Their aim was "to discover a source and standard of religious truth independent of the historic faith. Hence, the search for a new methodology became a prime consideration and often overshadowed the efforts to define the content of religious truth."[37] This modernist trend developed after liberal theology had begun and is represented by people like Shailer Matthews (1863–1941), Douglas Clyde Macintosh (1877–1948), Henry Nelson Wieman (1884–1975), and G. A. Coe (1863–1951).

SCRIPTURE IN LIBERAL THEOLOGY

Revelation

Liberal theology reacted sharply against the traditional orthodox view of the revelation and authority of the Bible. In orthodoxy, propositions or doctrines were seen as the content of God's revelation. Liberal theology tended to focus on revelation as Jesus Christ and "in a wider sense revelation includes the preparation for the revelation in Christ and the results of his influence in the lives of individuals and in the church since the time of Christ."[38] By conceiving revelation in this way, liberal theologians were able to speak about God's disclosure in history and also to use the tools of biblical scholarship and science to help in reconstructing theology.[39]

For liberal theology, God's revelation is the event in which God speaks God's word. This revelation took place supremely in Jesus Christ and more widely in these "great, cumulative series of divine acts to which witness is borne in the Bible."[40] But since every communication must have both one who speaks and one who hears, or one who writes and one who speaks and one who hears, or one who writes and one who reads, "the effectiveness of communication generally depends clearly on both the one who makes known and the one to whom something is made known."[41] In God's revelation, humans who receive the communication of God have the freedom to be either open or closed to God's revelation. So in the present day, "at every moment, our own decision affects the actual success or failure of the divine-human communication."[42]

This leads to the emphasis in liberal thought that the Bible as a revelation of God was written by human authors. The mystery of revelation, declared C. H. Dodd, who represents this view, is "the mystery of the way in which God uses the imperfect thoughts and feelings, words and deeds, of fallible men, to convey eternal truth, both to the men themselves and through them to others."[43]

The Nature of Scripture

Since the Bible was penned by human authors, liberals argued that "strictly speaking, the Bible itself is not the pure Word of God."[44] Similarly:

> God's word spoken to us through the Bible depends for the clarity and purity of its reception both upon our own open and understanding minds and also upon the reception and expression given his word by the ancient men who wrote the words of the Bible and, in some instances, others who related orally the messages later written down in the Scriptures.[45]

Thus "the Bible shows clearly that fallible men have written, edited, copied, and translated it."[46]

When liberal theologians approached Scripture, they pointed out various phenomena that showed how Scripture was conditioned by the culture in which it was written. These included what were considered contradictions or mistakes in Scripture, both of historical and religious natures.[47]

Thus in Scripture, "the level of truth varies greatly in different parts of the Bible."[48] It is sometimes the case, in this view, that people of later times will be prepared to receive new and higher revelations on the basis of earlier writings.

Inspiration

One is led to conclude that there are varying degrees of "inspiration" in the Scriptures. Some writings may indicate a maximized "divine element," while others display a minimal divine element.[49] As humans were "prepared through progressive stages of understanding, obedience and humble spiritual sensitiveness," God was able to show "increasing measures of His truth to humanity."[50] The writings of Scripture are by humans "conditioned and limited by their times and their individual peculiarities, though also rising frequently to great heights of expression under the illumination of God's self-disclosing presence. The reader who would hear the true word of God in the reading of the Bible must be prepared to discriminate between the word of God and the words of men."[51]

This sharp distinction between the word of God and human words leads to a definition of *inspiration*. As Harold DeWolf defines it: "The Bible as a whole was accomplished by an extraordinary stimulation and elevation of the powers of men who devoutly yielded themselves to God's will, and sought, often with success unparalleled elsewhere, to convey truth useful to the salvation of men and of nations."[52]

The biblical writers were often described as "religious geniuses" by virtue of their inspiration. The writers recorded their understanding of the ways of God with humanity on the basis of their special religious experience.[53] Yet since even their record or witness displays the marks of their own cultural conditioning, some have considered the Bible as nothing more than the ancient religious writings of an ancient people not varying significantly from other such ancient writings. Scripture had thus only a human origin.[54] But insofar as the biblical writers were "inspired" and their natural powers were stimulated and elevated to an extraordinary degree so that the Bible is a book of exquisite spiritual beauty, power, and dignity, Scripture possesses its own uniqueness as a witness to God's revelation.

Biblical Authority

As one proponent of liberal theology has written:

When the Scriptures are understood as human documents, they then are susceptible to all the canons of modern historical and literary analysis. To the liberal theologian, there is a considerable difference between viewing the Bible primarily through the eyes of faith and being equally open to a cultural and historical perspective. Historically, the resurrection of Jesus and the virgin birth are at best ambiguous as concrete occurrences. From the perspective of faith, however, they may have quite a different significance. But one should never conclude that the Scriptures are unimportant for the liberal Christian. Quite the contrary, they are central to the Christian faith. The fact that more attention is given to them as symbolic documents than as historical documents does not distort their importance.[55]

For liberal theologians, "at least one basepoint for all reflection and meditation is the symbolic forms present in Scripture and the traditions of the church."[56] Scripture functions as an "authority" insofar as "in the study of Scripture one learns, or refreshes one's acquaintance with, those stories which make reference directly or indirectly to all the grand questions surrounding human existence."[57] The value of Scripture as a "religious" book is separate from the questions of biblical scholarship in which the Scriptures are sent to be conditioned by historic time and culture. As Bishop James A. Pike noted: "Therefore, in the Scriptures we have quite a mixed bag of truth, of error, of sound ethics, unsound ethics, of myth in the best sense of the word, and legends— some useful, some apparently not so useful. The worldview of the time of writing and the public of the particular writer very much influenced what was said."[58]

But "what makes the Bible important is neither literalness nor historicity, but rather the images, as represented in story and parable and example, that challenge the moral imagination."[59] For

the authority of the word of God resides precisely in those teachings through which God speaks now to the living faith of the reader. . . . The reading of [the Bible's] pages renews our understanding of the faith by which we live as Christians. The teachings of the Bible, as tested in the life of the church, and in the open, critical thinking of innumerable devout scholars, call us back to the events through which the power of God came uniquely into human history for our salvation. By present study of the Scripture we correct our understanding of our faith and we renew our faith itself.[60]

SCRIPTURE AS EXPERIENCE

Liberal theology attempted to reformulate traditional orthodoxy in a way that would be acceptable to modern thought and persons. It did so by following the lead of Schleiermacher and focusing the locus of religious authority on religious experience. This experience was centered on one's appropriation of the teachings of Jesus, which Harnack summarized very succinctly.

In liberal thought, "experience" became a controlling feature. It was through the Bible that one's religious experience could come. The Scriptures themselves were the religious experiences of those who witnessed to their encounter with God. The Bible was a very "human" book and was not seen as "perfect" in matters of truth. The tools of biblical criticism could help establish fuller understandings of Scripture.

With the recognition of the humanness and culturally conditioned nature of the Bible came the question of how the thought forms and categories of the ancient writings could be meaningful to contemporary people in a modern and scientific world.

One liberal response to this was suggested by Fosdick, who spoke of "abiding experiences and changing categories."[61] He suggested that some basic human experiences always remain the same. But these are expressed in a variety of concepts and frameworks that change from time to time and place to place. The theologian, according to Fosdick, must search out these "abiding experiences" that stand underneath the categories of the Bible and then reinterpret and reformulate the meaning of these experiences in forms that are intelligible and meaningful to contemporary persons. The nature of these "abiding experiences" was defined by Pike: "What is true in the Scriptures, or what seems to ring true, whether a matter of fact or principle or ethic or inspiration or insight, is made true by its correspondence to what would seem to be plausible inferences from experienced reality."[62]

For liberal theology, the principle of autonomy is seen in this view because Christianity continues in the world not through a body of objective propositions or even in an institution but in the "abiding experiences" that are repeatable for each new generation. These experiences exist independent of any received authorities, such as church or Scripture.

The principle of dynamism is also seen in this view of Scripture as experience. The religious truth to which abiding experiences point will always be developing. These experiences will constantly need to be placed in "changing categories," thus being interpreted and reinterpreted again and again.[63]

With this shift to the category of "experience," liberal theology in the tradition of Schleiermacher opened a new way of perceiving the Bible and thus began a new era.

One of the finest liberal preachers in the twentieth century is William Sloane Coffin. In the following sermon, note how the experiences of Scripture witness to God in our experience, and observe the fusion of freedom and virtue, which are universal experiences available to faithful Christians in liberal democracies.

Sail On, O Ship of State

William Sloane Coffin

Matthew 14:22-33

What if modern scholarship should one day establish that the silver dollar George Washington hurled across the mighty Rappahannock had, in fact, splashed? Would George Washington still remain, as we were taught in grammar school, "first in war, first in peace, first in the hearts of his countrymen?" The answer, of course, is yes, for the story of the silver dollar is an expression of faith, not a basis of faith. It is the kind of story followers of George Washington, committed to him on other grounds, would love to tell of him around a good campfire.

Likewise, if Jesus never walked on the Sea of Galilee, he is still to Christians their Messiah. Christ is not God's magic incarnate, but God's love incarnate. He was not one to go around Houdini-like, breaking the laws of physical nature; but rather one who, beyond all limits of human nature, loved as none before nor after him has ever loved. In the face of such awesome love, even the waves must rise up and the winds bow down, even as at his birth a star stood still, and at his death the earth quaked, rending rocks and splitting graves wide open.

And what is the meaning of the story? Ask a crowd straining their necks to see on the ceiling of the Sistine Chapel what they find there, or ask an audience listening to Beethoven's Ninth Symphony what they are hearing, and no two answers will be the same. Such is the evocative power of great works of art. As biblical stories stimulate even more the imagination, no one should be surprised that I see in this story related in Matthew 14:22-33 a perfect three-act drama for a Fourth of July sermon.

As the first act opens, the disciples are boarding a boat for what appears to be a routine crossing. But, at some distance from the shore, they find themselves buffeted by an unexpected and terrible storm. Their boat begins to sink, not only because the winds are high and against them, but also, as it turns out, because Jesus is not there.

Well, were we not also taught in grammar school: " Thou too sail on, O Ship of State,/Sail on, O Union strong and great"? And in the middle of World War II, didn't Churchill send Roosevelt a morale-building telegram quoting that Longfellow poem more fully?

> Thou too sail on, O Ship of State,
> Sail on, O Union strong and great.
> Humanity with all its fears,
> With all the hopes of future years,
> Is hanging breathless on thy fate.

But nobody sends us telegrams like that anymore. We, too, seem at sea, caught in a storm with no compass to point us toward a promising future. That we've come a long way, there's no denying. Even though we were a white nation founded on the genocide and bondage of other races—and though we've a long way to go in our treatment of blacks and Native Americans, ethnic minorities and women (what's one woman on the Supreme Court but hollow symbolism when death comes to the Equal Rights Amendment?)—still, ours is the longest-lasting revolution in the world, over two hundred years old. And the liberties established way back then, in a remote agrarian backwater, have miraculously survived and at times positively flourished.

But today something has happened to our understanding of freedom, to our notion of democracy. Our eighteenth-century forebears were enormously influenced by Montesquieu, the French thinker who differentiated despotism, monarchy, and democracy. In each he found a special principle governing social life. For despotism, that principle was fear; for monarchy, honor; and for democracy—take heed!—virtue. "It is this quality," he wrote, "rather than fear or ambition, that makes things work in a democracy."

Samuel Adams agreed: "We may look to armies for our defense, but virtue is our best security. It is not possible that any state should long remain free where virtue is not supremely honored."

Freedom, virtue—these two were practically synonymous in the minds of our revolutionary forebears. To them it was inconceivable that an individual would be granted freedom merely for the satisfaction of institncts and whims. Freedom, virtue— they were still practically synonymous a hundred years later in the mind of Abraham Lincoln when in his Second Inaugural Address he called for "a new birth of freedom." Freedom and virtue seem to embrace each other in perhaps the greatest of all American hymns, written by Julia Ward Howe:

> In the beauty of the lilies Christ was born across the sea,
> With a glory in his bosom that transfigures you and me;
> As he died to make men holy, let us die to make men free!
> While God is marching on.

Today we Americans are not marching in the ways of the Lord but limping along in our own ways, thinking not of the public weal but of our private interests. Today tax-cutting is more popular than social spending, even for the poorest Americans. And because we have so cruelly separated freedom from virtue, because we define freedom in a morally inferior way, our "Union strong and great" is stalled in a storm, in what Herman Melville called the "Dark Ages of Democracy," a time when, as he predicted, the New Jerusalem would turn into Babylon, and Americans would feel "the arrest of hope's advance." America today is a cross between a warship and a luxury liner, with all attention concentrated on the upper decks. But below the water line there are leaks. Our ship is sinking.

But on to Act II, which opens with one person preparing to abandon ship. And can't you hear the cries? There are so many of those cries in every sinking ship: "For God's sake, Peter, sit down; you're rocking the boat!"

What do you suppose moved Peter, and not the others, to abandon ship? To most human beings there is something fundamentally unacceptable about unpleasant truth. Most of the time we seek to bolster our illusions, to protect ourselves from our fears. But in our more courageous and honest moments, some of us are willing to face the shallowness of our personal relations, the barbaric ladders on which we climb to success, the banality of our culture, the cruelty in our foreign policy. And when in the fourth watch of the night, that miserable 2:00 A.M. to 6:00 A.M. shift when we are most alone with ourselves, Jesus bids us come. Some of us, like Peter, are ready for that leap of faith.

Peter almost immediately begins to sink, and modern scholarship may one day establish that Jesus called him "the Rock" then, not for his foundational but for his sinking properties! And why not? "Whenever I am weak, I am strong," said Paul (2 Cor. 12:10), who had the vision to see that God's "power is made perfect in weakness" (2 Cor. 12:9). It is only when we realize that we can no more trust our own buoyancy than we can that of the ship we have just abandoned that we truly give ourselves to Christ. Then the true miracle takes place, the one that makes this story eternally, if not literally, true. "Lord, save me," cries Peter, and Jesus does (Matt. 14:31). There's the central miracle of every Christian life, which should take place on an average of about every other day. When, sinking in our sense of helplessness, we reach out for a love greater than we ourselves can ever express, when we reach out for a truth deeper than we could ever articulate, and for a beauty richer than we ourselves can ever contain, when we too cry out "Lord, save me," he who died to make us holy does indeed transfigure you and me. Cry out for a thimbleful of help, and you receive an oceanful in return.

Many people wish the story ended here. What greater relief to an unhappy soul than to find stability in a world of turmoil, certitude in a world of doubt, contentment amid pain? But the goal of the Christian life is not to save your soul but to transcend yourself, to vindicate the human struggle of which all of us are a part, to keep hope advancing. Peter doesn't say to Jesus, "Now that you have saved me, Lord, let's walk off, just you and me, into the sunrise of a new day and forget all about those fellows in the sinking ship." No, having abandoned the sinking ship for Jesus, Peter now returns with Jesus.

This is our Fourth of July message, our example for patriots who call themselves Christians: "America, love it and leave it." Leave it for Jesus, for America's sake as well as your own, and then return with Jesus. That's how to love America with Christ's wisdom, with Christ's compassion, with a concern for the whole, fusing once again freedom with virtue in order to renew "the patriot's dream, that sees beyond the years, her alabaster cities gleam, undimmed by human tears."

When Peter returned to the boat with Jesus, the winds abated. I think our own ship could once again recover headway and direction if only American Christians followed Peter's example. With faith in God, it's right to love one's country, love it as Jesus did Israel.

Longfellow may have been a bit triumphant in his view of America, but he was right in the fervor of his love. These are the more prayerful words he addressed to our nation at the end of his poem:

> Sail on, nor fear to breast the sea.
> Our hearts, our hopes are all with thee,
> Our hearts, our hopes, our prayers, our tears,
> Our faith triumphant o'er our fears,
> Are all with thee, are all with thee.

IV

FUNDAMENTALIST THEOLOGY

Scripture as Proposition

TWO OF ITS LEADING ADHERENTS SAID THAT "FUNDAMENTALISM IS THE RELIGIOUS phenomenon of the twentieth century."[1] This American religious movement, which has at times identified itself with the "establishment" and at other times with the "outsiders," is a movement that its supporters say is "here to stay."[2] As the two spokespersons wrote:

> For years it was ignored, criticized, and relegated to the backwoods of Appalachia. But like a rushing mighty wind, it has moved across the tide of secularism in America and left its sweeping imprint on virtually every level of society. The movement that was once despised and rejected . . . resurged as the religious phenomenon of the 1980s.[3]

It is estimated that fundamentalism involves some ten to twenty million Americans.[4] Commenting on the use of current technology, one historian has noted that "militant fundamentalists control a large percentage of the 1,400 radio and 35 television stations that make up the Protestant media network. . . . Moreover, fundamentalist leaders like Jerry Falwell and Pat Robertson—who take in more money than the Republican and Democratic parties—are mastering the mails."[5] From its inception, Falwell's publication *Moral Majority Report* had a greater circulation than any of the traditional "oldline" denominational magazines.[6]

The "identity" of fundamentalists has been variously described. But at its base, they see themselves as

> the legitimate heirs of historical New Testament Christianity. They see themselves as the militant and faithful defenders of biblical orthodoxy. They oppose Liberalism, communism, and left-wing Evangelicalism. True Fundamentalists hold strongly to the same basic tenets that they were debating seventy-five years ago. These defenders of the faith range from well-educated professors to backwoods preachers.[7]

BACKGROUNDS

Historical Interpretations

Historians of the movement known as fundamentalism have painted varying pictures of the movement at different times. In 1931 the early historian of the movement, Stewart Cole, interpreted fundamentalism as a form of social maladjustment. He wrote: "For a half century the church has suffered a conflict of social forces about and within it that accounts for the present babel of witnesses to Christian truth and purpose."[8] H. Richard Niebuhr, writing in the mid-1930s, set the "social sources" of fundamentalism in relation to "the conflict between rural and urban cultures in America."[9]

In the 1950s the "anti-intellectual" stance against evolution and other modern thought was emphasized.[10] Richard Hofstadter claimed that fundamentalist anti-intellectualism and paranoid style were "shaped by a desire to strike back at everything modern—the higher criticism, evolutionism, the social gospel, rational criticism of any kind."[11]

In the late 1960s revisions of these portraits began to be made. Paul Carter argued that fundamentalists were not anti-intellectual, just intellectual in a different way from their opponents.[12] Ernest Sandeen saw the roots of the fundamentalism of the twentieth century as reaching back to the alliance in the nineteenth century between the Old Princeton theology of Princeton Seminary Calvinists and advocates of millenarianism.[13]

The most detailed and persuasive vision of the nature of fundamentalism has been offered by George M. Marsden. His capsulized definition of fundamentalism is worth citing in full.

> Fundamentalists were evangelical Christians, close to the traditions of the dominant American revivalist establishment of the nineteenth century, who in the twentieth century militantly opposed both modernism in theology and the cultural changes that modernism endorsed. Militant opposition to modernism was what most clearly set off fundamentalism from a number of closely related traditions, such as evangelicalism, revivalism, pietism, the holiness movements, millenarianism, Reformed confessionalism, Baptist traditionalism, and other denominational orthodoxies. Fundamentalism was a "movement" in the sense of a tendency or development in Christian thought that gradually took on its own identity as a patchwork coalition of representatives of other movements. Although it developed a distinct life, identity, and eventually a subculture of its own, it never existed wholly independently of the older movements from which it grew.[14]

These varying historical interpretations of the fundamentalist movement showed "a much more complex phenomenon than previously imagined. It is urban and rural, sophisticated and simplistic, intellectual and anti-intellectual, moderate and militant. In short, fundamentalism is much more diverse—geographically, socially, politically, educationally, and theologically—than its negative public image portends."[15]

Historical Developments

The immediate context out of which the fundamentalist movement arose was the American scene from the 1870s to the 1930s. These decades were marked by rapid change and the rise of various new "philosophies of life" (such as pragmatism). More Americans were attending college, and strides in science were substantial.

At the beginning of this period, evangelical Protestantism was "the dominant religious force in American life."[16] But the changing social and intellectual scene presented new theological problems.

One such challenge was that of evolution. In 1859 Charles Darwin published *The Origin of Species*. This work presented the theory of the process of "natural selection," which came to be described as the "survival of the fittest." In its theoretical form, this theory of evolution suggested that only natural forces are involved in determining which species will be able to adapt to world conditions and thus perpetuate themselves. In 1871, with Darwin's *The Descent of Man*, the developmental hypothesis was extended to include humans. All of these ideas were unsettling and troublesome to those who understood the Bible to teach (as in Gen. 1:25) that God had made "the beast of the earth after his kind." The "argument from design," which had been a traditional proof for God's existence, was thus called into question, because the new theory seemed to rule out the need for a God through whose design the whole world itself was created and sustained.[17]

Another major challenge to traditional Protestantism was the rise of biblical criticism and the "scientific study" of religion. As the views of European "biblical critics" (most often German) began to spread in America, increasing controversies in seminaries and denominations developed.[18] Under attack by the "Higher Critics" and historians of religion were the views of Christianity as a unique religion founded on supernatural revelation; the miracles as recorded in the Bible; the historicity of various biblical characters, such as Abraham and Moses; and the historical accuracy of biblical accounts, because they were written from the perspectives of believers in Jesus. With the spread of these kinds of questions in America, traditional Protestantism faced another major challenge.[19]

A third major difficulty for American Protestantism from 1870–1930 was the rapid social change in America itself. During this period

America was changing rapidly from a culture dominated by small towns and the countryside to one shaped by cities and suburbs. Waves of "uprooted" immigrants, together with rapid industrialization, created virtually insurmountable urban problems. Industrialization, with the drive for efficiency, usually overcoming traditional moral restraints, created ethical, social, labor, and political problems beyond the capacities of traditional solutions.[20]

With these challenges in front of them, American Protestants had much to be concerned with and much to ponder.

Theologically, another force was making itself felt at this period. With the spread of biblical criticism and the "scientific" study of religion in America, an alternative theological force to the dominant American evangelicalism came to the fore. This was liberal theology, later called Modernism.[21] Liberalism sought to integrate the findings of science, biblical criticism, and historical studies within its structure and refashion Christian doctrine accordingly. But did scientific discoveries and "the assured results of higher criticism" offer a truth more secure than that of the Bible itself? For liberalism, they did. For traditional Protestants, they did not. But now, "for the first time in American history a broad and influential theology developed which was not evangelical."[22] To this challenge taking shape in the form of an organized theology, conservative American Protestants felt the need to respond.

RESPONSES

A threefold task may be seen as the agenda for evangelical American Christians at the beginning of the twentieth century: "(1) to defend the name of Christianity against the Modernists who wanted the sanction of Protestant tradition without the substance of Protestant faith, (2) to maintain the validity and integrity of evangelical theology in the face of the great changes in American life, (3) to make a convincing response to new forms of thought, particularly evolutionary science."[23]

One significant response to liberalism was the publication of twelve paperback books from 1910 to 1915 for a project called *The Fundamentals: A Testimony of the Truth*.[24] These books were financed by Lyman and Milton Stewart, who owned the Union Oil Company of Los Angeles. Approximately three million copies were distributed free to Christian leaders throughout the English-speaking world. They sought to defend the basics of traditional Christian faith and in that way answer the charges of liberalism. While some 200,000 reported letters of support were received, only a small number of religious journals reviewed the books or gave them notice.[25]

The writers of these volumes represented a broad coalition of denominational and theological affiliations. Included as authors were Methodists, Baptists, Presbyterians, Episcopalians, and pastors of independent churches. One fourth of the authors were British. An indication of the breadth of participation can be seen in that the writers included the staunch Calvinist B. B. Warfield of Princeton Seminary as well as C. I. Scofield, the leading exponent of dispensationalism— a theological position that differed on many crucial points from the Reformed orthodoxy of Warfield.[26] The editor of the series was A. C. Dixon, a prominent evangelist and author who was then pastor of the Moody Church in Chicago. He was succeeded by Louis Meyer, a Jewish-Christian evangelist, and Reuben Torrey, another well-known evangelistic preacher.

Approximately one-third of the articles concerned Scripture and sought to answer the attacks of the liberal theologians. Another third were devoted to traditional Christian doctrines, while the final pieces included polemics gainst modern "isms" (such as Russellism, Mormomism, Eddyism, and Romanism), personal testimonies, and articles on mission and evangelism. Political causes and issues were avoided. *The Fundamentals* represent a symbolic "starting point" for identifying a fundamentalist movement. It represents the movement "at a moderate and transitional stage before it was reshaped and pushed to extremes by the intense heat of controversy."[27]

From 1917 to 1920, many conservative American Protestants found themselves shifting from a moderate to a more militant stance. In that period many were drawn to the desire to save American civilization from the perceived dangers of evolutionism. With the social experience of World War I, a heightened interest in millenarian thought behind them, and the decline of the German civilization in front of them, many linked attacks on the Bible to the potential total collapse of civilization. Christian concern for the spiritual and moral welfare of the nation emerged with the theological concern for the place of the Scriptures as supreme authority to cause many to seek a return to the time when an evangelical theological consensus was the controlling factor in American life.[28]

In 1919 the World Christian's Fundamentals Association met in Philadelphia with 6,000 people in attendance. Other similar meetings were held throughout the century. Out of these meetings emerged what later became the "five points of Fundamentalism," which were to serve as an antidote to liberalism. Reflecting the fundamentals of Christian doctrine, they emphasized: (1) the inerrancy of Scripture, (2) the deity of Christ, (3) the substitutionary atonement of Christ, (4) Christ's bodily resurrection and (5) Christ's literal (premillennial) second advent.[29]

From 1920 to 1925, fundamentalism took shape as a definite movement. Active on two fronts, its adherents sought to gain control of the major denominations and to recover these bodies from drifting toward liberalism. In 1923, J. Gresham Machen of Princeton Seminary wrote a book entitled *Christianity and Liberalism,* in which he argued that modern religious liberalism was a separate religion from historic Christianity.[30] During this period, the Presbyterian Church underwent an ecclesiastical struggle over fundamentalism and modernism centered around the sermon preached by the Baptist Harry Emerson Fosdick, who was supply preacher for the First Presbyterian Church in New York City in 1922. His sermon was entitled "Shall the Fundamentalists Win?" In the Arch Street Presbyterian Church in Philadelphia, Clarence Edward Macartney preached a rejoinder: "Shall Unbelief Win?"[31]

Second, fundamentalists sought to influence American culture by stopping the teaching of evolution in the public schools. This effort was dramatized in the famous Scopes trial at Dayton, Tennessee, in 1925, pitting William Jennings Bryan against Clarence Darrow in the courtroom. The case concerned John Scopes, a biology teacher who was charged with violating a Tennessee law against the teaching of Darwinism in any public school. In this arena, the two lawyers represented the two sides of the "Fundamenalist-Modernist controversy."[32]

This "Scopes Monkey Trial" was a severe test for the fundamentalist movement. Though Scopes was eventually cleared of the charge, the effect of the trial was to discredit fundamentalism intellectually to many Americans. As Marsden has analyzed it: "Before 1925 the movement had commanded much respect, though not outstanding support, but after the summer of 1925 the voices of ridicule were raised so loudly that many moderate Protestant conservatives quietly dropped support of the cause rather than be embarrassed by association."[33]

Yet while fundamentalism as a movement receded from the center stage of American cultural life, it took further root through other means. In local congregations, independent agencies, Bible schools, and mission organizations, as well as through various media, fundamentalist theology and values continue to thrive.[34] The movement in the last fifty years can be seen as taking form within three major bodies: (1) major denominations, such as the Southern Baptist Convention, that self-consciously identify themselves with fundamentalism; (2) fundamentalist influence within non-fundamentalist denominations; and (3) separate fundamentalist denominations.[35] Thus through churches, theological schools, publishing houses, magazines, radio and television media, and vigorous leaders, fundamentalist theology remains an important force in American religious and cultural life.[36]

FUNDAMENTALIST VIEWS OF SCRIPTURE

As fundamentalism developed historically, its views of Scripture owed much to the formulation of the doctrine of Scripture made by the theologians of Princeton Seminary in the nineteenth and early twentieth centuries.[37] In a famous formulation of this view, A. A. Hodge and B. B. Warfield of Princeton presented what they considered to be "the great Catholic doctrine of Biblical Inspiration, *i.e.* that the Scriptures not only contain, but *are the Word of God,* and hence that all their elements and all their affirmations are absolutely errorless, and binding the faith and obedience of men."[38] For them, "every element of Scripture, whether doctrine or history, of which God has guaranteed the infallibility, must be infallible in its verbal expression." Since "infallible thought must be definite thought, and definite thought implies words," one is led to believe in "the truth to fact of every statement in the Scriptures."[39]

This doctrine of Scripture stressed the inerrancy of Scripture, which meant that the Bible is completely accurate on all matters of science, history, and geography about which it teaches. Today this doctrine of inerrancy is often said to be the "evangelical badge" by those who identify themselves as evangelicals and who stand in the tradition of American fundamentalism.[40]

From the 1940s to the present, American fundamentalism has had two streams. A new evangelicalism has emerged that stands in basic continuity with much fundamentalist doctrine but rejects the name "fundamentalist."[41] The second stream is those who maintain the name "fundamentalist." This latter group is often marked by a separatist stance toward those who do not agree with their doctrine.[42]

> Those who throughout the entire period persisted in calling themselves fundamentalists were marked by continued militant separatism. They were mostly dispensationalists and maintained a steadfast refusal to cooperate with apostates and even sometimes with friends of apostates. Some of their leading evangelists often preached anticommunism and American patriotism . . . others were more consistently separatist and apolitical.[43]

Thus fundamentalism today is a varied grouping and includes different ecclesiastical bodies; differing emphases, especially in eschatology; and different theological structures.[44] One strain of fundamentalism is influenced by evangelical pietism and expresses itself in missionary and Bible conferences.[45] Another strain is more confessional or scholastic in orientation; this group in particular perpetuates the Old Princeton theological formulation of the doctrine of Scripture.[46] Thus fundamentalism draws together diverse groups, even those with differing fundamental theological assumptions, such as dispensationalist and covenant theologians.[47]

The Nature of Scripture

As indicated, fundamentalist views of the Bible often stem from the doctrine of Scripture and its nature and authority as formulated by the Old Princeton theology.[48] Part of this view is capsulized in the statement of a contemporary fundamentalist theologian, Charles C. Ryrie: "Today, 'in order to affirm clearly a belief in the full inspiration of the Scripture,' it has become necessary to say, 'I believe in the verbal, plenary, infallible, unlimited inerrancy of the Bible.' "[49]

To gain a perspective on this fundamentalist view of the nature of Scripture, the following terms may be defined.

Verbal inspiration. According to Ryrie, it once was enough to say, " 'I believe in the inspiration of the Bible.' That said it all. Everyone understood those words to mean that the Bible was from God, completely accurate and reliable, and therefore authoritative."[50] But now it is important to emphasize "verbal inspiration" to say that "the very words were inspired, not only the thoughts. . . . God must have guided the very words used by the writers, or the Bible is less than inspired."[51] This view was also emphasized in "The Chicago Statement on Biblical Inerrancy," which affirmed that "the whole of Scripture and all its parts, down to the very words of the original, were given by divine inspiration."[52]

Plenary inspiration. Ryrie defined the term *plenary* as meaning "full" or "complete." This term assures that "no part of the Bible would be omitted" with regard to inspiration[53] and counters a view that "the inspiration of Scripture can rightly be affirmed of the whole without the parts, or of some parts but the whole."[54]

Infallible. With regard to inspiration, Ryrie wrote that the term *infallible* affirms that "the words were exactly the ones God wanted in the text, and therefore every word was authoritative."[55] In a wider sense, as the "Chicago Statement" said, Scripture is "infallible, so that, far from misleading us, it is true and reliable in all the matters it addresses."[56] A fuller definition follows: *"Infallible* signifies the quality of neither misleading nor being misled and so safeguards in categorical terms the truth that Holy Scripture is a sure, safe and reliable rule and guide in all matters."[57]

At this point it may be noted that most fundamentalists reject the charge that their view gives them a "mechanical" or "dictation" mode of inspiration. How did God inspire human authors to record God's Word? The "Chicago Statement" declared that "the origin of Scripture is divine. [But] the mode of divine inspiration remains largely a mystery to us."[58] Yet, leading fundamentalist preacher and writer John R. Rice appeared to argue in favor of the dictation theory when he wrote that "God raised up men, prepared the men and prepared their vocabularies, and God dictated the very words which they would put down in the Scriptures."[59] Rice also wrote:

> "Dictation," says someone, "dishonors the men who wrote the Bible." Shame! Shame! So you want big prophets and a little God, do you? You do not want a man simply hearing what God says and writing it down, do you? Well, then your attitude is simply the carnal attitude of the unbelieving world that always wants to give man credit instead of God, whether for salvation or inspiration. A secretary is not ashamed to take dictation from man. Why should a prophet be ashamed to take dictation from God?[60]

While owning the term *dictation,* Rice said it was not "mechanical dictation": "Face it honestly, if God gave the very words and men wrote them down, that is dictation. It was not *mechanical* dictation."[61]

Inerrancy and unlimited inspiration. For Ryrie, "inerrant inspiration" focuses on "the necessary relation between accuracy of the words and authority of the message."[62] Put positively, he said, "the inerrancy of the Bible means simply that the Bible tells the truth."[63] This quality was further defined in the "Chicago Statement" as meaning "the quality of being free from all falsehood or mistake and so safeguards the truth that Holy Scripture is entirely true and trustworthy in all its assertions."[64] Article XII of the "Chicago Statement" stated both "positive" and "negative" dimensions to inerrancy:

> We affirm that Scripture in its entirety is inerrant, being free from all falsehood, fraud, or deceit.
> We deny that Biblical infallibility and inerrancy are limited to spiritual, religious, or redemptive themes, exclusive of assertions in the fields of history and science. We further deny that scientific hypotheses about earth history may properly be used to overturn the teaching of Scripture on creation and the flood.[65]

In this view, the terms *infallible* and *inerrant* may be "distinguished but not separated."[66]

For the fundamentalist a distinction is sometimes made between what the Bible "says" and what it "teaches." When critics of inerrancy look at the book of Job and see the recorded speeches of the "comforters" of Job who espouse a wrong theology and thus conclude that the Bible teaches "error," inerrantists respond that "these 'errors' are *recited* rather than *asserted*. The literary form permits us to distinguish between the fact that they said this (the *veritas citationis*) and the truth of what they said (the *veritas rei citatae*)."[67] This distinction does not in the minds of fundamentalists diminish the concept of "unlimited inerrancy." For it is "where Scripture explicitly teaches truth about history and nature [that] it is wholly reliable."[68] Or, as Harold Lindsell has described it:

> This Word is free from all error in its original autographs. . . . It is wholly trustworthy in matters of history and doctrine. However limited may have been their knowledge, and however much they may have erred when they were not writing sacred Scripture, the authors of Scripture, under the guidance of the Holy Spirit, were preserved from making factual, historical, scientific, or other errors. The Bible does not purport to be a textbook of history, science, or mathematics; yet when the writers of Scripture spoke of matters embraced in these disciples, they did not indite error; they wrote what was true.[69]

Where "problem passages" such as apparent discrepancies, conflicting numbers, differences in parallel accounts, or purportedly unscientific statements occur in the Scriptures, inerrantists would respond that these were "due to errors in the transmissions of manuscripts over time, modern misunderstanding of what the texts really mean, or temporary confusion that would clear up with more time and scholarship."[70] Or, as Ryrie put it:

> The inerrantist, on the other hand, has concluded that the Bible contains no errors. Therefore, he exercises no option to conclude that any of those same problems is an example of a genuine error in the Bible. His research may lead him to conclude that some problem is yet unexplainable. Nevertheless, he believes it is not an error and that either further research will demonstrate that or he will understand the solution in heaven.[71]

It is this view of the nature of Scripture that underlies the sole doctrinal basis for the Evangelical Theological Society, founded in 1949: "The Bible alone, and the Bible in its entirety, is the Word of God written and is therefore inerrant in the autographs."[72] On this foundation the conclusion is drawn that "because the Bible is God's Word, he originally gave it to us in a form that was without error and that spoke truthfully on whatever subject it treated. God is true, and therefore his Word sets forth the truth without any admixture of falsehood."[73]

SCRIPTURE AS PROPOSITION

Behind the fundamentalist views of infallibility, inerrancy, and authority lies a specific view of the nature of God's revelation in Scripture. For fundamentalists and those in the fundamentalist tradition, Revelation is considered as "a set of propositional statements, each expressing a divine affirmation, valid always and everywhere."[74] Carl

Henry urges that God is revealed "in the whole canon of Scripture which objectively communicates in propositional-verbal form the content and meaning of all God's revelation."[75] Further, Henry writes: "God's revelation is rational communication conveyed in intelligible ideas and meaningful words, that is, in conceptual-verbal form."[76]

Because it is believed that "the biblical position is that the mighty acts of God are not revelation to man at all, except in so far as they are accompanied by words to explain them," the words of Scripture are seen as revealed by God and inspired by God.[77] These Scripture propositions themselves reflect the character of God— they are God's Word. Thus because God is perfect and cannot lie or deceive, God's Word in its propositional form also cannot lie or deceive. Put in syllogistic form, Ryrie proposes:

1. *Major Premise:* God is true (Rom. 3:4).
2. *Minor Premise:* God breathed out the Scriptures (2 Tim. 3:16).
3. *Conclusion:* Therefore, the Scriptures are true (John 17:17).[78]

Ryrie concludes that "a God-breathed Bible must be a *true* Bible."[79] This perception of truth is the foundation for the following sermon by James Borland, a fundamentalist scholar and preacher in Lynchburg, Virginia. Observe how scriptural images from both Testaments are woven into a three-point system of thought about the biblical principle of acts and consequences.

Sowing and Reaping

James Borland

The Bible frequently uses the motif of sowing and reaping. Eliphaz proclaims metaphorically that "those who plow iniquity and sow trouble reap the same" (Job 4:8). The psalmist notes that "Those who go out weeping,/ bearing the seed for sowing,/ shall come home with shouts of joy,/ carrying their sheaves" (Ps. 126:5).

Proverbs states both the positive and the negative aspects of this motif. "Those who sow righteousness get a true reward" and "Whoever sows injustice will reap calamity" (Prov. 11:18; 22:8). The prophet Hosea warns of the extreme consequences of sowing the wind and reaping the whirlwind (Hos. 8:7). Haggai cautions that sowing may be in vain if one's heart is not right and urges Israel to "consider your ways" (Hag. 1:6-7).

I would like to consider three stages in the sowing and reaping motif as they affect each of us today. First, there is a time to sow. This is followed by a period of growing, and subsequently a final stage of mowing.

I. A TIME TO SOW: THE FAITH STAGE

All of life presents opportunities to sow. For the farmer it takes willpower to get started, followed by seed and soil, work and water. In any case, one has to get started. It is obvious that sowing must begin if a harvest is to be reaped. What a paradox it is that failure to sow is itself the sowing of idleness or perhaps something worse than that.

Yet, many excuses can be found for not sowing. Solomon observes that one who watches the wind might use it as an excuse to avoid casting his seed into the field for fear it might blow away.

Again, the sowing stage is the faith stage. It takes faith to sow a crop. In fact, the planted seed appears to rot and decay. Will life spring forth or has the seed been wasted? One must trust God for the increase. One seed of sweet corn may yield five hundred kernels of ripe corn, but it takes faith to trust God for the result.

Solomon records the paradox that there is that which scatters and yet increases; and also that which refrains from scattering. The latter retains the seed, and yet it tends to poverty (Prov. 11:24). There is a time to sow, but it takes faith to do so. We may wonder if we'll get results, but if we fail to sow, the consequences are certain.

II. A TIME TO GROW: THE MYSTERY STAGE

After the seed has been sown, the second period of the sowing and reaping process unfolds. It is a time of mystery and magic. New life springs forth from the old. Somehow the seeming death and disintegration of the seed produces revival and life. It is not termination, but germination. The movement is from expiration to animation.

This second part of the drama is a time to grow. It is the mystery stage. Jesus captured the essence of this period in a brief parable about a farmer. He plants and then goes about the rest of his chores. Almost imperceptibly, the seed begins to sprout, grow, and mature—in a way quite inexplicable to the farmer (Mark 4:26-28). It is truly a mystery. Human beings may plant and scatter their seeds, but it is God who superintends the growing process.

It is a truism that some things take longer to grow than others. If one of my sons wants to help in the garden and see the fruit of his labors soon, we'll plant some radishes. They sprout, grow, and mature rapidly. Watermelons take much longer. But an acorn will take most of my son's life to grow large and strong, and even then it will not be finished.

Everything that is sown has its own growing cycle. God has encoded into the genetic fabric of every plant how it will grow and mature. Likewise, all that one sows during this life will grow to produce some harvest. The result may not be anticipated by some, but the reward, either good or bad, will be certain.

After a while the growing stage is complete. Then it is time to harvest, reap, pick, or combine. There is a time to sow, a time to grow, and a time to mow.

III. A TIME TO MOW: THE REWARD STAGE

Two principles in God's word are applied directly to sowing and reaping. The Apostle Paul declares both ideas. First, one will reap *what* he sows. "Do not be deceived; God is not mocked, for you reap whatever you sow" (Gal. 6:7). Second, one will reap *how* he sows. "The one who sows sparingly will also reap sparingly, and the one who sows bountifully will also reap bountifully" (2 Cor. 9:6).

The reward stage is full of precision. One who sows kindness will reap kindness. If I sow mercy, I will reap mercy. Love sown will result in love reaped. Joy will yield joy.

Purity exhibited in one's life will result in a pure harvest as well. Happiness sown in the lives of others will gain happiness for the sower. Sow patience; reap patience. Gentleness sown will reap the same.

If I am helpful, I will find help myself. Good deeds sown will later be reaped. A harvest of righteousness will come to the one who sows righteousness. The same could be said for fidelity, dependability, faithfulness, trust, meeting others' needs, sharing, and a host of other wonderful seeds to sow.

The contrary is also true. Corruption will yield corruption. Sinful acts will bring a sinful harvest. Wicked deeds will produce a harvest of wicked fruit, death, and destruction. One cannot mock God. The wicked may claim that serving God is useless and in vain, or that his own actions will bear no consequence. But claim and reality will be harmonized.

So, too, each of us will reap how we sow— that is, to the same extent. If I sow much, I'll reap much. If I sow little, my reward will be little. Great wickedness will result in great loss, but a bountiful harvest awaits those who sow plentifully.

The conclusion is this: First, we must get busy sowing. We have to get started. It takes willpower and energy. It also takes faith to sow for a future harvest. Get started sowing good things today.

Second, leave the growing and maturing process with God. He knows how to multiply the seed that is sown just fine. He will cause it to mature on schedule, and his timing is perfect. We may not understand it, but we can rest assured in the perfection of the process.

Third, remember that the reward will be according to what we sow as well as how we sow. This should be an encouragement to sow good things, deeds, ideas, thoughts, and actions. Similarly, it should challenge us to sow abundantly, realizing that nothing sown will ever be wasted, but will instead yield a proportionately large harvest, either here or hereafter.

V

SCHOLASTIC THEOLOGY

Scripture as Doctrine

THE MOVEMENT THAT MAY BE TERMED "SCHOLASTIC THEOLOGY" CAN BE ASSOCIATED with a distinctive theological movement that was particularly powerful in America in the nineteenth century. This movement is often called the "Old Princeton" theology. It is associated with a line of professors who taught at Princeton Seminary from its founding in 1812 until the seminary was split by a theological dispute in 1929. Throughout the nineteenth and into the twentieth centuries the "Princeton Theology" was very influential in the intellectual life of Americans.[1] It sought to maintain a continuity with the Reformation theology of John Calvin and his successors in the period of seventeenth-century Reformed orthodoxy.

One of the hallmarks of the Princeton theology was its developed doctrine of Scripture. In the 1920s and later, many Americans adopted the formulations of Old Princeton on Scripture as their own.[2] Both fundamentalists and Old Princeton adherents were united in their opposition to liberalism and modernism. However, they disagreed sharply on other points of doctrine, such as the covenant, predestination, and eschatology.

Contemporary controversies over the nature of Scripture and its authority have focused special attention on the doctrine of Scripture as formulated by the Old Princeton school.[3] In particular, the view of the inerrancy of Scripture, which was a crucial component of the Princeton position, is today carefully scrutinized and debated.[4]

BACKGROUNDS

Four Princeton Theologians

Princeton Seminary was founded in 1812. Until that time in America, the Presbyterian Church had no centralized location for providing theological training for its pastors. In 1808, the Rev. Archibald Alexander (1772-1851) preached a sermon to the General Assembly of the church lamenting this fact. Alexander who had been moderator of the church in 1807, found himself in 1811 as the chair of a committee that was to construct a plan for a theological seminary. In 1812, he was elected as the first professor of the church's first seminary located in Princeton, New Jersey. On August 12, 1812, he was inaugurated to this post.[5]

Archibald Alexander was to play a significant role in the shaping of what became the Princeton theology.[6] It was his task to construct the curriculum for the new institution, and the course of study for many years was directed largely by Alexander's own interests and concerns. Prior to assuming his position, Alexander had been pastor of the Third Presbyterian Church in Philadelphia and also President of Hampton-Sydney College in Virginia. His earlier pastorates were in Charlotte County, Virginia, and he had been for a time a circuit-rider preacher along the frontiers of Virginia and Ohio.[7]

Alexander's early education was received through his tutor William Graham, a graduate of Princeton College who studied there under its famous president, John Witherspoon. Graham conveyed Witherspoon's influence to Alexander, particularly Witherspoon's commitment to the Scottish Common Sense philosophy. Alexander's religious experience was also shaped by his exposure to various revivals in the Blue Ridge region, which he visited with Graham. Through Graham, Alexander also became familiar with the writings of Calvinist theologians, such as Jonathan Edwards, John Owen, and Francis Turretin.[8]

It is well said that "in Dr. Alexander is to be found, in germ, the entire Princeton theology."[9] This is true not only with regard to various doctrines but also in terms of the "grand motifs" of the Princeton theology. These have been summarized as devotion to the Bible, concern for religious experience, sensitivity to the American experience, and full employment of Presbyterian confessions, seventeenth-century Reformed systematicians, and the Scottish philosophy of Common Sense.[10]

One of Archibald Alexander's earliest and most brilliant students was Charles Hodge (1797–1878). Hodge was the son of a surgeon. He was born in Philadelphia and entered the sophomore class of Princeton College in the fall of 1812. From 1815 to 1819, Hodge attended Princeton Seminary, where he studied theology with Alexander. The first Princeton professor had become nearly a father to Hodge, who had lost his own father early in life.[11]

After graduating from the seminary, Hodge followed the course suggested by Alexander and made a special study of biblical Hebrew while also being licensed to preach. In June 1820, Hodge returned from his home in Philadelphia to become an instructor in the biblical languages to Princeton Seminary students. He was to remain on the faculty for fifty-eight years, during which time he taught approximately three thousand students.[12] Hodge became Professor of Didactic Theology in 1840. From 1826 to 1828, Hodge toured German theological institutions and gained appreciation for the benefits of the German approach to theology. Meanwhile he also saw the dangers of "rationalism," "mysticism," and "ritualism."[13]

Charles Hodge elaborated on the groundwork laid by Archibald Alexander and provided the Princeton theology with its most comprehensive systematic statement. In 1872, Hodge's 2,000-page, three-volume *Systematic Theology* replaced the *Institutio Theologiae Elenticae* of Francis Turretin as Princeton's principal textbook of systematic theology.[14] This text became one of the most widely used seminary textbooks and remains in print to the present day. Hodge's influences were substantial through his voluminous writings, which are marked by his unchanging commitment to orthodox Calvinism, his emphasis on logic as a tool of Christian theology, and also his concern for the personal and spiritual dimensions of theological doctrine.[15]

In 1877, one year before Charles Hodge died, he was joined at Princeton by his son Archibald Alexander Hodge (1823–86), who became his assistant and then his successor as Princeton's third Professor of Theology.[16]

A. A. Hodge was named in honor of Archibald Alexander and graduated from the seminary in 1847. He had served three pastorates in Maryland, Virginia, and Pennsylvania prior to becoming a Professor of Theology at Western Seminary in Allegheny, Pennsylvania, (now Pittsburgh Theological Seminary) in 1864.

Benjamin Breckinridge Warfield (1851–1921) was a close friend and colleague of A. A. Hodge as Professor of New Testament Language and Literature at Western Seminary. When A. A. Hodge died suddenly and without warning in 1886, Warfield was chosen to take his place. He served as Professor of Didactic and Polemical Theology at Princeton for thirty-three years.

B. B. Warfield entered Princeton College the same year (1868) James McCosh (1811–94) became its president. McCosh was the last great proponent of Scottish Common Sense realism on the American intellectual scene.[17] After initial interest in science, Warfield entered Princeton Seminary in 1873, where he studied under Charles Hodge until 1876. When he graduated, Warfield traveled and studied in Europe, became an Assistant Pastor of First Presbyterian Church of Baltimore, and in 1878 went to Western Seminary to teach New Testament. When the call to Princeton came, Warfield switched to the field of theology in the same way as had Charles Hodge previously.[18]

B. B. Warfield was a prolific writer who was a vigorous defender of the Princeton theology on all fronts. In particular he worked to refine the Princeton doctrine of Scripture to meet the rising tides of liberalism and the continuing assaults of biblical criticism. This took particular focus in Warfield's defense of the Princeton doctrine against the criticisms of Charles Augustus Briggs (1841–1913), who questioned its doctrine of inerrancy and charged the Princeton theology with deviating from the teachings of Calvin and the Westminster Confession.[19]

THE OLD PRINCETON TRADITION

The four theologians from Alexander to Warfield were the major shapers of the Old Princeton theology, but others made important contributions as well. The last major defender of the old Princeton theology at Princeton Seminary was J. Gresham Machen (1881–1937). Machen became a student of Warfield's in 1902 and from 1906 to 1929 taught New Testament at Princeton.[20] In 1923 Machen published a book entitled *Christianity and Liberalism,* in which he argued that the two were completely different religions. In 1929 the General Assembly of the Presbyterian Church gave its approval to the reorganization of Princeton Seminary. Under the leadership of president J. Ross Stevenson (president since 1914), the seminary was moving in the direction of including a variety of theological positions among its faculty.[21] When the seminary was reorganized in 1929, Machen and three other faculty members—Oswald T. Allis, Robert Dick Wilson, and Cornelis Van Til—left to found Westminster Seminary in Philadelphia to carry on the Old Princeton tradition. In its first semester, fifty students enrolled at the new seminary.[22] Today the Old Princeton tradition is self-consciously carried on in a variety of forms at Westminster Seminary; Covenant Seminary in St. Louis; the Reformed Seminary in Jackson, Mississippi and Maitland, Florida; and

Faith Seminary in Philadelphia. In addition, individual professors in other theological institutions may be found who self-consciously adhere to the Old Princeton theology.[23]

SCRIPTURE IN THE OLD PRINCETON THEOLOGY

The Princeton theologians were deeply committed to traditional Calvinism. As American Presbyterians, each professor at Princeton took a subscription vow to the Westminster standards.[24] In this they confessed their belief that a system of doctrine was taught in Holy Scripture and has been accurately systematized in the Westminster Confession of Faith. As professors at Princeton, they promised not to teach anything contrary to this system of doctrine.

The particular sources of the Princetonians' doctrine of Scripture has been studied and debated in recent years.[25] Some scholars have argued that the Princeton doctrine with its emphasis on the "inerrancy" of Scripture, particularly in the original (now lost) autographs, owes its origin to the scholastic theology of seventeenth-century Reformed orthodoxy and especially to the writings of the Swiss theologian Francis Turretin (1623–87). It is further argued that Turretin's theological method was a Protestant version of the approach of Thomas Aquinas (1225–74), in which reason is given a priority over faith and reason leads to faith. In this and in Reformed scholasticism's development of the concept of inerrancy, by which the Bible is said to provide technically accurate information on all subjects about which it teaches, some have seen a departure from the views of Calvin and of the Westminster Confession.[26] In this analysis, Calvin and the Westminster Confession stand in a tradition that stretches back to Augustine (354–430) and emphasizes that faith leads to understanding as a theological method. Scripture is seen as providing guidance for the life of Christian faith. Scripture is infallible for that purpose. Technical inerrancy is not required for this purpose to be accomplished.[27]

Others have stressed elements of continuity between the Reformers and Reformed orthodoxy. In their view, the orthodox developed the theology of the reformers to meet the challenges of their own context and times, and in many instances merely drew out the logical implications of what was already to be found in, for example, Calvin's teachings. In this view, the inerrancy of Scripture is seen as Calvin's own teaching with its roots in the earlier history of the church as well.[28] Scholars of this persuasion, while recognizing that Turretin was a "major influence at Old Princeton," do not see that Turretin and Reformed scholasticism were "dominant in the sense of determining the scope and sweep of their theology."[29]

Despite these scholarly disputes, it is possible to delineate the distinctive features of the Princeton theology's view of Scripture. Variations and developments from Archibald Alexander to B. B. Warfield can be discerned. But these took shape in the context of the new questions and issues with which the Princeton theologians had to deal.[30]

Reason and Revelation

From its inception, the Princeton theology placed a heavy emphasis on the powers and capacities of human reason. The original "Plan" of the theological seminary was concerned to train theologians who could combat Deism.[31] Deists believed that human reason could discover the moral law that was inherent in nature as the only revelation humanity needed. Princeton professors sought to demonstrate the proper use of reason in religion and the need for biblical revelation. As Archibald Alexander wrote: "Without reason we can form no conception of a truth of any kind; and when we receive any thing as true, whatever may be the evidence on which it is founded, we must view the reception of it to be reasonable. Truth and reason are so intimately connected that they can never with propriety be separated."[32]

Reason was also a useful tool with which to interpret Scripture. Again Alexander wrote: "It is reasonable to believe whatever God declares to be true."[33]

For all the Princeton theologians, there were two sources of the knowledge of God. "Natural revelation" was God's revelation in the course of nature and history. "Special revelation" was God's revelation in Scripture. The theistic proofs of God's existence, developed particularly by Aquinas and his followers, were logically valid according to the Princeton theologians, and thus through rational arguments one could come to a knowledge of God's existence.[34] Warfield wrote of the relationship between general and special revelation:

> Without special revelation, general revelation would be for sinful man incomplete and ineffective. . . . Without general revelation, special revelation would lack that basis in the fundamental knowledge of God as the mighty and wise, righteous and good, maker and ruler of all things, apart from which the further revelation of this great God's interventions in the world for the salvation of sinners could not be either intelligible, credible or operative.[35]

Thus reason and revelation went together. Both were necessary for a knowledge of God and each in its own way produced a reliable knowledge of God.

The Nature of Faith

Due to the presence and power of human sin, the Princeton theologians believed that humans could not come to a *saving* knowledge of God on their own. For this the "internal testimony" or "internal witness" of the Holy Spirit was needed.[36] This was the act of "regeneration," which occurs when the Spirit grants the gift of the faith in Jesus Christ to sinners.

But for the Princeton theologians, particularly Warfield, the means the Holy Spirit used were the methods of causing the human reason to acquiesce to logical "reasons for faith." Charles Hodge defined faith as "assent to the truth, or the persuasion of the mind that a thing is true."[37] For him, "The Scriptures teach that faith is the reception of truth on the ground of testimony or on the authority of God."[38] As Warfield developed this notion that faith is grounded in evidence, he taught that "the action of the Holy Spirit in giving faith is not apart from evidence, but along with evidence; and in the first instance consists in preparing the soul for the reception of the evidence."[39] Thus faith is not unreasonable. It is indeed *the* most reasonable action, because the "testimony" on which one's faith rests is the testimony of God by the Holy Spirit.

But for Hodge and Warfield, this testimony of the Holy Spirit was an action separate from the act of "faith" by which one came to believe in the divine origin of the Scripture. The "evidence" upon which this "faith" rested, Warfield called the *indicia* of the divinity of Scripture.[40] These *indicia* provided the proofs of the divine origination of the Bible. These *indicia* were "coworkers" with the Holy Spirit to bring one to the faith that Scripture was divine.[41]

Authority of Scripture

For the Princeton theologians, Scripture was authoritative because God has spoken through the biblical writers. As Charles Hodge put it: "The Bible claims to be the Word of God; it speaks in his name, it assumes his authority."[42] Warfield wrote:

> The authority of the Scriptures thus rests on the simple fact that God's authoritative agents in founding the Church gave them as authoritative to the Church which they founded. All the authority of the apostles stands behind the Scriptures, and all the authority of Christ behind the apostles. The Scriptures are simply the law-code which the law-givers of the Church gave it.[43]

This meant for Warfield that it was crucial to show that all the canonical books had apostolic sanction and authority.[44]

Verbal Inspiration

In his earliest expression of biblical inspiration, Archibald Alexander had distinguished among three kinds of inspiration: (1) *superintendence,* which was guidance of the authors but no new revelation of facts to them; (2) *suggestion,* which functioned to communicate new information to the author; and (3) *elevation,* which is seen when a biblical writer spoke or wrote in words or ways that were "far more sublime and excellent than they could have attained by the exercise of their own faculties."[45] Later Princeton writers rejected these degrees of inspiration.[46]

Charles Hodge, however, was the first to give systematic expression to the Princeton view of inspiration, which was defined in his *Systematic Theology* as "an influence of the Holy Spirit on the minds of certain select men, which rendered them the organs of God for the infallible communication of his mind and will. They were in such a sense organs of God, that what they said God said."[47] Earlier Hodge asserted that "the whole end and office of inspiration is to preserve the sacred writers from error in teaching."[48]

B. B. Warfield defined *inspiration* in his inaugural address at Allegheny Seminary in 1880 as the "extraordinary, supernatural influence (or, passive, the result of it) exerted by the Holy Ghost on the writers of our Sacred Books, by which their words were rendered also the words of God, and therefore, perfectly infallible."[49] Both human and divine dimensions were present in inspiration. As Warfield wrote:

> The Church, then, has held from the beginning that the Bible is the Word of God in such a sense that its words, though written by men and bearing indelibly impressed upon them the marks of their human origin, were written, nevertheless, under such an influence of the Holy Ghost as to be also the words of God, the adequate expression of His mind and will.[50]

Warfield used the term *concursus* to describe both of these dimensions, defining it as meaning that "every word is at once divine and human."[51]

Inerrancy

Charles Hodge recognized difficulties with what Warfield later described as *concursus*—that is, that God guided the language as well as the thoughts of the biblical writers. When "difficulties" in the biblical text arose, Hodge said the only proper course was "to believe what is proved to be true, and let the difficulties abide their solution."[52] Basically Charles Hodge believed that "the difficulties are so minute as to escape the notice of ordinary intelligence." An example of such, he said, would be when one writer might state that "on a certain occasion twenty-four thousand persons were slain; another, a thousand years after, says there were twenty-three thousand." While there may be other more serious objections, Hodge still believed these objections were "pitiful" and "miraculously small."[53] Hodge's view was captured in his famous description:

> The errors in matters of fact which skeptics search out bear no proportion to the whole. No sane man would deny that the Parthenon was built of marble, even if here and there a speck of sandstone should be detected in its structure. Not less unreasonable is it to deny the inspiration of such a book as the Bible, because one sacred writer says that on a given occasion twenty-four thousand, and another says that twenty-three thousand, men were slain. Surely a Christian may be allowed to tread such objections under his feet.[54]

For Hodge, the inspiration of Scripture was seen in the form that it comes to us—in verbal forms, or words. These words, because Scripture *is* the word of God, are also the *words of God*. Because God is perfect and cannot lie or err, Scripture too must be perfect in this way. Scripture, for Charles Hodge and the Princeton tradition, cannot deceive or err in what it teaches, even on matters of science, geography, and history. As Charles Hodge wrote:

> An inspired man could not, indeed, err in his instruction on any subject. He could not teach by inspiration that the earth is the center of our system, or that the sun, moon, and stars are mere satellites of our globe, but such may have been his own conviction. Inspiration did not elevate him in secular knowledge above the age in which he lived; it only, so far as secular and scientific truths are concerned, preserved him from teaching error.[55]
> Inspiration extends to all the contents of these several books. It is not confined to moral and religious truths, but extends to the statements of facts, whether scientific, historical or geographical. It is not confined to those facts the importance of which is obvious or which are involved in matters of doctrine. It extends to everything which any sacred writer asserts to be true.[56]

For Charles Hodge, biblical teachings were perfectly congruent with the findings and teachings of nineteenth-century science. As he put it in one example in 1857, "no man now pretends that there is a word in the Bible, from Genesis to Revelation, inconsistent with the highest results of astronomy."[57]

During the next three decades, with developments in biblical criticism, the natural sciences, and historical thinking, the Princeton position on Scripture also developed. In the 1879 edition of *Outlines of Theology,* A. A. Hodge explicitly introduced the notion that the "original autographs" of Scripture are "absolutely infallible when interpreted in the sense intended, and hence are clothed with absolute divine authority."[58] By careful definition, A. A. Hodge went on to assert that the present copies and translations of Scripture may contain apparent "discrepancies" arising from "frequent transcription." But these discrepancies do not damage a view of the plenary or full inspiration of the Scriptures, because in the most technical sense "the Church has asserted absolute infallibility only of the original autograph copies of the Scripture as they came from the hands of their inspired writers."[59]

This appeal to the "original autographs" of Scripture became an important part of the Princeton theology's view of Scripture in the writings of Warfield and particularly in the article he jointly authored with A. A. Hodge in 1881.[60] For A. A. Hodge and Warfield, *inerrancy* and *infallibility* were synonymous. Each logically implied the other. Both referred to "the complete trustworthiness of Scripture in all elements and in every, even circumstantial statement."[61] For the Bible "in all its parts and in all its elements, down to the least minutiae, in form of expression as well as in substance of teaching, is from God."[62] The Princetonians were not bothered by the argument that we no longer possess the original copies of Scripture. Warfield believed that God had providentially preserved texts that are close enough to the original that through textual criticism the autographic texts were within reach. As he wrote: "God has not permitted the Bible to become so hopelessly corrupt that its restoration to its original text is impossible."[63]

For the inerrancy of Scripture to be *disproved,* A. A. Hodge and Warfield set out their views on what would constitute a "proven error" in Scripture.

> (1). Let it be proved that each alleged discrepant statement certainly occurred in the original autograph of the sacred book in which it is said to be found. (2). Let it be proved that the interpretation which occasions the apparent discrepancy is the one which the passage was evidently intended to bear. It is not sufficient to show a difficulty, which may spring out of our defective knowledge of the circumstances. The true meaning must be definitely ascertained, and then shown to be irreconcilable with other known truth. (3). Let it be proved that the true sense of some part of the original autograph is directly and necessarily inconsistent with some certainly known act of history, or truth of science, or some other statement of Scripture certainly ascertained and interpreted. We believe that it can be shown that this has never yet been successfully done in the case of one single alleged instance of error in the Word of God.[64]

For Hodge and Warfield it was not the "common text" of Scripture but only "the autographic text that was inspired" and "no 'error' can be asserted, therefore, which cannot be proved to have been aboriginal in the text."[65]

With these criteria for "error" fully established, the Princeton theology's doctrine of the authority, inspiration, and inerrancy of Scripture was firmly in place.[66]

SCRIPTURE AS DOCTRINE

The Old Princeton theology has been explicated as an example of what may be termed "scholastic theology."[67] Generally this view can be categorized as emphasizing that God through the Scriptures has revealed certain doctrines to be believed. The Bible, then, is "primarily a source for doctrine, or religious *teachings*."[68] For

> Charles Hodge expressed a doctrinalist perspective when he insisted that "Revelation is the communication of truth by God to the understanding of man. It makes known doctrines. For example, it makes known that God is . . . that Christ is the Son of God; that he assumed our nature; that he died for our sins, etc. These are logical propositions."[69]

Similarly for Hodge's successor B. B. Warfield it can be said that "biblical texts, construed as containing a system of doctrine, strike with numinous power so that one's initial responses, as Warfield reports it are awe, trembling, and submission."[70] Thus "for the doctrinalist understanding of the Bible, the most important and fundamental way in which human beings are to respond to the Bible is with intellectual assent to the 'teaching' propositions asserted therein."[71]

This scientific approach exemplifies the self-understanding of the Old Princeton theology.[72] But it also meant that one of the doctrines of Scripture to be believed was the doctrine of Scripture itself. Thus the Princetonians called people to believe what may be called the "doctrine of the doctrine of Scripture." One came to believe, or have "faith," in Scripture by assenting to the truth of Scripture of which one was persuaded in one's mind by the "evidences" of Scripture that prove its divine origin. Methodologically, "reason leads to faith." When this occurs, one comes to believe, said the Princetonians, that "the Scriptures are the word of God in such a sense that their words deliver the truth of God without error."[73] For the Princeton theology, this was seen as the church's view of the Bible since the earliest times.[74] In the nineteenth and throughout the twentieth centuries, those of the Old Princeton tradition dedicate themselves to perpetuating this view of the Bible.[75] The following sermon by Roger Nicole, from Reformed Seminary, is a classic example of doctrinal preaching about the doctrine of Scripture.

All Scripture Is God-Breathed

Roger Nicole

2 Timothy 3:16

At first it would appear that Timothy did not need to be reminded in that way. He had a wonderful preparation. His mother and grandmother taught him. They had the Scriptures of the Old Testament. And from his youth he was instructed in what Paul there calls, "the sacred letters." Then he had been for some time a companion of Paul, and there is no doubt that he had occasion many times to study the Scripture, memorize it, meditate upon it. Thus it seems somewhat elementary that Paul should approach him and say: "All Scripture is God-breathed. Hold on to what you have learned; don't let anyone shake your foundation. From your youth you have known the Scriptures, and I encourage you to stay with it, because it is very essential for the man or woman of God."

In making that statement, the Apostle Paul has managed to encapsulate in just three words some of the most important features we must recognize in a biblical doctrine of Scripture. He says the Scripture is God-breathed—that tells us the nature of inspiration, the origin of the Scripture. He says the Scripture is God-breathed—that tells us about the object of inspiration. He says all Scripture is God-breathed—this tells us about the extent of inspiration. Thus this verse tells us something about the nature, something about the object, and something about the extent of inspiration. It is not surprising, then, that when people want to discuss the doctrine of the inspiration of Scripture, they should go to 2 Timothy 3:16; it is a classical passage.

Some people, unfortunately, get the idea that this is the only place in the Bible where inspiration is asserted. And that, of course, is not true at all. There are literally hundreds of passages that bespeak inspiration. There are more than 1,700 places in the Bible that say "this is God's Word" or "the Lord spoke to Moses and said" or "thus says the Lord"! If you examine the Scripture withthis in view, you will find a tremendous amount of information and specification on this great subject.

Now let us consider these three words in reverse order. First, the Scripture is God-breathed. This word was explored very carefully by the great Presbyterian scholar Benjamin Breckenridge Warfield. He wrote an immense article of more than fifty pages in the *Presbyterian and Reformed Review* on the actual meaning of that word. Some people had expressed the thought that in this passage that Paul was saying that Scripture is inspiring, that it breathes out God, so that when you are in contact with it, you are under the influence of that breathing out of the Scripture. That, of course, is true, but the fact that something is true does not necessarily indicate that this is the truth that is presented here. Warfield went to work to explore in depth what that word could well mean because this is a rare word. We don't find it anywhere else in the New Testament; we don't find it in the Greek translation of the Old Testament, either; and we don't find it elsewhere in Greek literature prior to the Apostle Paul. Obviously, after our Christian era, since this word was in 2 Timothy, there are people in the church who began to use it, but prior to Paul, nobody had expressed the matter in this way. Warfield made a very strong study of all the Greek words that begin with *theo* (meaning "God") and then end with a participial adjective, like *pneustos*. He gave a very impressive demonstration, so far unchallenged, that words of this type are passive—that is, they indicate something that has been done by God rather than something that is done about God or to God. With great scholarly rigor he draws the conclusion that the translation "God-breathed" is accurate: The Scripture has been breathed out by God; God is at the origin of Scripture. What distinguishes Scripture from all other books is that here God Himself is the author. Other books speak to me about God, but in the Scripture it is God who speaks to me.

In other places God may speak. In nature, for instance; although some people, who press that point to excuse their playing golf instead of worshiping on Sunday morning, may not hear the voice of God as clearly on the greens as they would joining with Christian people in Christian fellowship and studying the Word. Yet God does speak in nature. But in the Scripture He has given us a form of speaking that is beyond doubt, that is marked by the character of God Himself. The examination of the world gives us an ambiguous message because sin is so very commonly mixed with whatever we may see of the good creation of God. But in the Scripture, God has seen to it that we have His word in purity, without mixture of human errors that would tarnish the message. This is God-breathed, and therefore in this passage Paul makes it clear that God is the primary author of Scripture.

It is true, of course, that God spoke using human authors as the means whereby His message would come. God does not do very many things without using means in our lives. He uses parents as a means whereby the nurture of the children will be secured; He uses work as a means whereby the family will be fed; He uses the church as a means whereby the spiritual life of God's people is developed; He uses human authors as the means whereby His Word was consigned in its original form so it could remain a permanent norm for Christian people through all ages. In using these means, God has permitted them to mark, or to stamp as it were, the character of their own lives, personality, style, and preparation on the written record. But what He has also seen to is that no failures, no mistakes that are so common to humanity would be embedded in the record. If that were the case, we would never know when we have a pure message from God and when we have a message that has been tarnished and damaged by the process. You could compare the matter with a garden hose. The type of hose may determine the way the water comes out, but it does not modify the nature of the water that is gushing forth. It is especially important for the communication of truth that the message we get should not be mixed with fallible materials that could mislead us. Now this is precisely what God has done; He has given us a pure flow of divine truth and has permitted that truth to be shaped in some respects by the circumstances and personality of the authors.

At times this dual authorship surfaces. For instance we read in Acts 4:25: "It is you who [spoke] by the Holy Spirit through our ancestor David." God is still seen as the speaker, but He does not speak as a thunderbolt from heaven. Rather, He speaks through the mouth of the human being whom He has equipped for that purpose and is best on that account. It is therefore very important when we approach the Scripture that we should recognize its divine origin and character, for it is a divine impulse and guidance given to human beings whereby they are empowered to record precisely as God wants it done that which God wants to communicate to us for our blessing, for our salvation, and for our spiritual life.

Now in the second place we notice the object of inspiration: It is Scripture. Now this object is important, because most people would attempt to analyze inspiration as something terminating upon human beings. They think that it is their person or their condition that was influenced by the Holy Spirit so that they would be empowered to produce the Scripture. This is not a faulty view, because it is stated expressly in that way in 2 Peter, where we read that "no prophecy of scripture is a matter of one's own interpretation, because no prophecy ever came by human will, but men and women moved by the Holy Spirit spoke from God" (2 Pet. 1:20-21). So here we have the presentation that the Spirit influenced the men and women whose work is embodied in the Holy Scripture, but in 2 Timothy we have a different emphasis. It is Scripture, not writers of Scripture, about which divine inspiration is asserted. You might say, "Well that doesn't really make a difference. This may be proper for an academic situation where you are teaching seminary students, but we don't care whether it is the 'Scripture' or the 'writers of Scripture.' It is all the same." I wouldn't say that. If it was only the writers of Scripture that were inspired, we would not know to what extent they recorded accurately what God had given them by inspiration. If it was the writers of Scripture only who were inspired and not the result of their activity that was divinely controlled, we would be at a sharp disadvantage, because we are some 1,900 years distant from even the most recent one. We have to say that Moses is dead; David is dead; Paul is dead; John is dead; Peter is dead; even Jesus does not speak now as He did in the days of His flesh when He was in Palestine. And so we are beyond the range of the voices of all those people; they are not here anymore with us. Therefore, we would be at a serious disadvantage if only they were the object of inspiration and not what they produced, the text that came forth from their hand.

But that is precisely what Paul tells us: Scripture, what is written, the book that has been written and gathered under the guidance of the Holy Spirit, is the object of the control and of the blessing of God. Therefore, we can say we are at no disadvantage, because we have the Word of God.

Finally it says: All Scripture is given by inspiration, and that is refreshing because so often people say, "All Scripture is inspired, but . . . " and immediately after that there are qualifications and restrictions, some of which may seem to undercut very seriously the authority of the Word. Paul is not concerned here about limitations. He is concerned primarily about the great freedom and assurance that the inspiration of God can give us, and so he says all Scripture is inspired—not only what is contained in the New Testament, but the Old Testament as well. In fact, when he deals with Scripture, probably the scope he had in view is particularly the Old Testament, because that is what Timothy had studied from his youth. The Old Testament writings were the sacred Scriptures he was instructed in from an early age.

It is true that in two passages in the New Testament the word *Scripture* is used in relationship to a New Testament passage, or so it would seem. One of them is in I Timothy 5:18, where the Apostle Paul deals with the question of the salary or subsistence that must be provided for God's servants, and he says: "Scripture says, 'You shall not muzzle an ox while it is treading out the grain' "—a quotation from Deuteronomy 25:4. He continues, "The laborer deserves to be paid." The conjunction *and* is often used in the New Testament to connect one quotation with another. Now "the worker deserves his wages" is a statement that is not found in the Old Testament, but is found in Luke 10:7 in precisely that same form, word for word. And that is a statement by Jesus. It is, therefore, quite possible to construe that the Apostle Paul intended to prove what he said by two quotations, one from the Old Testament and the other from what has become the New Testament. He says, "This is what Scripture says." Thus the passage of Luke may be viewed as part of Scripture.

The other passage is 2 Peter 3:16, where we read that Paul writes the same way in all his letters, speaking in them of these matters discussed also by Peter. His letters contain some things that are hard for some persons to understand, and these may distort these Scriptures "to their own destruction." When Peter says "the other Scriptures," he implies that Paul's letters were Scriptures. The term *other* implies that whatever you talk of belongs to the same category as what you previously have mentioned. In 2 Peter, therefore, it is quite probable that Peter refers to the epistles of Paul as being already recognized as Scripture. It is not clear that this is what Paul does in 2 Timothy 3:16. However, what which is true of the Old Testament is true of the New Testament, for if God took care to provide an infallible norm for His people of old, the Israelites, when they had only the provisional economy of the Old Testament, how much more would God provide an infallible norm when He expressed the truth for all ages until the coming of Jesus Christ.

Now the statement "all Scripture" implies that this is not one book only but all the books of the canon. The statement "all Scripture" implies that this is not only when the Bible deals with some religious subject like Christian doctrine or ethics, but it is reliable in whatever it deals with and makes affirmation about. The confidence in Scripture is not limited to one time or to one people, but it covers up the "waterfront" in every way. We are glad that we have this unambiguous affirmation and that everything we read in Scripture can be received as the Word of God. It is true, of course, that the Scripture records certain things that are not endorsed by God. It records the words of Satan, the words of the friends of Job, the words of some disciples who are being rebuked, the words of the enemies of the gospel, the challenge of some of the heathen kings who assailed Israel—the fact that these things are recorded does not mean that God now says this is true. What is meant is that we have a proper record of what may be an improper statement. We need, therefore, to take notice of the context when we study Scripture, so that we may not ascribe to God something that does not have the divine authority otherwise than by being an appropriate and exact record of what happened or what was said. Yet we can say that from Genesis to Revelation the Scripture is God's Word, and that is what gives us our confidence in the authority of Holy Writ.

A Bible that remains unused is a Bible that is not effective. God has put His word in the Bible. If we do not open the Bible, we don't get God's Word. Therefore, a statement like "All scripture is God-breathed and useful" must challenge us anew to cherish the Word of God, to respect it, to guide our lives by it, to read it, to meditate upon it so that the message of God may come in and invigorate our lives and our church and our society. May it be so for all of us. Amen.

VI

NEO-ORTHODOX THEOLOGY

Scripture as Witness

THE THEOLOGICAL MOVEMENT VARIOUSLY KNOWN AS NEO-ORTHODOXY, NEO-reformation theology, or neo-Calvinism reacted simultaneously to contemporary forms of scholastic theology and to the theology of liberalism. Neo-orthodoxy gained impetus with the publication of Karl Barth's (1886–1968) biblical commentary *The Epistle to the Romans* (1919). This work went through six editions and marked a new approach to biblical scholarship. The movement is chiefly associated with Barth and with Emil Brunner (1889–1966). Together they began what was initially known as "dialectical theology" or the "theology of crisis."[1] Other early figures associated with neo-orthodoxy include Eduard Thurneysen (1888–1974), Friedrich Gogarten (1887–1967), and Rudolf Bultmann (1884–1976).[2] In the broader sweep of the movement, theologians like Hendrik Kraemer, Dietrich Bonhoeffer, Otto Weber, Wilhelm Vischer, Daniel Jenkins, and Thomas Torrance may be seen as related to it.[3] In America, Reinhold Niebuhr (1892–1971) was also seen moving with its direction.[4]

BACKGROUNDS

The term "dialectic theology" as a designation for the theology of what became also known as "neo-orthodoxy" can be traced back to the second edition of Barth's commentary on Romans, published in early 1922. There Barth wrote that he wished to exegete the Scripture in "a dialectic movement as inexorable as it is elastic," to attain "the *inner dialectic of the subject matter.*" Barth's commentary affirms: "The grace of creation, like the grace of redemption, is nowhere present as a given condition among other given conditions. It is the imperceptible relation in which all given conditions stand, and knowledge of it is always and everywhere dialectic."[5]

Barth's association with Gogarten was in part responsible for his reworking the first edition of *Romans* to produce the second. Behind Barth's understandings at this time were thinkers such as Luther and Calvin, Dostoevsky, Blumhardt, Kierkegaard, Nietzsche, and especially Franz Overbeck (1837–1905). Overbeck was a friend of Nietzsche who attacked Christianity and Christendom by arguing that Christianity and history do not belong together. When Christianity takes on a historical form, it is no longer Christian and becomes demonic.[6] A genuine religion, said Overbeck, must be based on a supernatural revelation that originates beyond history. In the course of Christian history, Christianity has become "historicized." In it, "the original message of Christ and the apostles, a message which spoke of the wholly supernatural kingdom of God, had been betrayed by the transformation of Christianity itself into a social, cultural, and political movement *within* history."[7]

Basic to Barth's thought as it developed into "dialectical theology" was the absolute contrast between God and humanity. The personal potency of this contrast for Barth was strong. As the son of a minister of the Swiss Reformed Church who was born in Basel, Switzerland, Barth was trained in the liberal theology of Adolf von Harnack, who passed on to him the theological approach of Schleiermacher. Schleiermacher's influence was to be prominent with Barth for many years.

In 1911 Barth became pastor of a Reformed church. For the next three years he preached as his theological training had taught him, emphasizing life and experience as the basis for his sermons.[8] When World War I broke out and Barth saw his former theological professors were supporting the war policy of Kaiser Wilhelm II, Barth said that "a whole world of exegesis, ethics, dogmatics and preaching, which I had hitherto held to be essentially trustworthy, was shaken to the foundations, and with it, all other writings of the German theologians."[9]

During the war years, Barth studied with his friend Eduard Thurneysen and was introduced to the thought of Johann Christoph Blumhardt (1805–80). Blumhardt's theology stressed eschatology and commitment to the kingdom of God. Barth sought the "signs" of the "breakthrough" of the kingdom while also "waiting patiently for God as he worked for the Kingdom as he could. During this time he said the one term which summed up his new insight from the New Testament was 'hope.' "[10]

Barth's constant need to preach and to produce sermons eventually led him to discover that he could not continue to follow Schleiermacher. Instead of life and experience, Barth began to believe that theology should begin with the Bible and with the God who encounters humans in "the strange new world of the Bible. . . . We have found in the Bible a new world, God, God's sovereignty, God's glory, God's incomprehensible love. Not the history of man but the history of him who hath called us out of darkness into his marvelous light! Not human standpoints but the standpoint of God!"[11]

This approach was seen in Barth's commentary on Romans. There Barth said he wished "to see through and beyond history into the spirit of the Bible, which is the Eternal Spirit."[12] Barth's method clashed with the historical-critical methods of biblical studies, which were taught and practiced by his own teachers, and led to heavy criticism of his book by biblical scholars and theologians, such as von Harnack and Adolf Jülicher.[13] While Barth did not want to negate totally the results of recent centuries of biblical scholarship, he did wish, as he was later to write, that criticism would stop serving "the foolish end of mediating an historical truth lying behind the texts." Instead, scholars should examine Scripture "as it actually is before us."[14] Barth's goal was to turn with "all the more attentiveness, accuracy and love to the texts as such."[15] For Barth this meant "theological exegesis" carried out from the presupposition of the church's basic confession that "Jesus Christ is Lord."[16]

With the second edition of Barth's commentary, the influences of his studies of Plato, Kant, Kierkegaard, and Dostoevsky as well as Calvin and Luther showed clearly, and the contours of dialectical theology began to take shape.[17] From Kierkegaard, Barth borrowed the phrase the "infinite qualitative distinction" between time and eternity, between God and humanity. In opposition to his liberal training, Barth stressed the *discontinuity* between God and humanity. God's transcendence and majesty meant that God is the "Wholly Other," the "Hidden One." Thus for Barth:

> God *is God,* not man writ large; and he cannot be spoken of simply by speaking of ourselves in a loud voice. He cannot be taken for granted as simply "there" in our religious sense, our spiritual depth, or our moral awareness, for he transcends, he stands over against all of these. He can be met, really met, only in the encounter in which we finite creatures of time and history are confronted by the One who is infinite and eternal, and who remains infinite and eternal and "wholly Other" than ourselves in that meeting.[18]

Yet for Barth at the same time, this God has been revealed in Jesus Christ in whom heaven and earth meet. This is the crisis under which the world stands, for all of history and all of humanity has been brought under judgment by this act of God in Jesus Christ. The Word of God in Jesus Christ is one of both mercy and judgment. It contradicts all human achievement, pride, self-sufficiency, ethics, politics, and even *religion.* All human securities, which the Apostle Paul calls the "righteousness of law," fall before the cross of Jesus Christ. There God speaks a decisive "No!" to all human claims for self and leaves humans with no source of security in themselves. This "No!" from God is only part of the picture, however. It is spoken so that humans may also hear the divine "Yes!" in Jesus Christ. In trusting Christ by faith, humanity is saved. The divine answer to the predicament of humanity (sin) is God's own righteousness in Jesus Christ. In Christ, "the Word of God is the transformation of everything that we know as Humanity, Nature, and History, and must therefore be apprehended as the negation of the starting-point of every system which we are capable of conceiving."[19] Faith comes from the pure promise and invitation of God and was not for Barth, as for Schleiermacher, a general awareness of "absolute dependence." Instead, faith was the response of the "moment" to the Word of God himself, Jesus Christ.[20]

The "dialectic" of Barth's thought made a considerable impact on the theological landscape of Europe for the next years. Later Barth said he was like a man who tripped in the darkness of a church tower, accidentally grabbing out and catching a bell-rope to gain his balance, and then with the sounding of the bell, alarming the whole countryside!

For Barth, as for Kierkegaard, the dialectic was in the total contrast between God and humans, the relationship of the "No!" and "Yes!" of God in Jesus Christ, and the implications that stemmed from this. For Barth this meant that no human speech about God could ever contain or even directly or indirectly express the truth about God. All statements by humans needed to be qualified and even negated. Only in this dialectical process may one ever hope to hear the Word of God. For Barth, God is the subject who must be revealed to humankind. Human beings can only "witness" to this wonder.[21]

Barth and his colleagues believed that their rediscovery of the essential message of Paul, and hence of the whole New Testament, stood dramatically opposed to the prevailing liberal theology. For the dialectical theologians, the liberals were seen as having replaced God with humanity and thus having turned theology into anthropology. They saw liberalism as secretly assuming that God and humans were in effect identical. This view meant that liberalism had no adequate doctrine of the revelation of God because it did not take with sufficient seriousness the nature and person of God. From this stemmed other inadequacies of doctrine, from that of Scripture as the vehicle of God's Word to humanity as sinful rather than just misguided, to the nature of authentic faith, which must be radical in its character. The person of Jesus Christ had been grossly distorted in liberalism, according to the dialectical theologians. In liberal theology, Jesus was a spiritual ideal, a "man among men" who set the great example and provided the ethical norms for others to follow. For Barth, Jesus Christ was the Word of God who intersected time and eternity, the finite and the infinite, and who is the One through whom all humanity might become reconciled with God. As Barth said in commenting on Romans 3:21, God in Jesus Christ "pronounces us, His enemies, to be His friends."[22]

Dialectical theology set out to reverse prevailing theological method. Its first emphasis was the "Godness of God." Its second was the reality of the Word of God in Jesus Christ, and third it stressed the impossibility of building theology on any other foundation.[23]

The year 1921 brought Barth the offer of a teaching post in Reformed theology at the University of Göttingen. In 1922 he was given an honorary doctorate of theology from the University of Münster and immersed himself in preparing lectures. At this time he became thoroughly familiar with the Reformed tradition while he taught courses on Calvin, Zwingli, the Heidelberg Catechism, and Schleiermacher.[24]

In 1925 Barth moved to the University of Münster, where he taught until 1930. During this time his *Christian Dogmatics in Outline* appeared in 1927. This work stressed the "Word of God" as the speech or act of God in which God was always the initiator, the "subject." It is the Holy Spirit who makes hearing and responding to God's Word possible. This gave a place for the human, existential situation in which God's revelation occurred. But because of his heavy use of Kierkegaard, Barth's thought was being misunderstood. So Barth began again. This time he reworked his whole theological methodology. He completely rethought the relationship between theology and philosophy. Barth wanted to maintain an emphasis on the knowledge of God, faith, Christian belief, and experience without letting them take on an independent status in themselves.[25]

Barth's new insight came when he taught a seminar in the summer of 1930 on Anselm's classic work *Cur Deus Homo? (Why Did God Become Man?)*. There at the University of Bonn, where he now taught, Barth lectured on what later became his book *Fides quaerens intellectum (Faith Seeking Understanding)*. This work studied Anselm's proof of the existence of God. For Barth the key was in Anselm's concept of theology proceeding through "faith seeking understanding." For Anselm and Barth, faith summons humans to knowledge. Theology was the quest for understanding, which saw behind all "logical understanding" to the inner meaning of the reality behind the words. God initiates faith in us, and from there we move on to further understanding.[26]

For Barth, faith seeks "understanding," which comes from Holy Scripture. Scripture must be read from the perspective of faith. It concerns more than merely trying to understand the meaning of words, paragraphs, and histories in the Bible. "Understanding" when reading the biblical texts comes through illumination by God. Thus theology is the task of the church. The theologian presupposes that God has acted and been revealed.[27]

From this insight, Karl Barth moved on to begin his monumental theological work, *Church Dogmatics*. This work was never completed but at the time of Barth's death ran to thirteen part-volumes, which were published between 1932 (vol. I/1) and 1967 (vol. IV/4, Fragment). In his *Dogmatics,* Barth moved away from the influence of Kierkegaard and tried to "rethink everything that I had said before and to put it quite differently once again, as a theology of the grace of God in Jesus Christ."[28] Barth's work was structured around the doctrines of the Word of God (vol. I), God (vol. II), Creation (vol. III), and Reconciliation (vol. IV). Each of these revolved around the trinitarian structure of God's being as Father, Son, and Holy Spirit. Barth's projected volume on Redemption was never begun. Throughout, Barth's beginning and ending points were Jesus Christ as the revelation of God. These emphases on Christ and the Word of God were to become hallmarks of Barth's theology.

SCRIPTURE IN NEO-ORTHODOX THEOLOGY

The Word of God

Barth's "prolegomena" to his *Church Dogmatics* began with two volumes on "The Doctrine of the Word of God." The term "Word of God" for Barth meant God's "self-revelation."[29] Barth said quite simply: "God's Word means that God speaks."[30] God's revelation and speaking are in Jesus Christ and in the reconciliation of the whole world accomplished in him, for "to say revelation is to say 'The Word became flesh.'"[31]

A special emphasis for Barth was that the Word of God comes in a threefold way. There is the Word revealed (Jesus Christ), the Word written (Scripture), and the Word proclaimed (preaching).[32] These three forms are mutually interrelated and not isolated from one another. There are not three different "Words" of God. There is only one Word of God—Jesus Christ—who meets us in this threefold way.[33]

For Barth, the Scriptures of the church as the church's canon prevented the church from merely proclaiming a human message of its own invention.[34] The canon of Scripture is self-authenticating for Barth, in that there are no "proofs" or "reasons" behind it. The content of the canon is what is decisive. As Barth wrote: "The Bible is the Canon just because it is so. It is so by imposing itself as such."[35]

The Bible Becomes God's Word

God has chosen to confront the church through the ages *via* the Bible. This was God's free decision, not humankind's. So "the Bible is God's Word to the extent that God causes it to be His word, to the extent that He speaks through it."[36] This was a confession of faith. It is not that "man has grasped at the Bible but that the Bible has grasped at man."[37] According to Barth, "the Bible, then, becomes God's Word in this event, and in the statement that the Bible is God's Word the little word 'is' refers to its being in this becoming. It does not become God's Word because we accord it faith but in the fact that it becomes revelation to us."[38]

The Bible is the key link between God's revelation in Christ and the church. Barth wrote: "The decisive relation of the Church to revelation is its attestation by the Bible. . . . The Bible is not itself and as such God's past revelation. As it is God's Word it bears witness to God's past revelation, and it is God's past revelation in the form of attestation."[39]

As a "witness," the Bible points in a definite direction "beyond the self and on to another."[40] In this respect the Bible as a witness claimed no authority for itself but let "that other than itself be its own authority." For Barth, "we thus do the Bible poor and unwelcome honour if we equate it directly with this other, with revelation itself."[41] The direct identification between revelation and the Bible only takes place as "an event." It happens "when and where the biblical word becomes God's Word."[42] In this "event," it is the revelation that "should be understood primarily as the superior principle and the Bible primarily as the subordinate principle."[43]

In "the event of inspiration," however, biblical writers "become speakers and writers of the Word of God."[44] They told of "the occurrence of God's revelation itself apart from their own existence," which had happened "once and once-for-all." This was nothing less than the fact that "God was with us," that "His Word became flesh of our flesh, blood of our blood." The "publishers of revelation," the prophets and apostles, witnessed that "this 'God with us' has happened. It has happened in human history and as a part of human history." This witness gave the biblical writers authority. Even though "they seek no authority, even with their fallible human word they can continually claim and enjoy the most unheard of authority."[45]

The biblical writers, according to Barth, were witnesses to the divine event of God's revelation. Barth said: "Revelation is originally and directly what the Bible and the Church proclamation are derivatively and indirectly, i.e., God's Word."[46] Thus both the Bible and the church's proclamation of the Bible (which is the basis for its preaching and message) "must continually become God's Word." When this happens, it is an act of God's free grace. Insofar as the church's preaching and the Scriptures themselves witness to God's revelation, "one may thus say of proclamation and the Bible that they are God's Word, that they continually become God's Word."[47]

The Authority of Scripture

For Karl Barth, the authority of the Bible was grounded in "the witness of the Holy Spirit."[48] To say this meant that Scripture *becomes* "authentic" and "authoritative" for humans through the work of the Holy Spirit. No reasons or logical proofs lead one to confess the authority of Holy Scripture. One makes this confession through the work of the Holy Spirit. In this sense, Barth was appropriating the theological method he learned from Anselm: "Faith leads to understanding." For Barth, "Scripture is holy and the Word of God, because by the Holy Spirit it became and will become to the Church a witness to divine revelation."[49] The Bible is a unique book. God has made it so. The special content of the Bible, as witness to the Word of God through which the Holy Spirit works to create faith and obedience, is what gives Scripture its authority in the church.

The Inspiration of Scripture

The Scriptures claim for themselves that they are witnesses to Jesus Christ, God's incarnate Word.[50] But it is through human beings who were "witnesses" that this revelation in Christ came to the world. These people were *witnesses* of the Word. To be more precise, they are primary witnesses, because they are called directly by the Word to be its hearers, and they are appointed for its communication and verification to other men. These men are the *biblical witnesses of the Word*, the prophetic men of the Old Testament and the apostolic men of the New. They were contemporaries of the history in which God established his covenant with men. In fact, they became contemporary witnesses by virtue of what they saw and heard of this history.[51]

These witnesses saw and heard God's revelation and then spoke it.[52] They served in a God-given capacity, unique to them, and what they did in this capacity was inspired by God.[53]

Barth viewed the inspiration of Scripture particularly in the light of the biblical passages from 2 Timothy 3:14-17 and 2 Peter 1:19-21.[54] He concluded that "the decisive center to which the two passages point is in both instances indicated by a reference to the Holy Spirit, and indeed in such a way that He is described as the real author of what is stated or written in Scripture."[55] For Barth the human authors of Scripture had a direct relationship to God's revelation.

> The special element in this attitude of obedience lay in the particularity, i.e., the immediacy of its relationship to the revelation which is unique by restriction in time, and therefore in the particular nature of what they had to say and write as eye-witnesses and ear-witnesses, the first-fruits of the church.[56]

This view led Barth to criticize early church views of the inspiration of Scripture as limiting the work of the Holy Spirit "in the emergence of the spoken or written prophetic and apostolic word as such."[57] Barth also complained that in the early church there was "a tendency to insist that the operation of the Holy Spirit in the inspiration of the biblical writers extended to the individual phraseology used by them in the grammatical sense of the concept."[58] The Reformers, however, corrected this. For Luther and Calvin inspiration was not "mantico-mechanical" nor "docetic." The Reformers rested Scripture's inspiration directly on the relationship of the biblical witnesses to the special content of their witness.[59]

In the seventeenth century, according to Barth, however, orthodox theologians turned the knowledge of the Bible as the Word of God into a part of one's eternal knowledge of God or the knowledge of God that humans can have on their own without the grace of God.[60] Barth asked whether, in these theologians when they speak of the biblical writers, there is not "a return to the idea that they are mere flutes in the mouth of the Holy Spirit."[61] Post-Reformation theologians separated the doctrine of the internal testimony of the Spirit from the witness of the Spirit in Scripture. They went on to justify the Bible as the Word of God by appealing to certain convincing characteristics of the biblical record.[62] To Barth this represented a "docetic" theory because it suppressed the human dimensions of the texts. For Barth, the orthodox had grounded the Bible upon itself "apart from the mystery of Christ and the Holy Ghost." Scripture had become a "paper Pope" and "was no longer a free and spiritual force, but an instrument of human power."[63]

Barth recognized that Christianity as a "book religion" taught that God through the Holy Spirit spoke the divine Word in human words. Thus it is proper to speak of "verbal inspiration" in that it is only in the *words* of Scripture that the *Word* of God is to be found.[64] Yet, said Barth, "the literally inspired Bible was not at all a revealed book of oracles, but a witness to revelation, to be interpreted from the standpoint of and with a view of its theme, and in conformity with that theme."[65]

SCRIPTURE AS WITNESS

Barth recognized that the words of the biblical witnesses were human words and were thus limited in terms of space and time. The Scriptures could not themselves be a substitute for the Word of God. He wrote: "It is quite impossible that there should be a direct identity between the human word of Holy Scripture and the Word of God, and therefore between the creaturely reality in itself and as such and the reality of God the Creator."[66] Scripture, for Barth, was included as part of God's act of revelation. But it in itself was not the central act of revelation. Jesus Christ was. Scripture's function was to point or witness to Jesus Christ. The written Word of Scripture "takes the place of the thing itself (i.e., the Word of God)."[67] The written Word directs its readers to the living Word. Thus scriptural statements must not be directly equated with the reality of the revelation in Jesus Christ. Like "the unity of God and man in Jesus Christ," Scripture for Barth was in its own way and degree "very God and very man, i.e., a witness of revelation which itself belongs to revelation, and historically a very human literary document."[68] Scripture's form for Barth was a very *human* form.

Scripture as witness to Jesus Christ written in human words meant that there was not a direct correlation between the Truth and the Scripture's statements about the Truth. In some sense the light of all truth was refracted through the lenses of the Scripture writers. This was what Barth meant when he spoke of the extent to which Scripture was the Word of God: "The Bible is God's Word to the extent that God causes it to be His Word, to the extent that He speaks through it."[69] Scripture statements were God's Word only to the degree that God by the Holy Spirit permitted them to witness to God's truth. Since the words of the biblical writers were "human and conditioned by time and space," they could never in themselves be infinite, perfect, or absolute. They could never let the whole truth of God shine through in all its fullness.

For Barth the limits of human language and the biblical writers "can be at fault in any word, and have been at fault in every word." Yet, "according to the same scriptural witness, being justified and sanctified by grace alone, they have still spoken the Word of God in their fallible and erring human word."[70] Barth resisted attempts to overemphasize divine dimensions of Scripture when he wrote that

> every time we turn the Word of God into an infallible biblical word of man or the biblical word of man into an infallible Word of God we resist that which we ought never to resist, i.e., the truth of the miracle that here fallible men speak the Word of God in fallible human words—and we therefore resist the sovereignty of grace, in which God Himself became man in Christ, to glorify Himself in His humanity.[71]

"Verbal inspiration" for Barth "does not mean the infallibility of the biblical word in its linguistic, historical and theological character as a human word. It means that the fallible and faulty human word is as such used by God and has to be received and heard in spite of its human fallibility."[72]

For Barth there was a pointed "distinction between inspiration and therefore the divine infallibility of the Bible and its human fallibility."

We cannot expect or demand a compendium of solomonic or even divine knowledge of all things in heaven and earth, natural, historical and human, to be mediated to the prophets and apostles in and with their encounter with the divine revelation, possessing which they have to be differentiated not only from their own but from every age as the bearers and representatives of an ideal culture and therefore as the inerrant proclaimers of all and every truth. They did not in fact possess any such compendium. Each in his own way and degree, they shared the culture of their age and environment, whose form and content could be contested by other ages and environments, and at certain points can still appear debatable to us.[73]

Because the biblical writers were "witnesses," there is a "vulnerability of the Bible," since the writers had a "capacity for errors."[74] Yet no one, even in the twentieth century, had the right to specify what was an error in Scripture and what was not. For Barth, when speaking of the biblical writers,

> within certain limits and therefore relatively they are all vulnerable and therefore capable of error and even in respect of religion and theology. In view of the actual constitution of the Old and New Testaments this is something which we cannot possibly deny if we are not to take away their humanity, if we are not to be guilty of Docetism. How can they be witnesses, if this is not the case?[75]

But through it all Barth recognized that God could use any particular portion of Scripture through which to speak the Word of God. No one has the right to say which portions of Scripture are more or less fallible: "We are absolved from differentiating the Word of God in the Bible from other contents, infallible portions and expressions from the erroneous ones, the infallible from the fallible, and from imagining that by means of such discoveries we can create for ourselves encounters with the genuine Word of God in the Bible."[76]

For Barth and other neo-orthodox theologians, such as Elizabeth Achtemeier, the genuine Word of God in the Bible, the center of Scripture, was Jesus Christ, to whom all the witnesses of Scripture, old or new, point with one accord.

Hatred and the Christian Life

Elizabeth Achtemeier

Jeremiah 11:18-20; Romans 12:14-21

There is a sense in which the Christian life consists in a growth into the fullness and the measure of the Scriptures. When we first start to study the Bible, we find ourselves agreeing with 2 Peter 3:16, which says of the letters of Paul that "there are some things in them hard to understand." But as we continue to study day after day, many ideas begin to come clear. Indeed, some of the words of Scripture begin to shape our own personal lives, and we know them to be true because we live them.

Through the years, then, the process continues. The more we read the Bible and speak of it and teach it, the more we find it molding our lives. Passages never understood before open up, because we experience their truth in our encounter with the world. A particular text shapes the way we look at some situation; a story from the Old or New Testament determines our reaction to a crisis; a verse from Deuteronomy or the Psalms or the Gospels becomes our guide in a difficult situation. And we find ourselves growing up into the dimensions of the life of faith set forth in this Word of God.

And yet there are some passages in the Scriptures that we never grow up into, because we do not consider them worthy or Christian expressions of the life of faith. And that is certainly true of our Old Testament lesson from Jeremiah. This is probably the earliest of Jeremiah's confessions, uttered while he was still in his hometown of Anathoth. The men of Anathoth, Jeremiah's friends and neighbors, are out after his blood, probably because of his preaching of the Deuteronomic reform. They are laying a secret plot to kill him, but God warns Jeremiah of the plot. And in response, Jeremiah prays, "O LORD . . . let me see thy vengeance upon them, for to thee have I committed my cause" (Jer. 11:20 RSV).

We find many prayers for vengeance like that in the Old Testament. The Psalms are full of them: "Make them bear their guilt, O God," prays one psalmist (5:10). "Let them fall by their own counsels." "Let them be caught in the schemes they have devised," prays another (10:2). Or "may their bellies be filled with what you have stored up for them" (17:14). Or "repay them according to their work,/ and according to the evil of their deeds;/ repay them according to the work of their hands;/ render them their due reward" (28:4). Yes, "O Lord . . . let me see thy vengeance upon them, for to thee have I committed my cause."

Now, none of those prayers seems to us to square very well with the Christian way of life, because our Lord has commanded us to love our enemies, to pray for those who persecute us, and to forgive those who wrong us, seventy times seven. And so we reject these biblical prayers for vengeance as sub-Christian and unusable leftovers from the lives of those who have not known Jesus Christ, unworthy portions of the canon of Holy Scripture. That is, we reject such prayers until we find ourselves in a situation where we hate. And then suddenly the marvelous, cleansing power of these prayers comes home to us.

Jeremiah prayed his prayer for vengeance when his neighbors were threatening his life, and certainly that is not our particular situation, although the lives of Christians were threatened and sometimes lost back in the sixties in the civil rights movement. And Christians still are threatened with death in China and parts of Africa and Central America.

But that is not our situation right now in our society. We do, however, suffer the slings and arrows of less menacing opponents. For example, a temptor or temptress enters our spouse's life and threatens to break up our marriage. A criminal or a drunk on the highway injures a member of our family. A vicious gossip undermines our Christian reputation, or someone in authority shakes our hard-won self-confidence to the roots and cuts us off from a future we had planned. Or some modern-day Pharisee casts scorn on our abilities and achievements. And in such a situation we become fearful and resentful and very angry—and we find ourselves hating the person who has done such an evil act toward us.

To be sure, our hatred may seem justified. We may in fact have been wrongfully injured. But still the question is over how we can get rid of the hatred. For we all know, hate festers in our souls and minds and poisons everything we do. We nurse it in the imaginations of our hearts; we let it grow and rankle, until it reeks of vengeance planned, through cutting words said and foul deeds done in retaliation. And no

Christian can long live with that and remain faithful to his or her Lord. The hatred must be overcome and the awful wound healed.

And this is where these psalms of vengeance come in and claim their due. "Let me see thy vengeance upon them, O Lord!" There! The hatred is expressed, in all its reality, all its anger, all its justified claim. But the hatred is expressed to God and turned over to his hands. That is the one avenue of retaliation the wrongfully injured Christian has. And if you believe this God of ours acts in the world, then you know that God will set things right. "Vengeance is mine. I will repay," says the Lord.

Now I am not at all suggesting that such a course should be turned into universal public policy; we are dealing with individual hatreds here, although certainly this teaching should inform our public life. If the cause is just, God will hear it and act. If it springs from our own illusion, God will take care of that, too. But there it rests. The case is in God's hands. The hatred has been turned over to him. And we no longer find it festering within us or affecting our daily life. "O Lord, let me see thy vengeance upon them, for to thee I have committed my cause." We can get on with our business of trying to lead faithful lives. Indeed, we may even find ourselves so able once again to forgive and love our enemies that the burning coals of repentance are heaped on them too, and their evil is replaced by good.

As to how God will work out his vengeance, well, that is up to him, isn't it? Our text from Jeremiah does tell us, however, that God judges righteously, and tries the heart and mind. God sees the hearts of all of us sinners. God knows what we are about. And he will deal with us all, according to our faith, in his justice and love and compassion. He is, you see, the Lord over all our lives, even over our hatreds and angers. Thanks be to God, who delivers us from our enemies and from ourselves. Amen.

VII

NEO-EVANGELICAL THEOLOGY

Scripture as Message

WITH THE DEATHS OF HAROLD JOHN OCKENGA AND FRANCIS SCHAEFFER (IN 1985 AND 1984 respectively), two of the most influential leaders of evangelicalism in America were gone.[1]

Ockenga, in a 1947 convocation address at Fuller Theological Seminary in Pasadena, California, coined the term "the new evangelicalism."[2] It was a distinguishable movement from that time on, and Ockenga and Schaeffer, along with Billy Graham, Harold Lindsell, and Carl F. H. Henry, gave leadership that established neo-evangelicalism as a major force in American religion.[3]

Today *neo-evangelicalism,* like the term *evangelicalism,* is defined and understood in various ways.[4] Those who accept this name as characteristic of their theological positions may not agree exactly on all or specifically on a few major doctrinal points. This is especially true as will be seen in terms of the doctrine of Scripture.[5] But before these diversities can be appreciated it is necessary to examine some definitions and backgrounds to the current scene.

BACKGROUNDS

The term *evangelical* has been prominent in America in recent years. In 1976, George Gallup, Jr., on the basis of a Gallup Poll, called 1976 "the year of the evangelical."[6] Commentators have written of an "evangelical renaissance," an "evangelical resurgence," and a "new evangelical majority."[7] In the Gallup poll, 34 percent of the respondents said they have had a "born again" experience, a turning point in life that led to a commitment to Jesus Christ. On a national scale, this percentage would mean that nearly 50 million Americans fit into this category. Among Protestants 48 percent and among Roman Catholics 18 percent said they have had a born-again experience.[8] According to Gallup, 30 percent of Americans accept the term *evangelical* to define their religious position.[9] A *Christianity Today* poll put the number at 22 percent.[10]

The statistics naturally raise problems for the definitions of *evangelical.* James Davison Hunter has provided a broad, contextual definition when he writes that evangelicalism is best understood as

a religiocultural phenomenon unique to North America though clearly related in intimate ways to other forms of theologically conservative Protestantism in other times and places. The world view of Evangelicalism is deeply rooted in the theological tradition of the

Reformation, in northern European Puritanism, and later in American Puritanism and the First and Second Great Awakenings in North America. Indeed, Evangelicalism has striven to remain entirely faithful doctrinally to this general conservative tradition. At the doctrinal core, contemporary Evangelicals can be identified by their adherence to (1) the belief that the Bible is the inerrant Word of God, (2) the belief in the divinity of Christ, and (3) the belief in the efficacy of Christ's life, death, and physical resurrection for the salvation of the human soul. Behaviorally, Evangelicals are typically characterized by an individual and experiential orientation toward spiritual salvation and religiosity in general and by the conviction of the necessity of actively attempting to proselytize all nonbelievers to the tenets of the Evangelical belief system.[11]

From this definition, several considerations can be noted. "Evangelicalism" in America does refer to "a fairly unified tradition." While this tradition over the centuries has

undergone considerable change, it has nevertheless maintained its identity and looked back to its origins with considerable sympathy and respect. Its origins lie in that revolution in Christendom which the English Puritan movement intended to accomplish. Only in North America, however, where ancient traditions had very little social and economic footing, were the full implications of this revolution borne out.[12]

The backgrounds of English Puritanism led to the Continental Protestant Reformation and to the Protestants who by the 1520s were identifying themselves as "Evangelical" over against Roman Catholicism. In that sense "when the Reformers called themselves Evangelicals, they did not think of themselves as a schismatic group within the church but as representatives of the true church—the church founded by Jesus Christ and based on the biblical gospel."[13]

After the Reformation, other movements—such as Puritanism and Pietism, which later had effects in America through various means—further developed the meaning of "evangelical."[14] Looking back to the Greek term *euangelion,* meaning the "evangel" or "good news" or "Gospel," the evangelical movement of the British Isles in the eighteenth century (whose leaders included John and Charles Wesley and George Whitefield) stressed the need for religious conversion or "the new birth," being "born again." This emphasis in these figures, however, was not made in isolation from the central theological theme of the Protestant Reformation: justification by faith. In America the "born again" theme became a hallmark of nineteenth- and twentieth-century revivalism and revivalists/evangelists, such as Charles G. Finney (1792–1875), Dwight L. Moody (1837–99), Rueben A. Torrey (1856–1928), William "Billy" Sunday (1862–1935), and William F. "Billy" Graham (b. 1918).[15]

Beyond the historical continuity of an American evangelical tradition is the theological or doctrinal basis that defines evangelicals. In the broad sense as noted, evangelicalism as an American theological tradition looks to the teachings of the sixteenth-century Protestant Reformers as the most faithful expositions of the basic gospel message of Scripture.[16] A further description of this would be that

if asked to list the key elements in a vital Christian faith, an evangelical in the classical sense might well reply: biblical fidelity, apostolic doctrine, the experience of salvation, the imperative of discipleship, and the urgency of mission. Holding firm to the doctrine taught by the prophets and apostles in Holy Scripture, evangelicals stress the need for personal experience of the reality of Christ's salvation as well as the need to carry out the great commission to teach all people to be his disciples and to call all nations to repentance.[17]

A specific focus of debate over the meaning of *evangelical* in recent years has been the issue of biblical authority. Particular controversy has centered on the use of the term *inerrancy* to describe Scripture and whether that specific concept must be used to qualify for having an "evangelical" view of the Bible. Harold Lindsell, in *The Battle for the Bible,* claimed that biblical inerrancy (as defined specifically by the theologians of the Old Princeton theology) has been the historic position of the Christian church throughout its history and must be maintained as "the badge of evangelicalism."[18] On the other hand, Donald Bloesch has argued that "today, some of the definitions of what it means to be evangelical are too narrow. To equate evangelicalism with a belief in biblical inerrancy is to leave out many in the past and present who staunchly affirm the gospel in all its breadth and depth and yet who recoil from applying the term 'inerrancy' to Scripture."[19] The debates among evangelicals on these issues have produced a great volume of literature.[20]

Among those who define *evangelical,* it is possible to see both those who use the term *inerrancy* as a guiding criterion and those who do not. In this latter category is Robert K. Johnston's definition: Evangelicals are those who believe in "(1) the need for personal relationship with God through faith in the atoning work of Jesus Christ, and (2) the sole and binding authority of the Bible as God's revelation."[21] Richard Quebedeaux, as well, defines them as those who believe in three major theological principles: "(1) the full authority of Scriptures in matters of faith and practice; (2) the necessity of personal faith in Jesus Christ as Savior and Lord (conversion); and (3) the urgency of seeking the conversion of sinful men and women to Christ (evangelism)."[22]

Emerging Evangelicalism

The Fundamentalist-modernist controversy dominated the decade of the 1920s in America.[23] Splits within denominations had occurred within the Presbyterian Church with J. Gresham Machen and others continuing the traditions of classical Calvinism at Westminster Seminary and in Methodist, Episcopal, and Church of Christ churches throughout America, particularly in the North.[24]

During the 1930s, fundamentalists struggled with "competing desires: they wished to separate themselves from a culture they thought was on its way to Armageddon, yet they still wanted to win that culture for Christ."[25] In the 1930s fundamentalist coalitions sought strength through evangelism and the building of religious communities. The economic depression of the 1930s was accompanied by a "spiritual depression" through which fundamentalism had "the popular support, structural strength, innovative flexibility, and reproductive potential to maintain its vitality."[26] In these terms fundamentalism "produced a message that attracted many at a time when Americans were searching for a heritage to remember and conserve. Thus the movement was prepared to play a leading role in the postwar evangelical revival."[27] The three major motifs of fundamentalism during these years were separation, the Second Coming, and revival.[28]

Through a variety of media, including radio, and marked by the outstanding successes of fundamentalist preachers, such as Charles E. Fuller and "The Old Fashioned Revival Hour," fundamentalists by the beginning of the 1940s began to examine again their place on the American scene. Fundamentalist emphasis on separation had made them "insular and defensive, but now their desire for revival was leading many of them to seek fellowship and cooperation with other evangelicals. Revival would come, many thought, only as evangelicals put aside their quarrels and formed a great united front to accomplish the task."[29]

On September 17, 1941, fundamentalists under the leadership of Carl McIntire, a former follower of Machen who split from Westminster Seminary to establish the Bible Presbyterian Church, founded the American Council of Christian Churches (ACCC). Their purpose was to attack the Federal Council of Churches and to provide a platform for those who were "militantly pro-Gospel and anti-modernist."[30] On April 7 and 8, 1949, a second group was formed in St. Louis with a more positive purpose in mind. From this emerged the National Association of Evangelicals (NAE), which was "a fundamenalist-initiated but genuinely inclusive fellowship that signaled the formation of a new evangelical coalition."[31] The leaders of this group said they were "determined to break with apostasy but . . . wanted no dog-in-manger, reactionary, negative or destructive type of organization." They wished instead for an organization "determined to shun all forms of bigotry, intolerance, misrepresentation, hate, jealousy, false judgment, and hypocrisy."[32]

While the ACCC and the NAE were completely united in doctrine, their policies were different. NAE membership was more inclusive with selective membership offered for members of the Federal Council of Churches. The ACCC held the attitude of "no cooperation, no compromise." The NAE adopted the position of "cooperation without compromise."[33] Soon the NAE had become "a major symbol and coordinating center of the evangelical resurgence." By 1947 it represented thirty denominations, totaling 1,300,000 members.[34] Today the NAE represents 30,000 churches and 3.5 million Christians.[35]

In 1947 Ockenga called for "the new evangelicalism." According to Ockenga, by 1942 evangelicalism had become synonymous with fundamentalism as seen in the choice of the name National Association of Evangelicals. Yet, said Ockenga, "the new evangelicalism differs from fundamentalism in its willingness to handle the societal problems that fundamentalism evaded."[36] He asserted that

> the new evangelicalism embraces the full orthodoxy of fundamentalism, but manifests a social consciousness and responsibility which was strangely absent from fundamentalism. The new evangelicalism concerns itself not only with personal salvation, doctrinal truth and an eternal point of reference, but also with the problem of race, of war, of class struggle, of liquor control, of juvenile delinquency, of immorality, and of national imperialism. . . . The new evangelicalism believes that orthodox Christians cannot abdicate their responsibility in the social scene.[37]

On a variety of fronts, ranging through religious radio and television programs, youth evangelistic organizations, periodicals, publishing houses, seminaries, and parachurch organizations, "the new evangelicalism" emerged as a significant American religious force. Among "the chief symbols of the evangelical establishment" have been, in addition to the National Association of Evangelicals, the Evangelical Theological Society (founded 1949); Billy Graham, America's foremost evangelist, who came to prominence in 1949; and the journal *Christianity Today*, founded in 1956 and edited by Carl F. H. Henry and later Harold Lindsell.[38]

Continuing Classifications

The varieties and diversities within evangelicalism have led to numerous attempts at classifying contemporary positions. Some approach the issue on the basis of theological doctrines, others via ecclesiastical traditions, while still others look to a more sociological analysis.

A basic type of distinction was made by James Barr, who designated "Fundamentalists" and "Evangelicals." Barr based his distinctions on doctrinal attitudes, particularly attitudes about Scripture.[39]

Hunter pointed out that generally four major religious and theological traditions are present in contemporary American evangelicalism: (1) Baptist, (2) Holiness and Pentecostal, (3) Anabaptist, and (4) Reformational-Confessional. He then provided denominational names for each of the four groups.[40]

Quebedeaux, in *The Young Evangelicals* (1974), distinguished among (1) separatist fundamentalists, (2) open fundamentalists, (3) establishment evangelicals, (4) the new evangelicals, and (5) the young evangelicals. For Quebedeaux, these divisions take shape primarily around an assessment of how socially and politically progressive each group shows itself to be.[41] In *The Worldly Evangelicals* Quebedeaux designated three subcultures within evangelical Christianity as (1) fundamentalists, (2) charismatics, and (3) neo-evangelical, whom he described as "the direct descendants of fundamentalism" but who "broke with what they saw in fundamentalism as theological and cultural excesses—anti-intellectualism, sectarianism, social unconcern, and an almost complete repudiation of the values of the wider society."[42]

Bloesch offered the most comprehensive classifications of contemporary evangelicalism. He distinguished fundamentalism from evangelicalism when he wrote:

Evangelicalism unashamedly stands for the fundamentals of the historical faith, but as a movement it transcends and corrects the defensive, sectarian mentality commonly associated with fundamentalism. Though many, perhaps most, fundamentalists are evangelicals, evangelical Christianity is wider and deeper than fundamentalism, which is basically a movement of reaction in the churches in this period of history. Evangelicalism in the classical sense fulfills the basic goals and aspirations of fundamentalism but rejects the ways in which these goals are realized.[43]

In his chapter on "The New Conservatism," Bloesch outlined the groups he considered part of the new conservatism in American Christianity today. He noted that

all of the various strands in the new conservatism would gladly accept the term "evangelical" with very few exceptions (mainly on the far right). Even pastors and theologians who stand in the theological tradition of Karl Barth and Emil Brunner have no compunction in identifying themselves as evangelical, though the left wing of the neo-orthodox movement might feel uncomfortable with this designation.[44]

Bloesch then described (1) fundamentalism, (2) neo-evangelicalism, (3) confession-alist evangelicalism, (4) charismatic religion, (5) neo-orthodoxy, and (6) Catholic evangelicalism.[45] He recognized, however, that these categories are "ideal types," for "no one theological or spiritual leader fits completely into any one type, and most have associations with various types."[46]

Within the category of neo-evangelicalism, Bloesch discerned two distinct strands. As he described them:

> the first signifies a cautious opening to modern trends which might best be described as neofundamentalism. The second is a more progressive evangelicalism which seeks to move beyond a rigid position on biblical inerrancy. Both these movements wish to be known as evangelical rather than fundamentalist, but only the second is inclined to reject the fundamentalist label.[47]

With these continuing classifications of evangelicalism comes the realization that labels and categories must be used with care. This is why so much time is expended here on the subject. The problem becomes particularly evident also when positions on the nature of Scripture are examined.

SCRIPTURE IN NEO-EVANGELICAL THEOLOGY

The distinctions made by Bloesch between the "right" and "left" wings of neo-evangelicalism are especially helpful in regard to their views of Scripture. As Bloesch put it: "While the right wing of the neoevangelical movement is particularly insistent on the inerrancy of Scripture, the moderate and left wings prefer to speak of the infallibility of Scripture."[48] He went on to point out that

> following Hodge and Warfield, the right-wing evangelicals nonetheless qualify inerrancy, claiming that only the original manuscripts or autographs (which are no longer available) are without error. This allows for critical textual work on the various copies and translations. When moderate neoevangelicals employ the term "inerrancy" in reference to Scripture, they generally have in mind its teaching or doctrine.[49]

In dealing with the doctrine of Scripture in neo-evangelical theology, attention will be turned to the views of those in the moderate and left wings of this movement. The views of those on the right wing are encompassed in scholastic theology, which shows the link between fundamentalism and the scholastic view of Scripture. Those who call themselves neo-evangelical and are on the right wing of that movement have come out of fundamentalism and have basically the fundamentalist view of Scripture as refined by the scholasticism of the Old Princeton theologians. Their primary identification now is "evangelicals" who hold to the Old Princeton view of the Bible, marked by their contention for the term *inerrancy*. This, as mentioned above, for some has become the distinguishing mark of an evangelical.[50]

The preference for the term *infallibility* when applied to Scripture is a distinguishing mark of those in the moderate and left wings of neo-evangelicalism.[51] They have attempted to approach the issue of Scripture without the emphasis on rational arguments to establish the Bible's authority and the attendant apologetic stance to defend the Bible's accuracy in matters of fact and history that are parts of scholastic theology.

In this these neo-evangelicals see themselves as returning to the tradition of the sixteenth-century Protestant Reformers, particularly Luther and Calvin. These evangelicals see themselves as carrying on the Reformation tradition, which in the nineteenth century was expressed by evangelicals like T. M. Lindsay (1843–1914) and James Orr (1844–1913) in Scotland and Abraham Kuyper (1837–1920) and Herman Bavinck (1854–1921) in the Netherlands.[52] Just as these scholars reacted against the inerrancy views of the Old Princeton theologians in the nineteenth century, so also neo-evangelicals see themselves doing the same in the twentieth century. Positively, these evangelicals emphasize the Bible as the Word of God with its central purpose being to proclaim God's message to the world, which comes through the human words of Scripture.

Faith and Reason

Many of the neo-evangelicals of this persuasion look also to the Dutch theologian G. C. Berkouwer (b. 1903) of the Free University of Amsterdam as a twentieth-century evangelical whose writings preserve the Reformation emphasis on the doctrine of Scripture.[53] Other significant writers on Scripture in this tradition have included Donald Bloesch, Jack Rogers, and Bernard Ramm.[54]

In this view it is emphasized that faith and the knowledge of God are not based on the powers of human reason. This tradition looks back to the theological method of Augustine, who saw that "faith leads to understanding."[55] Certain neo-evangelicals believe that the ability of humans to use their reasoning powers was not left untainted by the fall into sin. Because reason is affected by sin, reason itself (through theistic arguments or arguments about the divine origin of the Bible) cannot serve as the foundation on which humans build a knowledge of God. In writing on sin, Berkouwer said that "there is no limit or boundary within human nature beyond which we find some last human reserve untouched by sin; it is man himself who is totally corrupt."[56]

This means, too, that a "natural theology" that seeks to know God purely from human perceptions of the world and nature is impossible. As Berkouwer wrote:

> What is the background of this conception in which natural reason is considered capable of such knowledge? It is clear that specific anthropology is involved here, an anthropology or view of man which lifts the so-called rational soul out of the sin-depraved life of man, and then by way of this non-corrupt reason considers man capable of knowledge of God.[57]

As Bloesch put it, "Any attempt to take the fall of man seriously will radically call into question the capacity of reason to discover or come to the truth."[58] This position does not deny "the possibility of a believing apologetic," says Berkouwer, "but an apologetic will have to begin with faith, not with uncertainty and doubt, if it is to be fruitful and a blessing to anyone."[59] Formal, rational apologetics is thus not first on the theological agenda.

According to neo-evangelicals, Scripture is accepted in faith, and then through the use of reason one moves on to a further understanding of the message of Scripture. This use of reason is what the Westminster Confession referred to as that which "by good necessary consequence may be deduced from Scripture."[60] Believers use their reason in the service of further obedience and understanding. As Bloesch has written:

> Reason is not the foundation of faith, but it can be an exceedingly useful instrument of faith. We cannot share Leibniz's view that "faith must be grounded in reason," but we should certainly acknowledge that reason can serve faith. Natural reason can bring much light to bear upon such matters.
>
> It can be said that we reason *in* faith but not *to* faith. We do not arrive at faith by reason, but we can explicate faith by reason. It is not permissible to postulate a "Christian reason" (in the sense of a reason that is inherently Christian), but we can speak of a Christian exercise of reason.[61]

Authority of Scripture

For neo-evangelicals, the purpose of Scripture is to bring people to faith and salvation in Jesus Christ. It is the function of Scripture that is of primary concern.

Technically this is what the Refomers called the *scopus* or "goal" of Scripture, which means that the words of Scripture "are related to and tend toward a definite goal (Phil. 3:14)."[62] The Bible is a book that presents a gospel that does "not come to us as a timeless or 'eternal' truth or idea" but as "a message of salvation received, interpreted, and handed over by men."[63] This "intention and directedness" is made very clear in Scripture itself. There the words of Jesus are focused on a "concrete goal," which is salvation (John 20:31) that produces hope (Rom. 15:4) and is intended to equip the believer for every good work (2 Tim. 3:16).[64]

For Christian believers the Scriptures are authoritative. They are the inspired Word of God and as such present Jesus Christ to us by the work of the Holy Spirit. As Bavinck wrote, "Scripture is the word of God because the Holy Spirit witnesses of Christ in it, because it has the incarnate Word as its subject matter and content."[65] For Bloesch, "The Bible is authoritative because it is centered in Jesus Christ and conveys the truth about Christ."[66] In this the position of Calvin, who wrote that "the Scriptures obtain full authority among believers" only when they are regarded as "having sprung from heaven, as if there the living words of God were heard," is reaffirmed.[67]

The authority of Scripture is underlined by the neo-evangelical understanding that "Scripture *is* the Word of God." Berkouwer cited the many instances of Jesus and others using the words "It is written" (Matt. 4:4; 4:7: 10; Mark 1:2; Luke 2:23; Acts 7:42) to indicate the authority of Scripture. These words

> functioned prominently as a last appeal and as a redeeming and blessed limitation of all human meditation and speculation (1 Cor. 4:6). "It is written" points to the source with decisive authority and with the intent to awaken faith in the heart. . . . This arises out of a life with Scripture, to which all [Jesus'] followers are called because the written word comes to them with final saving authority.
>
> By its nature, the written Word can never be formally isolated, because precisely that written Scripture testifies of salvation and is directed toward that salvation. And in that context words can become living words (Acts 7:38).[68]

Thus there is an "authoritative function of the written Word."[69]

It is by the work of the Holy Spirit that the authority of Scripture comes to be known and established for believers. As Bloesch put it, "The truth of revelation can be apprehended through the medium of the human language which attests it but only by the action of the Spirit."[70] For Berkouwer, "it is of great importance that the Reformed confessions definitely do not view faith in Scripture as a preparation for true faith, or as a component of it which, if so desired, can be considered independent of it; but they connect faith in Scripture with the testimony of the Holy Spirit."[71]

The Holy Spirit, rather than the church or any other "authority," witnesses that the Scriptures are the Word of God.

> [For] only God himself is a sufficient witness to himself. The Word of God finds no acceptance until it is sealed by the inward witness of the Spirit, and the heart finds its rest in Scripture only through his inward teaching. Scripture is not subject to human argumentation and proof, and Scripture's own assuring power is higher and stronger than all human judgment.[72]

The witness of the Spirit is tied directly to the content of Scripture—the gospel message itself. Bavinck wrote that "the real object to which the Holy Spirit gives witness in the hearts of the believers is no other than the *divinitas* of the truth, poured out on us in Christ. Historical, chronological and geographical data are never in themselves, the object of the witness of the Holy Spirit."[73]

Accordingly, "our faith in Scripture increases and decreases according to our trust in Christ."[74] Scripture's authority is directed toward its purpose and goal: salvation in Christ.

Inspiration

For neo-evangelicals, Scripture is to be interpreted in the light of its central message of salvation. In line with Reformation emphases, Scripture is its own interpreter and is to be interpreted in the light of the analogy of faith.[75]

One image used to indicate the relationships of Scripture was expressed by Bavinck in his understanding of inspiration. He spoke of an "organic inspiration," using the picture of the human body to say that there is a center and periphery to Scripture just as in the human organism. "In the human organism nothing is accidental, neither the length, nor the breadth, nor the color, nor the hue; but all does not therefore stand in the same close connection with the life center. Head and heart have a much more important place in the body than hand and foot, and these again stand in worth above nails and hair."[76]

This did not mean for Bavinck that there were different levels of inspiration in Scripture but rather that each part has its own function. Some parts were more directly related to the central message of Scripture than others. All Scripture is inspired by God (2 Tim. 3:16). God has used human writers to communicate God's Word. There is both a divine and a human dimension to Scripture. Yet not all Scripture texts are related in the same way to the main gospel message God wishes to communicate:

> The hair of the head participates in the same life as heart and hand. . . . It is one Spirit, out of whom the whole of Scripture has come forth through the consciousness of the

writers. But there is a difference in the way in which the same life is immanent and active in the various parts of the body. There are varieties of gifts, also in Scripture, but it is the same Spirit.[77]

While neo-evangelicals assert the inspiration of Scripture, they generally avoid speculative theories on how Scripture *is* the Word of God. They do not wish to produce a theory of inspiration. Berkouwer wrote that "the mystery of the God-breathed Scripture is not meant to place us before a theoretical problem of how Scripture would possibly and conceivably be both God's Word and man's word, and how they could be 'united.' It rather places us before the mystery of Christ."[78]

Infallibility

The preference of neo-evangelicals for the term *infallibility* of Scripture rather than *inerrancy* is reflected by their views of faith and reason, Scripture's authority, and inspiration. This theology stresses the central purpose of Scripture to be theological in nature—the revelation or self-communication of God. The authority of Scripture is established not by rational arguments but by the witness of the Holy Spirit. The Spirit witnesses to Scripture's content—Jesus Christ. One does not go to Scripture to answer human philosophical questions or to gain accurate information about ancient history, science, geography, or astronomy. One goes to Scripture to learn how to be related to God and to find how God wants people to live their lives in faithful obedience.

Given these understandings, neo-evangelicals prefer to speak of the "infallibility" rather than the "inerrancy" of Scripture. Infallibility refers to Scripture's complete trustworthiness and its ability to accomplish its purpose. Scripture is infallible, in this view, because it will not deceive humans about matters of salvation. It will not lead them into "error," which according to Berkouwer is biblically conceived as "a swerving from the truth and upsetting the faith (2 Tim. 2:18)."[79]

"Error" in the sense of sin and deception should not be relegated to the same level as the concept of "error" as "incorrectness." This "infallibility" position stands in contrast to the "inerrancy" view of scholastic theology, which emphasizes the precision and accuracy of the original biblical texts in all matters on which they teach.[80]

SCRIPTURE AS MESSAGE

For neo-evangelicals who seek to stand in the tradition of how they read the Protestant Reformers, Scripture is the inspired Word of God that comes to the church through the words of human writers. Scripture contains a divine message expressed in human words. The thrust of Scripture is not to be a textbook of science or to offer information on every human topic. As Berkouwer noted, "It is not that Scripture offers us no information but that the nature of this information is unique. It is governed by the *purpose* of God's revelation."[81] Scripture is infallible in accomplishing its purpose. For neo-evangelicals, "the purpose of the God-breathed Scripture is not at all to provide a scientific *gnosis* in order to convey and increase human knowledge and wisdom, but to witness of the salvation of God unto faith."[82] God has used humans to communicate the Word of God. As Berkouwer put it, "When God speaks, human voices ring in our ears"; yet this "speaking of God through men is not a substitution of God's Word for that of man. It remains man's own speech through the Holy Spirit in the mission to speak words (Jer. 26:5): the authorization of this human speech is found in this mission."[83] Scripture gains its authority by the witness of the Holy Spirit, who brings one to faith in both Christ and Scripture. The Bible is God's active, living Word, which through a variety of scriptural forms presents God's message of salvation for the world. Through preaching, "the message of the gospel is expressed in living form."[84] One can live with Scripture "only when the message of Scripture is understood and is not considered 'a metaphysical document,' but a living instrument serving God for the proclamation of the message of salvation."[85]

Observe in the following sermon by Jack B. Rogers how neo-evangelicals place a greater emphasis on doing and living out the message of the gospel, without primary concern for persuading unbelievers or colleagues about their theories concerning the words of the Bible.

An Authority for Action

Jack B. Rogers

2 Timothy 3:16-17

I want us to turn our attention first of all to the Scripture itself, to Paul's second letter to Timothy, the third chapter, reading verses 16 and 17. Paul says to Timothy, "All Scripture is inspired by God and is useful for teaching, for reproof, for correction,, and for training in righteousness, so that everyone who belongs to God may be proficient, equipped for every good work."

Theologically, this is considered the classical text about the inspiration and authority of the Bible. We have to be careful with familiar texts in order not to bring to them a whole apparatus of presuppositions about what they ought to say. Let us try to think freshly about what it does say, and let us stay in the context of intimate, familial encouragement that Paul is giving to his friend and younger colleague, Timothy.

The text tells us that there are two things about Scripture and one thing about us that are essential. Scripture is inspired. Scripture is useful. And we are to be equipped to do every kind of good deed. Neither in this text nor anywhere else in the Bible do we get a nice, neat, theological definition of inspiration. But when we study what the Bible says here and elsewhere about its inspiration, and when we see what its character is, we discover that inspiration works through incarnation.

God has a style of communication. The Bible calls it incarnation, coming in the flesh. When God wanted to communicate most deeply with us, God became a human being in Jesus Christ.

C. S. Lewis was the twentieth-century writer who probably grasped the incarnational style of communication more than any other. He saw the connection between the incarnation in Christ and the incarnation in Scripture. In *Reflections on the Psalms,* Lewis wrote, "The Scriptures precede not by the conversion of God's Word to a literature but by the lifting up of a literature to become the vehicle of God's Word." Lewis thereby in modern times saw what the early church theologians and the Reformers had seen before him.

The theologians of the early church and the Reformation grasped God's incarnational style of communication, and they called it accommodation. Their model for understanding the way God worked with human beings was a human and relational one. God was likened to a parent or a teacher or a physician. God, they said, accommodated, condescended, became humble, in order to speak in the language and thought forms of human beings. God did that for our good.

Augustine said, "We can safely follow Scripture which proceeds at the pace of a mother stooping to her child, so to speak, so as not to leave us behind in our weakness." Origen said that God talks baby talk. Calvin said that God lisps like a nursemaid talking to infants. All of these are attempts to grasp the notion articulated in Isaiah 55:8: God's thoughts are not our thoughts. God's ways are not our ways. But God has chosen to use our thoughts and ways to communicate effectively with us. So Paul wrote to Timothy that the Bible was inspired.

Paul also said that the Bible is useful. For what? The purpose of the Bible is to restore relationships and guide us in right living. That is what Paul said in verse 15—the Bible leads to salvation through faith in Jesus Christ. In verse 16, Paul returns to that same premise, saying that Scripture is useful for teaching the truth, rebuking error, correcting faults, and giving instruction in right living.

These guidelines should not be taken out of their very human, relational context and put into some kind of academic or scientific context. That would not have occurred to Paul, and it would not have made sense to Timothy. We will save ourselves a great deal of argument and time and energy if we can just remember that the Bible's purpose is to teach salvation, not to give instruction in science.

The biblical message always comes concretely in a particular historical and cultural context. So the Bible always can be read at two levels. The first is the level of basic human need. That is the level of salvation. That is the level of guidance for right living. That is what ties the whole Bible together.

At the same time, you can always delve into the surrounding material, the cultural context. If you want to know all the details about a particular biblical concept, you need to do much study to get into the historical and cultural setting of that situation. That secondary kind of understanding is not essential for salvation, but it is very useful for our Christian growth and maturity and depth of understanding.

A great deal of what we do in seminary is at this secondary level, trying to understand all of the cultural matrix. One reason is so that we can separate and distinguish between what belongs only to that time and situation and, on the other hand, the dynamic, eternal, applicable message for everyone in all times. We all know this because we know that the Bible can be translated out of one cultural and historical setting into a whole variety of others. Groups like the Wycliffe Bible Translators and the various Bible societies have brought at least one book of the Bible into nearly 2,000 of the world's 6,000 languages and cultures.

The punch line of Paul's admonition to Timothy is not directed at the Bible but at us, at you and me. Paul says the Bible is inspired and the Bible is useful so that the person who serves God may be fully qualified and equipped to do every kind of good deed. We are saved in order to serve. The Bible has authority because it meets our deepest human needs. We will have authority as Bible-believing persons when we give ourselves in the service of our fellow human beings.

I learned this early on in my seminary career, and I have to keep relearning it. Between my first and second years in seminary, I went into an internship in Pittsburgh, Pennsylvania. It was an inter-denominational, experimental kind of internship in which I participated in all kinds of unusual ministries. Perhaps the most interesting for me was the opportunity to participate once a week in a lunchtime discussion group with mostly young lawyers at the Harvard/Yale/Princeton Club in Pittsburgh. The convener of the group was a Christian lawyer who gathered some of his atheistic and agnostic friends around him on the pretext that they were going to discuss religious matters.

Toward the end of the year, a man who described himself as a lapsed Jew came up with a remarkable suggestion: "You Christians take your religion from the New Testament, don't you? Why don't we read the New Testament?" We Christians were being much too sophisticated for that kind of approach! We quickly agreed that before the next weekly luncheon meeting, we would all read the Gospel according to Luke. I never read Luke so much, and I never prayed so much in one week. I was eager to see what that man's reaction would be—we all were. We waited for him to speak first. He said, "That was quite an experience! I've never encountered a person like Jesus! But, of course, it can't amount to anything because I've never seen any Christians act like Jesus!"

Friends, that is what business people call the bottom line. That is where it makes a difference. That is the challenge to you and to me in this text. Do we want people to believe that the Bible is inspired? Do we want them to believe that the Bible is useful? We must so read and incarnate the Bible in our own lives that we live as those who are equipped to do every good work.

Let us pray: We thank you, O God, for giving us the opportunity to be hearers of the Word. Help us by your Spirit to be doers as well. We pray in Jesus Christ's name. Amen.

VIII

EXISTENTIAL THEOLOGY

Scripture as Living Encounter

IN 1933 A FORTY-SEVEN-YEAR-OLD MAN FLED NAZI GERMANY AND BEGAN A NEW CAREER in a new country. His new language was to be English instead of his native German. The man was Paul Tillich (1886–1965). On April 13, 1933, Tillich's name was on the first list of professors to be dismissed from German universities. At that time he was dean of the philosophical faculty at the University of Frankfurt. Of the twelve suspended at Frankfurt, eleven were Jewish and Tillich was the other. Within one year, 1,684 German scholars were removed from their posts. On May 10, 1933, in Frankfurt, Tillich witnessed the Nazi burning of books, including his own book *The Socialist Decision.* By October 1933, Gestapo members were following him in Dresden, and after visiting family and friends, Tillich accepted the invitation to come to the United States to teach at Union Theological Seminary in New York City.[1]

Tillich's experiences helped to shape the formation of this theological work. By the time of his death in 1965, Tillich was one of the most well-known and influential American theologians.[2] He taught philosophical theology at Union Seminary until 1955. Then he became University Professor of Theology at Harvard until 1962 and Professor of Theology at the University of Chicago Divinity School until he died.[3] Throughout his career, Tillich was concerned to speak to the questions of human existence in a way that was meaningful to contemporary persons.[4] This led him to develop his theology in a philosophical form and in dialogue with historic Christian thinkers as well as secular philosophers.[5]

Tillich's personal development, which led him to emphasize both theology and philosophy, was but one aspect of how he perceived "the way my ideas have developed from my life."[6] The rubric he used to describe this development was the image of "the boundary." He wrote as early as 1929 that "the boundary is the best place for acquiring knowledge."[7] In his autobiographical sketch, *On the Boundary,* Tillich chronicled his odyssey through a series of "betweens" among which were two temperaments, social classes, theory and practice, theology and philosophy, church and society, religion and culture, and Idealism and Marxism.[8] Thus it is not surprising that Tillich's theological thought is marked by polarities or concepts in tension with each other—a dialectical thinking that Tillich described in volume 2 of his *Systematic Theology:*

> In a dialectical description one element of a concept drives to another. Taken in this
> sense, dialectics determine all life-processes and must be applied in biology, psychology,
> and sociology. The description of tensions in living organisms, neurotic conflicts, and

class struggles is dialectical. Life itself is dialectical. If applied symbolically to the divine life, God as a living God must be described in dialectical statements.[9]

Existential Theology

Tillich's concern to correlate the polarities of human life as expressed in his "boundary" symbol affected all phases of his religious thought.

During World War I Tillich served in the Germany army as a chaplain. As the war progressed, he faced the horrors of death and devastation, and he suffered a series of collapses. While he had initially been enthusiastic about the German war effort, he became increasingly disillusioned and disturbed by the role of political, ideological, and religious institutions in supporting such wholesale human death.[10] With the collapse of the old orders of German society, Tillich also recognized a collapse of the traditional concept of God. In the midst of a terrible battle, Tillich reported that he had a personal *kairos,* or crisis time, in which the philosophical underpinnings under which the war had been waged were destroyed. This was the philosophy of classical idealism, which Tillich had imbibed from his philosophical studies of Hegel (1770–1831) and Schelling (1775–1854).[11] According to Tillich, "the idealists claim that their system of categories portrays reality as a whole rather than being the expression of a definite and existentially limited encounter with reality."[12] But in Tillich's wartime experience, this perception of reality was shattered. During this time he reported that he became an *existentialist.* Now he moved "from pure abstraction to a realization of the importance of encounters in living contexts. The war, for example, brought to Tillich the experience of the abyss of existence."[13]

After the war, Tillich taught at the University of Marburg from 1924–1925 before moving to Frankfurt. At Marburg both Rudolph Bultmann and Martin Heidegger were lecturing. As Tillich later said, Heidegger's lectures at Marburg, his book *Sein and Zeit (Being and Time),* and his interpretation of Kant helped Tillich to clarify the relationship between theology and philosophy. His further studies on Schelling (on whom he had written two dissertations), Kierkegaard, and Nietzsche led Tillich to a full "acceptance of existential philosophy."[14] For Tillich, "existential philosophy asks in a new and radical way the question whose answer is given to faith in theology."[15] For Tillich, theologians have as their basic attitude a "commitment to the content" they expound, for "detachment would be a denial of the very nature of this content. The attitude of the theologian is 'existential.' He is involved—with the whole of his existence, with his finitude and his anxiety, with his self-contradictions and his despair, with the healing forces in him and in his social situation."[16]

Theological Method

Tillich's concerns and theological method are outlined in the introduction to his three-volume *Systematic Theology.* Tillich explained that theology moves back and forth between two poles, the "eternal truth of its foundation" and the "temporal situation in which the eternal truth must be received." This is seen in "kerygmatic theology," which emphasizes the unchangeable truth, and "apologetic theology," which is "answering theology"—addressing itself to the questions of the human "situation," humanity's own self-interpretation. Any honest theology must keep both aspects alive and synthesize them using a "method of correlation" to unite both message and situation.[17]

The theologian, Tillich maintained, enters into theological work with a concrete commitment to the validity of the Christian message. This comes by virtue of one's faith commitment in which one declares that the "ultimate concern" is with the Christian message, dealt with "scientifically" but yet nevertheless being acknowledged as unique and universally valid. This approach resolves the conflict between pietists and orthodoxy, which in turn stress "faith" and "objectivity." It makes this ultimate concern with the Christian message the criterion for being "inside the theological circle," being a theologian.

At this point, Tillich introduced two formal criteria of every theology: (1) that it is the *object* of theology which concerns us ultimately. Thus theological propositions are only those that make the object of theology a matter of concern for us; and (2) "Our ultimate concern," wrote Tillich, "is that which determines our being and non-being." Thus theological propositions are only those that "deal with their object in so far as it can became a matter of being or non-being for us."[18] "Being" is "the whole of human reality, the aim of existence." These two criteria point to the "boundary" situation between the "scientific" question of ultimate concern and the "faith" question of being.

For Tillich, "theology is the methodical interpretation of the contents of the Christian faith." As such it involves the *whole* activity of humans (not just "feeling" as in Schleiermacher) and is grounded definitively in "Jesus as the Christ," the Word become flesh, the union of the absolutely concrete and absolutely universal. This, Tillich argued, is "the only possible foundation for a Christian theology which claims to be *the* theology," for it is the only concept great enough to include *all* of thought and to conquer "cosmic pluralism."[19] If this assertion is accepted, Christian theology infinitely transcends all other theologies.

On the question of theology and philosophy, Tillich acknowledged that every theologian must be a philosopher in that the theologian questions reality as a whole, the quest of being. But there are three differences between the philosopher and the theologian. First, the philosopher remains objective and detached to questions. The theologian becomes involved in the object of the question and thus has an "existential concern." Second, there is a difference in their sources. The theologian is not only concerned with reality as a whole but also with one's ultimate concern, the *logos*. Third, there is a difference in their content. The philosopher deals with categories as they appear in different material. But the theologian relates questions to the quest for new being.[20]

There is also, however, a convergence between philosophers and theologians. Both are concerned with being. But while the philosopher argues in the name of universal *logos* or "reason," the theologian is shaped by the appearance of a "particular *logos*" that reveals the meaning of the whole. Thus "neither a conflict between theology and philosophy [is] necessary, nor is a synthesis between them possible." For there is no "common basis" for this relationship and no particularly "Christian" philosophy. The Christian claim of Jesus Christ as the *logos* need not "include the claim that wherever the *logos* is at work agrees with the Christian message." Also, "no philosophy which is obedient to the universal *logos* can contradict the concrete *logos*, the Logos 'who become flesh.' "[21]

Tillich's third section deals with the organization of theology in which he considers the difference between historical and systematic theology.[22] In his section on the method and structure of systematic theology, Tillich pointed to the three important questions of systematic theology: The questions of its sources, the medium of reception, and the norm determining the use of these sources.

The source for systematic theology may be thought to be the Bible, but Tillich argued that there is more, for the Bible arose out of the church's history and this too must be a source. Included in this for Roman Catholics are the decisions of church councils and the popes. A broader source is the history of religion and culture which interprets theologically the materials of pre-religious and religious humankind. In all this there are degrees of importance that correspond in direct and indirect relationship to the central event of the Christian faith, which is "the appearance of the New Being in Jesus as the Christ."[23]

But these sources can be so only to those who participate in them. Thus the element of existential or experiential concern is prominent. *Experience* today is used in an ontological, scientific, and mystical sense, said Tillich. But all of these fail as sources. The first excludes a divine being from its theology because it presupposes "an immediate participation in religious reality preceding any theological analysis of reality as a whole" in order to give one a concept of what a religious experience is.[24] Thus the different philosophical concepts of the nature of this religious experience arise.

The completely "scientific" description of experience fails, because the object of theology is not within scientific experience, and the object can be found only in acts of surrender and participation. Also, the "mystical experience" is not an acceptable criterion for theology, because it is secretly presupposed by the ontological and the scientific and does not mediate anything new in us. The real question is this: What does experience by participation reveal?

If all these fall short of an acceptable criterion of experience, the one true criterion must be the experience of the unique event of Jesus the Christ. "This event is given to experience and not derived from it. Therefore, experience receives and does not produce."[25]

But the decisive question of the norm of theology is not yet answered. This is "the question of the criterion to which the sources as well as the mediating experience must be subjected." This norm must grow out of the church, as the church is the home of the systematic theologian and also the place where the theologian works. Tillich maintained that the proper norm, "the material norm of systematic theology today is the New Being in Jesus as the Christ as our ultimate concern." The "new being" is based on Paul's concept of the "new creation" as the answer to the present and every human situation. This norm is "the criterion for the use of all sources of systematic theology."[26]

But how for Tillich is this norm to be related to the basic source for theology—the Bible? While the Bible is the basic source, as a "collection of religious literature, written, collected, and edited through the centuries," there must be a theological norm to determine canonicity. This norm must be the collective experience of the church in maintaining as its content the biblical message that grows within the medium of experience and is at the same time the criterion of any experience.[27]

In all this, systematic theology is not a history but a constructive task. Tillich raised the question of the place of reason or the rational character of systematic theology. The theologian is one who not only participates in the New Being but who can also express its truth in a methodical way. Yet reason is not a source of theology. It does not produce the contents of theology. While the theological norm must be a matter of personal and communal religious experience, it nevertheless must also be a matter of the methodological judgment of the theologian. Thus a problem is created that cannot be solved this side of the kingdom of God.[28]

However, certain directing principles can be brought forth. There is first the semantic principle, which points to the need for the language of the theologian not to be "sacred" or "revealed" language. The second principle is logical rationality, which points to the desire to give "logical expression of the infinite tensions of Christian existence." It means that God's actions, while perhaps superseding and transcending finite reason, do not destroy or annihilate it. Thus is born the concept of paradox. Yet for Tillich there is only one genuine paradox in the Christian message. It is "the appearance of that which conquers existence under the conditions of existence. Incarnation, redemption, justification, etc., are implied in this paradoxical event." The third principle is that of methodological rationality, which implies that theology follows a method and "a definite way of deriving and stating its propositions."[29]

The Method of Correlation

For Tillich, the method of correlation is the theological methodology of systematic theology. It is the forming of questions implied by the divine-human encounter and the corresponding answers implied in the divine self-manifestation under the guidance of the questions implied in human existence. Tillich argued that systematic theology has always used the method of correlation "sometimes more, sometimes less, consciously, and must do so consciously and outspokenly, especially if the apologetic point of view is to prevail. The method of correlation explains the contents of the Christian faith through existential questions and theological answers in mutual interdependence." Thus the answers of Christian "revelation" are "meaningful" only insofar as they are in correlation with questions concerning the whole of our existence, with existential questions.[30]

For Tillich, theology proceeds by making "an analysis of the human situation out of which the existential questions arise, and it demonstrates that the symbols used in the Christian message are the answers to these questions. The analysis of the human situation is done in terms which today are called 'existential.' " All areas of culture contribute to the analysis of the human situation: philosophy, poetry, drama, the novel, therapeutic psychology, and sociology. The theologian "organizes these materials in relation to the answer given by the Christian message" and may make a more penetrating analysis of existence than that of many philosophers.[31] In Tillich's view:

> the Christian message provides the answers to the questions implicit in human existence. These answers are contained in the revelatory events on which Christianity is based and are taken by systematic theology *from* the sources, *through* the medium, *under* the norm. Their content cannot be derived from the questions, that is, from an analysis of human existence. They are "spoken" *to* human existence from beyond it.[32]

This theological method of correlation replaces three inadequate methods: supranaturalistic, naturalistic, and the dualistic.

Thus Tillich's whole theological system proceeded in a question/answer fashion. Its parts were "Being and God"; "Existence and Christ"; "Life and the Spirit"; "The Kingdom of God"; and an epistemological section as Part I of volume 1 of his *Systematic Theology* on "Reason and Revelation."[33]

SCRIPTURE IN EXISTENTIAL THEOLOGY

Reason

The categories of "reason" and "revelation" are major ones in the thought of Tillich and his theology of human existence. For Tillich, reason and revelation may be distinguished but not ultimately separated. There is no chasm between the two but a basic continuity between humans and God, between the "natural" and the "supernatural." Yet these are not identical.[34]

In *Systematic Theology* (vol. 1) Tillich distinguished among various concepts of reason.[35] At its broadest, reason is the structure by which the mind grasps and shapes reality. The "depth of reason," in Tillich's thought, refers to the presence of the absolute (God) in the structures of both mind and reality. This presence is such that the mind never completely grasps the reality toward which it points, yet it is never fully separated from it either.[36]

Because humanity has fallen into "existence" where it is estranged from the ground of its being (God), human reason is separated from ultimate union with God. Because of the conditions of existence, "reason in existence expresses itself in myth and cult," which while they "contradict essential reason, they betray by their very existence the 'fallen' state of a reason which has lost immediate unity with its own depth."[37]

For Tillich, this implies that religious experience will naturally take expression in symbols. These symbols may participate in the reality to which they point and can unite a person with the depth of oneself and with the depth of all being, God.[38] Therefore, in Tillich's thought:

> all reality, especially the personal, participates in God and points to God symbolically when the ultimate manifests itself through its structures. All reality is thus potentially the material for religious experience and so potentially sacramental. On the other hand, no manifestation of God through created structure can be identified with God, for Tillich's system contains an inherent safeguard against idolatry.[39]

Because humans have fallen into "existence," salvation occurs only when the basic self is reunited with the ground of its being, God. This unity, or "essentialization," comes when the content, or *essentia,* the "definite power of being" is realized.[40] In its fallen state of existence, reason needs "essentialization" to come to its true essence.[41] For Tillich, this process of "salvation" comes by revelation.

Revelation

Tillich believed revelation is a special kind of knowledge, extraordinary in nature. In revelation, reason is driven beyond itself to "its 'ground and abyss,' to that which 'precedes' reason . . . to the original fact that there is *something* and not *nothing*." This is the *mystery* of revelation and positively in this mystery one comes in *actual revelation* to recognize that it is God who is the "ground" or "the power of being conquering nonbeing."[42] Thus in revelation God is manifest and one's intellect comes to face the transcendent God. Because humans are fallen into "existence" and their reason can grasp only the finite and objects, and because God is neither finite nor an object, God is the transcendent source of all being. God "cannot be reached by ordinary human knowledge. In order to acquire any genuine knowledge of God, therefore, it is necessary for the mind to overleap all finite categories and transcend the ordinary distinctions between subject and object. Extraordinary knowledge of this sort is what Tillich means by revelation."[43]

For Tillich, "revelation is the manifestation of what concerns us ultimately. The mystery which is revealed is of ultimate concern to us because it is the ground of our being." Tillich pointed out that "in the history of religion revelatory events always have been described as shaking, transforming, demanding, significant in an ultimate way. They derive from divine sources, from the power of that which is holy and which therefore has an unconditional claim on us."[44]

The "objective" side of revelation manifests the divine as the mysterious ground of being. These events are "miracles." The reception of such occurrences in which the mind "transcends its ordinary situation" is "ecstasy."[45] Thus in Tillich's view

> what is given to us, therefore, in revelation is no new body of information. There is no increase in our knowledge of nature, history and man. The insight which comes to us through a miracle and is acquired through ecstasy is perhaps best described as a new awareness of, or a new perspective on, that which is already known. We get knowledge about the revelation of the mystery of being, not just additional information. What we already know is clarified and its experiential value heightened by our discovery of its union with the ultimate.[46]

Revelatory events are united by common symbols. There is an "original" revelatory event in which, for example, a new religion is founded. In this both the "miracle" and the "ecstasy" are new and united for the first time. Specifically, Jesus with his disciples, Buddha with his disciples, or Moses and the people fleeing Egypt at the foot of Mt. Sinai would constitute original revelatory events. Original revelation is "given to a group through an individual. Revelation can be received originally only in the depth of a personal life, in its struggles, decisions, and self-surrender."[47]

A "dependent revelation" occurs in later generations where communities (and for Tillich, revelation always creates a community) find that they experience the power of the revelation for themselves. A dependent revelatory situation exists "in every moment in which the divine Spirit grasps, shakes, and moves the human spirit."[48] The original revelatory event is expressed through religious symbols. The symbols themselves become holy objects and then are the media through which new revelatory events occur. Thus for Tillich:

> religious symbols provide the continuity among a set of dependent revelatory events and link them all to the original event. In the case of Christianity, the disciples of Jesus created a verbal symbol, the "biblical picture of Jesus the Christ" which is cast in narrative form to express the fact that the original revelatory event had occurred and that they personally

had participated in it. This picture thereafter occasions dependent revelatory events as it is read or preached in church.[49]

In the Christian view, the final revelation is the biblical picture of "Jesus as the Christ."[50] This original revelation was given through Jesus to his disciples but continues to the present day as a dependent revelation in the church and through the church until the end of time. Christianity itself "as Christianity is neither final nor universal. But that to which it witnesses is final and universal."[51] This final revelation in Christ was "not an isolated event. It presupposed a revelatory history which was a preparation for it and in which it was received."[52] This is the "history of revelation." It is "universal" in the sense that it can take place anywhere at any time. The "concrete" revelations related to Christianity were to the Jewish people and are recorded in the Old Testament. In the New Testament are the basic documents relating to the final revelation of God in Jesus Christ. Thus the Bible is a record of God's revelation.

Revelation and Salvation

Crucial to Tillich's thought was that "the history of revelation and the history of salvation are the same history. Revelation can be received only in the presence of salvation, and salvation can occur within a correlation of revelation." For "Salvation is derived from *salus,* 'healthy' or 'whole,' and it can be applied to every act of healing: to the healing of sickness, of demonic possession, and of servitude to sin and to the ultimate power of death. Salvation in this sense takes place in time and history, just as revelation takes place in time and history."[53]

While "salvation and revelation are ambiguous in the process of time and history," for Tillich, "the Christian message points to an ultimate salvation which cannot be lost because it is reunion with the ground of being."[54] Salvation is not individualistic in that individuals are isolated from each other. Rather "fulfillment is universal" and in the symbol of "the kingdom of God" there is "complete transparency of everything for the divine to shine through it. In his fulfilled kingdom, God is everything for everything. This is the symbol of ultimate revelation and ultimate salvation in complete unity."[55]

Revelation and the Word of God

Traditionally the doctrine of revelation has been developed as a doctrine of the "Word of God." Tillich points out that in the concept of Jesus Christ as *logos*, "Logos points to a revelatory reality, not to revelatory words." For Tillich, "the doctrine of the Logos prevents the elaboration of a theology of the spoken or the written word, which is *the* Protestant pitfall."[56]

The term "Word of God" has six different senses, according to Tillich.[57]

1. The Word is "the principle of the divine self-manifestation in the ground of being itself." The ground of being has "the character of self-manifestation; it has *logos* character."

2. The Word is "the medium of creation." In contrast to Greek philosophical (neo-Platonic) emanations, the *Logos* as the medium of creation points to both the freedom of creation and the freedom of the created.

3. The Word is "the manifestation of the divine life in the history of revelation."

4. The Word is "the manifestation of the divine life in the final revelation." The "Word" is a name for Jesus as the Christ. It is not the words *of* Jesus but "the being of the Christ, of which his words and his deeds are an expression."

5. The Word is also applied to "the document of the final revelation and its special preparation, namely, the Bible." Yet for Tillich, to use the expression "Word of God" for the Bible will mean that "theological confusion is almost unavoidable." Scripture is the Word of God in two senses. It is the document of final revelation and "it also participates in the final revelation of which it is the document." In Tillich's view, "nothing has contributed more to the misinterpretation of the biblical doctrine of the Word than the identification of the Word with the Bible."

6. The Word is also "the message of the church as proclaimed in her preaching and teaching." Human words and language become "the Word" when they are spoken in power and their content received existentially by listeners.

In conclusion, for Tillich

> the many different meanings of the term "Word" are all united in one meaning, namely, "God manifest"—manifest in himself, in creation, in the history of revelation, in the final revelation, in the Bible, in the words of the church and her members. "God manifest"— the mystery of the divine abyss expressing itself through the divine Logos—this is the meaning of the symbol, the "Word of God."[58]

The Nature of Scripture

For Tillich the Bible is a source of revelation and participates in the revelation because the biblical writers wrote as living witnesses to the revelation they encountered.[59] Their participation was "their response to the happenings which became revealing events through this response." Tillich defined the "inspiration" of the biblical writers as

> their receptive and creative response to potentially revelatory facts. The inspiration of the writers of the New Testament is their acceptance of Jesus as Christ, and with him, of the New Being, of which they became witnesses. Since there is not revelation unless there is someone who receives it as revelation, the act of reception is a part of the event itself. The Bible is both original event and original document; it witnesses to that of which it is a part.[60]

The Bible for Tillich, while written in ordinary human words, is not merely the communication of information. If it were only "information," it would "not have the power of grasping, shaking, and transforming, the power which is attributed to the 'Word of God.' "[61] Words are the indispensable medium of all revelation.

But the word of revelation "cannot be spoken apart from revelatory events in nature, history and man." The words of the Bible would mean nothing apart from the revelatory events in history to which they witness. Thus, because "the knowledge of revelation can be received only in the situation of revelation, and it can be communicated—in contrast to ordinary knowledge—only to those who participate in this situation,"[62] the Bible does not convey new content but a new dimension of ultimate meaning. The nature of Scripture as revelation is such that it enables a person to enter into the same revelatory events described in the Bible and to share in the same ecstatic experiences as the biblical writers who witnessed to God's final revelation in Jesus Christ.

SCRIPTURE AS LIVING ENCOUNTER

The Bible for Tillich presents a collage of religious symbols that express the revelatory events witnessed to by the biblical writers. Revelation and salvation are identical so that through the Scripture one gains "an existential understanding of revelation, that is, a creative and transforming participation of every believer in the correlation of revelation."[63]

Biblical religious symbols are authoritative for Tillich

> because they fulfill two functions: They *express* the occurrence and content of the original revelation in Jesus as the Christ, and they *occasion* dependent revelatory events having precisely the same content as the original one. The continuity of content between the original and dependent events apparently hangs entirely on the fact that the same symbols function in them all. Thereby the symbols, and above all the "biblical picture," effectively link us with the healing power mediated to [humans] by Jesus of Nazareth.[64]

The climax of biblical revelation is the symbol of "Jesus as the Christ," for in this symbol the biblical writers witness to revelation by saying that in the unique event of Jesus of Nazareth the power of the "New Being" was present as nowhere else.[65] Through the symbols of the Bible, humans are brought into a living encounter with Jesus as the Christ. This biblical picture can and does mediate the power of new being to sinful, estranged humans today.[66] For Tillich it is "the Christian claim that the biblical picture of Jesus as the Christ does sometimes serve as the occasion for such healing events today."[67] These are "healing events" of "salvation" (*salus*) and thus "revelation." For the power of being is mediated to humans through holy objects (the Bible), which rescue humans in estranged existence from the threat of "nonbeing" and aid in their quest for healing and wholeness.

In the sermon by Gail R. O'Day, a homiletician at Candler School of Theology, observe how the symbols of sound and voice in human experience are used to help us hear the unsettling voice of Jesus in our midst. Then the abridged sermon by Robert Neville, philosopher and theologian, affirms the dialectic between judgment and love, which is explained through the scriptural correlates of justice, mercy, and virtue. This dialectic and these symbols confront our personal subjectivity about God.

Sounds and Voices

Gail R. O'Day

Mark 1:21-28

The Gospel lesson is a text of sounds and voices. Some stories that we read are visual texts; we are invited into the world they create by visual images and signs. The pictures those stories put before our eyes hold our imagination. This text from Mark, though, is distinctly aural—that is, our entrance into its world depends on what we are able to hear. Our ears provide the key to our imaginative participation in this text. We must therefore listen carefully to what are at times glaringly discordant voices if we are to accept the invitation of this text.

The story opens on the sabbath in the synagogue, itself a place of voices. Synagogue worship is a pattern of voices: the reading aloud of Scripture, prayer, teaching, and exposition of the meaning of Scripture—all oral, all offerings of voices to expectant ears. There is a calm to this speaking and listening, because we find ourselves in the realm of the expected, the conventional, the traditional. We are at worship, and we know what pattern the voices will take.

Jesus adds his voice to those who are reading, teaching, and praying and when he does, something unexpected happens. The people are astonished! They have never heard teaching like Jesus' teaching before, and they can only gape in amazement and whisper to one another. Such teaching! Such authority! Such a voice! The conventional world of the synagogue has been pried open ever so slightly by the power of Jesus, who teaches with authority.

There is no time for those of us who listen to sit and reflect on Jesus and his teaching, however, because immediately the conventional world of the synagogue is burst wide open and the calm of the worship service is gone forever. There is a rupture in the moment, in the text, and we are jolted from the conventional to the unconventional.

How are we jolted? By a voice, of course. There is a man with an unclean spirit in the midst of the gathered congregation, and we come to know of this man's presence because he cries out. Loud. At the top of his lungs. Probably right in the middle of the prayer. Or in a moment of silence. Or in the middle of Jesus' teaching. This man cries out, announcing himself, shouting uncontrollably. It is embarrassing. It is uncomfortable. No one in the synagogue knows where to look. No one knows what to say. People become remarkably fascinated with their own feet as the man continues to shout.

The man with the unclean spirit does not merely draw attention to himself with his shouts, though. His loud, discordant shouts also serve to lock the focus on Jesus. The man's words, three sentences, are all an assault on Jesus: "What have you to do with us, Jesus of Nazareth? Have you come to destroy us? I know who you are, the Holy One of God."

The cacophonous brashness of this voice is brought fully to bear upon Jesus. "I know you," the voice of the unclean spirit shouts, "and I do not want any part of you!"

It is the staggering, yet sobering, reality of this text that evil immediately recognizes Jesus and the voice of evil gives the fullest identification of Jesus. The unclean spirit (whose name is Legion) knows immediately what the stakes are in a confrontation with Jesus: "Have you come to destroy us?" The people in the synagogue were impressed with the authority of Jesus' teaching, but the unclean spirit knew that appreciation of Jesus' teaching barely touches the surface of who Jesus is. Jesus is the Holy One of God, the one with the power and authority to destroy that which destroys life. This meeting between Jesus and the unclean spirit is no simple meeting in a synagogue: this is a confrontation of cosmic proportions. What is at issue here is how the world will be shaped and governed—by the power of evil and death or by the power of God for life. The voice of the unclean spirit shouts into the calm of the sabbath worship that the reign of the principalities and powers has a crack in it, that it can no longer be business as usual, that something new has been set loose among us.

As this raging, shrieking voice rings in our ears, as this voice screams its protest in an attempt to drown out the tolling of its own death knell, another voice is heard. It is the voice of Jesus. Mark has told us about the authority of Jesus' synagogue teaching, but we have not heard his voice for ourselves until now. Now, faced with the full, screaming, crying voice of evil, Jesus speaks. He speaks sternly, directly, forcefully. He rebukes the unclean spirit and says to him, "Be silent and come out of him."

Note Jesus' first words: Be silent. Jesus knows the power of the demon's voice, the disruptive, destructive power of that voice, and so he commands him to be silent. Jesus speaks against the unclean spirit: health against disease and destruction, peace against chaos, voice against voice. Before Jesus can exorcise the demon, Jesus must silence the demon, because it is the voice that gives the unclean spirit its hold on the man.

That's it, you see, it is the voice of the unclean spirit that gives it power. The man (yes, somewhere behind this powerful, shrieking voice there is still a human being) lost his own voice, lost the ability to hear his own voice and to speak his own voice ages ago. Now he can only hear the voice that torments him and speak the voice that springs from his torment. He lost the voice of life, and he exists always, only in response to the voice of death.

We all know that voice. We all live daily on the edge of giving in to that voice. Sadly, we all live many days having that voice or voices—the voice that tells us that we are worthless, that we are failures, that we are irredeemable. The voice that fills us with guilt and shame, immobilizes us, paralyzes us, turns us away from the good, from what is life fulfilled, because it is full of risk. The voice that causes us indeed to treat our neighbors as ourselves, so that the harshness we feel toward ourselves issues in callousness and injustice toward others. The voice that tells us no one loves us, not even God, and so we live tormented, always fighting against, never rejoicing with. We rage at one another, at the world, at humanness given us by God, and we credit only the strident, cacophonous voice of death.

The jeers and raucousness of the unclean spirit have free reign until they meet the voice of Jesus. And then, with a loud scream (always loud, always grating) the unclean spirit comes out of the man. The spirit does not leave without a fight. The battle waged by Jesus for life is never easy, and the man is surely ravaged by the wracking convulsions that shake his body. But the voice of the unclean spirit is denied any determinative force by Jesus, and so, though the spirit protests, the spirit is indeed defeated. "The strife is o'er, the battle done, the victory of life is won." Jesus has won yet another victory over chaos and death. The voice of evil and death does not have ultimate authority over life when the voice of Jesus is heard, when the voice of Jesus is allowed to speak.

As the raucous, frenzied confrontation between the voice of the unclean spirit and the voice of Jesus in this story from Mark demonstrates, the determination of which voice will govern is never easy. The voice of death is loud, forceful, and with its own kind of compelling power. Once that voice takes hold, once our ears are attuned to its cadences, we soon forget that there are other options, that there is any other voice with a claim to a hearing. Yet, despite our deafness, there is always this other voice, the voice of God, which speaks to us through Jesus and says, "Be silent and come out of her." It may at times be a still, small voice; it may at times be a voice so out of tune with the other voices that beckon us that we doubt its credibility and its authority. It may be a voice that tells us things that are hard for us to hear, but it is there; it is always there, calling us away from death and on toward life.

There is, of course, one final voice in this story: the voice of the synagogue congregation, who know only to speak in amazement. They have heard the confrontation of the voices and have heard the amazing power of the voice of Jesus silence the unclean spirit. It is this voice of amazement that spreads the news of Jesus everywhere in the surrounding region of Galilee. "There is one," the voice of amazement says, "this one, this Jesus, who teaches with authority and who has the authority to silence the unclean spirits. What is this?" the people ask in their amazement. Over and over again they ask, "What is this? Who is this?"

Who is this, indeed? "I know you, you are the Holy One of God," Jesus of Nazareth. You are the one who speaks to us out of the darkness and torment, and calls us into life. May our ears never forget the powerful cadences of your gracious voice.

God the Witness

Robert C. Neville

Micah 1:2; 2:1-10; Luke 17:11-19; 2 Timothy 2:8-15

Surely God's mercy is shown in the placement of the harshest words of divine judgment in biblical books so short we hardly ever find them. Micah, Joel, Obadiah, Nahum, Habakkuk, Zephaniah, even 2 Timothy are called to our attention only by the lectionary, and pity to you if ever you are required to find a passage quickly at a public meeting!.

The judgment of God, however, is necessary to hear before the message of love and mercy makes sense. To be sure, we cannot inwardly believe the message of judgment until we encounter divine love. Yet we cannot understand God's love until we have accepted divine judgment. So long as our personal self-condemnation exceeds that for which we believe God judges us, divine love and mercy are opaque to us and ineffectual in renewing our lives.

Divine judgment is an unpopular topic, however. I am going to take the easy way out by discussing the preparatory topic of divine witness. Micah wrote, "Hear, you peoples, all of you;/ listen, O earth, and all that is in it;/ and let the Lord GOD be a witness against you,/ the Lord from his holy temple" (Mic. 1:2).

This passage, and the conception of divine witness it illustrates, is easy to reject in this modern day, for it depicts God as a heavenly voyeur peeking out from the temple at our affairs. Even more sophisticated interpretations of God as a super-fatherly being in some metaphorical sense who watches us from the outside are easy to reject because they suppose that God has some kind of personal subjectivity, a private divine consciousness. If God has a personal subjectivity, then it is limited and stopped when it encounters our subjectivity. That is what personal subjectivity means: to look out onto a world that is a bunch of objects; when one of those objects is another person looking back at us, we suddenly encounter another personal subject behind those eyes. The world is no longer merely objects but includes some other subjects as well, other people who are mysterious to us, who are as private behind what they do not reveal as we discover ourselves to be when we are misunderstood. We discover our own depths as we see signs of unrevealed depth in others. If our world contains only objects, no subjects, we never know that there is more to us than that of which we are self-conscious. Because we encounter other subjects, we can encounter ourselves as subjects and find signs for what lies behind consciousness.

Here's the rub for judgment and witness: Behind the presentation of our personal subjectivity lies the heart we don't want seen, the heart we cover up to ourselves except for telltale traces. Now, if God is another personal subjectivity, then we are safe! If God has to look out from a private divine standpoint, then we can hide, even better than we can hide from ourselves. When our theology depicts God as a super-personal consciousness, then we can play the infinitely postponing game of hide and seek. We hide from God's judgment while seeking God's love. But if by chance we find God's love, it cannot count because it does not address what we have to hide. God cannot forgive us what would be opaque to a divine consciousness, and we live in infinite guilt that God's love is wasted because neither God nor we ourselves have access to that for which mercy is needed. If God is a personal subject, we can deceive God as we deceive ourselves. Divine witness cannot mean this.

Return to Micah's text:

> Alas for those who devise wickedness
>   and evil deeds on their beds!
> When the morning dawns, they perform it,
>   because it is in their power.
> They covet fields, and seize them;
>   houses, and take them away;
> they oppress householder and house,
>   people and their inheritance. (Mic. 2:1-2)

Planning evil may very well be the stuff of dreams and unconscious motivations. We good people surely never sit around and consciously plan to do something wicked for its own sake. Even if we do have a jealous or vicious thought, we know it is private and unexpressed.

But then how is it that we do evil? By accident? Surely not! To seize a field we covet requires planning and connivance. We may hide the covetousness from ourselves, but organizing the seizure requires discipline and use of law. We may disguise love of oil as love of freedom, but it requires strategic intelligence and diplomacy to defeat an Arab state in the Middle East. We may think racism is only a bad dream, but it takes financial organization and elaborate cooperation to redline a neighborhood's real estate. We may think we do not want power over our family and friends, but it takes enormous wit and energy to play the games of status. We may think we feel for victims, but our national, social, and personal lives are shaped by the efforts to avoid the victim's lot through adjusting to the powers of oppression. According to Micah, God is witness to the stretch between heart and deed; from heart to deed we go, from deed to heart God sees, the witness is the whole, heart and deed, one piece, who we are.

The first lesson of divine witness is that the things we are, heart and deed, count ultimately. In divine witness there is no hiding, no game of self-revelation on our part, no divine mystery. What we are as a matter of fact is the ultimate witness in divine perfection. The witness is not a representation of ourselves in a separate divine mind but our own very being as measured in God. We can deceive ourselves, but we cannot deceive God because our very being, lodged in God, is the judgment on us. If only God were over there we could hide and dissemble. But God is the infinite creator in whom we have our being. In God's very being our lives are measured by the plumb lines of justice, piety, faith, hope, and love, and in each case we are found wanting. God's witness is the divine goodness in whose context we are judgment on ourselves.

God is faithful in love to us creatures, whatever the witness. When we dream of evil, God still finds us lovely, and sensing that love we can face our dreams. When we pursue wickedness not for gain but just because it is possible, God still finds us lovely, and sensing that love we can abandon our enslavement to the possible. When we covet our neighbor's field, God faithfully finds good in us, and knowing that we can rest in satisfaction. Where we can seize with impunity, God loves us for the guilty conscience, and knowing that we can put things aside. When we oppress others and live in ways that hold them in poverty and hurt, God's mercy is still offered, and seeing that, we can turn to righteousness and begin the small steps to justice and virtue.

In none of this is God's witness denied. We dream deeds of evil, and that is who we are. We let the dreams unfold in reality, and those deeds are who we are. We pursue wickedness not just for gain but merely because it is possible, and that is who we are. We covet our neighbor's field, and we are truly covetous. We seize the holdings of the weak and defenseless, and we are truly the abusers of power. We oppress others with poverty and pain, and the truth is that we are oppressors. These faults are who we are within the divine witness. But God loves us despite all this, finds a loveliness in us we cannot bear to accept, and offers us the power to surmount our sin, to transcend our suffering, to find light through our ignorance, and to return to the harmony of the divine peace.

IX

PROCESS THEOLOGY

Scripture as Unfolding Action

ONE OF THE MOST SIGNIFICANT CONTEMPORARY THEOLOGICAL MOVEMENTS AMONG professional theologians today is process theology. It has developed from process philosophy and has been evolving into its present sophisticated forms since the 1920s. The emphasis on the dialectical theology of neo-orthodoxy since the 1930s gave way to a host of particularized theologies in the 1960s, such as theologies of race, revolution, ecology, and feminism. But in the return of theologians to the search for a system of theology, process theology has offered a new and comprehensive way of viewing basic realities and theological concepts.[1] Process theology presents "an immanent God who is known by rational reflection on human experience."[2]

BACKGROUNDS

Whitehead

Contemporary process theology is built on the philosophical thought of Alfred North Whitehead (1861–1947). Whitehead taught mathematics at Cambridge University from 1885 to 1910.[3] From 1911 to 1924 he taught in London and with his former student Bertrand Russell wrote a three-volume work *Principia Mathematica* (1910–1913), which helped create a new framework for logic. In 1922 Whitehead's *The Principle of Relativity with Applications to Physical Science* presented an alternative to Einstein's theory of relativity.

When Whitehead was sixty-three years old in 1924, he moved to Harvard University to teach philosophy, although he had previously not taught in that discipline. During the next thirteen years, Whitehead produced eight books and a number of articles. His major work, *Process and Reality,* contained his Gifford lectures, which had been delivered at the University of Edinburgh in 1927–1928.[4] During his time at Harvard, Whitehead began to develop a new metaphysic that would present a comprehensive picture of reality. His work *Science and the Modern World* outlined his new views, which led him to deal with the nature of God and traditional static views of religion.[5] Other American thinkers, such as John Dewey, applauded Whitehead's work as offering an important new framework to relate personal values and scientific facts. Whitehead's 1926 book, *Religion in the Making,* argued that humanity's deepest vision of reality is embodied by religion.[6]

Metaphysics

Whitehead's metaphysic rested on the notion of process. This he spoke of as a "philosophy of organism." For Whitehead, the entire universe was

> a vast, creative movement, a "process," involving multifarious levels of interrelated elements which he called "actual entities." These ranged from God himself at one end of the scale to the slightest "puff of existence" at the other. Each of these entities was "bi-polar," with both a "physical" and a "mental" aspect—though only above a certain level did the latter attain the intensification which produced "consciousness." The mental aspect at all levels enabled what he called "prehension," by which the different entities linked up with and related to each other. Through the whole network of prehensions and interactions, the universe was integrated as a dynamic, developing whole, a cosmic symphony.[7]

Whitehead believed that

> the temporal process is a "transition" from one actual entity to another. These entities are momentary events which perish immediately upon coming into being. The perishing marks the transition to the succeeding events. Time is not a single smooth flow, but comes into being in little droplets. A motion picture suggests an analogy: the picture appears to be a continuous flow, whereas in reality it is constituted by a series of distinct frames.[8]

What Whitehead called "occasions of experience" stressed that actual entities arise, become, reach completion, and then are past. Yet "the things that endure are series of these occasions of experience. Electrons, molecules, and cells are examples of such enduring things. Likewise the human soul, or stream of experience, is composed of a series of distinct occasions of experience."[9]

All experiences are related to previous experiences through a multiplicity of relations. A momentary experience becomes distinct in itself by how it reacts to and is unified with these relations. Thus the ways these relate are called "prehension" and "feeling." The present occasion "prehends" or "feels" occasions that have gone before. The present occasion is "nothing but its process of unifying the particular prehensions with which it begins."[10]

To summarize this view:

> Each of Whitehead's occasions of experience begins, as it were, as an open window to the totality of the past, as it prehends all the previous occasions (either immediately or mediately). Once the rush of influences enters in, the window is closed, while the occasion of experience forms itself by response to these influences. But as soon as this process is completed, the windows of the world are again open, as a new occasion of experience takes its rise. Hence, the next molecular occasion within that series constituting the enduring molecule, or the next moment of human experience within that stream of experiences constituting the soul, is open to the contributions that can be received from others.[11]

This means, too, that "Whiteheadian process thought gives primacy to interdependence as an ideal over independence. Of course, it portrays interdependence not simply as an ideal but as an ontologically given characteristic. We cannot escape it. However, we can either exult in this fact or bemoan it."[12]

God

This basic view of reality has implications for the process view of God. For Whitehead, "one all-pervasive fact, inherent in the very character of what is real is the transition of things, the passage one to another."[13] Or again, he wrote: "It belongs to the nature of a 'being' that it is a potential for every 'becoming.' This is the 'principle of relativity.' "[14] Thus "how an actual entity *becomes* constitutes *what* that actual entity is. . . . Its 'being' is constituted by its 'becoming.' This is the 'principle of progress.' "[15]

Process philosophy, when it speaks of God, is sometimes called "dipolar theism." Charles Hartshorne (b. 1897), Whitehead's former teaching assistant and Professor of Philosophy at the University of Chicago from 1928 to 1955, describes God as having two "poles" or aspects. One is the abstract essence of God; the other is God's concrete actuality.[16] God's abstract essence is eternal, absolute, independent, and unchangeable. At every moment, the divine existence is marked by these aspects. God's concrete actuality is temporal, relative, dependent, and changing constantly. In God's life each moment produces new, unforeseen happenings in the world. God's concrete knowledge thus depends upon decisions made by people or actualities in the world. Thus God's knowledge is "always relativized by, in the sense of internally related to the world."[17]

Whitehead's description of the nature of God varied from that of Hartshorne. Whitehead spoke of the primordial and the consequent nature of God. The "primordial nature" may be defined as "the mental pole in God. The primordial nature is God's grasp of all possibilities. This grasp involves an ordering evaluation of possibilities into a harmony which is called the 'primordial vision.' "[18]

The "consequent nature" of God, according to Whitehead, may be said to be "the physical pole in God." This is "God's feelings of the world. It is 'consequent' in a twofold sense: first, it follows from the primordial nature in God, and second, it follows from the actual happenings in the world."[19]

God is intimately related to this world in that God participates in all that happens in the world and all that happens makes an impression on God. For Whitehead, "God related entities to each other on a grand order as God integrated the physical feelings of God's consequent nature with the conceptual feelings of God's primordial nature."[20] In contrast to traditional theism, which stressed the divine absoluteness and "simplicity," process thought stresses that the divine reality enters into the world of "feelings." This means that

the divine reality is not limited to a "bare knowledge" of the new things happening in the world. Rather, the responsiveness includes a sympathetic feeling with the worldly beings, all of whom have feelings. Hence, it is not merely the content of God's knowledge which is dependent, but God's own emotional state. God enjoys our enjoyments, and suffers with our sufferings. This is the kind of responsiveness which is truly divine and belongs to the very nature of perfection.[21]

The implication for Christians is that this view of God is also "the ideal for human existence. Upon this basis, Christian *agape* can come to have the element of sympathy, of compassion for the present situation of others, which it should have had all along."[22]

SCRIPTURE IN PROCESS THEOLOGY

Doctrine and Authority

Contemporary process theologians see the compatibility of Whitehead's analysis of reality with basic features of the Christian faith. Religious doctrine is a structured form that is given to beliefs that one consciously holds. For process theologians, these beliefs are derived from

> induction, deduction, and authority, as well as from immediate experience, and there is a great diversity among them. Belief at this level must be distinguished from the complex of prereflective beliefs that we all hold in common, since we all immediately apprehend a common reality in every moment of our experience. These deeper beliefs are originally preconscious and prereflective. They may or may not emerge into conscious awareness.[23]

When beliefs emerge into conscious awareness and take the forms of conscious beliefs, they have profound effects on human existence. Christian doctrines "which are explications of universal aspects of experience have importance in the same way. For example, they lift into consciousness certain aspects of the universal experience of deity, such as divine grace. . . . Christian doctrine, by selecting certain features of experience for conscious emphasis, shapes attitudes, purposes, and commitments, and even the structure of human existence itself."[24]

For process theologians following Whitehead, religious doctrines can be accepted only if they are self-evident.[25] This does not mean that the doctrine will be equally obvious to all people, because not everyone has the same ability to "perceive the previously unformulated factors in experience."[26] When these have been perceived consciously and then verbally expressed, others may recognize them. Whitehead used an analogy of a tuning fork and a piano. The piano responds to the note struck by the tuning fork only because it has a string that is tuned to the same note that the turning fork emits.[27] People may assent to and affirm doctrines as verbal expressions of a universally experienced fact because they have already perceived the fact. The verbal form (doctrine) brings the perception to the conscious level and will make it become more important in one's life. It could in fact become a central principle around which one's whole life might be organized.[28] Theology's task in this view is to state the basics of one's beliefs so they call forth a response of perception from others who find them self-evidently true.

Beside doctrines, other things are self-evident to humans as well. The reality of the external world is one of these. It is thus possible for one's "prethematic" or prereflective view of reality also to become conceptualized. When this happens it may receive validity as an expression of one's experience. In the philosophy of Whitehead, process theologians find an accurate description of the human experience of reality.[29]

The Functions of Scripture

For process theologians the Bible may serve several functions. First, it may be used as a source for doctrine. Because doctrine represents the explication of universal aspects of experience, it is entirely possible and likely that the Christian Scriptures may be used as a source for finding data or materials that will help to explicate these universal aspects of experience.

One example of how this works can be seen in process Christology and specifically in the doctrine of the incarnation of Jesus Christ. There are varieties among process theologians with regard to Christology just as there are on other topics.[30]

One process Christology proceeds as follows: "Special revelation" may be considered as taking place "through intensifying the image of God in human consciousness. While this may occur in an ultimate sense in Jesus, revelation begins far before that time in the long history of Israel."[31] Through the covenant in the Old Testament, God established a relationship with Adam, Noah, and Abraham. Through the covenant:

God's will toward justice in relationships is revealed; through the people's participation in the covenant, justice in relationships is enacted in society. Faithfully, God lures the people into being a people who will reflect the divine character. Insofar as the people become a society of justice, the image of God is created in human society; insofar as they fall away, the image is distorted. Always the constancy of God is like a goad, pricking the people into relationships which exhibit justice, and therefore fulfill the covenant.[32]

In a process world, "God acts with the world as it is, leading it toward what it can be. The aims of God will transcend the given, but must also reflect the given."[33] Throughout the Old Testament, God's revelation builds and "Christian history builds upon Israelite history. The richness of Judaism made Christianity possible. The revelation of the nature of God, seen and still seen through a whole people, was also given through the one person, Jesus. Through this one, yet another people are given birth so that they too might reflect the image of God."[34] In this one person, Jesus, according to the process theologian, both the nature of God and the nature of what humanity is called to be are revealed. This person may thus be called "Immanuel, God with us."[35]

In distinction from traditional Christology, however, in process thought:

if all this it to be achieved by a human person incarnation cannot be a once-for-all happening but must be a continuous process. In process thought a person is not one actual occasion but a series of many, many occasions. For incarnation to occur, there would have to be an assent to incarnation in every moment of existence. Incarnation would have to be continuous.[36]

From this one may examine the gospel accounts of Jesus of Nazareth and see his character. This character also reveals the character of God and thus Jesus becomes the special revelation of God. As Suchocki put it:

No matter which gospel text we take to consider the life of Jesus, we are confronted with one who consistently manifests the love to which he calls others. He breaks down all partitions that divide humans from each other; he embodies a love that is just, and a love that therefore variously exhibits judgment, affirmation, service, or sharing, depending upon the context of love. But this is the life which reveals the nature of God for us; this is the life which offers a concrete vision of the reality to which God calls us; this is the revelation of God to us for the sake of conforming us to that divine image. If we see in Jesus a revelation of God for us, then the way Jesus loves is the way God loves.[37]

In process thought, "to see the life of Jesus as God with us, incarnate in him, is to lift all that we see in that revelation to ultimacy."[38]

It is clear here that the Bible functions as a source for this "doctrine of the incarnation" because Scripture provides the data from which the doctrine springs. But the doctrine itself, as a Christian doctrine, formally expresses what people will find when they encounter the biblical picture of Jesus of Nazareth. In this sense it will confirm what is self-evident.[39]

However, doctrinal statements that originate from Christian Scripture are not to be accepted only through appeals to authority.[40] They must be judged on the basis of their self-evidency. In this case of the doctrine of the incarnation, the question would be about how the nature of God is revealed through God's presence in Jesus and how this perception about Jesus coincides with what process thought believes about God. As such, this doctrine with its source in the biblical data should be presented (as Cobb and Griffin state) "in such a way as to elicit a responsive perception of these as self-evidently true."[41]

Suchocki proposes the self-evident prehension of God's love:

How, then, is the nature of God revealed through God's presence in Jesus? Consider Jesus' openness to others in relation to the sense in which God, through the consequent nature, feels every reality in the universe precisely as that reality feels itself. What is added to the philosophical statement by the biblical revelation is that the openness to all which is stated philosophically is a loving openness. Jesus reveals the character of God as love. In Jesus, openness to the other is in the mode of love; in God, openness to the other which feels the other regardless of place, position, or power is an openness of love. Jesus is open to the other with a will toward the well-being of the other: the openness of God through the consequent nature must therefore be an openness which wants the well-being of the other. Process philosophy requires that every prehension be felt with a certain "subjective form" or qualifying feeling. The revelation of God in Jesus tells us that God's subjective form in feeling the world is love.[42]

Thus it is clear that the affirmation of God's presence of Jesus, which is verbalized as a "doctrine of the incarnation," is a self-evident perception arising from the biblical picture of Jesus of Nazareth and how that figure Jesus exemplified in his life and actions the consequent nature of God. The attitudes and actions of Jesus coincide with the experienced reality of a God who "feels every reality in the universe precisely as that reality feels itself." The biblical picture adds to the philosophical picture by presenting Jesus acting in the mode of love. This love can then be perceived as the feeling of the prehension or the feeling of the other in the universe. A further development of this model of process Christology occurs when Suchocki goes on to answer how Jesus, who "loves with a mutuality which invites giving and receiving," is like God. This is seen in that, for Suchocki, "the fullness of the revelation of God does not stop with the life of Jesus, but continues through the crucifixion and resurrection."[43] There is thus an "interplay" between human experience as understood via process modes of expression and doctrines derived from the Bible. In these discussions, too, Scripture becomes a source for helping to describe (in doctrines) the unfolding action of God in this world.[44]

A second function of Scripture in process thought is for the Bible to present possibilities of experience that go beyond the experience of a society not informed by Scripture. An example of this would be the Christian experience of the grace of God. Events or modes of relationships may be opened by Scripture even though they have not yet been a particular part of our own experience. In this sense again, the Bible introduces us to the unfolding action of God as people turn and return to the Scriptures and find their return continuing to bear new insights and inspiration. As Cobb and Griffin write:

> Nevertheless, our immediate experience is the final court of appeal. We have faith in the continued fruitfulness of returning to the first accounts of and reactions to Jesus' life for new insights because of the repeated fruitfulness of this return in the past. But this fruitfulness must finally prove itself in our own experience, or faith in the continuing relevance of Jesus will decline in company with other beliefs that do not ring true for us.[45]

As one turns to Scripture, one's own experience is both confirmed and enlarged by encountering the continual evolution of God and God's relationship with the world.[46]

SCRIPTURE AS UNFOLDING ACTION

From this survey, it is apparent that process theology is closely related to process philosophy. This philosophy is a comprehensive view of reality that stresses "becoming" rather than "being," and this fundamental direction significantly affects the whole of Christian theology. Traditional Christian doctrines are redefined within the process system.

Process theology views of Scripture and its nature are closely related to its views of reality and the nature of God. Scripture may be a source for "doctrine," but it derives its authority from its concurrence with one's own self-evident experience.[47] To interpret Scripture, the process view of reality is to be used, which itself is validated by its self-evidence.

Scripture may be seen in this system to be a source among others through which one perceives the unfolding action of God in the world. As one turns to the Bible and finds experience confirmed or enlarged, one may experience a way by which God can be known. By opening new avenues of experience, Scripture provides the means through which humans can relate to God and the avenue by which the divine relativity may become real to humans. As a source for insight and inspiration, Scripture opens new possibilities of experience to us. The process view of God presents a deity evolving with creation into the new possibilities of the future, which is much closer, process theologians argue, to the biblical witness of a God who is active in time and history and who relates to humans in responsive love. The traditional picture of God as static and absolute is discarded. The story of the Bible is thus continued in our own "stories" as humans progress into their futures with a God who grows with the world and works together with humanity for a better and more unified world of tomorrow. Scripture may introduce us to this unfolding action of God.

Marjorie Suchocki preaches below about the self-evident experience of human suffering, the same grief that is described in the Scripture and apprehended by God through Jesus in death and resurrection.

In Our Gethsemanes

Marjorie Suchocki

Psalm 139; John 20:24-28

Psalm 139 celebrates the height and depth and width and breadth of the divine presence—no heaven too high, no hell too low, but God is there. And in the incredible Easter passage we see God present to us in one crucified and risen—the anguished Thomas has cried out that not unless he sees and touches the nailprints will he believe. The answer is given; a hand is held out, and in the divine presence Thomas proclaims, "My Lord and my God."

Between these two texts are two other passages, not of presence but of denial and absence.

> They came to a place called Gethsemane; and he said to his disciples, "Sit here while I pray." He took with him Peter and James and John, and began to be distressed and agitated. And he said to them, "I am deeply grieved, even to death; remain here, and keep awake." And going a little farther, he threw himself on the ground and prayed that, if it were possible, the hour might pass from him. He said, "Abba, Father, for you all things are possible; remove this cup from me; yet, not what I want, but what you want." (Mark 14:32-36)

Within twenty-four hours Jesus had his answer:

> When it was noon, darkness came over the whole land until three in the afternoon. At three o'clock Jesus cried out with a loud voice, "Eloi, Eloi, lema sabachthani?" which means, "My God, my God, why have you forsaken me?" (Mark 15:33-34)

How can it be that this one who shows us so surely that God is present to us and present for us should in this Gethsemane and on this Golgotha witness with such anguish to God's denial and absence? The hour did not pass him by, and the cup was not removed.

We, too, have the hours we beg to pass by, and the cups we cry out not to drink. We, too, have our Gethsemanes that raise the question of divine presence.

We know our mortality, and we accept our finitude. But sometimes we lose a friend in his prime, and we say "Not yet!" It's one thing to know we will die someday, and quite another to know the date. Gethsemane, for us, is the grief of a dying friend. For that friend, it is the pain and the confluence of the daytime knowing and the nighttime knowing—the daytime when rationality shines like a winter sun and preparations are made. The nighttime darkness brings a different mode of knowing, and no preparation guards against it.

We have yet other Gethsemanes. Recently a woman received the word that her daughter was missing. She simply disappeared from campus, with no note or indication of any intentions left behind. Where is this woman's daughter? Are you a mother? A father? Can you feel this parent's anguish and fear? Where is her daughter? Is she even alive? We pray for this mother and her daughter, begging that like the prodigal in Luke 15 she will return; hoping that like that prodigal, she can.

I know that each of you here has your own Gethsemane that you could likewise share with me, the prayer from a pain that knows no easy answer. But I would be remiss if I related Gethsemane only to these private matters.

There have been very public matters: the crisis in Bosnia, in Waco, and the mounting tension and violence in South Africa. We read of each event and hear the reports on our newscasts. We feel distress, but there is, after all, a distance, because every week brings news of someone else's violence. Yet that distance is an illusion. The pain, anguish, and grief caused by these events are just as deep as what we feel for our own Gethsemanes. The reality is that our whole earth seems like a contemporary Gethsemane, and we cry out to God for our relief, all the while fearing in our souls that our own answer, too, might force out the cry, "Why hast thou forsaken me?"

Is there no connection between the Markan passages and those that speak of presence? Hear again the psalmist: "If I make my bed in [hell], you are there." We are so accustomed to the beauty of the psalm that we sweep the starkness of that statement into the rhetoric of joy and confidence. But hear it in all its defiant literalness: If I make my bed in hell, you are there! In Gethsemane, you are there!

And think of it again: This one who prayed so uselessly in that garden is the one we call God incarnate, God revealed, God with us. Is it not so that Jesus reveals God's presence not just sometimes, but at all times? Is he not revealing God's presence in Gethsemane and on Golgotha? The very cry of God-forsakenness from the God-revealing one shouts out that even in the hell of God-forsakenness, God is there present with us, though we have no sense of it! God is present and for our good even when it is against all the evidences of our emotions.

Follow the effect of such presence. Its purpose cannot be simply to comfort, for scant comfort is found. Its purpose is a steadfast redemptiveness, a determined will toward our good. God's presence with us is necessarily God's deep and experiential knowledge of us, tasting with us each drop of the bitter cup; feeling each fighting gulp and the nauseating response. In being present, God is not protected from our anguish; the cross tells us that! And I dare to think that precisely because God is so thoroughly present to us, knowing us even more fully than we know ourselves, God is able to fashion for us the mode of resurrection hope we can bear, and the mode of resurrection life we can follow.

What will that resurrection hope and life be? What was it for Jesus? What is it for each person and nation suffering from oppression? Gethsemane's answer on Golgotha tells us that the answer will not necessarily be a removal of the suffering. The world is hard, and as dangerous as it is beautiful. It is full of competing realities, the vulnerability of interdependence, and the awesome ability to choose evil. The hour of suffering may not pass, and the cup of suffering may not be removed. Yet if Jesus is a revelation of God he is as surely that revelation in Gethsemane and Golgotha as in the pretty manger of Bethlehem, and the revelation is simply that God is present for our good.

In the Gospel of Mark, the redemptiveness of that presence is not given as a shout of triumph, and oddly enough, in the midst of our own Gethsemanes I do not think we could hear such a shout if it were given. It would be hidden by its clash with our perceived world, and there is no room in the grief of our hearing for shouts of triumph. Mark gives us not a shout but a whisper, and the whisper comes twice.

The whisper comes first in the very naming of suffering as a cup. Has it never struck you as peculiar that Jesus asks that the cup be removed from him on the very night when the Gospel also records that he took a cup, gave thanks, and gave it to his disciples to drink? He receives a cup of denial and death, but gives a cup of affirmation and life, and the two cups are so connected that the cup of denial made the cup of affirmation possible. And in all the years of our faith since, the cup of affirmation has also been a cup that proclaims presence and strength and community. The connection between the cups is so quietly there, like a whisper, but it says to me that the God who is present to me in Gethsemane is the God who, in the very midst of denial and death, is nonetheless affirmation and life for us.

And Mark whispers to us yet again in the conclusion of the book through recounting a resurrection that can scarce be believed, so deep has been the pain: "Do not be alarmed; you are looking for Jesus of Nazareth, who was crucified. He has been raised; he is not here. Look, there is the place they laid him. But go, tell his disciples and Peter. . . . So they went out and fled from the tomb, for terror and amazement had seized them; and they said nothing to anyone, for they were afraid" (Mark 16:6-8). This account of resurrection is a whisper, not a shout. Yet it is just as surely resurrection as those more joyous responses in Matthew, Luke, and John.

A portion of John's account, however, can add yet more insight to the mode of resurrection that comes to us in whispers. In the passage we read, Thomas, like the women in Mark, dares not to believe. Only when he sees the nailprints does he recognize his risen Lord. The resurrection has not wiped them away, as if they had never been. To the contrary, the resurrection bears the scars of crucifixion, and those very scars make the resurrection recognizable. The whisper comes: Resurrection is fitted to the mode of suffering we bear; it is fashioned through that suffering, and bears its marks. The fit is close, shaped to us, like a garment only we can wear.

The whisper tells us that God's presence with us is so deep that God's knowledge of us is complete. From the completion of that knowledge, God shapes for us a resurrection suitable for us. The God who is present is a God of resurrection.

There is a mode of resurrection for all who suffer. I cannot tell you beforehand what that resurrection will be, but I will recognize it by its own peculiar nailprints. For some, will it be a healing of the spirit, a deepening of love? I dare not think it will be any finite healing of a wracked body. What is resurrection for that mother, particularly if no living daughter is found? Far better that she not be made to drink from that cups. But she does drink, and God drinks with her, knowing her, and therefore knowing what mode of resurrection she can bear. God is resurrection power for her, for us, for all the world.

Take this cup, and dare to drink. Are you in Gethsemane, on Golgotha? There is a whisper of resurrection for you. Drink; listen.

X

NARRATIVE THEOLOGY

Scripture as Stories That Shape

NARRATIVE, OR STORY, THEOLOGY IS A GENERAL NAME FOR A NUMBER OF contemporary attempts to emphasize the dimension of narrative in theology and Scripture. As one writer has put it: "There is currently a stir among students of religion about 'narrative theology'—the way or ways in which the ideas of religion may be expressed in story form."[1] While there is a variety of approaches, "these 'theologies of story,' or 'narrative' theologies as they are sometimes called, broadly agree that the way toward theological renewal lies in the reconception of theology as story."[2] Put in its widest context, "narrative theology is discourse about God in the setting of story. Narrative (in its narrow sense) becomes the decisive image for understanding and interpreting faith. Depiction of reality, ultimate and penultimate, in terms of plot, coherence, movement, and climax is at the center of all forms of this kind of talk about God."[3]

These theologians contend that the most potent and vital religious, theological, and biblical insights are transmitted through narrative structures, especially stories. To those engaged in narrative theology, significant help and insight can come from a variety of fields of study. Literary criticism is a natural source for learning the structures and flow of narratives. Psychology with its insights into the human mind and perceptions can help in seeing how narratives may function in shaping behavior. Linguistics offers clues on how human language itself is constructed and how it operates when certain semantic forms are employed. Social ethics can examine how stories function in shaping the identities and actions of whole communities or religious groups. Communications theory can probe the way stories are transmitted and how they are perceived by their various receptors. So in the study of "story," a number of disciplines can contribute important dimensions.

The variety of approaches for the study of narratives in themselves is seen in the multiple ways by which narrative theologians operate. Some are more heavily influenced by a particular discipline than are others. It is important to recognize that theology and the study of Scripture in themselves are crucial components for the establishment of narrative, or story, theology. Within the Christian context, the Bible and Christian tradition provide the basic data both in which narratives are found and from which stories can be constructed or analyzed. Thus a number of background features go into the formation of story theology and the work of theologians who stress "narrative" today.

BACKGROUNDS

The Importance of Stories

Contemporary studies of preliterate cultures have well underlined the significance of storytelling in these societies. Through the power of verbal narratives—tribal myths, legends, tales—the intellectual, social, and religious shape of the world was formed. Oral traditions passed from "generation to generation" and included sacred stories about gods and heroes, tales of the cosmos wisdom about human behavior, nature, and the miraculous. Personal and social identities were shaped by these stories. Leadership roles, systems of kin, social structures, and accepted behavior patterns were transmitted through these stories. In other words:

> these stories served the metaphysical function of linking the individual to the mystery of the universe as a whole, intelligible and heuristic image of nature, the sociological function of articulating and enforcing a specific social and moral order, and the psychological function of marking a pathway to guide the individual through the various stages of life. Ritually enacted and socially imposed, these stories patterned the thinking and living of all members within a given tribe or culture.[4]

Yet despite the vast differences between earlier cultures and our own industrialized, technological society, stories have not disappeared. Television, movies, advertisements, books, magazines, records, and even little children repeatedly tell us stories. Personal and cultural stories are still enacted and transmitted. While they are more fragmented and diverse than those of previous societies, nevertheless, "stories still give the fundamental shape to personal and social identity in the modern world."[5]

The Power of Stories

From ancient times the inherent power of stories has been recognized by people in all walks of life. Besides helping to shape personal and corporate understandings, stories have also the power to evoke action. How stories are formed, how they function, and how they are perceived have been extensively analyzed and probed so a clearer view of the power of the story can be established.[6]

In terms of structure, stories can be characterized as to plot, setting, characterization, and point of view. Various types of stories include tragedy, comedy, and elegy. The modes of narrative embrace myth, legend, folktale, epic, romance, allegory, fable, chronicle, satire, biography, autobiography, novel, and short story. Yet, "the careful articulation of these various narrative elements has only clarified what the unlettered folklorist and the growing child know—stories have power over human imagination and behavior because they ring true to life."[7] Stories have the uncanny knack of revealing insights in a moment of time or saturating our consciousness with penetrating truths about our own lives, our cultures, and our world. They convey this power often in moving and memorable ways.

More technical explanations have been given as to the common features of narrative, why stories generate their power, and how this happens. In summary, today many narrative theologians hold that the power of great stories, including the sagas of faith, lies in the resonance with who and what we most essentially are. Robert Roth points to their purposiveness as kindling a universal human hope; Stephen Crites views them as reflecting the "tensed modalities" of memory, attention, and anticipation; Metz finds them honoring the facts of suffering and conflict; Robert Alter stressed the place they give to human decision. In each case the constituents of story structure appear: cumulative action in all its suspense and tension depicted as moving toward resolution, led there by narrator vision.[8]

The intimate relationship between human language and perceptions of life has led contemporary philosophers, social scientists, and literary artists to see that "the impact of a story is not limited to the life exemplified or the principle illustrated in the story. Stories have the power to shape life because they formally embody the shape of life."[9] As one observer has put it: Stories have their beginning, end, and "in-between time" featuring characters interacting through critical and dramatic moments through relationships that progressively unfold. All elements of the story advance this story line. When the themes of the story have run their course, the story ends either happily or unhappily. The individual stories presuppose others, as parts of larger episodes that shape and color these stories.[10]

Our lives as well begin and end with the times "in-between" spent "making sense" of the people we know and experiences we have. We have "givens"—age, sex, education, and health—as well as personalities and circumstances that frame the limits of life. The patterns that emerge from life may take any shape as we continually fashion them as we wish within the parameters of our situations. Further, "life is always a movement toward completing the life forms we are living, and thus human life is always seen from ending rather than beginning."[11] Our individual lives take their meaning within the context of larger communities: family, society, culture, race, earth, cosmos, and "whatever 'other worlds' there might be."[12]

There seems to be an inherent narrative quality underlying all human experience. Thus

both time and space are experienced in all their concrete expressions in an inherently narrative way. The human experience of time would be impossible without memory and anticipation. Without memory, experience would lack all coherence. Without anticipation, experience would lose all direction. But memory and anticipation can be held together without dissolving the present into sheer succession only if the remembered past and anticipated future are taken up in stories.[13]

If there is a narrative structure underlying human experience, it is entirely understandable why storytelling is a universal method of cultural expression and why it appeals so powerfully to personal experience.

NARRATIVE THEOLOGIES

Several typologies or models have been suggested as ways of categorizing various contemporary story or narrative theologies.[14]

Introduction to Religion. This approach uses narrative or story as a way to understand the study of religion in general or Christianity in particular. It is represented by a number of contemporary writers. Among them are Sam Keen, *To a Dancing God*;

Harvey Cox, *The Seduction of the Spirit*; Michael Novak, *Ascent of the Mountain, Flight of the Dove*; Robert Roth, *Story and Reality*; Gabriel Fackre, *The Christian Story*; and John Shea, *Stories of God*.[15]

In this approach, "narrative" is used to "describe and explain the location of religion in human experience and the meaning of 'faith in relation to a person's encounter with other people and the world."[16] Human experience is perceived as having a "religious" dimension, which is related to the stories people tell about themselves and those that help structure their worlds.

Life Story. The relationship of narratives to human experience is explored by a number of writers. Stephen Crites's "The Narrative Quality of Experience" argued that "the formal quality of experience through time is inherently narrative."[17] In sacred stories, mundane stories, and temporal experience itself this "narrative quality of experience" is expressed with each of these dimensions "constantly reflecting and affecting the course of the others."[18]

Two significant works fit into this category. John S. Dunne, in *A Search for God in Time and Memory,* argues that by seeking to bring the past into the present of our consciousness we may find "what God tends to be for us."[19] In Dunne's method of "passing over by sympathetic understanding to others" he claimed one can enter into others' lives and find what is distinctive about one's own life story. Thus we can "enter into the life stories of Paul, Augustine, and Kierkegaard and discern the different forms a Christian life assumes and in turn come to a new understanding of ourselves."[20] Modern life stories, he said, could function in the same way. For Dunne, the result of the "passing over" process was that a person "discovers the shape of the life story in other ages, the story of deeds, and the story of experience, and coming back from this to his own time is how he discovers by contrast its current shape, the story of appropriation."[21] From these life stories one finds "God's time, the greater and encompassing time which is that of the stories of God and [one] experiences companionship with God in time."[22]

A second important contribution to "life stories" is in the hearing of another's story. This approach is practiced by James William McClendon, Jr., in his *Theology as Biography.* In it he claims that "by recognizing that Christian beliefs are not so many 'propositions' to be catalogued or juggled like truth-functions in a computer, but are living convictions which give shape to actual lives and actual communities, we open ourselves to the possibility that the only relevant critical examination of Christian beliefs may be one which begins by attending to lived lives. Theology must be at least biography."[23]

Thus "biography" provides the primary tools by which the meaning of Christian doctrine may be known. McClendon then examines the lives of Dag Hammarskjöld, Martin Luther King, Jr., Clarence Jordan, and Charles Ives as the biographical "stories" that can give perspective on (in these cases) "atonement" in a way that differs from the traditional Christian doctrinal formulations. This approach links theology and ethics, and it focuses attention on Christian doctrine as lived beliefs that directly affect ethical decisions and judgments.[24]

Biblical narrative. A third category of story theologies focuses specifically on the Bible and on the category of narrative in Scripture. Theologians who concentrate on this approach find examples of narrative texts in Scripture and seek to answer how these texts function as "authority" in the life of Christian communities. Biblical scholars have long been aware of the role of historical narratives in Scripture. These help to form what some refer to as *heilsgeschichte,* or "salvation history," throughout the Bible.[25]

Particular lines of work on biblical narratives have emerged among scholars. Many have been influenced by the work of literary critics like Amos Wilder, who argued that "the narrative mode is uniquely important in Christianity" and "when the Christian in any time or place confesses his faith, his confession turns into a narrative."[26] In a highly significant study of the style of biblical narratives, Eric Auerbach concluded that

> the text presents the reader with a vision of the way things are, a representation of reality in which Scripture makes an imperialistic claim. The text depicts a world, and it is "not satisfied with claiming to be a historically true reality—it insists that it is the only real world, is destined for autocracy." The challenge the biblical text presents to the reader is not whether the reader can appropriate the text and its claims within the reader's world; the challenge is whether the reader can and will enter into the world of the text; "we are to fit our own life into its world, feel ourselves to be elements in its structure of universal history."[27]

These insights have led theologians to examine the history of biblical interpretation and to see how in the eighteenth and nineteenth centuries the distinction began to be drawn between a text's literal sense—the world it claimed to show—and its historical reference—what the narrative referred to historically. When this occurred, readers could come to an understanding of the text's original setting and meaning, but (as Auerbach describes the process of fitting one's own life into the text's world) readers did not enter automatically into the realities that the biblical texts claimed to present. In other words, "once meaning was separated from reference it is no longer possible to read the text realistically."[28]

Related also to the study of the functions of narratives has been the recent emphasis by biblical scholars on "canonical criticism." James Sanders has argued that the meaning of any portion of Scripture must be seen in the context of the whole canon itself.[29] Another Old Testament scholar, Brevard Childs, has defined "canonical criticism" as seeking "to understand the peculiar shape and special function of these texts which comprise the Hebrew canon."[30] Childs has emphasized the final form of the biblical text instead of concentrating on how it came to be formed. His views have been challenged by James Barr.[31]

Of closer direct connection to the story theologies, which function as introductions to religion and life stories, has been the work of Sallie McFague.[32] McFague reflects the insights of literary critics and biblical scholars by arguing that "metaphorical thinking constitutes the basis of human thought and language."[33] Human thought worlds are constructed through metaphors. A metaphor, most simply, is

> seeing one thing *as* something else, pretending "this" is "that" because we do not know how to think or talk about "this," so we use "that" as a way of saying something about it. Thinking metaphorically means spotting a thread of similarity between two dissimilar objects, events, or whatever, one of which is better known than the other, and using the better-known one as a way of speaking about the lesser known.[34]

McFague has argued that "the parables of Jesus are typically metaphorical" in that "they bring together dissimilars (lost coins, wayward children, buried treasure, and tardy laborers with the kingdom of God); they shock and disturb; they upset conventions and expectations and in so doing have revolutionary potential." A "metaphorical theology," says McFague, "starts with the parables of Jesus and with Jesus as a parable of God."[35] Parables are extended metaphors that set in tension both the familiar and the unfamiliar and in so doing open up new dimensions of life and fresh visions for us.[36]

SCRIPTURE IN NARRATIVE THEOLOGY

The Functions of Language

Fundamental to these major views of narrative theology is the emphasis on the shaping power of language. Language shapes human consciousness. Language also defines our boundaries and ourselves as people. McFague pointed this out when she wrote that "the language of a people is their sense of reality; we can live only within the confines of our language."[37] The images that emerge through the language we use is what Dunne referred to as "personal mythos" when he wrote that "out of this feeling for life or this pattern of feelings there emerge images or a coherent set of images which could be called the 'personal mythos.' The personal mythos has all the elements of drama—plot, characters."[38]

The language humans use, metaphorical in character according to the story theologians, is the shaping agent through which new insights arise, for "metaphor is basically a new or unconventional interpretation of reality."[39] Through life experience and language about it, a "grid" is constructed through which one's own existence is interpreted. This set of images, "personal mythos," or grid also becomes the guide for interpreting new experiences.[40] Some story theologians refer to this grid or vision as one's religion. McClendon writes: "By 'religion' . . . I mean life lived out under the governance of a central vision. I will seek, therefore, some central image, or cluster of images, by which our subject understood himself and his horizons, and through which that vision may be expressed."[41] Language, specifically metaphor, enables us to look beyond and to shape our lives, for "metaphor is movement, human movement; without it we would not be what we are—the only creatures in the universe to our knowledge who can *envision* a future and consciously work toward achieving it."[42]

Story theologians draw on linguistic insights that show that narratives invite response and are thus highly participatory forms. Violence is done to the fundamental nature of the narrative form itself (particularly parables) if one tries to restate the "meaning" of the story in conceptual terms. "Metaphorical language," writes McFague, "conveys meaning through the body of the world. It makes connections, sees resemblances, uniting body and soul—earthly, temporal, ordinary experience with its meaning. But the 'meaning' is not there to be read off conceptually; we only get at the meaning through the metaphor."[43]

The participatory nature of narratives means that they are always tremendously personal and elicit the self-involvement of the reader or hearer. To understand a narrative in the view of narrative theologians is not to gain more conceptual or "intellectual" knowledge but rather to be faced with viewing one's life in a new way as one encounters new metaphorical images. One's life, existence, or "vision" is thus shaped by the encounter with the metaphor. As McFague writes of parables: "The impact of the parables is directly tied to their qualities as aesthetic objects, their insistence that insight be embodied, incarnated . . . in human *lives,* not in the head alone but in and through the full scope and breadth of a human life." Human lives themselves as "stories" are examples of "lived out images."[44]

Thus one's own life can be seen as a "story" or a "coming to belief." From the Christian perspective, "Christian belief must always be a process of coming to belief—like a story—through the ordinary details of historical life (as it is in the parables, though in a highly compressed way)."[45] A "narrative theology" will use stories "to confront people with their own possibilities of coming to belief."[46] The examination of the lives of those who have sought to live according to their "visions" (including here the life of Jesus) will enable one to see the validity of the images they used and be led to further understanding of one's own "story."

As a narrative form, autobiographies are most helpful here to the story theologian, for

> autobiography is metaphoric story through and through. The story of the self can only be told indirectly and incarnationally since the mystery of the self only comes to appearance in and through concrete speech and action. When we write autobiographically, we move from the known to the unknown, through the details of our lives to the mystery of our selves. Each speech remembered and incident reported is a metaphoric unfolding of the "master form" of the teller's life—a form that is not only communicated through but constituted by the story told.[47]

As McFague put it: "In autobiographies, finally, intermediary theology has a source for understanding how language and belief move into a life, how a life can itself be a parable, a deformation of ordinary existence by its placement in an extraordinary context."[48]

The Functions of Scripture

For Christian narrative theologians, the Scriptures provide the central set of metaphors by which one's vision and life can be shaped.[49] As Stanley Hauerwas and David Burrell put it, "Religious faith . . . comes to accepting a certain set of stories as canonical. . . . We discover our human self more effectively through these stories, and so use them in judging the adequacy of alternative schemes for humankind."[50] And, as Hauerwas indicates, "whatever else it is the message that appears central to the Christian faith is in the form of a story."[51] The gospel is "a story that gives you a way of being in the world."[52] For those whose lives are being shaped by the story of the Christian gospel, "the stories we find in Scripture are crucial for living our lives truthfully."[53]

Scripture functions as an authority for Christians. By this, Christians mean to indicate that "they find there the traditions through which their community most nearly comes to knowing and being faithful to the truth,"[54] for "by trying to live, think, and feel faithful to its witness they find they are more nearly able to live faithful to the truth. For the scripture forms a society and sets an agenda for its life that requires nothing less than trusting its existence to the God found through the stories of Israel and Jesus."[55] The Bible assumes an ongoing relevance, both for individuals and for the Christian community. The Scriptures have the "power to help us remember the stories of God for continual guidance of our community and individual lives. To be a community which lives by remembering is a genuine achievement, as too often we assume that we can ensure our existence only by freeing ourselves from the past."[56] The shaping power of scriptural narrative not only " 'renders a character' but renders a community capable of ordering its existence appropriate to such stories."[57] To claim the Bible as authority is the church's testimony that "this book provides the resources necessary for the church to be a community sufficiently truthful so that our conversation with one another and God can continue across generations."[58]

Scripture in narrative theology thus provides the reminder that "the church is a community that lives by memory."[59] As the Bible is read, studied, and proclaimed through preaching in the church, those in the Christian community may locate their own "stories" in "God's story" as told in Scripture. Hauerwas writes:

> It is our conviction that we are provided with a truthful account of reality that enables us to see our life as more than a succession of events when we learn to locate our story in God's story. That does not mean our life has a singular goal or meaning; rather, the story of God we learn through Christ gives us the skills to go on even when no clear goal is present. We rightly seek neither happiness nor pleasure in themselves; such entities are elusive. Rather we learn happiness and pleasure when we find in a faithful narrative an ongoing and worthy task that is able to sustain our lives.[60]

The Scriptures are the narratives to which the church returns over and over, since Christians are "people of a book," a "community which lives through memory." As Hauerwas writes,

> We do not seek a philosophical truth separate from the book's text. Rather, we are a people of a book because we believe that "the love that moves the sun and the stars" is known in the people of Israel and the life of a particular man, Jesus. Such "truth" is inherently contingent; it can only be passed on from one generation to another by memory. We test our memory with Scripture as we are rightly forced time after time to seek out new implications of that memory by the very process of passing it on.[61]

The story in Scripture, told in and through the church, "creates a people capable of being the continuation of the narrative by witnessing to the world that all creation is ordered to God's good end." Thus "the church is the necessary context of inquiry for the testing of that narrative. The church must always remain open to revision since the subject of its narrative is easily domesticated."[62]

The power of scriptural narratives to give vision, to form character, and create community also shapes human perception of what the world should be. The scriptural stories shape our understandings of reality. The biblical narratives "were not meant to describe our world—and thus in need of translation to adequately describe the 'modern world'—but to change the world, including the one in which we now live."[63] For narrative theologians, this distinguishes the biblical stories from mere theories. "A theory is meant to help you know the world without changing the world yourself; a story is to help you deal with the world by changing it through changing yourself." This means that "ethics cannot be separated from theology."[64] The social ethical task of the church, then, may be construed as "to be the kind of community that tells and tells rightly the story of Jesus," whose own "story defines the nature of how God rules and how such a rule creates a corresponding 'world' and society."[65] For the story of Jesus forms the church, and "there is no way to speak of Jesus' story without its forming our own. The story it forms creates a community which corresponds to the form of his life."[66]

The Scriptures are the stories that shape existence and human community in the church. Those whose lives are being shaped by Scripture find that "the Scriptures are exhibited in communities that are capable of pointing to holy lives through which we can rightly see the reality that has made the Scriptures possible."[67] As Christians see the different ways the lives of others in the community are shaped, they understand their own stories better. For "through the lives of the saints we begin to understand how the images of Scripture are best balanced so that we might tell and live the ongoing story of God's unceasing purpose to bring the world to the peace of the kingdom."[68]

SCRIPTURE AS STORIES THAT SHAPE

Narrative theologians emphasize the power of stories to shape consciousness, belief, and action. Human language, metaphorical in character, is the medium through which new insights arise and life itself is directed. One's existence or "vision" is shaped by the encounter with metaphorical images. Human lives themselves have a narrative, or "story," character. These stories naturally invite participation and comparison.

Scripture as "God's story" invites readers to set their life "story" in relation to its "story." The Scriptures provide a new grid or set of images by which one may "come to belief" and interpret one's own life experiences.

The vision of life offered in Scripture receives its validation as it is lived out in the concrete lives of those in the Christian community who enter into its narrative and are affected by its metaphors. Christians claim or attribute authority to Scripture because "it is the irreplaceable source of the stories that train us to be a faithful people. To remember, we require not only historical skills, but examples of people whose lives have been formed by that memory. The authority of Scripture is mediated through the lives of the saints identified by our community as most nearly representing what we are about. Put more strongly, to know what Scripture means, finally, we must look to those who have most nearly learned to exemplify its demands through their lives."[69] The church "returns time and time again to Scripture not because it is trying to find the Scripture's true meaning, but because Christians believe that God has promised to speak through Scripture so that the Church will remain capable of living faithfully by remembering well."[70]

In the following sermon from the most outspoken advocate of narrative theology, Stanley Hauerwas, we see an example of how narratives about waiting in Scripture are a metaphorical vehicle for teaching the disciplines and ethics of our Christian community. This use of Scripture and story in preaching is not to be confused directly with recent methods in homiletics, which are known as "narrative proclamation."

THE BIBLE IN THEOLOGY AND PREACHING

Like Those Who Dream

Stanley Hauerwas

Psalm 128; Luke 3:1-6

I always loved Mrs. Peter's Sunday school class. She enthralled our five-year-old imaginations with her unparalleled flannel-board talks. Indeed, that is the way I learned most of the early stories of the Bible. If you could not make the story fit on the flannel-board, you could live without it.

For example, I have never forgotten Mrs. Peter's rendering of the sacrifice of Isaac. I remember the large green felt Abraham and Isaac and the donkeys in the lower lefthand corner, the mountain in Moriah in the upper righthand corner. Mrs. Peters told us that God had told Abraham that he must sacrifice Isaac. She knew that this might disturb some five year olds who were beginning to feel the threat of their fathers. So, rather than keep us in suspense, she quickly took out a large wooly ram and placed it on the mountain, saying, "Don't worry, God is going to supply a ram so Isaac won't have to be killed."

I was in seminary before I realized, through reading Kierkegaard's *Fear and Trembling,* that God did not tell Abraham or Isaac that there was going to be a ram in the bush. Abraham had to walk all the way up that mountain, thinking, "This is it. I am going to have to kill Isaac." God was not playing, and there was no assurance that things were going to come out all right.

I tell this story because I think that when we enter the season of Advent it is as if we Christians say to ourselves, "Let us play like we need to wait for a while. Let us play like we need time. Let us play like we are Jews."

This playing at Advent, of course, invites the most invidious of contrasts between Christians and Jews: Jews do not know fulfillment because they do not believe the Messiah has come. They are, therefore, a people permanently on hold. They have plenty of hope and some patience, but their essential task is to wait. In contrast, we Christians are people of fulfillment because we know the Messiah has come. We do not need to wait. We have been given the truth, so our task is to simply get on with it. We remind ourselves one time a year that we ought to play like we have to wait, but in truth that is not our game.

In this respect, of course, the practice of receiving gifts at Christmas becomes our paradigmatic experience for "waiting," for we cannot help thinking of Advent like wanting to get a bicycle for Christmas. When we were between the ages of six and ten we were pretty sure we were going to get a bicycle. But we subjected ourselves to doubt about whether we were really going to get a bicycle (or a puppy) because we wanted to be surprised. After all, surprises are half the fun. In like manner, we Christians play at being Jews for a month so we can be surprised every year. But we know we are not "waiters."

The difficulty we Christians have with learning to wait has spawned the well-known genre of the Advent sermon. Since we Christians really do not believe that we are a people who have to learn to wait, we turn waiting—and correlatively, hope—into general anthropological characteristics intrinsic to the human condition. So we say things like, "Without hope, we die." Without dreams, life is meaningless. So Advent is that time of hopeful waiting in which we are reminded that life is always about living suspended between our hopes and their fulfillments.

There can be profound ways of displaying this tension, such as William Lynch's extraordinary reflections in his *Images of Hope* on the relationship between the absence of hope and mental illness. American capitalism gives us quite another account of the relationship between hope and fulfillment by suggesting that if we just learn to be patient and work hard, our hopes will be rewarded. Thus we believe that if we just keep working hard we may eventually graduate college, complete graduate school, get a Ph.D., or become a full professor. I often think that about the cruelest thing that can ever happen to anyone is to have his or her profoundest desires fulfilled.

These general anthropological characterizations about the relationship between waiting and hope, of course, have nothing to do with Jesus. Indeed, they have nothing to do with the Jews. The waiting and hoping, for Christians and Jews, is hope in a very specific, fleshy, material fulfillment that requires an equally specific form of waiting. Those who gave us Psalm 126 wanted Zion restored. Then they would be like those who dream, a dream formed by the material appearance of that fortress city. Then and then alone would the nations see that "the Lord has done great things for them." This hope is as concrete as the restoration of the watercourses of the Negeb. They want real water to drink.

We Christians, of course, have tended to spiritualize our hopes because we fear Jewish hopes. After all, Jesus is the Messiah of the Jews, and we are not quite prepared for Jewish rejection of our Messiah. Jews note, after all, that they also hope in a Messiah, but a Messiah capable of restoring Zion.

For example, it was a Jewish hope that Jesus read and appropriated in the synagogue:

> He has anointed me
> to bring good news to the poor.
> He has sent me to proclaim release to the captives
> and recovery of sight to the blind,
> to let the oppressed go free,
> to proclaim the year of the Lord's favor."
> (Luke 4:18-19)

But the Jews ask: "What happened? That does not sound like the world we live in." Like John sending his disciples to Jesus, they ask, "Are you the one to come or are we to wait for another?" Jesus answered, "Go and tell John what you have seen and heard; the blind received their sight, the lame walk, the lepers are cleansed, the deaf hear, the dead are raised, the poor have good news brought to them. And blessed is anyone who takes no offense at me."

The Jews ask, "What happened?" If this Messiah is the Messiah of the golden age, we still seem to live in a world of war, of blindness, of lameness, of the oppressed and the down troddened. Where is this golden age we were promised as the Messianic age? Surely this cannot be the Messiah.

There is no easy way to avoid these questions. Indeed, I have always been fond of the Apostate Julian's attempt to defeat Christianity. Julian hated Jews only a little less than he hated Christians. However, as a committed pagan, he had not suffered directly at the hands of Jewish tutors the way he had by Christian teachers. Accordingly, he called the Jews to him and gave them money to rebuild the temple in Jerusalem, since Christians made so much of the fact that the temple had been destroyed and not rebuilt.

Julian clearly understood the heart of the matter because he knew better than to separate issues of truth from the issues of Zion. He had learned much from his Christian tutors after all.

He thus reasoned that if the temple were rebuilt, it would show that Christians were at a disadvantage when compared to Jews. Christians subsequently made much of the fact that soon after the rebuilding began an earthquake struck Jerusalem, destroying the beginnings of the new temple. Julian was, moreover, killed in short order.

We are embarrassed by such polemics. We want to say that truth is spiritual. Yet, Christians no less than Jews were and are people whose hopes are material. That is why we cannot play at waiting. Jesus is no Messiah who promises us that if we just learn to wait our hopes will be fulfilled. Rather, Jesus is our Jewish temple who has made us, Gentiles, part of God's promise to be God's own material presence in the world, so that the world might know what kind of God governs the sun, the stars, and our lives.

As Christians we badly distort our faith when we think that our Messiah has made us other than the Jews. Rather, the salvation that has been wrought in Christ has established a new time when even we Gentiles can become part of God's promising people who rightly witness to the world that our lives, after Jesus, are eschatologically determined. It is the world's presumption that our existence has an outcome, but it is one that we can guarantee through our hopes. It is the Jew and the Christian who stand in the world, reminding the world that our outcome is not in our own hands but in God's.

I often suggest that Christians are not called to nonviolence because we believe nonviolence promises to rid the world of war, but in a world of war we cannot imagine being anything other than nonviolent as faithful followers of Christ. Christians can wait in nonviolence in a world at war because we know the material appearance of our God in the person of Jesus of Nazareth. We, therefore, do not hold out any vain hope in the general notion of peace separate from the peace that is embodied in this man Jesus. That is hard and painful waiting in a world of so much injustice. But we Christians must so wait not because the Kingdom did not come, but because it did, taking the form of this man—God who would not have the Kingdom violently.

Therefore, if we play at waiting during Advent we will destroy ourselves and fail to be witnesses to the God who calls us to be the eschatological people of the new age. We will be like those who submerge Christ's cross in the resurrection as if Christ went to his death knowing he would be raised. That makes the gospel a dumb show, and our lives a dumb show, as if we are only playing at death and life. Christ's death is as real as the land of Palestine. If his death is not at least that real, then his resurrection is equally an illusion.

That is why this fleshy meal of Christ's body and blood is absolutely crucial for us to learn what it means to be a people trained to wait and hope. For here time and time again we feed on God's bodily presence so that we might rightly learn to hope and wait. This meal is Kingdom come, it is our waiting feast, through which the world is given hope by being made part of God's dream. So come, celebrating here our inclusion as "people of the dream" who rightly have learned what a joy it is to have been engrafted into God's promise called Israel.

XI

LATIN AMERICAN LIBERATION THEOLOGY

Scripture as the Foundation for Freedom

VARIOUS FORMS OF "LIBERATION THEOLOGIES" OR "THEOLOGIES OF LIBERATION" HAVE emerged as the biblical theology movement faded in the 1970s and as white male theologians were succeeded through affirmative action in many of the academic guilds. Since 1965 the term *liberation* has taken on a more technical character when used to describe theological movements. Liberation theologies have altered traditional theological perspectives by affirming the importance of experience and social location in the formulation of theological statements. Thus the liberation theme has been expressed in a variety of contexts and by many different voices. While a thorough survey is not possible, three major theological movements—Latin American liberation theology, black theology, and Asian theology—are concerned with the liberation theme.[1]

Latin American Liberation Theology

In Latin America the desperate plight of the poor, standing in stark contrast to the rich in the various modernized cities, has led to many revolutionary uprisings. From this context has come a theological movement with its watchwords: *liberation* and *freedom*. While it shares features with other forms of liberation theologies, Latin America liberation theology is forged out of its own particular history and struggles. Like black theology, this theology

> arises out of a specific context of oppression. Like feminist theology, it contends that the reversal of these oppressive conditions will require a significant revision of Christian belief and practice. Like both, it promises liberation to all the bodily oppressed through deliverance from one particular form of oppression. In this case, however, *class* oppression is viewed as the underlying source and model of all other forms of human bondage.[2]

Because theologians in the Latin American context have been active in defining the theological bases and program of liberation theology, attention will be given to some of them and their views of the nature and function of Scripture.[3]

BACKGROUNDS

In August 1968, the Second General Episcopal Conference of Roman Catholic bishops (CELAM) was held at Medellín, Colombia. From that conference the theological meaning of *liberation* began to be shaped, for Medellín was "the first instance in which a significant portion of the Roman Catholic hierarchy has acknowledged the structural nature of evil and has analyzed violence as a component of the unjust structures."[4] While the conference was designed to examine the Latin American church in the light of the Second Vatican Council, the sixteen documents that emerged often went far beyond what Vatican II had stated forthrightly.[5]

In the texts of these documents a number of social issues and problems were addressed. The underdevelopment of Latin America was described as "an unjust situation which promotes tensions that conspire against peace." Not only is there "a lamentable insensitivity of the privilege sectors to the misery of the marginated sectors" but also a calculated "use of force to repress drastically any attempt at opposition."[6] Also denounced were social inequality, unjust use of power by the powerful, the perpetration of economic dependency through distortion of trade, and "institutionalized violence" that takes shape through "a structural deficiency of industry and agriculture, or national and international economy, of culture and political life."[7] The task of peace is a "permanent task" and is "not the simple absence of violence and bloodshed. Oppression by the power groups may give the impression of maintaining peace and order, but in truth it is nothing but the 'continuous and inevitable seed of rebellion and war.' "[8]

In this situation, the oppressed must be able to determine their own lots and future and thus be liberated from "cultural, social, economic and political servitudes" that oppose "human development."[9] Yet liberation is set forth in a Christian context in that it is "an anticipation of the complete redemption of Christ"[10] and peace is "the fruit of love," since "love is the soul of justice."[11] The Medellín conference represents what has been called the "formulation of the 'Theology of Liberation' (1968–1972)."[12]

The path begun by Medellín as the first focused writing on the liberation theme was continued in a further Conference planned for April 1972 in Santiago, Chile. The First Latin American Encounter of Christians for Socialism met there.[13] After Medellín, the momentum built to the point that Roman Catholic priests who spent their lives living with the poor began to be convinced that mere "reformist" movements progressed too slowly to bring needed social change. Additionally, these movements seemed ineffective. Priests discovered that many of the people were influenced by the Marxist analysis of society. Thus it became important to relate Marxist social analysis to the Christian faith.

In 1971 a group of eighty Chilean priests (*Los Ochenta*) issued a statement calling for their bishops to relate their Christianity to political commitment in socialist terms. From this group came the plans for the April 1972 meeting in Santiago. In comparison to the Medellín Conference, it can be said that

> if the distance between Vatican II and Medellín constitutes a step, the distance between the Medellín conference of bishops and the Santiago conference of Christians for Socialism resembles a leap. Medellín was in tune with Vatican II, even if beginning to move beyond it, whereas Santiago is more self-consciously "post-conciliar." Medellín usually leans toward a "third way" between capitalism and Marxism, whereas Santiago sees no "Christian solution" as such, denounces the collapse into a "third way," and insists that Christians be involved in the liberation process in socialist terms. With a few important exceptions . . . Medellín speaks of inequality between persons, whereas Santiago consistently links inequality to class struggle and the exploitation of the poor by

the rich. Medellín presses strongly for basic reform, whereas Santiago sees no solution without revolution, not necessarily violent. Medellín hopes that love, working for justice, can provide solutions, while Santiago argues that love is not a historic force apart from engagement in class struggle. Medellín offers theoretical analyses of Marxism, while Santiago calls upon Christians to "form a strategic alliance with Marxists." At Medellín the theologians were summoned by the bishops, at Santiago they were summoned by the militant.[14]

The final document of the Santiago meetings captures the mood and thrust of the movement. After asserting that two-thirds of the human race was being oppressed while "a relatively small sector of humanity is making greater progress and growing richer every day" at the expense of the oppressed poor, it goes on to say that imperialist capitalism is the reason this is so. Imperialist capitalism has exploited the poor for centuries and uses *de facto* forms of violence to maintain its power. Reformism alone is not enough, for "the structures of our society must be transformed from the roots up."[15] Therefore, delegates made a commitment to "the task of fashioning socialism [as] the only effective way to combat imperialism and to break away from our situation of dependence."[16] The basis for this action was to be theological in nature. Christianity's historic alliances with ruling classes had to be broken by siding with the exploited.

The section "Faith and Revolutionary Commitment" of this document urges Christians to realize that there is a "convergence between the radicality of their faith and the radicality of their political commitment." This means that "faith intensifies the demand that the class struggle move decisively towards the liberation of all men—in particular, of those who suffer the most acute forms of oppression." To be a Christian is to be committed in the midst of the struggle of the classes. To be neutral is not possible, for "faith has a critical role to play in criticizing complicity between faith and the dominant culture. But faith's reality will not come by detached theorizing; it will come only 'by joining parties and organizations that are authentic instruments of the struggle of the working class.' "[17]

In this context, as the Santiago document said, the attempt is made for "a new reading of the Bible and the Christian tradition."[18]

THE THEOLOGY OF LIBERATION

Latin American liberation theologians have focused attention on a number of particular themes rising from their experiences and social context. Among the prominent voices and works of these theologians are the following.

Camilio Torres (1929–66) who, though he did not directly participate in the emergence of Latin American liberation theology, is recognized by contemporary Latin American liberation theologians as pointing the way by calling for changes in fundamental economic and social structures. Torres was deprived of his university post and left the priesthood in 1965 to join a guerilla group. On February 15, 1966, he was ambushed and killed, and he became a pioneer martyr of the liberation movement. Torres had said: "I am a revolutionary because I am a priest."[19] His statement that "in my view, the hierarchy of priorities should be reversed: love, the teaching of doctrine, and finally [formal] worship" foreshadowed emphasis on praxis as the starting point for theology.[20] For him, "revolutionary action is a Christian, a priestly struggle."[21] In terms of significance, Torres "incarnated for Latin America the significance of the slogan, *conscientization.*"[22]

In 1969 Rubem Alves (b. 1933) published *A Theology of Human Hope,* which was his doctoral dissertation at Princeton Theological Seminary. This Brazilian has "produced the first systematic exploration of the theme of liberation."[23] In his analysis, Alves turned to the philosophy of language rather than political science or sociology for his analytical tools. In this regard he also focused attention on biblical hermeneutics.

For Alves, language is "an expression of how a community has programmed a solution to its existential problems" so that behind language stands a community. For him (drawing on the Hebrew concept), truth is found not in the realm of pure ideas but takes shape as "action," as "the name given by a historical community to its historical deeds, which were, are, and will be efficacious in the liberation of man."[24] Alves sees in "messianic humanism" that the goal is the humanization of life, which comes as God's gift of grace and opens a new future for God's people. The paradigm here is the event of the Exodus in the Old Testament, in which "God manifests himself as the power of liberation who rejects the objective and subjective impossibility of liberation of the 'given' condition of the Israelite tribes."[25] For Israel, "the future that was closed because of Egypt's oppressive power and Israel's own slave consciousness is broken open by a God who is free from the determinisms of history and is active in history."[26] Humans participate in the quest for freedom as they struggle in human communities.[27] This means that "liberation is not simply a history that breaks in from a future totally unconnected with the present: it is a project which springs from the protest born of the suffering of the present; a protest to which God grants a future in which man enters through his action."[28]

The emphasis on the concrete situation as the focus for theological work was struck also by the Brazilian priest Hugo Assmann. For Assmann, theology is done "beginning from concreteness," from "particular realities."[29] Action is the truth so that truth is found in history and not in speculative ideas. Thus Assmann wrote:

> The criteria for a good theology are not any more strictly theological, just as the criteria for an effective love of God belong to the historical and human order of the neighbor, i.e., to the order of the nondivine. In fact, just as the *divine* dimension in the love of the neighbor is the God-reference in the neighbor, so the *theological* in the reflection on the historical praxis is present in the dimension of faith. If the divine, therefore, can only be found through the human, it is entirely logical that a Christian theology will find its ultimate theological character in the human references of history.[30]

The Peruvian priest Gustavo Gutiérrez (b. 1928), in his *A Theology of Liberation* (1971), has given fullest expression to the basics of liberation theology.[31] Many of his themes are captured in the concern he exposed when he wrote that

> in a continent like Latin America ... the main challenge does not come from the nonbeliever but from the nonhuman—that is, the human being who is not recognized as such by the prevailing social order. These are the poor and exploited people, the ones who are systematically and legally despoiled of their being human, those who scarcely know what a human being might be. These nonhumans do not call into question our religious world so much as they call into question our *economic, social, political, and*

cultural world. Their challenge impels us toward a revolutionary transformation of the very bases of what is now a dehumanizing society. The question, then, is no longer how we are to speak about God in a world come of age; it is rather how to proclaim him Father in a world that is not human and what the implications might be of telling nonhumans that they are children of God.[32]

Here social analysis shows that the exploited and oppressed need to be humanized. The structures of society have deprived them of their basic dignity as children of God. A "revolutionary transformation" of social structure is needed for a free humanity to begin to take shape. This is the process of liberation.

For Gutiérrez, liberation takes shape on three levels. There is political liberation. Here *liberation* expresses "the aspirations of oppressed peoples and social classes, emphasizing the conflictual aspect of the economic, social, and political process which puts them at odds with wealthy nations and oppressive classes."[33]

Second, on the level of history *liberation* may refer to humans taking conscious responsibility for their own destiny. In the quest for true freedom, a new humanity and a "qualitatively different society" may take shape.[34] Finally, theologically, *liberation* in the Bible is found in Jesus Christ, who liberates humanity. Christ the Savior liberates humans from sin, which is "the ultimate root of all disruption of friendship and of all injustice and oppression."[35] Christ makes people truly free and enables them to live in fellowship with him. This is the basis for all human community.

Gutiérrez sees that while these three levels of liberation may be distinguished, they form a basic unity and one is not to be found without the others. As Gutiérrez wrote:

> Without liberating historical events, there would be no growth of the Kingdom. But the very process of liberation will not have conquered the very roots of oppression and exploitation of man by man without the coming of the Kingdom which is above all a gift. Moreover, we can say that the historical, political liberating event *is* the growth of the Kingdom, and *is* salvific event, but it is not *the* coming of the Kingdom, not *all* of salvation.[36]

Thus "political, historical, and spiritual liberation are inseparable parts of a single, all-encompassing salvific process."[37] For "in Christ the all-comprehensiveness of the liberating process reaches its fullest sense."[38]

It has been argued that the "originality" of Gutiérrez's theology is "not to have discovered these three levels of meaning but to have started from their *unity* as the fundamental point of departure."[39] Gutiérrez is repeatedly concerned with "the elimination of dualism"[40] in all realms, which leads him to argue that "history is one" so that "there is only one human destiny, irreversibly assumed by Christ, the Lord of history. His redemptive work embraces all the dimensions of existence and brings them to their fullness. The history of salvation is the very heart of human history." There is "only one history—a 'Christo-finalized' history."[41] In the one call to salvation there is given "religious value in a completely new way to the action of man in history, Christian and non-Christian alike. The building of a just society has worth in terms of the Kingdom, or in more current phraseology, to participate in the process of liberation is already, in a certain sense, a salvific work."[42]

The integration of the three levels of liberation for Gutiérrez is possible because of his "new way of doing theology."[43] This is to do theology as "critical reflection on praxis."[44] For Gutiérrez, the emphasis of the early church on "theology as wisdom" and of medieval scholasticism, which stressed "theology as rational knowledge," are to be replaced now by a new vision. Gutiérrez says that while "theology as a critical reflection on Christian praxis in the light of the Word does not replace the other functions of theology, such as wisdom and rational knowledge," it rather "presupposes and needs them."[45] Thus the aim for theology is not "the discovery or refinement of doctrine as timeless truth but for the transformation of the world through reflection on praxis."[46] Praxis is not only "involvement in a situation" or "practice" but carries with it too the Marxist emphasis of "participation in a class struggle to bring about the creation of a new socialist society. Theology is totally internal to this praxis and deepens one's commitment within it."[47]

> Theology as critical reflection on historical praxis is a liberating theology, a theology of the liberating transformation of the history of mankind and also therefore that part of mankind—gathered into *ekklesia*—which openly confesses Christ. This is a theology which does not stop with reflecting on the world, but rather tries to be part of the process through which the world is transformed. It is a theology which is open—in the protest against trampled human dignity, in the struggle against the plunder of the vast majority of people, in liberating love, and in the building of a new, just, and fraternal society—to the gift of the Kingdom of God.[48]

Other significant Latin American liberation theologians have focused attention on biblical studies, such as José Porfirio Miranda, an ex-Jesuit, who wrote *Marx and the Bible: A Critique of the Philosophy of Oppression.*[49] Hermeneutical considerations are developed by Juan Luis Segundo (b. 1925), a Uruguayan Jesuit, in his *The Liberation of Theology.* This was a development of initial ideas set forth in his earlier five-volume *A Theology for Artisans of a New Humanity.*[50] Segundo emphasizes among other things that the social sciences can be valuable tools for biblical interpretation. Major Christological studies have been produced by Jon Sobrino, a Spanish Jesuit, in his *Christology at the Crossroads: A Latin American Approach,*[51] and Leonardo Boff (b. 1938) in his *Jesus Christ Liberator: A Critical Christology for Our Time.*[52] Perhaps the best overview of how liberation theology has developed and its themes in general has been written by the Methodist scholar José Miguez Bonino in his *Doing Theology in a Revolutionary Situation.* His 1976 book, *Christians and Marxists: The Mutual Challenge to Revolution,* analyzes the interrelationships between Christianity and Marxism.[53] Justo L. González, writing from a Hispanic American perspective, has made significant contributions with his *Mañana: Christian Theology from a Hispanic Perspective* and (with Catherine González) *Liberation Preaching: The Pulpit and the Oppressed.*[54]

SCRIPTURE IN LIBERATION THEOLOGY

It is clear that the historical situations and contexts in which Latin American liberation theology developed significantly shape its approach to the Bible. In the 1960s, attitudes of Latin Americans about their futures changed. The 1950s were "characterized by great optimism regarding the possibility of achieving self-sustained economic development"[55] For this to happen, however, the pattern of dependence upon foreign trade in which nations exported primary products and imported manufactured products had to end. Internal development and industrialization were needed. But in the 1960s, "a pessimistic diagnosis of economic, social, and political realities replaced the preceding optimism."[56] Development was not proceeding in many nations, and the larger theory of development was questioned. In the emerging view, it was argued that "the dynamics of the capitalist economy lead to the establishment of a center and a periphery, simultaneously generating progress and growing wealth for the few and social imbalances, political tensions, and poverty for the many."[57] The imbalance between the developed and underdeveloped countries created further relationships of dependence so that "the poor, dominated nations keep falling behind; the gap continues to grow."[58]

In this context a new posture of "liberation" arose. This took political form in revolutionary political action in a variety of places.[59] As theologians became participants in these situations, many of them joined with others in calling for the overthrow of the capitalistic system they found so oppressive. Liberation and the call for freedom became the focus toward which all energies were directed. As Gutiérrez put it: "The untenable circumstances of poverty, alienation, and exploitation in which the greater part of the people of Latin America live urgently demand that we find a path toward economic, social, and political liberation. This is the first step towards a new society."[60]

Theological Method

The themes of Latin American liberation theology show that the basic starting point for theological inquiry must be with the poor of the world. The "marginalized," the poor who are the largest group in the human family, "are not inconsequential. And it is with them that theology must start; not with theories, not with views from above, but with 'the view from below.' "[61] As Frederick Herzog put it, theology must start "where the pain is."[62]

This commitment to beginning with the poor is a theological commitment. Liberation theologians see that in the Bible it is in the lives and plight of the poor that God is to be discovered. For

> the God of the Old Testament is the God of the poor and the oppressed, a God who sides with them, taking their part and identfying with them. The God of the New Testament is the same God, a God who becomes incarnate not in one who possessed wealth or influence or a good name, but in one who belonged to the "poor of the land" (the *am ha'aretz*), a lower class/working class Jew who cast his own lot with the poor to such a consistent degree that the rich and powerful found it necessary to destroy him.[63]

This means the "poor" have what Assmann has called an "epistemological privilege." The way the poor view the world is "closer to the reality of the world than the way the rich view it. Their 'epistemology,' i.e., their way of knowing, is accurate to a degree that is impossible for those who see the world only from the vantage point of privileges they want to retain."[64]

This starting point of the poor exemplifies the theological method of liberation theologians who stress the priority of praxis. The historical situation is the context and where theological reflection must begin. Because theology is "critical reflection on praxis," there is a continuing dialogue between theology and life situations, between action and reflection (theory). Action causes one to look at theory, and one's theory causes another look at one's action.

For liberation theologians, truth is found in action. Gutiérrez wrote that "knowledge is not the conformity of the mind to the given, but an immersion in the process of transformation and construction of a new world."[65] Appealing to the Old Testament prophets and the New Testament Johannine writings, these theologians argue that true knowledge of God is not to be found in speculation and abstract theories of "truth." Rather it is in active obedience to God, in participation, that truth is found. As Bonino put it: "Correct knowledge is contingent on right doing. Or rather, the knowledge is disclosed in the doing."[66] Theology is a "second act," in that it follows praxis as "critical reflection on praxis." The "first act" is the commitment of oneself to the transformation of society on behalf of the poor. In the "second act," theological reflection on the first act is done and is the attempt to see this action in the light of the resources of Christian faith. Clearly, "Christians can think their faith only as they practice it."[67]

The Functions of Scripture

From this context and theological method, liberation theologians reexamined Scripture. What they found was that the "poor," who are the starting point for theological reflection and who are so prominent in the Bible itself, have not been seen so in traditional classical theology or biblical exegesis. This led to the suspicion that Western biblical interpretation was actually ideologically controlled. Because biblical commentaries were written by established scholars in positions of safety and power, the suspicion is that these have brought certain presuppositions and "ideologies" to Scripture and thus have been blind to any scriptural challenge of these ideologies. Biblical scholars did not hear what Scripture said about the importance of the poor because they were ideologically captive to the social status quo. As Brown wrote: "This bending of the evidence, in an effort to make reality conform to what one wants reality to be, is a prevailing tendency of ideological thought, and suggests the ideology will work on the side of conformity, of maintenance of things as they are, particularly as it is employed by those in power."[68] In "ideologization," the text of Scripture and tradition "is forced into the Procrustean bed of ideology, and the theologian who has fallen prey of this procedure is forever condemned to listen only to the echo of his own ideology. There is no redemption for this theology, because it has muzzled the Word of God in its transcendence and freedom."[69] Put simply, in Gutiérrez's words, an ideology "rationalizes and justifies a given social and ecclesial order."[70]

With regard to reading Scripture, the pervasiveness of ideology leads to what the theologians called a "hermeneutics of suspicion." This is the suspicion that the usual interpretation of biblical texts does not take into account certain data that if considered would lead to a dramatically different interpretation. In the light of the social analysis and "suspecting" taught by Freud and Marx, Bonino writes that "every interpretation of the text which is offered to us (whether as exegesis or as systematic or as ethical interpretation) must be investigated in relation to the praxis out of which it comes."[71] Thus "very concretely, we cannot receive the theological interpretation coming from the rich world without suspecting it and, therefore, asking what kind of praxis it supports, reflects, or legitimizes."[72] The examples cited are the plainly political themes and implications of the life of Jesus that have remained "hidden" aspects of interpretation until recently. Or, as Brown asks, "Since the God of the Bible is on the side of the poor, why are we undisturbed by the fact that we are among the nonpoor?" His answer is that "we read what we can bear to read, we hear what is tolerable to hear, and we evade (or 'spiritualize') those parts which leave us uncomfortable, if not outraged."[73]

Latin American liberation theologians use Scripture in a variety of ways. The chief appeal, however, is to the Exodus event in the Old Testament because, for liberation theology, "the Exodus experience is paradigmatic."[74] As Brown puts it, "If there is a single passage that encapsulates the liberation themes of the Bible, it is the exodus story, describing a God who takes sides, intervening to free the poor and oppressed."[75] This event is "the center of Scripture" in that "God's saving action is focused in the exodus, the liberation of a people from political, cultural, and religious bondage."[76]

A second area of appeal to Scripture by liberationists is to the ethical teachings of the prophets. Here the concern of the prophets for the oppressed is particuarly prominent. This theme is capsulized in the statement "To know God is to do justice" (see Jer. 22:13-16).[77] According to the prophets, "where there is justice and righteousness, there is knowledge of Yahweh; when these are lacking, it is absent." To love God is to establish just relationships among people and "to recognize the rights of the poor. The God of biblical revelation is known through interhuman justice. When justice does not exist, God is not known; he is absent."[78]

The doctrines of eschatology and the future coming kingdom are another area of Scriptural appeal for Latin American liberation theologians. The Scriptures link the coming of Jesus with the Old Testament Exodus and also to the coming future *eschaton,* which will embody the values and concerns that Jesus himself embraced: peace, justice, love, and freedom. For Gutiérrez, eschatology is "the very key to understanding the Christian faith" as it looks to "that which is to come, towards a new action of God."[79] The establishment of the future kingdom by God means that "peace, justice, love and freedom are not private realities; they are not only internal attitudes. They are social realities, implying a historical liberation." In the struggle for liberation now, "the elimination of misery and exploitation is a sign of the coming of the Kingdom."[80]

SCRIPTURE AS THE FOUNDATION FOR FREEDOM

In Latin American liberation theology, traditional questions about revelation, inspiration, and the authority of the Scriptures are not as important as how the Bible functions in a Christian community. The Scriptures are validated continually as they are employed in the concrete action of liberation. The Scripture serves as a "foundation for freedom" in this theology because it provides the paradigms, the goals, and ultimately introduces humanity to the ultimate human liberator, Jesus Christ.

Latin American liberation theologians appeal to various strands of Scripture, including narratives, ethical teachings, and eschatology. But central through it all is the contention that Scripture as liberating word is powerful because it is interpreted in the context of a praxis that involves one with the poor and oppressed who hunger for freedom. It is not theoretical evaluations that give validity to any scriptural interpretation. An interpretation is shown to be true or false only as it works itself out in action through the struggle for liberation. "Only by doing this truth will our faith be 'verified,' in the etymological sense of the word."[81] The truth of any theological statement will be "confirmed in the *praxis* of the Christian community."[82]

The following sermon by theologian and preacher Justo González is not intended to represent an explicitly Latin American perspective because he reminds us that only Latin Americans can speak authentically from Scripture about their particular quest for freedom. González speaks for Hispanic Americans in search of freedom to speak their own language in their own culture. Observe how the sermon focuses on language as a social process and then creates a dialectic between unity and diversity in Scripture, based on the theme of Pentecost.

Confusion at Pentecost

Justo L. González

Genesis 11:1-9*a*; Acts 2:1-13

From ancient times, it is commonplace to set the story of the ascent at Babel in contrast with the descent of the Spirit at Pentecost. Both stories have to do with language and communication. In the Genesis story, humans come together to try to ascend to the heavens; in the other story in Acts, the Spirit descends upon those who are gathered. Babel was the epitome of sin and pride; Pentecost is the advent of grace and renewal. Usually, the main point of all these comparisons is that, whereas in Babel unity gave way to confusion, at Pentecost that confusion was overcome by unity.

But look again at the text in Acts. In verse 6 we read that the crowd "gathered, and was bewildered." The word that the NRSV translates as "bewildered" can also be translated as "confused." Indeed, it is the same word that appears in the ancient Greek translation of Genesis 11:7 where God says, "Come, let us go down, and confuse their language." If Pentecost produces unity, it is not a simple, straightforward unity,

Pentecost is not simply the reversal of Babel. Before Babel, according to the story, there was unity of language. After Pentecost, according to the story, there was a multiplicity of languages. In Babel, God intervenes to cause confusion. In Pentecost, God's intervention causes confusion among the crowd. In both stories, the flow of the text is from unity to diversity. At the beginning of the Babel episode, they all spoke one language and could come together in a single project. At the end, they can no longer understand each other, and they have to go their separate ways. At the beginning of the Pentecost narrative, they "were all together in one place," presumably speaking the same language. At the end, these same people are speaking a variety of languages, and they have caused confusion and even division among those who hear them.

Nor can we simply say that at Pentecost the Spirit brought together all these different people. The text tells us that they were already in Jerusalem. What the text does not say, but history tells us, is that the presence of all these various people in Jerusalem was the result of a long history of many conquests, exiles, and oppressions.

The text tells us that "there were devout Jews from every nation under heaven living in Jerusalem." How did these Jews come to represent so many nations? They did so, precisely because they represented a long history of empire building at the expense of weaker nations. There were people from Mesopotamia, Parthia, and Media, probably descendants of those who had not returned after the exile in Babylonia. And these people stood as a reminder of that exile. There were Jews from Egypt and Libya as far as Cyrene, a reminder of the ambiguous relation Israel has always had with her more powerful neighbors to the southwest. There were Jews from Cappadocia, Pontus and Asia, Phrygia and Pamphylia, a reminder of the more recent Macedonian conquest, and of the long struggle against the attempt to impose Hellenistic culture and religious practices on the people of Yahweh. And there were "visitors from Rome, both Jews and proselytes," a painful reminder that even now Judea was part of the Roman Empire.

All these people are brought together by a curious and complex intersection of religion and empire. Presumably they have come to Jerusalem because they are devout Jews and proselytes. But they also represent, as the text says, "every nation living under heaven" because of a long history of painful empire building.

It is a situation we all know. Even as we study the history of Christian missions, it is clear that mission has frequently been connected with colonialism and imperialism. How are we to deal with this situation? Are we to reject the unity that worldwide mission has brought, because of its connection with colonialism? Are we to bless colonialism and imperialism, because of their connection with the unity we now have?

In the fourth century, after the Roman Empire became Christian, it was customary to say that the empire had provided the means for the expansion of the gospel. This is a view that is still found in many textbooks on church history, and it is partially true. Yet the famous *Pax Romana* was wrought at the cost of much bloodshed and much injustice, and it is a terribly church-centered view of history to claim that all the wars and oppression connected with the Roman Empire were brought about by God simply so that Christian missionaries and evangelists could travel from land to land, and so that Paul's epistles could be safely carried from one corner of the empire to another. Somehow, while acknowledging the fact that Paul and his letters did travel along Roman roads, we must do so without blessing all the horrible, cruel, unjust events that brought about Roman imperial unity.

In a way, that is the crucial issue we must face as we deal with the last five hundred years of history on this continent, and our hopes for the future. It would be a blindly church-centered view of history to claim that the horrible genocide that began five hundred years ago, and in some ways still continues, was ordered by God so that the gospel might be preached. Yet, painful as it is to acknowledge, it is still true that we are here, and even that we can understand each other in a common language, as a result of that long and continued history of conquest, genocide, slavery, exploitation, and empire building.

Look again at the story of Pentecost. In some mysterious way, God's purpose of unity was being worked out in the very fact that there were in Jerusalem "Parthians, Medes, Elamites, and residents of Mesopotamia"—and in that those people, even apart from the miracle of Pentecost, were able to use some common language to say to each other: "What does this mean?"

In that story, we see that the Spirit uses, but also undercuts, the unity of empire. Those who gathered were able to understand each other. No matter whether they spoke in Aramaic or in Greek, their very ability to communicate was the result of a long history of conquests, in which their various languages, cultures, and traditions had been pushed aside as conquest led to empire, and empire to communication.

That is a story with which we are all familiar. When the All Africa Council of Churches meets, they must communicate in English and French. Last May, I was speaking in Nanjing Union Theological Seminary, in the People's Republic of China. In order to communicate with my Chinese friends there, I found it necessary to speak

English, a language that is neither mine nor theirs, but that we have both learned as a result of a long history of political, economic, and cultural empire-building. And here this evening, we are using a common language that has become ours through a long history of conquest and empire building.

Note, however, that in the story in Acts the Spirit undercuts the unity of empire. Empire leads to all these people being able to understand each other in a language that is not their own, whatever it might have been. But by the power of the Spirit, these people are able to hear, as they say, "each of us, in our own native language." I do not know whether there was a Hebrew-only movement in Palestine, as there had been in the time of Ezra and Nehemiah. I do not know whether there was an Aramaic-only movement. I do know whether among the cultured elites there was a Greek-only movement. And I certainly do know that, whatever attempts there might have been at imposing uniformity, the Spirit did undercut it, for all these various people, from different parts of the world, were made to hear, not in the language of empire, not even in the language of the apostles, but each in his or her own native language (and, for our purposes here, we could also say, "each in her or his own native culture").

If we then look back at the story of Babel, we see that the parallels between these two stories are more complex than we thought at first. In Babel, God intervenes to confuse the unity of a rebellious humanity. In Pentecost, God's intervention confuses the unities that empire has built. What is new about Pentecost is not that all persons speak the same tongue. They do not. What is new about Pentecost is that God blesses every language on earth as a means of divine revelation, and makes communication possible even while preserving the integrity of languages and cultures.

But that is not the whole story. The Holy Spirit also causes confusion among some who do not believe. As the text says: "Others sneered and said, 'They are filled with new wine.' " How can this be? In the face of such a miracle, with all sorts of different people hearing, each in his or her own native language, how can anyone be so dense not to see that this is a miracle?

The author does not tell us. But there is only one explanation I can imagine. Those who sneer do so because they do not see the miracle. They do not see the miracle, because to them nothing extraordinary is happening. To them, being able to understand what is being said is not unusual. All hear what is being said in their own native tongues. So do the mockers. But they don't see the miracle, precisely because they are natives. They are used to hearing everything in their own native tongue. They see all these people excited, and all they can say is, "What's the big deal?" In other words, they did not understand what was going on, precisely because they expected to understand.

The miracle that is taking place is that God is taking all these people, whose native tongues and native cultures make them outsiders, and is bringing them inside, making them insiders. They—the Medes, the Elamites, and the Phrygians—can understand that something extraordinary is taking place. But those who are already insiders, those who expect to hear their own language, those who are already at home, those who expect to understand, can do nothing but sneer.

What could those insiders, who did not perceive the miracle, have done? They could have turned to their Cappadocian or their Egyptian neighbor and asked what was going on. Perhaps then, through the witness of those who were not supposed to understand, such a person could have understood and would not have sneered.

The implications for the church gathered should be obvious. Those of us who belong to cultures and traditions that are often marginal in the life of the church, may rejoice, because at Pentecost God declared that our language, our culture, and our traditions are as good a vehicle as any for divine revelation. And those of us who belong to cultures where we expect that God will naturally speak in our language, those of us who represent the big churches and the established programs and the large endowments had better beware, lest we fail to see what God is doing in our world. Perhaps, like those who sneered because they could not see the miracle, we may need to turn to others, who are still astounded that the message is proclaimed in their own native tongue, and ask them to give us a glimpse of the miracle that is taking place all around us.

For the miracle is taking place all around us. There are "portents in heaven above, and signs on the earth below." Do you not see them? Ask the young people who are seeing visions, and the old people who are dreaming dreams. Ask your daughters and sons who are prophesying. Ask your servants, both men and women, on whom the Spirit is being poured. Ask the Native American, whose ancestors were in these lands since time immemorial. Ask the most recent undocumented immigrant. God is speaking to all of us, each in her or his own native tongue. And that—that is Pentecost!

XII

BLACK THEOLOGY

Scripture as Liberation for the Oppressed

THE TERM *BLACK THEOLOGY* CAN BE APPLIED TO THEOLOGIES ARISING FROM EITHER African or African-American contexts. Both are concerned with oppression and racism. Both focus on issues of liberation, political freedom, and justice. Despite their differences, both forms of theology find a common root in the experience of being black.

Black theologies share themes with Latin American liberation theologies as well. Yet because their contexts differ, so do some of their emphases. Whereas Latin American theologies of liberation are focused on socioeconomic and political questions, Africans, for example, "are more and more aware that 'anthropological poverty' (denial of their culture and very humanity) is more significant for them, while black Americans are particularly conscious of the history of slavery and their experience of being uprooted."[1] The issue of race binds African (both northern and South African) theology and African-American theologies together. Historically, suffering and powerlessness have been directly related to race and color.[2]

NORTH AMERICAN BLACK THEOLOGY BACKGROUNDS

Black theology in North America is rooted in the African-American experience. It reaches back to the philosophical heritage and religious sensibilities of African forebears and is now "best understood as the convergence of an African-derived worldview, the complexities of the experience of slavery, oppression, survival, rebellion, and adjustment in the New World, and their encounter with the biblical text." These realities have "shaped the African-American intellect and spirit."[3] It reflects African-American Christianity's passion, feeling, and expressiveness.

In the twentieth century, black theology in America arose out of the context of the civil rights/black power movement. This was consistent with the history of blacks in America, shaped by the experiences of slavery, discrimination, and injustice. As one scholar put it: "Black religion has always concerned itself with the fascination of an incorrigibly religious people with the mystery of God, but it has been equally concerned with the yearning of a despised and subjugated people for freedom—freedom from the religious, economic, social, and political domination that whites have exercised over blacks since the beginning of the African slave trade."[4]

The leadership of Martin Luther King, Jr., in the civil rights movement gave major impetus to the rediscovery of African-American religious roots, particularly as they were expressed in autobiographical writings, personal narratives, and journals of women and men who testified to their faith in God. Contemporary scholars agree that "the radical critique of American racism inherent in the black power movement is the source of contemporary black theology and prophetic black Christianity."[5] Black theology has provided a way of response to the issue of "the relationship between black religion and the quest for identity and power" among black people.[6]

The conscious development of black theology has been seen as emerging through three stages.[7] From 1966 to 1970 it developed mainly in black churches. Black church leaders responded to various questions through meetings and pronouncements. A second stage came in the early 1970s when black theology began to be discussed in universities and seminaries. Black theology became an academic discipline, building on black studies courses also in curricula. Influence by black churches declined, and the theologizing became less radical. A third stage developed by the mid-1970s when various links were made with other groups. The "Theology in the Americas" project in 1975 provided a dialogue point for black theologians with Latin American liberation theologians. It also involved other North American minorities, such as Native Americans, Hispanics, Roman Catholics, and women. In 1976, the Ecumenical Association of Third World Theologians (EATWOT) was formed, further widening opportunities for black theologians to be in discussions with others on a global scale. Among major voices in the ongoing development of black theology are James H. Cone; J. Deotis Roberts; James H. Evans, Jr.; and Cornel West, as well as Womanist theologians such as Delores Williams, Jacquelyn Grant, Toinette M. Eugene, Kelly Brown, and Katie Cannon.[8]

BLACK THEOLOGY AS LIBERATION THEOLOGY

On June 13, 1966, the National Committee of Black Churchmen issued a statement usually considered to be a founding document for the beginning of a consciously developed black theology. It said:

> Black theology is a theology of liberation. It seeks to plumb the black condition in the light of God's revelation in Jesus Christ, so that the black community can see that the gospel is commensurate with the achievement of black humanity. Black theology is a theology of "blackness." It is the affirmation of black humanity that emancipates black people from white racism, thus providing authentic freedom for both white and black people. It affirms the humanity of white people in that it says no to the encroachment of white oppression.[9]

This statement makes explicit what the history of African-Americans has shown—namely, that black theology "has always been intrinsic to the struggle for black liberation." It has "always been expressed in the idiom of the black community" and is thus "inseparable from its social context or surroundings," for black theology "addresses the question, What does the gospel of Jesus Christ have to do with the struggle of black people for liberation from white oppression?"[10]

Black theology as liberation theology has been expressed in many forms throughout African-American history. Black freedom fighters such as Henry Garnet, David Walker, Nat Turner, Gabriel Prosser, Harriet Tubman, and Sojourner Truth used the Scriptures in support of their resistance to slavery and oppression. Black spirituals, seen in the past as "other-worldly" or eschatological in orientation, are now recognized to contain double meanings. "Steal Away," for example, referred not only to believers' ultimate destiny with Christ, but was also used by Harriet Tubman as a signal of freedom for slaves intending to run away with her to safety.[11] Unambiguously, slaves sang:

> O Freedom! O Freedom!
> O Freedom! I love thee,
> And before I'll be a slave
> I be buried in my grave
> And go home to my Lord and be free.

As Cone notes, the true liberation theologian "is compelled to hear the cries and the moans of the people who sing 'I wish I knew how it would feel to be free, I wish I could break all the chains holdin' me.' "[12]

Black theology as liberation theology is also born out by "the two stubborn facts of African-American Christian existence," which are that "God has revealed Godself to the black community and that this revelation is inseparable from the historic struggle of black people for liberation."[13] The focus of black theology is on black history as "a source for its theological interpretation of God's work in the world because divine activity is inseparable from black history."[14] It is clear both theologically and historically that "black theology is a theology that equates liberation with salvation. It proclaims that the gospel affirms the black quest for freedom because the gospel of Christ is freedom."[15] Thus "the history of revelation and the history of liberation are the same history."[16]

James Evans has pointed out that liberation is God's work and intention and as such is a "permanent, final, and ultimate feature of one's existence." God's will is "irresistible, and God's work cannot be thwarted. All Christian hope stands or falls with this conviction." Yet this liberation is also "partial, fragile, and incomplete, because the drama of the struggle is yet being played out on the stage of history." It is not sufficient to limit liberation to the end of history, for this leads to "quietism and leaves the forces of dehumanization in the world unchallenged."[17] Instead, he proposes that liberation is "multidimensional." It includes physical liberation, or the "innate desire of all human beings to enjoy freedom of movement and association and the rights of self-determination"; spiritual empowerment, which includes "walking in the newness of life, no longer fettered by self-doubt and flagging confidence," freedom from "the sin of slavery as well as the slavery of sin"; and cultural liberation, which refers to "freedom from negative self-images, symbols, and stereotypes."[18] All three of these dimensions are interrelated; where one aspect has dominated, difficulties have emerged. In the contemporary world, Evans writes, "the reality of racism, sexism, and classism both inside and outside the African-American community requires a multidimensional view of liberation. Liberation involves more than what humans alone can accomplish. It is a powerful symbol for the ultimate destiny of humankind."[19]

Supremely, God's revelation and liberation are joined in Jesus Christ. With deep roots in the African-American religious experience, black theology has developed Christology as a central theme. Historically, the black community has been "convinced of the reality of Jesus Christ's presence and his total identification with their suffering." A "black messiah" or "black Christ" means "a messiah who sees his existence as inseparable from black liberation and the destruction of white racism."[20] To say that Jesus Christ is black is a counter to the white image of Jesus and was a way of saying that

> his cross and resurrection represented God's solidarity with the oppressed in their struggle for liberation. The oppressed do not have to accept their present misery as the final definition of their humanity. The good news is: God, the Holy One of Israel, has entered the human situation in Jesus and has transformed it through his cross and resurrection. The poor no longer have to remain in poverty. They are now free to fight for their freedom, because God is fighting with them.[21]

Thus, as Cone indicates, the "norm of black theology must take seriously two realities, actually two aspects of a single reality: the liberation of blacks and the revelation of Jesus Christ." For these two realities form the norm of black theology: "The norm of all God-talk which seeks to be black-talk is the manifestation of Jesus as the black Christ who provides the necessary soul for black liberation."[22]

SCRIPTURE IN BLACK THEOLOGY

Revelation

Black theologians agree with traditional definitions of God's revelation as God's self-disclosure, or God in "personal relationship with humankind effecting the divine will."[23] Yet they do not stop there, for according to black theology, revelation must mean more than just divine self-disclosure. Revelation is God's self-disclosure to humankind *in the context of liberation*. To know God is to know God's work of liberation on behalf of the oppressed. God's revelation means liberation, an emancipation from death-dealing political, economic, and social structures of society. This is the essence of biblical revelation.[24] The dynamism of the black view of revelation is captured by Cone, who wrote that for black theology "revelation is not *just* a past event or a contemporary event in which it is difficult to recognize the activity of God. *Revelation is a black event*—it is what blacks are doing about their liberation. I have spoken of the black experience, black history, and black culture as theological sources because they are God at work liberating the oppressed."[25] A goal of black theology, according to Cone, is "to create a theological norm in harmony with the black condition and biblical revelation."[26]

The Nature of Scripture

Black theologians agree that black theology is biblical theology.[27] "One cannot do theology in and for the African-American community without coming to terms with the influence of the Bible."[28] Cone calls Scripture "the primary source of theological speech," and Evans says that Scripture is "the primary, though not exclusive, conduit of the community's understanding of God's being and acts. It is the church's book in this sense, and it serves as a plumbline for the life and practice of the Christian community."[29] For Cone, "there can be no theology of the Christian gospel which does not take into account the biblical witness."[30]

J. Deotis Roberts has written of the theological significance of Scripture for black theology:

> The Bible, for blacks, is a "living book." Recognition of the creative and providential involvement of God in the history of the people of the Old Testament is basic to black interpretation. A direct relationship through faith exists between God's acts of liberating Israel and the freedom struggle of blacks. In black theology there is no "quest" for the historical Jesus. Jesus is present as a Divine Friend. The prophets speak for God in judgment against the dehumanization of the poor and the weak. But there is also an awareness of sin and guilt and the need for forgiveness among blacks. Black theology also recognizes God's forgiveness of the oppressor who meets God's demands for justice and love toward the needy and the helpless. This is not "cheap grace," for it includes the acceptance of the dignity and equality of all human beings and the sharing of power.[31]

The emphasis on Scripture as a liberating word is apparent here, as well as the centrality of Christ and themes of God's justice, love, and forgiveness.

Cone, too, speaks of the importance of the Exodus event as the focus of God's actions with Israel when he writes: "The import of the biblical message is clear on this point: God's salvation is revealed in the liberation of slaves from socio-political bondage. . . . Of course, there are other themes in the Old Testament, and they are important. But their importance is found in their illumination of the central theme of divine liberation." Similarly, in the New Testament, Cone continues, "the meaning of Jesus Christ is found in God's will to make liberation not simply the property of one people but of all humankind. God became a poor Jew in Jesus and thus identified with the helpless in Israel. The cross of Jesus is nothing but God's will to be with and like the poor. The resurrection means that God achieved victory over oppression, so that the poor no longer have to be determined by their poverty." Here the resurrection is "the divine victory over suffering, the bestowal of freedom to all who are weak and helpless. This and nothing else is the central meaning of the biblical story."[32] The biblical meaning of the resurrection becomes contemporary, according to Cone, because it means "the human being no longer has to be a slave to anybody, but must rebel against all the principalities and powers which make human existence subhuman. It is in this light that black theology is affirmed as a twentieth-century analysis of God's work in the world."[33]

For black theologians, Scripture must be taken seriously and prevents "making the gospel into private moments of religious ecstasy or into the religious sanctification of the structures of society." The Bible serves as "a guide for checking the contemporary interpretation of God's revelation, making certain that our interpretation is consistent with the biblical witness." Cone rejects views of Scripture that turn biblical writers into "mere secretaries" and argues that "efforts to prove verbal inspiration of the scriptures result from the failure to see the real meaning of the biblical message: human liberation!" His view is that "emphasis on verbal infallibility leads to unimportant concerns. While churches are debating whether a whale swallowed Jonah, the state is enacting inhuman laws against the oppressed. It matters little to the oppressed who authored scripture; what is important is whether it can serve as a weapon against oppressors."[34]

Biblical Interpretation

It is clear that in black communities whatever is said about the nature of Scripture is inseparable from the way Scripture is interpreted. Cone has indicated that "the chief mistake of contemporary white theology" is found "in its separation of theory from praxis, and the absence of liberation in its analysis of the gospel."[35] Black experience has shaped ways of understanding Scripture just as Scripture has helped to interpret black experience. Roberts writes that "because of their suffering, black people have always seen the Bible as a Book of Consolation. But because of their understanding of God, they have also recognized the Bible as a prophetic book. It has been, and still is, for blacks an incendiary document against injustices, but at the same time it speaks of the salvific assurance of forgiveness for each sinner before God."[36]

James Evans has indicated how African-American experience has made an impact on black views of Scripture and its interpretation. He indicates that blacks suffered from "invisibility and vulnerability" in Puritan America. During the slavery period, white slave owners took a literalistic view of the Bible to justify slavery. They appealed to the curse of Ham (Gen. 9:25), Abraham's ownership of slaves, and the view that neither Jesus' nor others in the New Testament condemned slavery (Eph. 6:5-9; Col. 3:22). In the face of these views, blacks developed three strands of African-American interpretation about views defending slavery. These three pillars were "the means by which African-Americans read the Bible with 'new eyes.' They were also forged in the context of the struggle for liberation."[37]

The first interpretive paradigm was the Exodus experience. This biblical narrative served as an "archetypal myth that, while drawn from Scripture, became the lens through which the Bible was read." Second, biblical references to Ethiopia, Cush, and Egypt (Num. 12:1; 1 Kings 10:1-10, 13; Ps. 68:31) in which black people are being referred to (see Song of Sol. 1:5, where an unnamed bride states that she is "black and beautiful") became sources of racial pride. Third, Jesus' stance toward the downtrodden and oppressed, wherein "his ministry among the marginalized persons of his day was seen to be the key to the Gospel," became a source of faith in God's personal attention to the black plight. In Paul's writings, blacks saw "an autobiographical narrative rather than an infallible guide to social behavior" so that Paul was perceived as a human being struggling with his faith and who moved on to ultimate victory. These avenues of interpretation enabled African-Americans to view the Bible as a "polyvalent narrative," always in need of interpretation so that Scripture must be read as "an imaginative text and a historical narrative."[38]

This means, according to Evans, that "in the African-American religious community the Bible continues to be read as a unified text whose central thrust guides the interpretation of its individual parts."[39] Katie Cannon confirmed this perspective when she wrote:

> The second lesson I learned from Black storefront clergy and laity is that every passage of literature does not have the same importance. These women and men understand the Bible to be a divinely inspired book but not every jot and tittle has the same significance. In explaining the full meaning of God's revelation, Bible study leaders give consideration to the whole Scripture and its unfolding movement. Afterward, they decide the priority which should be given to selected texts.[40]

This means, says Evans, that

> African-American Christians have seen and understood the Bible as a whole text, at the center of which is the Exodus myth, the cornerstone of the Hebrew model of interpretation. They have exercised a theological imagination that, like a prism, first focuses and then refracts the biblical text. Or to put it another way, African-American Christians have generally refused to dismember the biblical text without first remembering the biblical story.[41]

Biblical texts "come alive" in the context of the black community, particularly in preaching during worship. As the preacher enters into the biblical text, embodying it so that the text speaks out of the depths into the community's experience, black preachers know that when they hear "Amen" they have "correctly, or authoritatively, interpreted the Bible or some aspect of human experience." As William A. Graham put it, "A text becomes 'scripture' in active, subjective relationship to persons, and as part of a cumulative communal tradition. No text, written or oral or both, is sacred or authoritative in isolation from a community."[42] African-American models of biblical interpretation have resulted in a communal tradition, "forged in the need to transform their reality through an imaginative reconstruction of the biblical world and to participate in God's salvific activity by finding one's place in the biblical world."[43]

SCRIPTURE AS LIBERATION FOR THE OPPRESSED

Black theology has emerged out of the experiences of an oppressed community as African-Americans have heard, read, and interpreted Scripture. They have read the Bible as "an imaginative text that served the self-revelation of God and as a historical narrative that confirmed God's active presence in human affairs."[44] Like Latin American liberation theologies, black theology focuses on liberation as the content of the Christian gospel. It also shares with these theologies emphases on praxis, concrete theological formulations, and liberation as salvation.[45]

From these emphases and the unique African-American experience, Evans suggests four "biblical foundations" for black theology to indicate what the history of the experience means.

First, it means that "social location conditions biblical interpretation," since the marginality of African-Americans has affected the ways in which Scripture is perceived and interpreted. Second, "what the Bible means takes priority over what the Bible meant." In black theology emphasis is placed on the contemporary meaning of Scripture for the community, rather than the original meaning of biblical texts when they were first written. Third, "the story takes priority over the text." The narrative retelling of biblical stories in African as well as African-American slave communities has meant that the black cultural heritage emphasizes that the religious experience of the community with the text is of primary value. Fourth, "the African-American theologian must articulate the liberating hermeneutic that grants authority to Scripture in the experience of black Christians." The Bible has been used both to oppress and to liberate African-Americans and others. As the Bible is interpreted, the theologian must remember that "the Bible in the African-American community achieved its status as 'Scripture' in the heat of a liberation struggle, and that it is only within the contemporary struggle of the oppressed for liberation that the continuing authority of the Bible can be validated."[46]

In the following sermon by Stephen Breck Reid, observe how a dialectic is created between waiting and hoping. As the preacher calls the people to action, ironically he transforms a white male's wartime political rhetoric into a plea that we never give in.

Worth the Wait, or Reasonable People Don't Wait for Nothing

Stephen B. Reid

Psalm 130:5-8

When we hear this psalm we remember those times in our lives when we have called out to God. We remember those times we called out from the valleys of our lives. Those times when we almost gave up. The hardest word we could hear was *wait.*

The Hebrew term *qwh,* "wait," occurs twice in verse 5. It parallels the comparative in verse 6, "more than the sentry waits for the morning, more than the sentry waits for the morning." Further, the *qwh,* "wait, hope," parallels the verb *yhl,* "wait, hope." You would expect these two verbs to somehow be distinguishable, but they are not. Both terms make the connection between waiting and hoping. However, we should not miss the way that the *yhl* in verse 5 prepares us for the same term in verse 7.

Hope and wait go together. When one cannot find hope, one finds nothing to wait for. As a black child growing up in an alcoholic family, I hated to wait. I was no good at what we called in college "delayed gratification." The less hope I had, the less I could wait. Why wait until you can afford those things of which you do not have a realistic hope of ever affording? In a credit card culture often it is not the impatience that drives the insatiable lust for credit but the lack of true hope. Reasonable people do not wait for nothing; if nothing is what you expect, you will not wait.

The psalmist says, "I wait, my soul waits." "My soul," the Hebrew *nephesh,* refers to the personality, the very identity of the person. The core of the person waits. Our core self hopes.

A friend of mine, during his trip to Germany, went to Christmas dinner with a German family. A Romanian couple also came to that same Christmas dinner in that fateful year 1989. Suddenly a picture of the murdered Romanian dictator, Ceausescu, came on the TV screen. Such violence on the television on Christmas shocked my friend. Then he noticed that the woman was crying at the site of the dead bodies. She said quietly, "I knew God would not let us be slaves forever." Like people on both sides of the Iron Curtain, they lived, waiting and hoping.

African slaves likewise waited and hoped. Those who had no hope died. Sometimes the bliss of death meant the escape from this world. Sometimes the death in African-American communities past and present resembles the zombie-like death of one who must walk in the world of the living only to be dead to those things that make a person a person. We know this zombie-like life from Indian Reservations and ghettos where people live the death of alcoholism or drug abuse.

The character Celie waits in the Alice Walker novel *The Color Purple.* She waits beyond all reasonableness for reconciliation with her sister. She waits for the relationship with Shug, the woman her husband loves. She waits to come to terms with the anger that grows from her experience as an abused child and later as an abused wife. But in the waiting she does not stand still; she transforms herself.

How many abused children and battered wives wait for us as the messengers of God? How many children near and far in the clutch of hunger and poverty wait on the people of God?

Like Celie, we wait on the Lord; our souls wait, hope in the Lord. Not idly but in a constant metamorphosis. We don't wait alone. We wait like a woman in childbirth. After having four children, I can assure you that waiting through the labor is not idle. It is transforming. Even as the coach I was transformed.

We do not wait alone. Paul reminds us that the whole of creation waits with us (Rom. 8:22). But even the creation does not wait idly, but rather groans in anticipation. This travail is labor—that we know because of the death and resurrection of Jesus.

Someone in our midst today waits on the Lord. For that one, I remind us of the conclusion of the psalm. The New Revised Standard Version changes the word order from that of the Hebrew. The NRSV reads: "O Israel hope in the LORD." That is good, smooth English, but it misses the psalmist's emphasis. A more literal translation might be: "Hope! O Israel, in the LORD!" (Ps. 130:7a).

Our hope is the soil that nurtures our tenacity. We are instructed by Winston Churchill, who gave a short speech at Harrow School for Boys during World War II. He said: "Never give in. Never give in. Never, never, never, never. In nothing, great or small, large or petty. Never give in." If we are in the depths today, we hang on, for the God of loyalty and steadfastness is there for us. If we know someone who is in the depths, we continue to minister to him or her, even when it is inconvenient and annoying, for we shall never give in or give up on the promise of God made to us all in the message of Christ our Lord.

The world God has planned for us is worth the wait. We are reasonable people. We have not waited this long for nothing. We wait in hope so we shall never give in, never give in, never, never, never, never. Amen.

XIII

ASIAN THEOLOGY

Scripture as Stories for Freedom

THE CONTINENT OF ASIA CONTINUES TO PRODUCE A NUMBER OF SIGNIFICANT theological voices. In the Asian context, each nation has its distinctive history and traditions. Each has its own history of encounter with Western nations and culture. Some estimate that more than 85 percent of Asians live in poverty and oppression.[1]

In addition, Asia is a land of diverse religions. Hinduism, Buddhism, Confucianism, and other faiths coexist in Asia in a bewildering number of forms or relations. Religious oppression—against women, for example—is compounded by these relationships. Asian Christians, as approximately 3 percent of the population, are in a decided minority status. All of these factors present countless challenges to Asian Christian theologians. As Kosuke Koyama, one of the leading Asian theologians, has written:

> Theology responsible to a particular locality of culture, history, and people focuses itself upon the question posed by Jesus: "Who do [people] say that the Son of man is? . . . But who do you say that I am?" (Matthew 16:13, 15). This question comes to Asian Christians, who live in a world of great religious traditions, modernization impacts, ideologies of the left and right, international conflicts, hunger, poverty, militarism, and racism. Within these confusing and brutal realities of history the question comes to them. Here the depth of soul of the East is challenged to engage in a serious dialogue with the Word of God. Jesus refuses to be treated superficially.[2]

The Asian context drives Asian Christian theologians to have a keen interest in the relation of Christianity to other faiths. In addition, Asian theologians seek to develop their theology from an Asian perspective, from "the womb of Asia." C. S. Song has called this "third-eye theology," indicating that Christians must "train themselves to see Christ through Chinese eyes, Japanese eyes, Asian eyes, African eyes, Latin American eyes."[3] "Doing theology with Asian spirituality" is a goal, and the shape of this theology will be highly influenced by the Asian cultural context. The hope is to gain "freedom for our theological mind—freedom to meet God in Asian humanity, freedom to identify God's world within our Asian world, freedom to intertwine biblical history and Asian history, and freedom to encounter Jesus the savior in the depth of the spirituality that sustains Asians in their long march of suffering and hope."[4]

BACKGROUNDS

Koyama has listed six themes that have been expressed in Asian theology since 1945, the year when the atomic bomb was dropped on Hiroshima, Japan. These are (1) revolutionary social changes, (2) massive poverty, (3) ethnic and economic minorities, (4) creative and destructive aspects of cultures, (5) the people of other faiths, and (6) the reality of a divided church.[5] While these particular issues take shape in varying ways in differing countries, it is still possible to agree with the sentiments of M. M. Thomas of India, who said that "in spite of its plurality of cultures, political ideologies, and social structures, we can discern certain common features in what Asian peoples are revolting against and are struggling for." This justifies using the term "Asian theology" in the singular.[6]

Asian theology "seeks to take the encounter between life in Asia and the Word of God seriously."[7] It does not seek merely to mimic or reflect Western theology, but instead to respond to the biblical proclamation of Christ. This is its basic orientation toward a responsible "contextualization" of theology.[8] As Saphir Athyal put it, "A Western systematization of theology may not fit in the Asian scene. Asian theology should take a systematization which is dictated by the emphasis of the culture and leading thoughts of Asia."[9] C. S. Song proposes a radical contextualization of theology to the Asian setting when he writes:

> Let our theology come from a deep resonance in the heart of Asia. Let our theology be the *hibiki* ["echo"] of the Asian soul. And let our theology echo the silence broken by human suffering that grips most Asian peoples. With that theology let us turn once again to our own Bible, to the Christian faith. We may then become aware that we are standing beside an ancient pond, hearing deep resonance from human hearts touched by the Bible, by the Bhagavad Gita, or by the Sutra of the Lotus Flower of the Wonderful Law. What we encounter there are not cold doctrines, rigid laws, and menacing taboos, but human beings powerless before the power of fate and gripped by the touch of death; human beings in need of divine grace to sustain their hope in this world and beyond it. To be able to *image* such human beings is the beginning of theology in Asia.[10]

Asian Theology and Liberation Theology

The ongoing challenge of developing a Christian Asian theology has led Asian theologians in a number of directions. One theme of central and continuing significance is that of liberation. In January 1979, the Asian Conference of Third World Theologians met in Wennappuwa, Sri Lanka, and developed a common statement on the theme of the conference: "Asia's Struggle for Full Humanity: Toward a Relevant Theology." This statement affirmed that in the Asian context where "large numbers of men and women find themselves socially deprived and progressively thrown further and further away from the center of life and meaning," to be relevant, "theology must undergo a radical transformation."[11] The theologians said that "in the context of the poverty of the teeming millions of Asia and their situation of domination and exploitation, our theology must have a very definite liberational thrust."[12] While the "first act of theology, its very heart, is commitment" to the poor and oppressed of Asia toward a "full humanity," to be "truly liberating," this theology "must arise from the Asian poor with a liberated consciousness." The "oppressed community" will express this theology, with the help of trained biblical scholars and others. It can be "expressed in many ways, in art forms, drama, literature, folk stories, and native wisdom as well as in doctrinal-pastoral statements." The statement recognized that because "every theology is conditioned by the class position and class consciousness of the theologian," a "truly liberating theology must ultimately be the work of the Asian poor, who are struggling for full humanity." While they may use the help of specialists in theology whose knowledge can "complement the theologizing of the grass-roots people," ultimately, their theologizing "becomes authentic only when rooted in the history and struggle of the poor and the oppressed." Theology, to be "authentically Asian must be immersed in our historicocultural situation and grow out of it. Theology, which should emerge from the people's struggle for liberation, would spontaneously formulate itself in religiocultural idioms of the people."[13]

In his address to this conference, the Sri Lankan theologian Aloysius Pieris spoke on "Toward an Asian Theology of Liberation: Some Religiocultural Guidelines."[14] In this address, Pieris recognized the revolution in theology that occurred from the 1960s onward when Latin American liberation theologians "effected a complete reversal of method" by beginning their theology with "praxis" or the combination of action and reflection that seeks to alter social oppression. Pieris claimed that for Asians, "liberation theology is thoroughly Western, and yet so radically renewed by the challenges of the Third World that it has a relevance for Asia which the classical theology does not have."[15] "What Latin Americans claim," he continued, "and what we Asians must readily grant, is that it is not perhaps a new theology, but a theological *method,* indeed the *correct method* of doing theology."[16] Pieris sees the task of Asian theology as "to complement the Latin American method with an Asian critique of classical theology."[17]

Asian Theological Concerns

While an important theme in Asian theology is liberation, it is by no means the only theme among Asian theological concerns. The writings of a number of important Asian theologians make this clear.[18] Two of the most prominent writers include Kosuke Koyama (b. 1929) and Choan-Seng Song (b. 1929).

Koyama was born in Japan and has taught in Asia and since 1980 at Union Theological Seminary in New York. He has been highly influenced by the work of Kazoh Kitamori, *Theology of the Pain of God* in which Kitamori argued that pain is a part of God's nature and that the relation of this dimension of God to human oppression is the primary task for Japanese theology. Among the leading themes in Koyama's theology are God and idolatry, the encounter with Buddhism, and the phenomenon of greed. Koyama has sought to develop a "rice-roots theology," beginning from the *praxis* or everyday experience of the people. In his *Waterbuffalo Theology,* emerging from his work in Thailand, he wrote:

> On my way to the country church, I never fail to see a herd of waterbuffaloes grazing in the muddy paddy fields . . . it reminds me that the people to whom I am to bring the gospel of Christ spend most of their time with the waterbuffaloes in the rice field. The waterbuffaloes tell me that I must preach to these farmers in the simplest sentence-structure and thought-development. They remind me to discard all abstract ideas, and to

use exclusively objects that are immediately tangible. "Sticky-rice," "banana," "pepper," "dog," "cat," "bicycle," "rainy season" . . . these are meaningful words for them.[19]

This "theology from below" is the starting point for all the rest of theology.

Koyama's other concerns are expressed in his numerous writings. His emphasis on the dangers of idolatry is also reminiscent of Latin American liberation theologies. Western idols of speed and efficiency are one way idolatry is expressed. Koyama's book titled *Three Mile an Hour God* is a way of expressing the view that God works slowly in the conversion process, as seen in the biblical phrase "forty years in the wilderness."[20] Koyama has sought a dialogue between Asian spirituality and biblical spirituality as illustrated in the title of his book *Mount Fuji and Mount Sinai*.[21] He also joins hands with other liberation theologians in his concerns for the poor: "The oppressed want justice not charity. The rich want to give charity not justice. In particular, the powerful members of the community want to give 'religion' to the poor. 'Religion' will take away the complaints of the poor. . . . But God's politics must hear the unuttered cry of one fallen and unable to cry."[22]

Choan-Seng Song was born and taught in Taiwan. He once worked for the World Council of Churches, and is currently Professor of Theology and Asian Culture at the Pacific School of Religion in Berkeley, California. Song is concerned with many themes in Asian theology, as his numerous writings indicate. One continuing motif has been the theological motif of the meaning of the salvation history of Israel and the Christian church in relation to the nations of Asia. Song's contextualization of theology stems from his method of "transposition," which he defines as a transposition from "the Israel-centered view of history to the view that regards other nations as constructive parts of God's design of history." This is required, Song says, "for a more realistic perception of God's work in the world. Such a new theology of history contains a tacit admission that Israel alone cannot explain world history."[23] This means that the people of Israel were used by God as "a symbol of how God would also deal redemptively with other nations." Thus

> in the light of the experience unique to Israel, other nations should learn how their histories can be interpreted redemptively. An Asian nation would have its own experience of exodus, captivity, rebellion against Heaven, the golden calf. It would have its own long trek in the desert of poverty or dehumanization. . . . An Asian nation will thus be enabled to find its place side by side with Israel in God's salvation.[24]

Song sees redemptive elements in all human history that are witnesses to the presence of God in the world. Thus, in terms of a religion such as Buddhism, "the expression of Buddha's compassion for the masses in his vows and the way he toiled unselfishly for their emancipation from pain and suffering are not without redemptive significance. Can we not say that Buddha's way is also a part of the drama of salvation which God has acted out fully in the person and work of Jesus Christ?"[25] For Song, Christians should see the mission of the church "as consisting not of conquering members of other faiths but of growing with them in the knowledge and experience of God's saving work in the world." Specifically, the mission of the Christian church in Asia is the fundamental task of "informing the Asian spirituality shaped by Asian cultures and religions with the love and compassion of God in Jesus Christ. In addition,

Asian Christians together with people of other faiths and ideologies must seek to transform Asian society on the basis of freedom, justice, and equality."[26] In the end, "the Word has to assume Asian flesh and plunge into the agony and conflict of the mission of salvation in Asia."[27] Song's own theological method is to use parables and folktales to help Christians reinterpret and enlarge their vision of God's mission in the world.[28]

SCRIPTURE IN ASIAN THEOLOGY

Although the Final Statement of the Asian Conference of Third World Theologians (1979) considered the issue of liberation to be of primary concern, it also indicated that one of the issues for a relevant Asian theology was a "Biblical Perspective." Here the theologians stated:

> Because theology takes the total human situation seriously, it can be regarded as the articulated reflection, in faith, on the encounter of God by people in their historical situations. For us, Christians, the Bible becomes an important source in the doing of theology. The God encountered in the history of the people is none other than the God who revealed himself in the events of Jesus' life, death, and resurrection. We believe that God and Christ continue to be present in the struggles of the people to achieve full humanity as we look forward in hope to the consummation of all things when God will be all in all.[29]

The theologians also stated the need for theology to be "liberated from its present race, class, and sex prejudices" so that it can be in the service of the people and become "a powerful motivating force for the mobilization of believers in Jesus to participate in Asia's ongoing struggle for self-identity and human dignity." For this to happen, new areas of theology need to be developed, such as "understanding the revolutionary challenge of the life of Jesus, seeing in Mary, the truly liberated woman who participated in the struggle of Jesus and her people, bridging the gaps of our denominational separation, and rewriting the history of the Asian churches from the perspective of the Asian poor."[30]

Revelation

The perspectives developed by Song and other Asian theologians strongly stress that theology involves both God and humanity: "Our theology must begin with humanity and all that it means because it is in humanity that God is theologically engaged. Humanity to theology is something like water to fish. Fish die when taken out of water. Theology dies when divorced from human life and history."[31] As such, theology is always shaped by human forces. For "there is no such thing as a theology immune from cultural and historical influences. Theology is culturally and historically not neutral. A neutral theology is a homeless theology. It does not belong anywhere. Theology really begins in earnest when it identifies its home and discovers its belonging."[32]

Theology is thoroughly contextualized because God's revelation is totally contextualized as well. Song rejects what he calls "gravity-free" theology—the idea that "God's help comes from the august sky. When heaven opens, God speaks. This is essentially revelation. Heaven is the context of God's revelation. God creates separate contexts irrespective of what and who we are." A "gravity-free" theology "speculates about what God is like as an ontological being," spending most of its time "trying to figure out how many angels can dance on a needlepoint. It makes every effort to draw a line between the saved and unsaved."[33] Instead, Song insists that God's theology is "gravity-bound" theology, since God so loved the *world* (John 3:16).

> Love is essentially gravity-bound . . . [and] God is drawn to the world through gravity-bound love. God's love in Jesus Christ is grace, acceptance, communion, salvation, and life. The mark of this gravity-bound love is suffering: the cross. No magic can bring context and revelation together in theology. No theological method needs to be invented to test how revelation is at work in a particular context. Such a test is blasphemous and sacrilegious, for God has already united our context with revelation through gravity-bound love: God's suffering love.[34]

Thus "human longings and struggles for grace, acceptance, communion, salvation, and life in Asian settings are the contexts of revelation for Christian theology in Asia. This is where gravity-bound theology should begin and end."[35] An important implication of this view of revelation is that revelation is not God's breaking into history from outside history so much as it is God as present in the common events of human life here and now. Thus revelation is to be found in such an ordinary experience as seeing a peach tree in full bloom.[36] This means that "context and revelation are no longer separate entities. Context is not just a receptacle of revelation. Context and revelation become united to tell the world what truth is."[37] This view is contrasted to traditonal theologies in which Asians were "supposed to confront our context, dissect it, exorcise it, and expose its godlessness." Traditional theology taught that "revelation cannot be inherent in Asian existence and history" and decreed that "God works only tangentially within Asian cultures." It maintained that "we face only God's anger in Asian religious milieus." Instead, the example of Jesus was "to free his followers from fear of their context and to make them realize its revelatory significance. He helps them see the world as God sees it and not through taboos their religion has imposed on them" (see Matt. 6:26, 28-29).[38] This thoroughly incarnational theology and contextualized sense of revelation, joined with a *praxis* method, gives Asian theology strong affinities with Latin American, black, and feminist theologies.[39]

The Use of the Bible

Asian theologians who seek dialogue with other faiths and who see in the culture of Asia folktales and parables to be combined with biblical themes find the Bible to be a source for discerning God's presence and action in the world. Just as the stories of the people of Israel disclose God's work within that nation, so also the stories of Jesus, the "master storyteller," did "not remain mere stories. In the mouth of Jesus they became parables of God's kingdom and of human life. God and humans meet in Jesus' story-parables. And as we now know, Jesus' own life is the story-parable of suffering and hope in which God embraces humanity through the death on the cross."[40]

The Bible is the source of the stories about Israel, of Jesus' parables, and of his life, death, and resurrection to reveal "the compassionate God." The parables of Jesus are "powerful because they powerfully echo the longings in the hearts of those who suffer injustice of various kinds. And parables we find in abundance in religious cultures in Asia can also theologically reflect God's power at work in Asians when they echo strongly the aches and pains inflicted on the hearts and persons of millions and millions of their fellow Asians."[41]

Contemporary Asian theologians who combine a passionate concern for liberation with the desire to use Asian resources in doing theology now see traditional biblical stories with new eyes and find "many exciting and creative ways of rereading the Scripture."[42] They see the Scriptures as presenting stories for freedom as they make readers "aware of God who is the power of freedom and who gives that power of freedom to us." As the Christian Scriptures are read in conjunction with Asian resources, Asia is witnessing "the birth of this power of freedom in Asian humanity bound by centuries of fate not instituted by God but by emperors, kings, warlords, and landlords."[43]

Kwok Pui-lan has written that interpreting the Bible in the Asian context "must involve a powerful act of imagination. . . . Asian Christians have recognized the dissonance between the kind of biblical interpretation we inherited and the Asian reality we are facing. We have to find new images for our reality and to make new connections between the Bible and our lives."[44] What Choan-Seng Song has called "imaging theology" and Kwok Pui-lan "dialogical imagination" involves dialogue and the constant conversation between various religious and cultural traditions. For "it looks at both the Bible and our Asian reality anew, challenging the established 'order of things.' . . . Dialogical imagination attempts to bridge the gap of time and space, to create new horizons, and to connect the disparate elements of our lives into a meaningful whole."[45] Thus Maen Pongudom, a biblical scholar from Thailand, uses northern Thai creation folktales to contrast with the Genesis creation story, "arguing that people of other faiths and traditions share certain essential ideas of creation found in the biblical story." Archie Lee, an Old Testament scholar from Hong Kong, reinterprets the parable of Nathan (2 Sam. 12:1-4) from the point of view of Chinese tradition and finds that the "story has the unlimited power to capture our imagination and invite the readers to exert their own feeling and intention." Similarly, Asian women "are discovering the liberating elements of Asian traditions as powerful resources to re-image the biblical story." Kwok Pui-Lan herself has used Asian poems, a lullaby, and a letter from a woman in prison to interpret the meaning of suffering and hope and the story of Southeast Asian boat people to reappropriate the diaspora theme.[46]

In Korea, minjung theology refers to the theology of the masses of people who have been subjugated and oppressed. Minjung theology "reclaims minjung as protagonists in the historical drama, for they are the subject of history." Old Testament scholar Cyris H. S. Moon reinterprets the Old Testament story through the social biography of the minjung in Korea, showing how the story of the Korean people helps in understanding the Old Testament while the social biography of the Hebrew people has illuminated the meaning of the Korean minjung story. Thus, "through powerful theological imagination, Moon has brought the two social biographies in dialogue with one another."[47]

The great diversity and variety of Asian experience means that the Bible has been and will be appropriated in differing ways. As Kwok Pui-lan notes, "different communities pose critical questions to the Bible and find diverse segments of it to address their situations."[48] Concerns for dialogue across faiths, the use of imagination, appropriation of Asian resources, the contextuality of revelation, and the need for contextual theology to "explore and experience 'God-meaning' in human sufferings and hopes that take form in cultures, histories, and religions" all affect the use of the Bible in Asian settings.[49] A tremendous sense of the need for liberation in the Asian context, however, also strongly shapes how the Bible functions and is used. One way to express this perspective is to see Scripture as providing "stories for freedom."

Asia's struggle for a "fuller humanity in the socio-political as well as the psycho-spiritual aspects" means that "the liberation of all human beings is both societal and personal."[50] The Bible speaks to both dimensions for Asian Christians, and directs its readers toward a future that begins with the reality of life today. As Song puts it:

> Christians and theologians in Asia are learning that our vision of the future must begin within the reality of life today. This is how biblical faith came into being. The vision of the exodus began with the reality of life of enslavement in Egypt. The call to God's love and justice was issued by prophets from within a society that had become corrupted with human avarice and violence. And the vision of that great prophet Second Isaiah was born in the midst of a life of exile in a foreign land. That biblical faith never let the future run away by itself. The future was always in the firm grip of the present that had just struggled out of the past. It is that kind of future that made sense to the prophets. And only a vision built on the life of reality as actually lived made an impact on it.[51]

As Asian Christians read and study the Scriptures, reinterpreting them in the light of their own contexts and experiences, they find that "the Bible offers us insights for our survival." For, as Kwok Pui-lan puts it:

> historically, it has been more than simply a tool for oppression, because the *minjung* themselves have also appropriated it for their liberation. It represents one story of the slaves' struggle for justice in Egypt, the fight for survival of refugees in Babylon, the continual struggles of anxious prophets, sinners, prostitutes, and tax-collectors. Today, many women's communities and Christian-based communities in the Third World are claiming the power of this heritage for their liberation. These groups, which used to be peripheral in the Christian church, are revitalizing the church at the center. It is the commitment of these people which justifies the Biblical story to be heard and shared in our dialogue to search for a collective new religious imagination.[52]

In the following sermons by Choan-Seng Song, a Chinese professor, and Kosuke Koyama, a Japanese professor, observe how the biblical praise of God is easily contextualized in a theology of freedom and justice for the people of God in particular Asian cultures.

ASIAN THEOLOGY

Wisdom and Knowledge of God

Choan-Seng Song

Romans 11:28-33

Paul, who penned this letter to the Christians in Rome, is agitated. His spirit is in turmoil. He is torn between Jews and Gentiles. He is a Jew and remains a Jew. He could boast and say he was "circumcised on the eighth day, a member of the people of Israel, of the tribe of Benjamin, a Hebrew born of Hebrews" (Phil. 3:5). But exasperated by the Jews who opposed and reviled him at Corinth, he declared to them: "From now on I will go to the Gentiles" (Acts 18:6).

As a Jew, Paul knows his Hebrew Scripture inside out. He must have revered it as a holy book containing God's covenant with his own people and believed in God's promise of salvation for them. This is Paul's faith, and he remains committed to it. The sermon he preached in the synagogue at Antioch in Pisidia testifies to this: "You Israelites, and others who fear God, listen," he began. "The God of this people Israel chose our ancestors" (Acts 13:16-17). The rest of the first half of his sermon was a condensed history of Israel with its focus on God's promise to Israel. If he had stopped there, if this had been his entire faith, and if this had been his whole theology, he would have at most been an enlightened Jew, but would never have gone out of his way to become a missionary to the Gentiles.

But Paul did not stop there. His sermon took a radical turn. Leading the history of Israel up to King David, he suddenly broke it off and introduced a fresh starting point. "Of this man's [David's] posterity God has brought to Israel a Savior, Jesus" (Acts 13:23). Jesus! This Jesus makes all the difference! Jesus did make a radical difference to the life of Paul. Paul is no longer simply and solely a Jew. He is now a Jew and a follower of Jesus. The law and all that it stands for in his own religion cannot make up his faith entirely. He does not disown the law. He does not throw it out the window. But it has to be the law illuminated by what Jesus said and what he did. It has to be reshaped by Jesus, who has fulfilled "what God promised to our ancestors" (13:32-33).

Jesus, and not the law, is the final court of appeal. Jesus, and not your religious tradition, is the arbiter of truth. Jesus, and not your faith, is the measure with which you measure yourself and others. Jesus, and not your likes and dislikes, tells you what is good and what is evil, what is right and what is wrong, what is just and what is unjust. And it is Jesus, not your idea of God, not what you think God must be, that discloses to you who God is and what God is like. This is what it means to follow Jesus. This is what faith in Jesus requires. This is why you call yourself a Christian, someone who belongs to Jesus, who believes in Jesus, who becomes a member of the community gathered in the name of Jesus. Again this is not to reject everything you stand for and hold dear, but it does mean that what you stand for and hold dear, including the way you think God speaks to you through the Bible and in the church, has to be tested by him.

Thoughts such as these must have been uppermost in Paul's mind when he wrote to the Christians at Rome. What a challenge! And what a mystery! This is not something that you can work out with the help of a neat logic. It is not set out in your catechism. It is not written in your theological textbook. Before a mystery such as this you can only burst out in doxology. And this is what Paul does when he says in his letter: "O the depth of the riches and wisdom and knowledge of God!" (Rom. 11:33). Those riches of God render the grandeur of your religious systems and edifices poor. That wisdom of God makes you think over and over what you believe to be true. That knowledge of God compels you to take a second look, a third look, any number of looks, at the knowledge you have of God and of God's activity in history, in the world, in creation.

How deep all this is, all that concerns God, and all that regards what God is doing in the world! This is liberating, is it not? It liberates you from your stereotypical idea about God. It liberates you from your tunnel vision of God's saving activity. It liberates you from your inhospitable and often hostile relations with people who think and believe differently from you. And it liberates you from taking the Bible, the very source of your Christian faith, as a book closed once for all, as if nothing new and fresh is to be found in it, as if no mystery is left buried in it, as if you have seen through the mind of God in it, as if you hold God captive in it.

But we do not find Paul doing any such things. "O depth of the riches and wisdom and knowledge of God!" The riches of God are the depth that has no bottom. The wisdom of God is the depth that cannot be reached. And the knowledge of God is the depth that knows no end. It is this kind of riches, wisdom, and knowledge of God that we Christians are confronted with in our Bible. How can we treat the Bible as if it is a closed book? How can we use it as a proof text for our ideas and convictions? And can we worship it as if it has replaced the living and acting God, the God who goes ahead of us as well as behind us, the God whose judgments are unsearchable and whose ways are inscrutable (see Rom. 11:33)?

Paul does not treat his own Hebrew Scripture like a closed book. He does not believe the last chapter of the history of Israel has been written. And he resists any religious attempt to own God, to domesticate God, to turn God into a tribal god. With Jesus "crucified, dead, and risen" it becomes a whole new game altogether. The wall separating Jews and Gentiles is broken down. As a Jew, Paul must now reach out to the Gentiles. And he has to tell his own people that God is the God of Gentiles as well as Jews, that God saves both Gentiles and Jews; that before God no one, Jew or Gentile, can make a claim on God on the basis that he or she is as a member of a particular religious and ethnic community.

We have known Paul as a missionary to the Gentiles. This is true, but not entirely. He was also a missionary to Jews, to his own people. He was eager to let them know that with Jesus things have changed, a new horizon of history has loomed, a fresh vision of faith is no longer a matter of option but a matter of necessity. There is now a new role for Israel to play in the arena of God's saving activity. God continues to deal with Israel, but God has also been dealing with Gentiles. God has chosen Israel, but God has also chosen all nations. God has a future for the people of Israel, but God has a future for all humanity, too. Liberation from an ethnocentric religion! Liberation from an ethnocentric God! Paul must have been overwhelmed by an insight into the depth of God, an insight inspired by Jesus. No wonder he is led to say: "For God has imprisoned all in disobedience so that he may be merciful to all" (Rom. 11:32). He could have underlined the word *all* or written it in bold letters.

If an insight such as this overwhelms Paul and liberates him, it should also overwhelm and liberate Christians in Asia. For too long we have been taught to take the place of Israel and consider ourselves to be particularly favored by God for salvation. As to millions upon millions of people outside the Christian church, the

168

people that make up most of the people in Asia, almost half of the world's population, we name them as "Gentiles" who have no place in God's favor. For most of us the Christian Bible is a closed book, in which everything to be known about God and about God's saving activity is revealed to us completely. In it we perceive no depth of God's riches, feel no depth of God's wisdom, and confront no depth of God's knowledge. The Bible is a dead book. We have imprisoned God in it. We have replaced God with our Bible. The Bible is our God!

But the world of Asia is showing us something very different. People of Asia, those "Gentiles" and "pagans," are telling us different stories. In the midst of suffering and poverty, these "Gentiles" and "pagans" are capable of self-sacrifice in their struggle for a better society. They can respond to the call to work for the good of the community. They can band together to strive against the forces that oppress them and dehumanize them. Sometimes you cannot help thinking that Jesus may be more at home with them than with Christians in the church. Is not God, then, working with them and among them? Is not God the God of those people of Asia outside the Christian church as well as those inside it?

That Jesus, crucified and risen, changed Paul. It is not the law that interprets Jesus. The religious leaders of Jesus' day, including Paul himself before his conversion, interpreted Jesus in the light of the law, and they had Jesus die on the cross. For Paul it is Jesus that must interpret the law. Then the Sabbath is made for human beings and not human beings for the Sabbath. Is it not what we Christians in Asia should also be doing? It is not the Bible as we are taught to understand, as we take it to be, that should interpret Jesus. It must be the other way around. We must let Jesus tell us what the Bible is, who God is, and what God wills for all humanity. The Bible is not a rigid tradition, a compendium of our beliefs and doctrines. Jesus makes that same Bible a living book, a book that unfolds story after story of God's dealing with the world, a book that compels us to exclaim with Paul in doxology, saying: "O depth of the riches and wisdom and knowledge of God! How unsearchable are God's judgments and how inscrutable God's ways!"

Our faith should begin with such a doxology. Then in spite of ourselves we may hear echoes of it from the womb of the vast continent of Asia. We may feel the reverberations of it in the depth of the community of women, men, and children there. And we may realize that our Christian doxology and the doxologies that well out of the heart of Asian humanity join together in the confession that God's judgments are unsearchable and God's ways are inscrutable. This is at once a humbling and an exciting thought, for in such doxologies we shall meet Jesus working in the power of the Spirit to fulfill the promise of God to all humanity, both Jews and Gentiles, both Christians and those who are not Christian.

The Book That Can Speak to All Peoples

Kosuke Koyama

Exodus 20:3

My grandfather read the Bible to our family at the breakfast table every morning. Observing him, as a small boy, I was impressed with the importance of the Bible. The wonderful stories—the creation of the world, the Tower of Babel, Noah's Ark, Moses and the burning bush, Elijah and the prophets of Baal on Mt. Carmel, the miracles of

Jesus, the crucifixion of Jesus, and the conversion of Saul on the way to Damascus—stirred my imagination and filled me with excitement.

Our family discussed the stories of the Bible freely. We were encouraged to say whatever we thought about each day's lesson. Honest and concise comments were commended. We did not know about "biblical inerrancy" or "verbal inspiration." The small Christian church in Tokyo to which our family belonged was ignorant of such difficult theological controversies. For us, the Bible was simply a book to be heard and enjoyed, and by which we lived. Most of all, the lively, fast-moving stories of the Bible fascinated me.

"You shall have no other gods before me" is a major focus of the biblical message. This is not an abstract principle of exclusion, but a condensation of the long story of human experience. The thought that false gods must be rejected in the light of the true God forms a central theme of the biblical narratives. "You shall have no other gods before me" is the first Emancipation Proclamation in human history. Freedom from the power of false gods is emancipation from all possible forms of slavery.

This fundamental biblical message was impressed on me in 1945 when Japan, with its imperial cult, was destroyed in its war against fifty nations. Although I was young, I gave a biblical interpretation to the fall of Japan: Japan was defeated by its own idolatry, the emperor worship cult. The war experience of my country bound me to the Bible. Ever since that time, the Bible has been a very concrete book to me.

> Their idols are like scarecrows in a cucumber field,
>   and they cannot speak;
> they have to be carried,
>   for they cannot walk.
> Do not be afraid of them,
>   for they cannot do evil,
>   nor is it in them to do good.
> (Jer. 10:5)

Ever since World War II, I have lived with these unforgettable words. The greatness of the Bible is that it can express such a profound truth about human life with such simple picture language. Once you have heard, you do not forget its images!

The mysterious and solemn divinity cult of Imperial Japan was, in the language of the Bible, "a scarecrow in a cucumber field." The Japanese people were forced by their government to believe that the emperor was not an ordinary human being, but he was divine. The cult even led us to suppose that the Japanese people were unique and their land was a "divine land." We were told that something that cannot walk can walk. For a brief period, the teaching of the false god was able to generate enormous spiritual energy toward the war effort, but soon we found that we were becoming immobile, losing our own ability to walk. The Imperial cult became increasingly self-destructive. The words of Jeremiah were true!

The official propaganda of the Japanese imperial cult commanded the people of Japan to "have no other gods before 'the emperor.' " The emperor, they said, is incomparable, most sacred, and inviolable. But this fanatic ideology enslaved people. It did not emancipate anyone. The peoples of Asia, particularly the Koreans, suffered greatly from this Japanese "theological ideology."

But when "you shall have no other gods before me" comes from the biblical God, it means emancipation. Why is that so? Because this God is Love.

"The LORD, the LORD,
a God merciful and gracious,
slow to anger,
and abounding in steadfast love and faithfulness."
(Exod. 34:6)

The love of the merciful and gracious God upholds us and confirms us. This is the wonderful, hidden truth about human life. Any imperial cult, in whatever form, will eventually bring ruin to human community. The person of biblical faith knows this.

The depth of the message "you shall have no other gods before me" is unfathomable. The words of Jesus at the Last Supper—"This is my body which is given for you"—are also unfathomable. The divine affirmation of the first commandment is united and deepened by the divine self-giving of the Lord's Supper. Both words emancipate humanity from slavery. They contain, hidden within them, the life-giving message of the Bible. Every time we participate in the sacrament of the Lord's Supper, we taste and feel the innermost message of the Bible, the love of God for us and all creation. The unity of the Old and New Testaments is located in our experience of the love of God.

The biblical God of love is deeply concerned with social justice in our world. Love without concern for justice is a deception. Our God demands that we do justice, and love kindness, and walk humbly with our God (see Mic. 6:8). That is how we fulfill the first commandment and experience the mystery of the Lord's Supper. Christ has done justice, loved kindness, and walked humbly with God. Followers of Christ must do the same.

Yet we are challenged, judged, and humbled by the words of the Sri Lankan theologian Tissa Balasuriya: "Why is it that in spite of hundreds of thousands of eucharistic celebrations, Christians continue as selfish as before? Why have the 'Christian' people been the most cruel colonizers of human history?"

Over a thousand years, in serious engagement with human events, the Bible was written. Its language is concrete. It tells truth about human life without fear. Even as a child I noticed the difference between the biblical God and Japanese gods. I saw that the biblical God criticizes and judges God's people, while the Japanese gods speak only words of flattery for the Japanese people. The biblical God confronts God's own people, without hesitation calling them "stubborn," "unfaithful," "idolatrous," "greedy," and so on. The Japanese gods approve of whatever the Japanese leaders want to do.

The contrast is important. While the biblical God is universal, the Japanese gods are parochial. The biblical God understands all the languages of humanity; the Japanese gods understand only the Japanese language. The biblical God judges the quality of all cultures; the Japanese gods have no knowledge of cultures other than the Japanese. Japanese gods are globally ignorant. So these gods brought the nation to destruction.

We each have a need to be free from idols that destroy us, so we look to the God of the Bible. The Bible is not God; God speaks to us through the Bible. This God is the God of love and justice. Even nature is emancipated by this God because justice for all of creation is the will of this God. This God emancipates us from the powers that enslave us, and thus we are called to participate in God's work of love and justice in our world.

XIV

FEMINIST AND WOMANIST THEOLOGIES

Scripture as the Mother of Models

MOST FEMINIST THEOLOGY, AS IT HAS EMERGED SINCE THE 1970s, IS A FORM OF liberation theology. It has centered on the struggle of women for liberation. Like other forms of liberation theology, feminist theology is a protest against traditional forms and methods of doing theology. It is concerned with the central theme of liberation, variously defined as "equality," "freedom," and "humanization." The voices of women theologians are being heard today in increasing numbers.[1]

Among those womens' voices being heard are those of black women and women of color. While sharing common perspectives with the movement known as feminist theology, "womanist theology" also offers points of contradistinction to white feminist perspectives on issues of culture, society, and theology.

FEMINIST THEOLOGY

Prominent women theologians have made significant impact on all the theological disciplines. Emerging forms of feminist theology are being developed that call into question traditional modes of theological thought and practice. While not all women who do theology today would wish to identify their theological work as "feminist," reformulations of classic Christian understandings are developing from women who find themselves drawn to the wider, cultural feminist movement. Janet Kalven, who has worked with women in an international Christian renewal movement for about forty years, has said: "Feminist theology is not a matter of 'add women and stir.' Rather, feminist theology involves a profound rethinking of theology, its sources, methods and themes."[2]

Feminist theology is ecumenical in orientation. It has cut across traditional denominational lines and over barriers between Roman Catholics and Protestants. It has sought relations with people on many levels and in many contexts. As Beverly W. Harrison writes:

> To be a truly ecumenical person, is, from a feminist theological viewpoint, to live out a praxis that works to heal the brokenness of life in the world, however differently feminists construe the meaning of that brokenness. Hypothetically, feminist "ecumenism" requires address to all conflicts and differences that divide us from one another and

from the full potential of creation and that prevent us from living into our power as bearers of God's image. But this is not yet clarified in the feminist theological process.[3]

Feminist theology, therefore, has varied constituencies with many degrees of involvement apparent. There are varieties within the feminist theological process about precisely *what* tasks should be done and about *how* these tasks should be accomplished.

There are also diversities within feminist theology on the issue of Scripture. A basic recognition in feminist thought is that the Bible is a book composed in cultures that had patriarchal biases. Basic too is the contention that the Bible has been interpreted predominantly by males and that in many ways sexist interpretations have been dominant ones. In the light of this, feminist theologians face the fundamental questions posed by Katharine Doob Sakenfeld: "How can feminists use the Bible, if at all? What approach to the Bible is appropriate for feminists who locate themselves within the Christian community? How does the Bible serve as a resource for Christian feminists?"[4] While feminists differ in their specific responses to these questions, almost all would agree with Letty M. Russell:

> Fresh insights are needed as the rising consciousness of women and people in the Third World or in other oppressed circumstances leads them to challenge accepted biblical interpretations that reinforce patriarchal domination. From this perspective the Bible needs to be liberated from its captivity to one-sided white, middle-class, male interpretation. It needs liberation from the privatized and spiritualized interpretations that avoid God's concern for justice, human wholeness, and ecological responsibility; it needs liberation from abstract, doctrinal interpretations that remove the biblical narrative from its concrete social and political context in order to change it into timeless truth.[5]

Thus Russell speaks of "the liberating Word," "liberating the Word," and "the liberated Word" to describe the process of emerging feminist hermeneutics.[6] This is the attempt of women searching today for "a feminist interpretation of the Bible that is rooted in the feminist critical consciousness that women and men are fully human and fully equal. This consciousness is opposed to teachings and actions that reinforce the social system that oppresses women and other groups in society."[7]

BACKGROUNDS

Feminist Consciousness

The development of a "feminist consciousness" has taken place through the last few centuries.[8] In the Western world, until the early nineteenth century, most "intellectual and theological work was done out of a prefeminist perspective. There was no conscious awareness that women's experience *as* women's experience was relevant to intellectual work. It was a man's world. Women were part of the male story. As women they remained invisible. This prefeminist consciousness acknowledged that women's lives did have some unique aspects, but the differences were unimportant."[9]

With the growing rise of the self-consciousness of women as women, issues related specifically to the Bible arose. For opponents of the women's rights movement used the Bible to argue that it was not legitimate for women to name or value their female experience. Women in the churches tried to reconcile their commitment to the authority of the Bible with emerging feminist activism. They also became interested in questions of biblical interpretation. How did the Bible affirm their lives? When a text was insensitive to women's experience, what was its authority?[10]

Questions about the use of the Bible in relation to the position of women in society were not new in America. In 1837 the noted antislavery lecturer and women's rights author Sarah Grimke charged that part of a specific plot against women included a masculine bias in biblical interpretation and thus called for a new feminist scholarship. Antoinette Brown, the first ordained woman in Congregationalism, studied theology at Oberlin College and looked at the Pauline epistles with feminist questions. At her ordination, the Reverend Luther Lee, who preached the sermon, quoted Galatians 3:28—"There is neither Jew nor Greek, there is neither slave nor free, there is neither male nor female; for you are all one in Christ Jesus."[11]

Many feminist theologians today, however, trace the direct beginnings of a feminist consciousness about the Bible to the leadership of Elizabeth Cady Stanton. Stanton was involved as a suffragist and thus had a political awareness of what certain actions could mean. She established a committee of twenty women who found all major biblical passages relating to women, discussed them, and wrote extended commentaries on them from their own interpretive perspectives. Stanton said she undertook this task because she continued to hear so many "conflicting opinions about the Bible, some saying it taught woman's emancipation, and some her subjection."[12] The result was *The Woman's Bible,* published in two volumes in 1895 and 1898.[13]

Stanton's work is "not a treatise in modern biblical criticism," but rather "a passionate feminist criticism of biblical religion which anticipates many of the themes of feminist theology."[14] But two crucial insights for a feminist theological hermeneutics arose. According to Elisabeth Schüssler Fiorenza, these are: "(1) The Bible is not a 'neutral' book, but a political weapon against women's struggle for liberation. (2) This is so because the Bible bears the imprint of men who never saw or talked with God."[15] For Stanton, a scholarly and feminist interpretation of the Bible was politically necessary because

i. Throughout history and especially today the Bible is used to keep women in subjection and to hinder their emancipation.

ii. Not only men but especially women are the most faithful believers in the Bible as the word of God. Not only for men but also for women the Bible has a numinous authority.

iii. No reform is possible in one area of society if it is not advanced also in all other areas. One cannot reform the law and other cultural institutions without also reforming biblical religion which claims the Bible as Holy Scripture. Since "all reforms are interdependent," a critical feminist interpretation is a necessary political endeavor, although it might not be opportune. If feminists think they can neglect the revision of the Bible because there are more pressing political issues, then they do not recognize the political impact of Scripture upon the churches and society, and also upon the lives of women.[16]

The Woman's Bible project was not popular among many leaders. Female scholars who did not participate were in Stanton's view "afraid that their high reputation and scholarly attainments might be compromised by taking part in an enterprise that for a time may prove very unpopular."[17] The National American Woman's Suffrage Association formally rejected the project as a political mistake.

It has also been argued that *The Woman's Bible* was opposed because of "its radical hermeneutic perspective which expanded and replaced the main apologetic argument of other suffragists that the true message of the Bible was obstructed by the translations and interpretations of men."[18] Instead, Stanton maintained that the degrading ideas about women, which the churches said came from God, actually originated from the heads of men. For "over and against the doctrinal understanding of verbal inspiration of the Bible as the direct word of God, she stresses that the Bible is written by men and reflects the male interests of its authors. 'The only point in which I differ from all ecclesiastical teaching is that I do not believe that any man ever saw or talked with God.' "[19]

Stanton proposed that the Bible be treated like any other book and that the cultural limits of its authors be recognized. The Bible was not to be accepted or rejected wholesale. There are varieties of teachings in Scripture. So every biblical passage on women must be analyzed and carefully evaluated. In this way its androcentric implications may become clear. For Stanton, "Men have put their stamp on biblical revelation. The Bible is not just interpreted from a male perspective, as some feminists argued. Rather, it is man-made because it is written by men and is the expression of a patriarchal culture."[20]

In the early twentieth century a new concern about the equality of the sexes began to surface. "Women's studies" were begun to show that while the sexes were different, men and women shared a common humanity. Women and men are both the creatures of God. One did not have the proper perspective of human history if women's experiences were not noticed or appreciated. In that sense "history" was also "her story." In literature, psychology, sociology, economics, and politics many dimensions of women's experiences were explored.

Women's studies continue and have greatly expanded knowledge in a variety of ways. In biblical studies "the advent of women's studies expanded women's understandings of biblical authority. By helping everyone appreciate the place of women in the Bible and in the early church, it stretched orthodox assumptions about tradition. It offered alternative images of women. It suggested that more inclusive language could be important for the faith and the church." Women now may claim their equality in God's world, and through the development of a feminist critical consciousness can develop "an authentic inclusive interpretive framework for all biblical, historical, and theological work."[21]

Further women's studies have led both to the critique of past assumptions and ways of perception about women as well as to the shaping of completely new interpretive methods for a feminist critical consciousness. Feminist studies developed in relationship with other liberation movements and began to ask questions about "every biblical text and every event in church history: What difference did it make that women were or were not included? If women were not taken into account, why? The answers to these questions challenged many sacred principles of doctrine and practice."[22]

Emerging feminist critical consciousness "attacks majority positions and points out the injustices of history. Feminists are angry, iconoclastic, and revolutionary. A feminist critical consciousness does not always state positively what it stands for, but it knows and names its enemies. Feminism does not simply stretch the horizons of knowledge, it alters the landscape by tearing down many of the old patriarchal buildings."[23]

Put in a religious context, this means that

> the religious feminist movement is about women's claim to freedom to relate to God in the church and wider outside world. They are coming out of their experiences and consciousness and are expressing themselves, at times, through their own definitions. They are acting out these new freedoms. What follows among Christian feminists is a critique of the institutional church—traditionally controlled and defined by men—which, these women say, has misunderstood, ignored, denigrated and blocked women's consciousness.[24]

Ultimately, the aim of a feminist consciousness is, as one feminist writer put it, "to make the experience and insights of women available to the entire world, not simply to know more about women in and of themselves. Yet if we are to include women in the total picture, we are called to rethink how we interpret everything."[25] This comprehensive vision of the interpretation of reality shapes the feminist approach to theology and to the study of Scripture.

Feminist Critiques

An important early article in the area of feminist theology was published in 1960 by Valerie Saiving. In "The Human Situation: A Feminine View," Saiving argued that a crucial dimension to how one perceives theology is one's sexual identity.[26] She contended that

> there are significant differences between masculine and feminine experience and that feminine experience reveals in a more emphatic fashion certain aspects of the human situation which are present but less obvious in the experience of men. Contemporary theological doctrines of love have, I believe, been constructed primarily upon the basis of masculine experience and thus view the human condition from the male standpoint. Consequently, these doctrines do not provide an adequate interpretation of the situation of women—nor, for that matter, of men, especially in view of certain fundamental changes now taking place in our own society.[27]

A 1968 book by Mary Daly, *The Church and the Second Sex,* claimed that the church has encouraged the view that women are inferior to men and that the church has been a leading instrument in the continuing oppression of women.[28] Daly moved to the concept of "sisterhood" in 1971 to urge "the bonding of those who have never been bonded before for the purpose of overcoming sexism and its effects, both internal and external."[29] This signaled Daly's move outside the traditional boundaries and language of the Roman Catholic church and her growing identification with the feminist and women's liberation movements.

Daly's theological critique of the doctrine of God was stated in *Beyond God the Father* (1973). In it she argued that the essential core of Christianity is belief in the God of the Bible but that this is hopelessly patriarchal in nature.[30] The characteristic designation of God as "father" has the effect of legitimizing the image of a supreme heavenly patriarch who rules his people and thus sanctions a male-dominated order of society. The church has equated the biblical Eve of the book of Genesis with evil and made her responsible for sin. Thus women become equated with sin. "God" must be recast, argued Daly, from noun to verb. God is the "Be-ing" in which we participate. In her 1975 revised edition of *The Church and the Second Sex* she wrote a "new feminist postchristian" introduction, claiming that it was impossible to work with men who are the "oppressors" or with the church as the institution of oppression of women. Her goal was to sketch a new vision grounded fully in women's experience. The distinctiveness of women's experience will give insight into how women are related to the cosmos.[31]

The line begun by Daly is followed by others into what has been called the stream of "revolutionary feminism."[32] Revolutionary feminists look to women's *traditional* experiences as the norms and starting points for theology. These experiences, including motherhood and marriage, must be reappropriated by women from a feminist perspective. All sexist traditions must be rejected, including the oppressive authority structures of Judaism and Christianity. New symbols and traditions are to be found rising from women's experience of ultimate reality.[33]

To indicate their stance, revolutionary feminists often claim the title "post-Christian" or "post-Jewish." Some see women's spirituality merging into the broad stream of pagan spirituality, including the practice of witchcraft.[34] The image of the "goddess" is invoked to return to a spirituality prior to the biblical traditions and among the most primitive known. For revolutionary feminists "the goddess symbol found in many traditions can aid modern women's liberation by providing an image of female power that can counteract the symbol of God as male."[35]

Among the new sources of "revelation" and "authority" for these feminists are dreams and fantasies, the present and future vision of sisterhood, and Daly's androgynous future created by God the verb.[36] A metaphorical image for this stream of thought and practice is that feminists must "spook, spark and spin." This is in order that women's creative energies for survival may be used to break with male-dictated definitions of women's vocations so "sisters" may reach to the depths of themselves and let the creative powers of women flow in the midst of a world of death.[37] Among revolutionary feminists are Daly, Naomi Goldenberg, Judith Plaskow, Starhawk (Miriam Simos), Zsuzsanna Budapest, Carol Christ, and Penelope Washburn.[38]

A second stream of feminist theology may be labeled "reformist feminism." These theologians appeal to women's *feminist,* rather than traditional, experience. Here the religious traditions of Christianity and Judaism are not to be forsaken but rather may be renewed, reformed, and reinterpreted to provide resources for freedom. Oppression can be recognized, sexist cultures and institutions confronted, and liberation occur when women's experience provides the source of critique and analysis.[39]

While these Christian feminists recognize the radical critique of Christianity from other feminists, they "continue to struggle with the symbols and their transformation." Yet they also realize that "both historically and in the present, the Christian symbols of God, Jesus, sin and salvation, the Church and the Holy Spirit have been life-giving and liberating for women."[40]

The task is to search for resources within the biblical, theological, and intellectual traditions that enable Christian feminist theology to be understood as an intrinsic theological task . . . i.e., applications of Christian themes to contemporary issues.[41]

This task, says Anne Carr, "implies not only a Christian critique of sexist or patriarchal culture but a feminist critique of Christianity."[42]

A metaphorical image for this group of feminist theologians is "reweaving the web of life."[43] Many see their central task to be the active pursuit of making and keeping peace, which, they believe, women are better equipped to achieve than men. Nonviolence is a priority value. For the realization of this vision, the resources of the Christian faith are considered to offer some help.

In order to appropriate the resources of the Christian tradition, a reexamination of Christian roots is needed. This has led feminist theologians, who have a basic allegiance to the biblical tradition but who reject the sexism that has accompanied it, to be active in biblical studies, church history, theology, and ethics. Among the feminist theologians working in these areas are Phyllis Trible, Elizabeth Schüssler Fiorenza, Eleanor McLaughlin, Joan Morris, Letty Russell, Rosemary Radford Ruether, Patricia Wilson-Kastner, and Beverly Harrison.[44] Thus the diversities among feminist theologians are apparent. Their critiques of established traditions are similar; their positive prescriptions for constructive feminist theology vary. But in most general terms

the religious feminists' critique is wide-ranging. Among other matters, it addresses religious authority and government and names as inauthentic the bases on which much of these rest. It puts the biblical writers and the early fathers into their historical context. It identifies systems of oppression—sexist, racist, classist—and makes the connections between them both in the church and in the world. It identifies with the poor and hurting. It insists that liberation in one area must lead to liberation in all. It denies the split between spirit and matter. It honors sexuality and women's bodies. It calls for reintegration with nature rather than its subjection.[45]

Further: "it insists that intuitive, subjective, creative, even 'emotional' ways of thinking are as necessary as the rational, abstract, linear, reputedly objective models of exploring reality. It demands that women's experiences, as interpreted by women themselves, be regarded as valid and redemptive. It recognizes new spiritualities and theologies that grow out of these experiences. It attempts new ways of speaking of God—rescuing God from the 'he' categories. It incorporates dance, song, visual arts and poetry into its worship and revelation. Its images and icons come out of women's historic and contemporary lives."[46]

SCRIPTURE IN FEMINIST THEOLOGY

Authority and Interpretation

The varieties among feminist theologians show themselves also on the issue of Scripture. The questions raised by Sakenfeld on how feminists can use the Bible are crucial. The problem feminists have with the Bible is clearly stated by Rosemary Radford Ruether:

The feminist critique of sexism finds patriarchy not only in contemporary and historical Christian culture but in the Bible as well. The Bible was shaped by males in a patriarchal culture, so many of its revelatory experiences were interpreted by men from a patriarchal perspective. The ongoing interpretation of these revelatory experiences and their canonization further this patriarchal bias by eliminating traces of female experience or interpreting them in an androcentric way. The Bible, in turn, becomes the authoritative source for the justification of patriarchy in Jewish and Christian society.[47]

To speak of "the authority of the Bible" in a constructive or positive sense for feminist theologians means that substantial hermeneutical or interpretive problems must be overcome. As Russell puts it: "The authority of the Bible has to be understood in a way that accounts for the fact that, frequently, the texts are not only contradictory but also sexist, racist, and triumphalist. No interpretation of authority that reinforces patriarchal structures of domination would be acceptable for feminist interpretation."[48] Thus authority and interpretation of the Bible are intimately bound up together for feminist theologians.

Implicit in Russell's statement is her recognition of what feminist theologians often call the "critical principle of feminist theology." Ruether defines this as

> the affirmation of and promotion of the full humanity of women. Whatever denies, diminishes, or distorts the full humanity of women is, therefore, to be appraised as not redemptive. Theologically speaking, this means that whatever diminishes or denies the full humanity of women must be presumed not to reflect the divine or authentic relation to the divine, or to reflect the authentic nature of things, or to be the message or work of an authentic redeemer or a community of redemption.[49]

This feminist critical principle means for Ruether the demand that "women stand outside of and in judgment upon this patriarchal bias of the scriptures."[50] Schüssler Fiorenza also applies this directly to the Bible when she writes that

> feminist biblical interpretation must therefore challenge the scriptural authority of patriarchal texts and explore how the Bible is used as a weapon against women in our struggles for liberation. It must explore whether and how the Bible can become a resource in this struggle. A feminist biblical interpretation is thus first of all a political task. It remains mandatory because the Bible and its authority has been and is again today used as a weapon against women struggling for liberation.[51]

The relationship of the feminist critical principle to the Bible is a crucial one for feminist theologians.[52] If the Bible were *only* the "authoritative source for the justification of patriarchy in Jewish and Christian society," then, as Ruether points out, "the principle would also demand that feminism reject the scriptures altogether as normative for its own liberation. The Bible would reveal only a demonic falsification of woman's being; it would not provide touchstones for a liberating alternative."[53]

On the other hand, if a hermeneutic or practice of interpretation could be found that could meaningfully use the Bible as a source for understanding human life and persons, then a sense of the authority of Scripture could be acknowledged. For feminists to acknowledge the authority of Scripture in this sense *could* mean that

(1) at least scripture contains something more than a patriarchal view of human life, a support for sexism, and (2) the "more" that scripture embodies rings at least in harmony with the truth of women's reality as it is understood in feminist consciousness—touches it, perhaps unfolds it, makes it resonate with other truths, perhaps can help to test fidelity to it. For those for whom scripture has this authority, the interpretive task becomes imperative.[54]

Feminist Hermeneutics

There are several models to describe feminist biblical interpretation. "Feminist interpretation" can mean simply "the reading of a text (or the writing of an analysis, or the reconstructing of history) in light of the oppressive structures of patriarchal society."[55] Trible refers to it as "critique of culture in light of misogyny."[56] This reading may be "negative" in that it seeks to expose patriarchal orientations or oppressive intentions in the text or it may be "positive" in that it tries to point out social, religious, and political power of women which has previously been neglected.[57] While all "reformist" feminist theologians acknowledge that "the Bible came into existence in a strongly patriarchal environment and is a product of its time," the question of "how strong that bias is and how it should be dealt with are points on which feminists differ."[58]

Three general approaches of feminist theologians to feminist interpretation may be distinguished.[59] These interpretive procedures carry with them hermeneutical theories. The task of each approach is "to ground its analyses in the experience of women's oppression."[60]

Reclaiming texts. In the light of feminist perceptions of patriarchal biases and traditional sexist interpretations, some feminists seek to reclaim biblical texts. This may take the form either of reinterpreting well-known texts in the light of feminist consciousness or focusing attention on texts that are "forgotten" or distorted by patriarchal hermeneutics. Examples of fresh interpretations that do not portray women in so negative a light as before would be Genesis 2–3, 1 Corinthians 14, and Ephesians 5. Texts formerly overlooked would include Galatians 3:28 and the stories of the relationship of Jesus with women in the Gospels as well as those texts about women leaders, such as Miriam, Deborah, the women at the tomb of Jesus, Priscilla, and others.[61]

An important practitioner of what might be called the "remnant" standpoint in trying to reclaim texts is Phyllis Trible. Trible seeks to uncover countercultural impulses within biblical texts about women and, by the use of rhetorical criticism, see interpretation as "participation in the movement of the text."[62]

Theological Perspectives. A second approach to interpreting biblical texts from a feminist standpoint may be said to look not so much at specific biblical texts but from a theological perspective to see the message of Scripture as a whole. This view "approaches the Bible in the hope of recognizing what the gospel is really all about and then works from that recognition toward a specificity about women."[63]

One leading proponent of this approach is Rosemary Radford Ruether. For Ruether "the Bible can be appropriated as a source of liberating paradigms only if it can be seen that there is a correlation between the feminist critical principle and that critical principle by which biblical thought critiques itself and renews its vision as the authentic Word of God over against corrupting and sinful deformations. It is my contention here that there is such a correlation between biblical and feminist critical principles. This biblical critical principle is that of the prophetic-messianic tradition."[64]

This "prophetic tradition" becomes for Ruether the "central tradition" of Scripture and functions as the norm by which biblical texts are judged. By this, aspects of the Bible are determined as to whether or not they are authoritative. This prophetic tradition has as its central theme the call for the liberation of the oppressed.[65]

The work of Letty Russell shows another approach to interpreting biblical texts from a specifically theological perspective. For Russell, "the Bible is 'scripture,' or sacred writing, because it functions as a 'script,' or prompting for life." Scripture's authority, says Russell, "stems from its story of God's invitation to participation in the restoration of wholeness, peace, and justice in the world. Responding to this invitation has made it my own story, or script, through the power of the Spirit at work in communities of struggle and faith."[66]

Russell's approach distinguishes between scriptural *form* and *content*. The patriarchal language of the Bible is its form but not its content.[67] The theological message of Scripture is God's redemptive and liberating activity in Jesus Christ. This message is found in Scripture through

> God's intention for the mending of all creation. The Bible has authority in my life because it makes sense of my experience and speaks to me about the meaning and purpose of my humanity in Jesus Christ. In spite of its ancient and patriarchal worldviews, in spite of its inconsistencies and mixed messages, the story of God's love affair with the world leads me to a vision of New Creation that impels my life.[68]

The Bible also is the source of her "expectation of justice and liberation."[69]

From this, Russell urges a shift in paradigm to a new model of authority. She rejects the traditional picture of *authority as domination* in favor of *authority as partnership*. This means that people "participate in the common task of creating an interdependent community of humanity and nature."[70] According to Russell, this "shift in feminist interpretive framework means that we no longer need to divide feminist experience and biblical witness."[71]

Historical Reconstructions. A third approach to feminist hermeneutics seeks to reconstruct biblical history. Practitioners of this approach attempt to show that "the actual situations of the Israelite and Christian religions allowed a greater role for women than the codified writings suggest."[72] In this view, the earliest phases of Christianity were egalitarian. Thus "the patriarchalization process is not inherent in Christian revelation and community but progressed slowly and with difficulty. Therefore, a feminist biblical hermeneutics can reclaim early Christian theology and history as women's own theology and history."[73]

This emphasis has led Schüssler Fiorenza to propose a "feminist-critical and a historical-concrete model of biblical interpretation" that is "multidimensional" in its approach. This model, she says:

> should not search for a feminist formalized principle, a universal perspective, or a historical liberating dynamics but should carefully analyze how the Bible functions

concretely in women's struggle for survival. Key elements in such a model, as far as I can see, are the following: (1) suspicion rather than acceptance of biblical authority, (2) critical evaluation rather than correlation, (3) interpretation through proclamation, (4) remembrance and historical reconstruction, and (5) interpretation through celebration and ritual.[74]

Common Themes

Sharon Ringe has noted that despite these varieties in feminist hermeneutical approaches, they all share two perspectives in common. First, "they all honor insights into the nature of God and of the will of God deriving from the interpreters' own contexts and experiences." This enables interpreters to dialogue with biblical texts instead of being forced into choosing either to accept or reject them outright. Second, "these hermeneutical approaches all require that one approach the reading of scripture from praxis or engagement on the side of justice and advocacy for the poor and oppressed, and particularly for women."[75] As starting points for feminist theology and biblical interpretation, these perspectives are basic.

The primary task both for feminist theology generally and feminist hermeneutics particularly is "the critique of patriarchy" as understood to encompass "the web of intersecting patterns of oppression that find systemic expression in racism, classism, imperialism, and other relationships of domination, as well as in the sexism to which the term seems more apparently to refer." These relationships produce a domination expressed philosophically in "a dualistic ideology, according to which reality is perceived in patterns of opposition of male to female, rich to poor, powerful to powerless, pure to impure, white to black, 'good' to 'bad' and so forth." These dualistic categories, Ringe says, "identify not merely differences but also relative values, with qualities shared by persons possessing greater power understood as not just *other*, but also *better*."[76]

This means that "a sustained critique of the ideology of patriarchy and a commitment to engage in the struggle to change the social systems in which it is expressed are thus crucial to a feminist reading of the Bible, which is a reading from context to context."[77]

WOMANIST THEOLOGY

Womanist theology has emerged as a way for many women of "affirming them-selves as *black* while simultaneuously owning their connection with feminism and with the Afro-American community, male and female," for "the concept of womanist allows women to claim their roots in black history, religion, and culture."[78] The issue of self-naming is important, and womanist theology signifies a theology that "permits African-American women to define themselves, to embrace and consciously affirm their cultural and religious traditions, and their own embodiment." Womanist theology "directly taps into the roots of the historical liberation capability of black women."[79]

BACKGROUNDS

Pulitzer Prize-winning novelist Alice Walker gave expression to "womanist" in her *In Search of Our Mother's Gardens,* linking it to the black folk expression "You acting womanish." According to Walker, this means "wanting to know more and in greater depth than is good for one . . . outrageous, audacious, courageous and willful behavior." A womanist is also one who is "responsible, in charge, serious." A womanist is "committed to survival and wholeness of entire people, male and female." A womanist is "a black feminist or feminist of color."[80] Walker distinguished between "feminist" and "womanist" by saying that "Womanist is to feminist as purple to lavender."[81] Walker's suggestion is that "the experience of being a Black woman or a White woman is so different that another word is required to describe the liberative efforts of Black women."[82] By naming themselves in this way, womanists assert "the freedom to explore the particularities of black women's history and culture without being guided by what white feminists have already identified as women's issues."[83] By building on biblical, theological, historical, and economic bases, womanist theology searches for the "voices, actions, opinions, struggles, and faith of African American women in order to shape a distinctive perspective that takes seriously their experiences and traditions in response to the liberating activity of God." This means that womanist theology strikes a "critical posture toward sexism, misogyny, and the objectification and abuse of black women, both within African American communities and within the dominant patriarchal culture."[84]

Womanist theology has agreed with feminism in its criticism of sexism and the need for unity of women, just as it has agreed with black theology in its critique of white racism and the need for black unity.[85] But womanist theologians have also been critical of the inadequacies of feminist theology. As Jacquelyn Grant writes, "Feminist theology is inadequate for two reasons: it is *White* and *racist*. . . . Feminist theologians are white in terms of their race and in terms of the *nature of the sources* they use for the development of their theological perspectives."[86] While acknowledging that individual feminists may not be racists, Grant affirms that

> the movement has been so structured, and therefore takes on a racist character. In a racist society, the oppressor assumes the power of definition and control while the oppressed is objectified and perceived as a thing. As such, White women have defined the movement and presumed to do so not only for themselves but also for non-White women. They have misnamed themselves by calling themselves feminists when in fact they are White feminists, and by appealing to women's experience when in fact they appeal almost exclusively to their own experience. To misname themselves as "feminists" who appeal to "women's experience" is to do as "feminists" what oppressors always do; it is to define the rules and then solicit others to play the game.[87]

Brenda Eichelberger listed five categories of reasons for black women's rejection of white feminism:

> 1) Class differences mean that while Black women are dealing with "survival" issues, White women are dealing with "fulfillment" issues. 2) Negative imagery of Black women derived from physical and cultural stereotypes has resulted in the debased treatment of Black women. 3) The naiveté, or basic lack of knowledge, of Black women about the women's movement results in their inability to see the relationship between feminist issues and the Black struggle. 4) Black women perceive White feminists to be racists who are interested in them only in order to accomplish the White women's agenda. 5) There is a concern that an alliance of Black women with White women in a feminist agenda may be "detrimental to black men" and therefore divisive of the Black community.[88]

Theological Method

Emerging elements of theological method associated with womanist theology include the following: "(1) A multidialogical intent, (2) a liturgical intent, (3) a didactic intent, and (4) a commitment both to reason *and* to the validity of female imagery and metaphorical language in the construction of theological statements." According to Delores Williams, the womanist participates in dialogue throughout many diverse social, political, and religious communities. A major concern is for human survival and a productive quality of life for oppressed people. The liturgical intent focuses on the black church and allows womanist theology "to challenge the thought/worship/action of the black church with the discordant and prophetic messages emerging from womanist partiicipation in multidialogics. . . . The Bible, a major source in black church liturgy, must also be subjected to the scrutiny of the justice principles."[89]

The main focus of womanist ethics is on justice for women, survival, and "a productive quality of life for poor women, children, and men." This means the womanist theologian "must give authoritative status to black folk wisdom (e.g., Brer Rabbit literature) and to black women's moral wisdom (expressed in their literature) when she responds to the question, 'How ought the Christian to live in the world?' "[90] Language for theology in womanist perspective will be "rich in female imagery, metaphor, and story." Its appropriateness will "ultimately reside in its ability to bring black women's history, culture, and religious experience into the interpretive circle of Christian theology and into the liturgical life of the church. Womanist theological language must, in this sense, be an instrument for social and theological change in church and society."[91]

Womanist theology "begins with the experiences of Black women as its point of departure." As Grant puts it: "Black women must do theology out of their tri-dimensional experience of racism/sexism/classism. To ignore any aspect of this experience is to deny the holistic and integrated reality of Black womanhood. When Black women say that God is on the side of the oppressed, we mean that God is in solidarity with the struggles of those on the under side of humanity." In womanist theology, "the daily struggles of poor Black women must serve as the gauge for the verification of the claims of womanist theology."[92]

Place of the Bible

Womanist theology also holds a distinctive view of the place of the Bible. Womanists see that on one hand the Bible has been used by those in power "to restrict and censure the behavior of African American women. On the other hand, the Bible has significantly captured the imagination of African American women because extensive portions of it speak to the deepest aspirations of oppressed people for freedom, dignity, justice, and vindication."[93] The experience of black women reveals the Bible as a major source of religious validation in their lives. For although "Black women's relationship with God preceded their introduction to the Bible, this Bible gave some content to their God-consciousness." In this respect, "the source for Black women's understanding of God has been twofold: first, God's revelation directly to them, and secondly, God's revelation as witnessed in the Bible and as read and heard in the context of their experience."[94]

Black women are able to "identify and reflect upon those biblical stories in which poor oppressed women had a special encounter with divine emissaries of God." For example, the story of Hagar in the book of Genesis "is most illustrative and relevant to Afro-American women's experience of bondage, of African heritage, of encounter with God/emissary in the midst of fierce survival struggles."[95] In the New Testament, Christian womanist theologians focus on the beginning of the salvation story when the Spirit comes upon Mary, a woman of the poor (Luke 1:35).[96] In the Bible

> Black women have learned how to refute the stereotypes that depict Black people as minstrels or vindictive militants, mere ciphers who react only to omnipresent racial oppression. Knowledge of the Jesus stories of the New Testament helps Black women to be aware of the bad housing, overworked mothers, underworked fathers, functional illiteracy, and malnutrition that continue to prevail in the Black community. However, as God-fearing women they maintain that Black life is more than defensive reactions to oppressive circumstances of anguish and desperation. Black life is the rich, colorful creativity that emerged and reemerges in the Black quest for human dignity. Jesus provides the necessary soul for liberation.[97]

The prophetic tradition likewise "empowers Black women to fashion a set of values on their own terms, as well as mastering, radicalizing, and sometimes destroying the pervasive negative orientations imposed by the larger society." The prophetic tradition also enables black women to "articulate possibilities for decisions and action which address forthrightly the circumstances that inescapably color and shape Black life. Black women serve as contemporary prophets, calling other women forth so that they can break away from the oppressive ideologies and belief systems that presume to define their reality."[98] As Grant summarizes, for black women:

> The understanding of God as the creator, sustainer, comforter, and liberator took on life as they agonized over their pain, and celebrated the hope that as God delivered the Israelites, they would be delivered as well. The God of the Old and New Testaments became real in the consciousness of oppressed Black women. Though they were politically impotent, they were able to appropriate certain themes of the Bible which spoke to their reality. . . . The Bible must be read and interpreted in the light of Black women's own experience of oppression and God's revelation within that context. . . . To do Womanist Theology, then, we must read and hear the Bible and engage it within the context of our own experience. This is the only way that it can make sense to people who are oppressed.[99]

SCRIPTURE AS THE MOTHER OF MODELS

Feminist theologians in the "reformist" stream wish to look to the Bible as "providing resources in the struggle for liberation from patriarchal oppression, as well as models for the transformation of the patriarchal church."[100] For this to occur, feminists reject the view of Scripture that sees the Bible as "some special canon of texts that can claim divine authority."[101] Rather, the Bible is viewed not as an "archetype"—as an ideal form that sets an unchanging, timeless pattern—but as a "prototype," as critically open to the possibility of its own transformation.[102] The Bible is "an open-ended paradigm that sets experiences in motion and invites transformations."[103]

For womanist theologians, the Bible is relied upon as a major resource because of its vision and the promise it holds for a world where a productive quality of life ("wholeness") will be a reality.[104] Womanist theology "engages in a liberationist hermeneutical interpretation of the Bible in spite of numerous voices from within and without the Christian tradition that have tried to equivocate on the biblical vision and promises made to oppressed and marginal persons and communities."[105]

Scripture is a "mother of models," for the Bible is "an instrument by which God shows women their true condition as people who are oppressed and yet who are given a vision of a different heaven and earth and a variety of models for how to live toward that vision."[106] This understanding does not identify biblical revelation with "androcentric texts." It maintains, rather, that "such revelation is found in the life and ministry of Jesus as well as in the discipleship community of equals called forth by him."[107] Scripture provides a place where the feminist critical consciousness may find congruence with certain of the biblical witnesses.

In the feminist and womanist approaches to Scripture, "many voices and many visions seek a biblical faith that brings wholeness and well-being."[108] Feminist and womanist theologians see their tasks of biblical interpretation as ongoing ones that to this point have only just begun. What, then, comes next? As Phyllis Trible has put it: "More work in exegesis and in the historical and social milieu of scripture; the expansion of the enterprise to welcome other women and men; and, perhaps, in God's good time, a biblical theology of womanhood."[109]

With moving narrative redescription, pastor Gail Ricciuti combines her personal experiences of tragedy with careful exegesis, in order to rescue Lot's wife from false traditions that punish her and her descendants. Then Jacqueline Carr-Hamilton adapts the theme of Cain Felder's book *Troubling Biblical Waters* into a sermon refrain, as she takes the liberation theme (when Moses "troubled the waters") in Scripture to new heights, by modeling elements of the black rhetorical style.

Salted and Holy (In Memory of Lot's Wife)

Gail A. Ricciuti

Genesis 19:15-29; Luke 19:41-44

> There is no fear in love, but perfect love casts out fear; for fear has to do with punishment, and whoever fears has not reached perfection in love. (1 John 4:18)

The moving van has pulled out of the driveway and lumbered off down the street toward the highways, the thruway entrances, the state lines that mark the way to your new home. The kids are corralled in the back seat of the car, the dog between them, along with pillows and snacks and favorite toys and the suitcases you'll live out of for a while. The windows of the house have been locked up one last time, and dust bunnies swept out of corners now nakedly exposed in the absence of the furniture. You look around, check around, just once more.

There's the bit of plaster chipped off the corner by the kitchen door, where someone bumped it with the Christmas tree stand years back . . . and the smallest room, where you laid the new baby, with crayon marks on the lower wall where she conducted her first art project . . . and the dogwood tree just out the back window over the kitchen

186

sink, the tree you contemplated so many thousands of times, dreamily or fretfully, with hands in dishwater.

And then, after this final circuit, you walk out the front door, almost ceremonially, and lock it (knowing just how hard to pull the loose doorknob in order to fit the dead bolt into its casing) and drop the key back through the mail slot, where you told the new people it would be when they arrive next week. Down the flagstones of the walk your feet know by heart . . . you slip behind the wheel, click in the seatbelt, turn the ignition, back into the quiet street. And just at the corner, just where one more turn of the wheel will put this street and this home behind you forever, what is the last thing you do?

"Lot's wife, behind him, looked back, and she became a pillar of salt." Sunday school always taught us not to be like Lot's wife—silly woman, disobedient woman, paying no attention to God's warning like that. She disobeyed, and so this unpredictable God, jealous even of her glance, turned her into a pillar of salt. Even modern commentaries like The Anchor Bible series observe: "Though the deserving minority proves to be in this instance too small to affect the fate of the sinful majority, the innocent, here *Lot and his daughters,* are ultimately spared."

But *wait:* What the cultures of patriarchy have said was *never* how the biblical story *read.* "She *became* a pillar of salt." Looking back upon the smashed possibilities of her ruined home, weeping in the desert sun, unable to staunch the bleeding of her heart, unable to ignore the human suffering, she became her tears. It was one of those moments when you think you will never stop crying.

I know her feeling. Almost a year after my cousin was murdered, just when I thought the heaviest grief was over, at breakfast one day I remembered him, such a wonderful, bright, and witty man . . . and looking back, I began to cry. I did not go to work that morning but wandered around the house, crying my heart out. It is a sign of our institutional preoccupation that while part of me said, "This is okay, let it happen," the other part was fretting, *"Presbytery* meets this afternoon! How can I go and moderate with my eyes all swollen?"

Looking back, being consumed have somehow gained moral overtones, as if it is weakness of character to feel too much. As children, my generation heard her story and sensed the danger. Practicing air raid drills in school hallways, we were reminded of residents of Hiroshima and Nagasaki who turned to look in the direction of the unearthly roar over their homes and were blinded, their eyes literally melted from their sockets by the heat and light.

So she makes us uncomfortable, like an ancient bag lady out there, wandering crazy-eyed and recalcitrant. The world is afraid of such "fierce tenderness," to use Mary Hunt's phrase. And yet we too are full of passion for our friends, *we* live in relationship, and we long not to commit the very offense for which the prophet Isaiah claimed Sodom was destroyed: turning away from suffering and need.

Was she punished for disobedience, as we have been taught? If so, well, look at Lot: bargaining with the angels not to have to walk so far, dragging his heels, so to speak, in leaving home. Lot hesitated when told to flee to the hills, dickered for an easier destination, argued to be allowed to stop on the plain ("This little town nearby, it's hardly anything: no big loss if You let it be."). The weary angels all but booted him out on the road, at last. But *he* was not punished.

187

And she, suntanned and strong-muscled from maintaining a household, *reached* Zoar, that "little thing," with him. It was not midway in the desert when she turned and wept!

If her offense was in looking back over the devastated city, consider that Abraham *too* surveyed the smoking ruins the next day, from a far hill. Abraham the patriarch, with promised descendants too many to be numbered, his gaze is intentionally noted as the climax of this episode of faith history. But *he* was not punished.

And if the ghastly symbol of her supposed transgression is so much salt, then follow the trail of "salt" throughout the sacred texts and discover that salt in all its uses is holy and valued: for healing, for covenanting, for blessing, for preserving, for zesting. "Have salt in yourselves," Jesus said. "You are the salt of the earth. . . . " Only *here*, in this single sentence of Genesis, this terse biography of one nameless woman, is saltiness considered horrifying.

Our very core is salt. The delicate saline balance in our veins sustains our heartbeat. Perhaps we must also claim our *spiritual* core as salt, that ability to weep with compassion but to be empowered rather than consumed by it. *These* tears must be understood as *creative,* not sacrificial. Letting yourself be touched to the core is a fearless act. But there is no fear in love, for fear has to do with punishment.

You see, our labor is only in order to bring birth; it is hard work, but it is not punishment or atonement. A contemporary rabbi said, "No woman is required to save the world by sacrificing herself." And in the poetry of Marge Piercy, a strong woman doesn't *mind* crying while she shovels out the cesspool of the ages!

There was Another who gazed across sand and Kidron cemetery and wept with womb-love at the city he saw there. And then what did he do? He went into its midst. Lot's wife is the archetype for Jesus' tears, and he the divine response to hers. As Rita Nakashima Brock has written: "No one else can stop the suffering of brokenheartedness in our world but our own courage and willingness to act in the midst of the awareness of our own fragility" (*Journeys by Heart,* 106).

But first, we look back, lest in forgetting our past we inherit no future. Some of us, looking behind us, see in that conflagration across the valley the church in which we came to faith, but now in the grip of retrenchment to an exclusionary "orthodoxy" and we hope that we *can* continue to move into the heart of it, reopening each door slammed summarily shut.

Some of us look back toward beloved homelands left years ago and wonder how our children will ever learn to sing their native song in this foreign culture.

Some of us look upon the spectacle of a Senate enraged by a woman's story of sexual harassment . . . responding with political posturing and turning judgment back upon the vulnerable. Some of us suddenly look back upon forgotten incest suffered as children, or the rape of our bodily integrity . . . and cry out.

And some of us, perhaps this very day, turn around and behold, with tears of anger, the loss of our theological and ethical "innocence."

Some days it feels as if our tears are running into our boots. They threaten to choke our hearts, to paralyze our finest impulses for change, to undo us. It is the price of attentive compassion that we will weep. But the tears cannot be allowed to be the last word about us.

I wonder whether Lot's wife would have been paralyzed if *sisters* had stood beside her. Marge Piercy writes: "Strong is what we make/each other. Until we are all strong together/a strong woman is a woman strongly afraid" ("For Strong Women," in *The Moon Is Always Female*, 56-57). *Love casts out fear.*

What of Lot's wife? I picture her moving into her old age, a tower of wisdom, making a crone of herself, her wounds becoming her strength. She goes into the centuries without a name, salt tears her only memorial. Today, let our claiming of our own saltiness be the living monument, not only to her, but to all those women in history who have purchased justice, struggled for liberation, and given birth to a new day with their blood and their tears.

Thank God the Scriptures have instructed us well. Now we know it is not Scripture, but *tradition* that has promoted such lies. I will no longer believe that the wife of Lot transgressed. To her, I say: You are free, my sister, from these centuries of entombment. You were not afraid to love. May *we* grow to be like you. Amen.

Troubling the Waters

Jacqueline D. Carr-Hamilton

Luke 18:1-6

Beloved, we take our text from the first six verses of the Gospel of Luke, the eighteenth chapter. The exegetical focus of this parable of Jesus is on a poor widow who continuously comes before an unjust male judge. Her one repeated cry being, "Avenge me of my adversary." Now the text does not say, but we can surely imagine the feeling of a single woman (unprotected by a husband) in a patriarchal culture who must prosecute her own case without the assistance of expert legal advice. And further, adding to her anxiety, she must have that case heard before a judge who neither "fears God, nor regards man."

Yet because of her faithful persistence, constantly "troubling the waters," working on the judge's last nerve, if you will, she in her own way simply wore him out: "Yet because this widow keeps bothering me, I will grant her justice, so that she may not wear me out by continually coming." And it is so characteristic of Jesus to focus on the plight of women as a reference for the kingdom of God, wrought through prayer, faith, and righteous retribution. An active stance in which one is not expected to bow passively before adversaries, but rather to stand and demand justice and righteousness without fainting, without giving up, until the barriers of oppression cease to stand.

Now, it does not take any great act of genius or specious revelation (especially in this instance) hermeneutically to apply this text to the situation of African-American women and our womanist or feminist struggles for liberation. Any honest look at the development of Black women in America and worldwide easily reveals a heritage of having to "trouble the waters" of interstructured oppression with respect to the simultaneous effects of racism, sexism, and classism on our lives globally.

Furthermore, how willing we are to take such a stance when we perceive that the source of unrighteousness is from without, in the dominant societal structures whether systemically or individually. Then our heritage reveals mass efforts through the NAACP, the civil rights movement, and the various Black women's movements. Then we have no problem with inclusion.

Yet when the adversary of unrighteousness confronts us from within, and especially from within the church, then we hypocritically become confused. Too often we allow ourselves to participate in oppression through a continued code of silence that supports the "man of God" (spiritually, economically, socially, and politically) while ignoring the needs of the "woman of God." We fall back on shallow excuses: "We know it's not quite right to refuse to ordain women and salary them as we do men, but after all the men are the pastors and the deacons . . . and don't worry because the Lord will make a way somehow." Silence without righteous confrontation permits oppression to continue to foster its seeds. Silence permits scriptural proof texts to be taken out of context and used as a means to discriminate against women, in the same way that Scripture was taken out of context to foster racism and slavery. It allows the egregious act of attributing the narrowmindedness of people to the divine attributes of God. It permits the misconception through language and biblical images of a God who only fathers us and never mothers us. We forget the prayers of our own ancestors and ancestresses: "God you have been a mother to me and a father to me . . . a sister and a brother." We forget the very examples of Jesus, who compared faith in the kingdom of God to a courageous poor widow who refuses to give up, but actively becomes our example through "troubling the waters."

Neither was she discouraged by the position of the judge. Obviously his legal veneer couldn't shake her faith and determination to pursue righteousness. She doesn't even have the benefit of a crowd or collective body of supporters, but singularly she stands and she demands. Singularly she lifts up a standard that ignores the religious legalists and busybodies.

Beloved, how tragic it is when the words of our spiritual African-American sister, Jarena Lee, in the early nineteenth centure (before AME Bishop Richard Allen, making a plea for a preaching license) ring just as true for so many women today. "O how careful ought we to be, lest through our by-laws of church government and discipline, we bring into disrepute even the word of life. For as unseemly as it may appear now-a-days for a woman to preach, it should be remembered that nothing is impossible with God. And why should it be thought impossible, heterodox, or improper, for a woman to preach, seeing that the Savior died for the woman as well as the man." How tragic when congregational majorities allow themselves to be ruled by the patriarchal despotism of minorities in the church and its related associations, thus allowing the troubling voices of prophecy to be shut up while everyone professes to be at ease in Zion, allowing cases like the arrest of the Reverend Lainie Dowell in Columbia, Maryland, (1992) for refusing to be railroaded into giving up her position in the Black Baptist Church. Cases that are just as disturbing as the efforts for desegregation and efforts for civil rights. These are cases that demand our attention and prophetic insistence for justice and righteousness within the church, as well as without. How separate are church and state?

And if in these causes we perish, someone has not been "troubling the waters"! If we fail to lift up our voices and actions in righteous indignation to demand "Avenge us of our adversaries," then we have failed to take an active part in the kingdom of God. Love and truthful confrontation go hand in hand. You see, it's what our sisters and mothers realized through civil rights struggles, "Our feets may be tired but our souls gonna be at rest." It's what Rosa Parks meant when she refused to give up her seat. Troubling the waters.

And with Sister Rosa's troubling, the whole infrastructure of desegregation came tumbling down! Why would it be any less in society than in the church when Jesus has already given a clear mandate by precept and example? Beloved, we're not tired yet! We're gonna keep on walking, marching, and talking! We're gonna keep on praying, demanding and standing. "Avenge us of our adversaries" until the whole infrastructure of gender oppression in church and society (as with racisim and classism) comes tumbling down! Troubling the waters!

The songwriter says "I don't feel noways tired (Come on Somebody) . . . I've come too far back from where I've started from. . . . Nobody told me that the road would be easy but I don't believe . . . just won't believe that God brought me this far to ever leave me!"

AFTERWORD

THE DIFFERENT THEOLOGICAL VIEWS JUST PRESENTED ARE ALL CURRENT OPTIONS ON the contemporary theological scene. They all have adherents who perceive the Bible in the ways portrayed. While it may seem that such views can coexist together, there have often been severe theological struggles between devotees of the different positions. Since the issue of the nature of Scripture is so basic theologically, the importance of the stance adopted is great. Because a view of Scripture is so foundational to a theological system, it can have tremendous effects throughout the spectrum of one's whole theological beliefs. Often these consequences are hidden, because they flow so naturally from the position on Scripture. Yet the results are significant on a wide range of theological topics. As one views what is said about a theological topic, one can push back to the presuppositions about Scripture undergirding the assertions. While differences on what is said about Scripture can appear slight, they often go on to have important consequences when specific issues or topics are addressed.

Contemporary controversies over the nature of Scripture have dramatically affected a number of church denominations in America. Among these are Lutheran, Presbyterian, and Southern Baptist.[1] Many of these controversies have been of long standing. Views of Scripture, of how the Bible has authority, how it functions, and how it is to be interpreted have played major roles in what some today see as the division of American religion into equal camps of "conservative" and "liberal."[2] This division, it is argued, now crosses denominational lines.[3] Thus it is not surprising to read that "in the fall of 1989, approximately one hundred fifty people gathered at Christian Theological Seminary in Indianapolis to hear eleven speakers, representing seven different denominations or traditions, discuss the nature of biblical authority."[4] The ongoing questions are persistent. The nature and authority of Scripture continue both to unite and to divide groups of people.

On the academic theological scene, issues continue to be debated by professional theologians and biblical scholars. The theological positions outlined in the preceding chapters are not the only ones existent. Nor are the identifications of these positions or their descriptors ("bumper stickers") the only ways to perceive and group the plethora of current viewpoints. There are other ways to "slice the pie" or discern models about the nature of Scripture. A number of scholars have written about the contemporary landscape and offered their views on how the prevailing panorama can be construed.

One of the earliest writers to do this was David H. Kelsey. His work *The Uses of Scripture in Recent Theology* identified ways in which theologians have appealed to Scripture as a functioning authority. These include the appeal to Scripture's doctrines, concepts, narrative, presentation of the identity of an agent, images, symbols, and Scripture's presentation of a form of self-understanding.[5] Each position is presented through the lens of a theologian who perceives Scripture to function in these ways.

Kelsey organized his work around the responses of seven theologians to a basic question: "1. What aspect(s) of scripture is (are) taken to be authoritative? Is it the concepts in scripture, or the doctrines, or the historical reports, or the liturgical utterances, or the 'symbols,' or some combination of these, or something else?"[6]

The responses of the theologians broke into three streams: doctrinal or conceptual; recital or narrative; mythic, symbolic, or imagistic expression of a saving event. In the course of each of the three chapters highlighting these approaches, three further questions were posed:

> 2. What is it about this aspect of scripture that makes it authoritative?
> 3. What sort of logical force seems to be ascribed to the scripture to which appeal is made? Has it the force of a descriptive report, of an injunction, of an emotive ejaculation; is it self-involving?
> 4. How is the scripture that is cited brought to bear on theological proposals so as to authorize them?[7]

Kelsey does not claim that the theologians use Scripture exclusively in these ways nor that these are typologies that are exhaustive. He sees this way of understanding to be "a series of illustrations of the diverse ways in which biblical writings can be construed when taken as authority for theological proposals."[8]

Representatives of Kelsey's views are as follows: Doctrinal and Conceptual—in which either doctrine or biblical concepts are perceived as authoritative—B. B. Warfield (doctrine) and W. W. Bartsch (concepts).[9] Recital and Presence representatives—in which it is "the story rendering an agent" that makes Scripture authoritative—are G. Ernest Wright (narrative) and Karl Barth (rendering identity of an agent). Those representing Event and Expression—in which Scripture is perceived as linking humans with revelatory events—are: L. S. Thornton (image and mystery), Paul Tillich (symbol and miracle), and Rudolf Bultmann (myth and eschaton).

Kelsey's work has been important in focusing on the relationship between how Scripture is perceived as authoritative and how it is used. His illustrations from the seven theologians, and his groupings of the "construals" by each are meant to show "what theologians are actually doing as they pursue their craft."[10] Kelsey has helped to show the varieties of approaches to Scripture and also presuppositions behind them. In addition, he has highlighted the intrinsic relationship between what is said about the "nature" of Scripture and how the Scriptures "function" in one's theology.[11]

Another major work that compares contemporary views of Scripture is Avery Dulles's *Models of Revelation* (1983). Dulles had earlier written an influential work on ecclesiology entitled *Models of the Church* (1974) using "models" to typologize the various currents of ecclesiological thought. In *Models of Revelation,* Dulles employed the same approach to "classify the main varieties of revelation theology." His focus is on "the structural features of the systems." In Dulles's view, contemporary systems "may be divided into five major classes according to their central vision of how and where revelation occurs."[12] Since God's revelation includes revelation in Scripture according to Christian theology, Dulles's work has a heavy focus on what each view has to say about what the Bible is and how it functions. Yet, since "revelation" is wider than Scripture alone, his work also deals with significant theological statements about such topics as God, Christ, authority, grace, faith, and experience. The second part of the book is devoted to Dulles's development of his own view called "symbolic mediation."[13]

Before capsulizing his descriptions of the five types, Dulles indicates how he came to the groupings he did. He wrote:

> Inasumuch as the types are free theological constructions one cannot give definitive status to any given typology. Most typologies are empirically based in the sense of being derived from actual cases rather than aprioristic considerations. One notes that theologians wrestling with similar questions can be classified in groups according to the answers they give, not only to individual questions but to a whole series of questions, as a result of a certain mindset. The theologians thus fall into clusters with certain common characteristics. Although every major type can be broken down into smaller sub-types, it is usually desirable, in an initial exposition, to propose a relatively small number of types, all of which can be kept simultaneously in mind. The typology will be more successful if the types are sharply delineated, so that their differences are evident, and if each is capable of being characterized by a single orientation or metaphor that gives the key to the positions taken on a larger number of questions.[14]

Throughout his expositions, Dulles interacts each model with the others and assesses their strengths and weaknesses.[15]

Dulles's five models are: (1) Revelation as Doctrine, where "revelation is principally found in clear propositional statements attributed to God as authoritative teacher." Protestants usually identify revelation with the Bible, which is seen as a collection of inspired and inerrant teachings. Roman Catholic adherents connect revelation with official church teachings viewed as "God's infallible oracle."[16] Protestant representatives fall in the category of "conservative evangelicalism" with their primary inspiration the Old Princeton theologian B. B. Warfield. These include Gordon H. Clark, James I. Packer, John Warwick Montgomery, and Carl F. H. Henry.[17] A similar view is found within Roman Catholic neo-Scholasticism (1850–1950) in authors such as Reginald Garrigou-Lagrange, Christian Pesch, and Hermann Dieckmann, as well as in conciliar documents from Vatican I (1870), Vatican anti-Modernist documents (1907–10) and Pope Pius XII's encyclical letter *Humani generis* (1950).

(2) Revelation as History maintains that God is revealed through the great acts of God, which form biblical history's major themes. Scripture and church teaching embody revelation to the degree they are reliable reports of God's actions. They "witness" to revelation.[18] Leading proponents are: G. Ernest Wright, Oscar Cullmann, Jean Daniélou, and Wolfhart Pannenberg. This model is characteristic of the "biblical theology" movement. A major distinction between Wright and Cullmann and Pannenberg, however, is that while Wright and Cullmann speak of God's

revelation as focused on "salvation history," for Pannenberg, revelation is found in universal history.[19]

(3) Revelation as Inner Experience is a theological model that rejects both objective truths and events of history as the nature of revelation but sees it instead as an interior, personal experience of communion with God. This is a direct, mystical encounter with God (through Christ, for some theologians).[20] Among those who fit this model are liberal Protestant theologians such as Friedrich Schleiermacher, Albrecht Ritschl, Wilhelm Herrmann, and Auguste Sabatier. Early twentieth-century Roman Catholic Modernists, such as George Tyrrell and Baron Friedrich von Hügel, fit this mystical model as well. In later times, Anglicans such as Evelyn Underhill and Dean W. R. Inge, as well as the Swedish Lutheran Nathan Söderblom and the idealist William Ernest Hocking, emphasized revelation as occurring in mystical experience. The biblical scholars H. Wheeler Robinson and C. H. Dodd (early works) also represent this aspect, according to Dulles. Among current writers, the English Protestant John Hick is cited as well as mid-twentieth century Catholic transcendental theology represented by Karl Rahner's system of "transcendental revelation" and Piet Fransen's view that inner experience is where revelation concretely occurs.[21]

(4) Revelation as Dialectical Presence is a mark of "Neo-orthodoxy" as developed in Europe after World War I (see chap 6 above). The utterly transcendent God is seen as encountering human subjects by means of "God's Word," which is recognized as such by faith. God's "word" both reveals and conceals God's presence—giving credence to the term "dialectical presence."[22] Leading representatives, according to Dulles, were Karl Barth, Emil Brunner, and Rudolf Bultmann. Later "word-theologians" include Ernst Fuchs, Gerhard Ebeling, and Eberhard Jüngel.

(5) Revelation as New Awareness has emerged as a type of revelatory model since the middle of the twentieth century. Theologians typifying this model hold that "revelation takes place as an expansion of consciousness or shift of perspective when people join in the movements of secular history." Here, God is "mysteriously present as the transcendent dimension of human engagement in creative tasks."[23] The theologians here deny there are revealed "truths" and seek meaning as found by the illumination of experience as the hallmark of "revelation." Rooted in the subjective idealism of the nineteenth century, twentieth-century representatives include Paul Tillich, Gregory Baum, Leslie Dewart, Gabriel Moran, Ray L. Hart, and William M. Thompson.[24]

Quite helpful in Dulles's book *Models of Revelation* is his chapter "The Bible: Document of Revelation." In it he assesses how each of the models sees the relationship between the Bible and revelation. Succinctly, Dulles asks:

> Is the Bible a divinely authoritative book, propositionally containing God's very word (Model one)? Does it give access to events in which revelation is signified (Model two)? Does it express and induce immediate experiences of the divine in the depths of the human psyche (Model three)? Does it simultaneously reveal and conceal the God to whom it bears witness in fallible human language (Model four)? Or does it provide paradigms that enable us to interpret our own history and situation in the light of God's plan and purposes (Model five)?[25]

Dulles's own answer is in terms of his "symbolic mediation" view of revelation. For him, "God communicates both through symbolic realities and through the inspired images whereby believers express the meaning they have found in those realities."[26] This insight he sees as necessary correctives to the deficiencies of each of the models so that "by adverting to the symbolic character of revelation we may find it possible to escape certain dilemmas and overcome certain clashes among the models."[27]

Dulles's work provides an elaborate and sophisticated set of models for identifying contemporary views of Scripture. By focusing on the theological category of "revelation" he differs from Kelsey, who asks what makes Scripture an "authority." This also enables Dulles to widen the scope of issues with which he deals so he can helpfully show the implications of a revelation-model for questions of Christology, ecclesiology, world religions, eschatology, and the like. The Bible is a major dimension of this study of revelation, hence its usefulness for determining views of the nature of Scripture. Dulles's work differs from the present work in not accounting for Process, Story, Liberation, and Feminist theologies, in providing less detailed analysis on Scripture views themselves and in not tracing historical developments of theological movements or how they are expressed in preaching. But his work is an outstanding "model" of a comparative approach enhanced by his own interaction with the views he presents as well as the explication of his own.

A very useful book focused directly on the issue of the nature of Scripture is Robert Gnuse's *The Authority of the Bible: Theories of Inspiration, Revelation and the Canon of Scripture* (1985). With detailed documentation and nearly twenty pages of bibliography, Gnuse looks at five categories of models for the authority of Scripture. These are Inspiration (with chapters on strict verbal inspiration, limited verbal inspiration, non-textual inspiration, and social inspiration), Salvation History, Existentialism, Christocentric Models, and Models of Limited Authority. Each category is subdivided throughout. Gnuse focuses most strongly on "inspiration" because, he says, "it has received the greatest attention in the greater Christian tradition."[28]

Inspiration. As an extensive guide to the literature on each position, Gnuse's work is excellent. The strict verbal inspiration view, which holds that the text of Scripture is directly and divinely inspired, includes the positions delineated as Fundamentalism and Scholastic Theology above.

Limited Verbal inspiration adherents include many Protestant Evangelicals (see "Neo-Evangelical Theology," chap. 7 above) and "Roman Catholic positions on verbal inspiration in the nineteenth and twentieth centuries." This view is described as believing that the words of Scripture are communicated by God but are "historically conditioned or accommodated."

Non-Textual inspiration shifts attention away from the biblical text itself and suggests that only the ideas of Scripture or its message is inspired while others would limit inspiration only to the experience of the biblical authors (see "Liberal Theology," chap. 3 above).

Social inspiration refers to the view that it is the community as a whole and not individual writers who have been given the gift of "inspiration."[29]

Salvation History. Over against views of the Bible as containing "inspired" ideas or propositions, some twentieth-century biblical scholars proposed understanding the central message of the Bible and the locus of Scripture's authority to be in its account of God's salvific events. Major Scripture scholars such as George Ernest Wright,

Reginald Fuller, Oscar Cullmann, John Bright, and Paul Minear have pointed to Scripture's role as the testimony to God's gracious actions in history as the locus for its authority.[30]

Existentialism. Shifting away from biblical texts or history as the source for Scripture's authority, the existential mode focuses on the individual's response and acceptance to the written or preached word of God. Gnuse groups Karl Barth and Rudolf Bultmann together as leading models of existential interpretation or "the theology of personal encounter" (see "Neo-Orthodox Theology," chap. 6 above). These two represent "classic existentialism," while Paul Tillich (see chap. 8 above) represents "symbolic existentialism."

Christocentric Models. Those who select a part of the biblical text or an important theological concept to serve as a norm by which to intepret the rest of the Bible and by which Scripture thus gains authority Gnuse describes as using a Christocentric model. He cites Martin Luther as using this christological principle, as well as Karl Barth, whose views are paralleled by P. T. Forsyth, Friedrich Gogarten, Hubert Cunliffe-Jones, J. K. S. Reid, C. H. Dodd, and George Tavard. As an exponent of the doctrine of justification by faith as a norm, Gnuse cites the work of Ernst Käsemann.[31]

Models of Limitation. To declare the Bible should not be given such a prominent place as other views contend is characteristic of a range of writers Gnuse considers under this model. "Open canon" advocates claim all authority belongs to Christ and no limits on the particular documents to be received (as with the church's acceptance of a "canon") should be imposed. Some also have sought to limit biblical authority in order to elevate other "authorities" to an equal or greater status. Examples here include pre-modern Roman Catholics, who sought to limit the Protestant emphasis on *sola scriptura*, as well as Protestants influenced by Romanticism and the place of human experience—such as Schleiermacher, J. G. Herder, J. D. Michaelis, and J. J. Griesbach.[32] Some contemporary scholars note the diverse theological traditions in Scripture and argue that these demand a limit on the Bible's authority. Others emphasize awareness of all sources for theology. They claim Scripture takes its place along with other intellectual and cultural presuppositions as norms of authority. Gnuse here mentions "phenomenological theologians" who are "particularly concerned with groundsweeping so as to begin reconstruction of theology in balanced fashion on these norms."[33]

Two chapters conclude his book: "Historical Emergence of the Authoritative Bible" on the rise of the canon and "Ecumenical Discussion of Scripture and Tradition." By focusing particularly on Scripture and delineating especially the varieties among views stressing the inspiration of Scripture as a category, Gnuse has given a detailed road map to current views (exclusive of Process, Liberation, and Feminist thought). He indicates that he has not sought to be "theologically profound" in his analysis, but to be "comprehensive in scope" and provide an easily accessible text for interested students.[34] In this, Gnuse has well succeeded.

The three books just mentioned have laid out contemporary views with some comparisons among them. One other typology of approaches to Scripture has recently been offered by William C. Placher. He wrote an essay introducing the papers from the 1989 conference at the Christian Theological Seminary.[35] Here he suggested that the terms *conservative, moderate*, and *liberal*, often used to described views of biblical authority, are essentially political terms and embody "some deep mistakes," for "it is dangerous to continue to think that the only question to ask about the authority of scripture is 'how much authority?' " Instead, Placher contends, "There are different ways of thinking about the Bible as authoritative that we cannot rank on a single scale—not less authority or more, but just different, functioning as authority in different ways."[36]

Drawing on Kelsey's work, Placher proposes three models of how the Bible functions as authority in Christianity: (1) as a set of true propositions; (2) as a transforming word; or (3) as the narrative of God's identity.[37] Placher cites Charles Hodge and Clark Pinnock as proponents of the first view.[38] The desert father Anthony, St. Augustine, Albert Schweitzer, and Rudolf Bultmann are examples of the second model as well as "existential" theologians such as Kierkegaard, Paul Tillich, and current liberation theologians.[39] The third view is indebted to Karl Barth through the work of two Yale University scholars, Hans Frei and George Lindbeck.[40] Placher believes people will find Scripture functioning in each of three ways and that each approach has something to learn from the others.[41] While Placher's analysis is not extensive, he has helpfully focused on three major motifs and given a useful broad-brush outline for each.

Emergent trends in biblical studies and theology will produce new models or paradigms about the nature of Scripture. Sustained attention to the text of Scripture in the current day, along with the development of new hermeneutical approaches influenced by varying disciplines, means that issues dealt with in this book will continue to provoke disagreement and discussion in both church and academy.[42] Unfortunately, at times these controversies will be devisive. One can only hope, however, that churches will heed this counsel from an ecclesiastical document: "The Church needs always to remember that the use of Holy Scripture is more important than debates about its authority."[43] As conversations continue, both the use of Scripture and its nature will be considered, for these issues are crucial to Christian theology and to Christian faith. Thus we can fully expect to observe ongoing discussions of what Christians believe about the Bible.

NOTES

1. ROMAN CATHOLICISM

1. The primary source for many Roman Catholic documents in their original languages is *Enchiridion Symbolorum, Definitionum, et Declarationum de Rebus Fidei et Morum*, eds. H. Denzinger and A. Schonmetzer, 32nd ed. (Freiburg: Herder, 1963); hereafter cited as *DS*. In English, a most helpful collection is *Bible Interpretation*, ed. James J. Megivern, Official Catholic Teachings Series (Wilmington, N.C.: Consortium Books, 1978). The documents of Vatican II are translated into English in *The Documents of Vatican II*, ed. and trans. W. M. Abbott and J. Gallagher (New York: America Press, 1966).

2. See the relevant sections in Megivern, *Bible Interpretation*.

3. See Avery Dulles, "The Authority of Scripture: A Catholic Perspective," *Scripture in the Jewish and Christian Traditions: Authority, Interpretation, Relevance*, ed. Frederick E. Greenspahn (Nashville: Abingdon, 1982), 16.

4. Ibid., 17.

5. Ibid., 16.

6. Cited in Jaroslav Pelikan, *The Emergence of the Catholic Tradition (100-600)*, The Christian Tradition: A History of the Development of Doctrine (Chicago: University of Chicago Press, 1971), 333. The Latin is *ubique, semper, ab omnibus*.

7. Ibid., 333.

8. Ibid., 334.

9. See Geoffrey W. Bromiley, ed., "Authority," *The International Standard Bible Encyclopedia*, 4 vols. (Grand Rapids: Eerdmans, 1979), I:366; hereafter cited as *ISBE*.

10. On these, see standard histories of the early church and early Christian doctrine. Of particular note are Pelikan, *Emergence*; J. N. D. Kelly, *Early Christian Doctrines*, rev. ed. (New York: Harper & Row, 1978); and the classic work by Adolf von Harnck, *History of Dogma*, trans. Neil Buchanan, 7 vols. (New York: Dover, 1961).

11. *Paradosis*, the Greek word for "transmission" or "that which is transmitted," orally is used positively in the New Testament for Christian traditions in 1 Cor. 11:2 and 2 Thess. 2:15; 3:6. See also 1 Cor. 11:23 and 15:3. See *Teaching Authority & Infallibility in the Church:Lutherans and Catholics in Dialogue VI*, eds. Paul C. Empie, T. Austin Murphy, and Joseph A. Burgess (Minneapolis: Augsburg, 1978), 300 n. 24.

12. See R. P. C. Hanson, *Tradition in the Early Church* (Philadelphia: Westminster, 1963), 7ff.

13. See J. C. Turro and R. E. Brown, "Canonicity," *The Jerome Biblical Commentary*, eds. R. E. Brown, J. A. Fitzmyer, and R. E. Murphy (Englewood Cliffs, N.J.: Prentice-Hall, 1968), no. 67; and F. F. Bruce, *Tradition: Old and New* (Grand Rapids: Zondervan, 1970).

14. G. L. Robinson and R. K. Harrison, "Canon of the OT," in *ISBE* I:598. See also Kelly, *Doctrines*, 52.

15. The interpretation of the Old Testament from a Christian perspective is a recurrent issue in the history of exegesis. Of particular interest as formative influences are the ways the Old Testament was interpreted by Jesus, Paul, and the New Testament writers. See Robert M. Grant, "Jesus and the Old Testament" and "Paul and the Old Testament" as well as C. K. Barrett, "The Interpretation of the Old Testament in the New,"

in *The Authoritative Word: Essays on the Nature of Scripture*, ed. Donald K. McKim (Grand Rapids: Eerdmans, 1983), chaps. 2, 3, and 4.

16. F. F. Bruce, "Tradition and the Canon of Scripture," from *Tradition: Old and New*. Cited in McKim, *Authoritative Word*, 62-63.

17. On the New Testament canon, see R. P. Meye, "Canon of the NT" in *ISBE*, I:601-6; Kelly, *Doctrines*, 56-60; Werner Georg Kummel, *Introduction to the New Testament*, trans. Howard C. Kee, rev. English ed. (Nashville: Abingdon, 1975), Part II; Bruce, "Tradition" in McKim, *Authoritative Word*, 68-76; and Hanson, *Tradition in the Early Church*, chap. 5.

18. See Hanson, *Tradition in the Early Church*, chap. 5, and Kümmel, *Introduction to the New Testament*, 484ff., for a full discussion.

19. See Bruce, "Tradition," in McKim, *Authoritative Word*, 75. See also the discussion in Carl A. Volz, *Faith and Practice in the Early Church: Foundations for Contemporary Theology* (Minneapolis: Augsburg, 1983), 138-44.

20. See C. H. Dodd, *The Apostolic Preaching and Its Development* (London: Hodder & Stoughton, 1936); J. N. D. Kelly, *Early Christian Creeds*, 3rd ed. (London: Longmans, Green & Co., 1972); Hanson, *Tradition in the Early Church*, chap. 1.

21. See Kelly, *Creeds* and A. S. Wood, "Creeds and Confessions" in *ISBE*, I:805-12.

22. Irenaeus, *Against Heresis*, I.1.20. Cited in Hanson, *Tradition in the Early Church*, 75. The Greek phrase is *kanōon tēs alētheias*.

23. See Hanson, *Tradition in the Early Church*, 77.

24. Ibid., 128.

25. The Nicene Creed came to its present form at the Council of Constantinople in 381. Thus the familiar creed is actually the Niceo-Constantinopolitan Creed. See Kelly *Doctrines*, chap. IX.

26. See Kelly, *Creeds*, and Jack Rogers, *Presbyterian Creeds: A Guide to the Book of Confessions* (Philadelphia: Westminster, 1985), chap. 4.

27. See "Common Statement" in *Teaching Authority*, 19, and Volz, *Faith and Practice in the Early Church*, 160-70.

28. "Common Statement" in *Teaching Authority*, 20.

29. Ibid., 21.

30. Ibid.

31. See Volz, *Faith and Practice in the Early Church*, 173. Stephen I (254–257) was seemingly the first bishop of Rome to assert that he held the see of Peter by succession. See *Teaching Authority*, 301 n. 37; Geoffrey Barraclough, *The Medieval Papacy*, History of European Civilization Library, ed. Geoffrey Barraclough (Norwich, Eng.: Harcourt, Brace & World, 1968), chap. 1; and Robert B. Eno, "Some Elements in the Pre-History of Papal Infallibility" in *Teaching Authority*, 238-58.

32. See Barraclough's "Bibliographical Notes," 197-205 for reference works on the history of the papacy.

33. Pelikan, *Emergence*, 352.

34. Epistle *In requirendis* (Dss 217); E. Giles, *Documents Illustrating Papal Authority* (London: SPCK, 1952), 201. Cited in "Common Statement" in *Teaching Authority*, 21.

35. *DS* 363. Cited in "Common Statement" in *Teaching Authority*, 21.

36. Gregory the Great, *Epistles* 5.37. Cited in Pelikan, *Emergence*, 352. See also Jaroslav Pelikan, *Reformation of Church and Dogma (1300-1700)*, The Christian Tradition: A History of the Development of Doctrine (Chicago: University of Chicago Press, 1984), 114ff. for examples of later exegesis of the Matthew 16:18 passage.

37. Cited in Jaroslav Pelikan, *The Growth of Medieval Theology (600-1300)*, The Christian Tradition: A History of the Development of Doctrine (Chicago: University of Chicago Press, 1978), 47.

38. Ibid., 48. Leo I (440–461) was the first to use the term *pontifex maximus* to refer to the bishop of Rome.

39. Ibid.

40. On this period, see Barraclough and Maurice Keen, *The Pelican History of Medieval Europe* (Middlesex, Eng.: Penguin Books, 1969), Section One.

41. See Barraclough, *The Medieval Papacy*, 77ff.; Keen, *The Pelican History of Medieval Europe*, 77-80 n. 41. Jeffrey Burton Russell, *A History of Medieval Christianity: Prophecy and Order* (New York: Thomas Y. Crowell Co., 1968), chap. 10, speaks of "The Offensive of the Papacy" in the twelfth and thirteenth centuries. See also Steven Ozment, *The Age of Reform 1250–1550: An Intellectual and Religious History of Late Medieval and Reformation Europe* (New Haven, Conn.: Yale University Press, 1980), 141-43.

42. Barraclough, *The Medieval Papacy*, 113.

43. Cited in Ozment, *The Age of Reform,* 143. Ozment notes that "in canon law 'plenitude of power' (*plenitudo potestatis*) was something the head of a corporation derived from the corporation members and exercised only in conjunction with them, not an all-embracing authority conferred on the pope directly by God." He cites Brian Tierney, *Foundations of the Concilar Theory: The Contribution of the Medieval Canonists from Gratian to the Great Schism* (Cambridge: Cambridge University Press, 1955), 141-53.

44. On this history, see the works of Barraclough, Keen, and Ozment.

45. See Ozment, *The Age of Reform,* chap. 5: "On the Eve of the Reformation."

46. Dulles, "Authority," 18.

47. See Megivern, *Bible Interpretation,* 48, for the Council of Hippo (393).

48. See ibid., 175, for the Council of Florence and 180 for the Council of Trent.

49. Ibid., 191.

50. Dulles, "Authority," 18.

51. Ibid., 19.

52. On this see R. H. Pfeiffer, "Canon of the OT," and F. W. Beare, "Canon of the NT," in *The Interpreter's Dictionary of the Bible,* ed. George A. Buttrick, 4 vols. (Nashville: Abingdon, 1962), I:499-32.

53. See Dulles, "Authority," 21-22.

54. Among other sources, see Bruce Vawter, *Biblical Inspiration,* Theological Resources, eds. John P. Wahlen and Jaroslav Pelikan (Philadelphia: Westminster, 1972), hereafter cited as *BI*; and Louis Alonso Schökel, *The Inspired Word: Scripture in the Light of Language and Literature,* trans. Francis Martin (New York: Herder and Herder, 1972).

55. Megivern, *Bible Interpretation,* 175 (*DS* 1334). Vawter notes that it is here that "the term 'inspire' first entered into conciliar language," *BI* 70. See also *Statuta Ecclesiae Antiqua* (*DS* 325).

56. Megivern, *Bible Interpretation,* 191 (*DS* 3006; See also 3029).

57. Ibid., 191, see also 178. See Vawter's discussion, *BI* 70ff.

58. On the various notions of the meaning of *author* for Vatican I, see Schökel, *The Inspired Word,* 77ff., and Vawter, *BI* 70-71.

59. Megivern, *Bible Interpretation,* 216 (*DS* 3293).

60. Ibid., 215.

61. Vawter, *BI* 74, 138. See the discussion by Raymond E. Brown, *The Critical Meaning of the Bible* (New York: Paulist Press, 1981), 14ff. Vawter and Brown point out that in Brown's words, "Already in 1893 Pope Leo XIII in *Providentissimus Deus* (DBS 3288) excluded natural or scientific matters from biblical inerrancy, even if he did this through the expedient of insisting that statements made about nature according to ordinary appearances were not erorrs" (15). (An example might involve the sun going around the earth.) Vawter notes that formulation could be traced "all the way back to Aquinas and Augustine" (121; citing Augustine, *Gen. ad. litt.* 2.9, *Patrologia Latina 34:270; Aquinas, Summa Theologiae,* Ia 70.1 ad3). Leo had further stated that the same principles "will apply to cognate sciences, and especially to history" (see Megivern, *Bible Interpretation,* 214; *DS* 3290). See also Bruce Vawter, "The Bible in the Roman Catholic Church," in *Scripture in the Jewish and Christian Traditions,* 124.

Brown goes on to note that "thirty years later Pope Benedict XV attempted to close this door in *Spiritus Paraclitus* (1920) when he stated that one could not apply universally to the historical portions of the Scriptures the principles that Leo XIII had laid down for scientific matters, namely, that the authors were writing only according to appearances (DBS 3653)," 15.

62. *Dei Verbum* 11 in Megivern, *Bible Interpretation,* 409.

63. Dulles, "Authority," 23.

64. Ibid., 23.

65. Ibid., 24.

66. *Dei Verbum* 11 in Megivern, *Bible Interpretation,* 409.

67. See Vawter, *BI* 147, for a discussion of the various drafts of the Vatican II document on Scripture. See also Avery Dulles, "Scripture: Recent Protestant and Catholic Views," in McKim, *The Authoritative Word,* 246-48.

68. Vawter, *BI* 147. For interpretations of *Dei Verbum* on inerrancy, see A. Grillmeier, "The Divine Inspiration and Interpretation of Sacred Scripture," *Commentary on the Documents of Vatican II,* ed. H. Vorgrimler, trans. W. Glen-Doepel et al. (New York: Herder and Herder, 1968), III:199-246; N. Lohfink, "The Truth of the Bible and Historicity," *Theology Digest* (1967): 26-29; and Brown, *The Critical Meaning of the Bible,* 18-19.

69. Brown, *The Critical Meaning of the Bible,* 19, further notes that "in the inerrancy question Vatican II assumes as *a priori* that God wants the salvation of His people. The extent to which truth in Scripture conforms to that purpose is an *a posteriori* issue." The question of the nature of "truth" is also important

here. Vawter maintains that "the concept of biblical inerrancy is not to be confused with the venerable Jewish and Christian affirmation that the Bible is the true Word of God communicated without falsehood. *Falsehood,* not *error,* is the antinomy of the *truth* of the Bible that was sustained by the Fathers and the theologians of the medieval church." See Vawter, "Bible," 128, and *BI* 132ff., where he writes, while discussing Oswald Loretz, *The Truth of the Bible* (New York: Herder and Herder, 1968), that "the root idea of Biblical truth is thus reliability, permanency, steadfastness. Its opposite is not error, but deliberate *lying"* (150). Vawter states: "The fact is that in no council of the Universal Church, either before or after the Reformation, has the formula of inerrancy been applied to the Bible." See "Bible," 130.

70. For discussions of Roman Catholic biblical studies, see James T. Burtchaell, *Catholic Theories of Biblical Inspiration Since 1810* (Cambridge: Cambridge University Press, 1969); Vawter, *BI* chap. 5: "Inspiration and Contemporary Thinking"; Brown, *The Critical Meaning of the Bible,* chaps. 1–4; and Megivern, *Bible Interpretation,* Introduction. Pope Pius XII's encyclical *Divino Afflante Spiritu* (September 30, 1943) on "The Most Opportune Way to Promote Biblical Studies" [see Megivern, *Bible Interpretation,* 316-42] has been called *l'encyclique liberatrice* ("the encyclical of freedom"), because it gives recognition to the literary forms of Scripture (see *BI* 125). It marked "an undeniable about-face in attitude toward biblical criticism. The encyclical . . . instructed Catholic scholars to use the methods of a scientific approach to the Bible that had hitherto been forbiden to them." (Raymond E. Brown, *Biblical Reflection on Crises Facing the Church* [New York: Paulist Press, 1975], 6-7. Cited in Megivern, *Bible Interpretation,* xxv.

One of the major Roman Catholic theologians of the twentieth century whose views cannot be dealt with here is Karl Rahner (1904–1984). Among his numerous works, see *Inspiration in the Bible,* trans. W. J. O'Hara (New York: Herder and Herder, 1964); and for his position after Vatican II: "Bible. I.B. Theology," *Encyclopedia of Theology: The Concise "Sacramentum Mundi"* (New York: Herder and Herder, 1975), 99-108. On Rahner, see Dulles, "Scripture," 243-45.

71. Heiko Augustinus Oberman, *The Harvest of Medieval Theology: Gabriel Biel and Late Medieval Nominalism,* rev. ed. (Grand Rapids: Eerdmans, 1967), 6. Oberman calls these "Tradition I" and "Tradition II." See 371.

72. Ibid., 372.

73. Ibid., 372. This is the stream in which John Wycliffe (1330?–1384) stands.

74. Pelikan, *Reformation,* 119.

75. From Occam, *Dialogue* 1.2.2. Cited in Pelikan, *Reformation,* 120.

76. Oberman, *The Harvest of Medieval Theology,* 380, see also 381. Occam's nominalist philosophy shows here. See Jack B. Rogers and Donald K. McKim, *The Authority and Interpretation of the Bible: An Historical Approach* (San Francisco: Harper & Row, 1979), 48ff. on Occam.

77. In this stream, Oberman names Occam, Pierre d'Ailly (d. 1420) and Jean Charlier de Gerson (d. 1429).

78. Pelikan, *Reformation,* pp. 120-21.

79. Ibid., 122.

80. Augustine, *Against the Epistle of Manicheus Called Fundamental, 5 (Corpus scriptorum ecclesias-ticorum latinorum* [Vienna, 1866], 25, 197); Biel, *In Defense of Apostolic Obedience.* Cited in Pelikan, *Reformation,* 125.

81. Vawter, "Scripture," 119 (*DS* 1501). On the proceedings of Trent on this topic, see George H. Tavard, *Holy Writ or Holy Church: The Crisis of the Protestant Reformation* (New York: Harper and Bros., 1959), chap. 12. The standard history of the Council of Trent is Hubert Jedin, *A History of the Council of Trent,* trans. Ernest Graf (London: Nelson, 1961). See also *The Canons and Decrees of the Council of Trent,* trans. H. J. Schroeder, 2 vols. (St. Louis: Herder, 1941).

82. Tavard, *Holy Writ or Holy Church,* 208. See also Vawter, *BI* 154, who writes that "Catholic belief has consistently maintained that the biblical word must be read and heard within the context of tradition, whose truth is safeguarded by the Church's teaching authority. That authority, in turn, functions within the tradition and is constantly informed by the hearing of the word, for the Church is essentially the pupil of the Holy Spirit (*Dei Verbum,* art. 23)." The Vatican II document states that the Church "has always regarded, and continues to regard the Scriptures, taken together with sacred Tradition, as the supreme rule of her faith." See *Dei Verbum,* art. 21 in Megivern, *Bible Interpretation,* 414, see also art. 24.

83. See Brian Tierney, *The Origins of Papal Infallibility, 1150-1350* (Leiden: E.J. Brill, 1972), and his "Origins of Papal Infallibility," *Journal of Ecumenical Studies* 8 (Fall 1971): 841-64.

84. Guido Terreni, *Question on the Infallible Magisterium of the Roman Pontiff.* Cited in Pelikan, *Reformation,* 107.

85. See "Common Statement" in *Teaching Authority,* 23.

86. *DS* 3037, 3074. This translation is in Peter Chirico, *Infallibility: The Crossroads of Doctrine*, Theology and Life Series 1 (Wilmington, Del.: Michael Galzier, 1983), xxxix.

87. See the extensive treatment by Chirico, *Infallibility*. The following points are taken from 143ff.

88. See Avery Dulles, "Infallibility: the Terminology," in *Teaching Authority*, 78.

89. See Chirico, *Infallibility*, 146, and Dulles, "Infalliblity," 80.

90. See Dulles, "Infallibility," 90.

91. Ibid., 90.

92. See "Roman Catholic Reflections" on "Common Statement" in *Teaching Authority*, 49. The documents are in *DS* 2803, 3903.

93. See Hans Küng, *Infallible? An Inquiry*, trans. Edward Quiin (New York: Doubleday, 1971), and Carl J. Peter, "A Rahner-Küng Debate and Ecumenical Possibilities," in *Teaching Authority*, 159-68.

94. See Megivern, *Bible Interpretation*, 407. See also article 10, which states that "sacred tradition and sacred Scripture make up a single sacred deposit of the Word of God, which is entrusted to the Church" (Megivern, *Bible Interpretation*, 408).

95. See Dulles, "Authority," 35.

2. PROTESTANTISM

1. There are numerous fine treatments of the history of the Protestant Reformation. See among the many: Roland Bainton, *The Reformation of the Sixteenth Century* (Boston: Beacon, 1952); Harold J. Grimm, *The Reformation Era 1500-1650* (London: Macmillan, 1965); John M. Todd, *Reformation* (New York: Doubleday, 1971); and Hans J. Hillerbrand, *Christendom Divided: The Protestant Reformation*, Theological Resources, eds. John P. Wahlen and Jaroslav Pelikan (Philadelphia: Westminster, 1971).

The larger context of the Reformation is explored in works such as: A. G. Dickens, *Reformation and Society in Sixteenth-Century Europe*, ed. Geoffrey Barraclough, Library of European Civilization (London: Thames and Hudson, 1977); Peter J. Kalassen, *Europe in the Reformation* (Englewood Cliffs, N.J.: Prentice-Hall, 1979); and S. Harrison Thomson, *Europe in Renaissance and Reformation* (New York: Harcourt, Brace & World, 1963). A very excellent source for numerous aspects of the Reformation is Steven Ozment, ed., *Reformation Europe: A Guide to Research*, 3rd. ed., (St. Louis: Center for Reformation Research, 1982).

2. The literature on Luther is enormous. Among the one-volume biographies, Roland Bainton, *Here I Stand! A Life of Martin Luther* (Nashville and New York: Abingdon, 1950), and Heiko A. Oberman, *Luther: Man Between God and hte Devil* (New Haven: Yale University Press, 1990) are most notable.

There is scholarly debate as to whether Luther actually posted his Ninety-five Theses. Erwin Iserloh, *The Theses Were Not Posted: Luther Between Reform and Reformation*, 2nd ed. (Boston: Beacon, 1968) argued that he did not. Other Luther scholars do not agree, however. But the formal scholarly debate Luther sought through his Theses was never held.

3. *Luther's Works*, eds. Jaroslav Pelikan and Helmut Lehmann (Philadelphia and St. Louis: Fortress and Concordia Publishing House, 1955).

4. See Heiko Oberman, *Forerunners of the Reformation: The Shape of Late Medieval Thought* (Philadephia: Fortress, 1981). See also Luther's teachings as described in Paul Althaus, *The Theology of Martin Luther*, trans. Robert C. Schultz (Philadelphia: Fortress, 1966), 234ff.

5. Renaissance humanism originated in Italy as a philosphical and literary movement in the second half of the fourteenth century and spread throughout Europe. It looked back to antiquity to seek a revival and development of the human capacities of the ancients. This meant the full education of humans and the cultivation of the "humanities"—the study of poetry, rhetoric, history, ethics, and politics. Leading humanists included Gianozzo Manette (1396–1459), Marsilio Ficino (1433–1499), and Pico della Mirandola (1463–1494). Christian humanists applied methods of historical and linguistic scholarship to the Bible. Among the leading Christian humanists were Desiderius Erasmus (1469–1536) and John Colet (1466?–1519). See Paul Oskar Kristeller, *Renaissance Thought: The Classic, Scholastic, and Humanist Strains* (New York: Harper & Row, 1961), chap. 1; Nicola Abbagnano, "Humanism," trans. Nino Languilli, *The Encyclopedia of Philosophy*, ed. Paul Edwards, 8 vols. (New York: Collier Macmillan, 1972), IV, 69-72; hereafter cited as *EP*. See also James D. Tracy, "Humanism and the Reformation," in *Reformation Europe*, 33-57, for a valuable discussion and review of the literature. Humanism with its emphasis on history and rhetoric stood as a markedly different approach to learning than was taken by the reigning methods of medieval scholasticism in the Aristotelian tradition, which emphasized philosophy and logic. See Kristeller, *Renaissance Thought*, chaps. 2 and 5.

6. See Eric. W. Gritsch, *Martin—God's Court Jester: Luther in Retrospect* (Philadelphia: Fortress, 1983), chap. 9; and Althaus, *The Theology of Martin Luther,* chap. 18, among other treatments of Luther's theology for Luther's view of justification by faith.

7. Zwingli became aware of humanism when studying at the University of Vienna. The 320 books and 28 manuscripts in his library also reveal his knowledge of German humanists. See Robert C. Walton, *Zwingli's Theocracy* (Toronto: University of Toronto Press, 1967), 22. See also G. R. Potter, *Zwingli* (Cambridge: Cambridge University Press, 1976); *Zwingli and Bullinger,* ed. G. W. Bromiley, Library of Christian Classics (Philadelphia: Westminster, 1973); and Gottfried Locher, *Zwingli's Thought: New Perspectives, Studies in the History of Christian Thought,* ed. Heiko A. Oberman (Leiden: E.J. Brill, 1981). See also Robert C. Walton, "Zwingli: Founding Father of the Reformed Churches," *Leaders of the Reformation,* ed. Richard L. DeMolen (Sellingrove, Pa.: Susquehanna University Press, 1984).

8. On Erasmus's text of the New Testament, see Roland Bainton, *Erasmus of Christendom* (London: Wm. Collins Sons & Co., 1969), chap. 6.

9. See Walton, "Zwingli," 82ff. for details.

10. See John T. McNeill, *The History and Character of Calvinism* (New York: Oxford University Press, 1954); *Major Themes in the Reformed Tradition,* ed. Donald K. McKim (Grand Rapids: Eerdmans, 1992). John H. Leith, *Introduction to the Reformed Tradition* (Atlanta: John Knox, 1977), chap. 2; and *International Calvinism,* ed. Menna Prestwich (Oxford: Clarendon Press, 1985). For theological understandings, see *Encyclopedia of the Reformed Faith,* ed. Donald K. McKim (Louisville: Westminster/John Knox, 1992).

11. See *Calvin's Commentary on Seneca's 'De Clementia,'* eds. and trans. Ford Lewis Battles and André Malan Hugo (Leiden: E.J. Brill, 1969), particularly the first nine chapters of essays by Battles and Hugo. For a discussion of the importance of Calvin's training as a Christian humanist for his understanding and interpretation of Scripture, see Jack B. Rogers and Donald K. McKim, *The Authority and Interpretation of the Bible: An Historical Approach* (San Francisco: Harper & Row, 1979), 89ff.; hereafter cited as *AIB.*

12. See *Institution of the Christian Religion* (1536), trans. Ford Lewis Battles (Atlanta: John Knox, 1975), and *Institutes of the Christian Religion,* ed. John T. McNeill, trans. Ford Lewis Battles, 2 vols., Library of Christian Classics (Philadelphia: Westminster, 1960), for the English texts of the 1536 and 1559 editions.

13. See T. H. L. Parker, *John Calvin: A Biography* (Philadelphia: Westminster, 1975); François Wendel, *Calvin: The Origins and Development of His Religious Thought,* trans. Philip Mairet (London: William Collins, Sons & Co. Ltd., 1965); and Alister E. McGrath, *A Life of John Calvin* (Cambridge, Mass.: Basil Blackwell, 1990) for several of the best studies of Calvin's life and work.

14. See *The Book of Concord: The Confessions of the Evangelical Lutheran Church,* ed. and trans. Theodore G. Tappert (Philadelphia: Fortress, 1959) for the standard English translation.

15. Collections of Reformed Confessions are in Arthur C. Cochrane, ed., *Reformed Confessions of the 16th Century* (Philadelphia: Westminster, 1966); Philip Schaff, *Creeds of Christendom,* 6th ed., 3 vols. (Grand Rapids: Baker, 1977); John H. Leith, ed. *Creeds of the Churches* (New York: Doubleday, 1963); Lukas Vischer, ed., *Reformed Witness Today: A Collection of Confessions and Statements of Faith Issued by Reformed Churches* (Bern: Evangelische Arbeitsstelle Oekumene Schweiz, 1982); as well as in *The Constitution of the Presbyterian Church (U.S.A.): Part I The Book of Confessions* (New York and Atlanta: The Office of the General Assembly, 1983); hereafter cited as *The Book of Confessions.*

16. See *The Book of Confessions*; Edward A. Dowey, Jr., *A Commentary on the Confession of 1967 and an Introduction to "The Book of Confessions"* (Philadelphia: Westminster, 1968); and Jack Rogers, *Presbyterian Creeds: A Guide to The Book of Confessions* (Philadelphia: Westminster, 1985).

17. This approach is adopted rather than focusing specifically on the teachings of Luther and Calvin. For these see *AIB,* 75-116.

18. It is thus sometimes said that the Reformed Confessions are built on the "formal principle" of the Reformation—the authority of canonical Scripture—while the Lutheran Symbols are built on its "material principle"—the doctrine of justification by grace through faith. See Edward A. Dowey, Jr., "Revelation and Faith in the Protestant Confession," *Pittsburgh Perspective* (March 1961): 9. This was noted earlier by Karl Barth. In *Church Dogmatics,* trans. G. T. Thomson and Harold Knight (Edinburgh: T.& T. Clark, 1956), I/2, 547; hereafter cited as *CD..*

19. Edmund Schlink, *Theology of the Lutheran Confessions* (Phialdelphia: Fortress, 1961), 24.

20. Ibid. Schlink also writes: "This intense concern with the Gospel suggests that the Gospel is the norm in Scripture and Scripture is the norm for the sake of the Gospel. From this point of view we can understand why none of the Confessions before the Formula of Concord contain a section on Holy Scripture, because not only do individual articles specifically treat the Gospel, but in the final analysis all articles on the Confessions are concerned with the Gospel."

21. Cochrane, ed., *Reformed Confessions*, 146. See also Brian A. Gerrish, ed. *The Faith of Christendom: A Sourcebook of Creeds and Confessions* (Cleveland: World, 1963), 126ff., for an introduction to this Confession and the English text.

22. Cochrane, ed., *Reformed Confessions*, 165. The original language of the Confession is in Schaff, *Creeds of Christendom*, 3:437ff.

23. *The Book of Concord*, 464. Lutheran dogmaticians later affirmed this clearly. Abraham Calov (1612–1686) wrote that the first requirement for a Symbol was that it "must agree with Scripture and contain nothing which is not in Scripture either literally or virtually." Cited in Robert D. Preus, *The Inspiration of Scripture* (Mankato, Minn.: Lutheran Synod Book Company, 1955), 132, from Calov, *Exegema Augustanae Confessionis* (1665). The Lutherans often made the distinction between Scripture and the Confessions by designating Scripture as "the *norma normans* of theology" ("the standard which rules all") and the Confessions as "the *norma normata*" ("that ruled by the standard"). Thus "in controversy the appeal must be made from the Symbols to the higher authority of Scripture." See Robert D. Preus, *The Theology of Post-Reformation Lutheranism* (St. Louis: Concordia, 1970), 38.

24. See Barth, *CD* I/2, 475-76.

25. See Calvin, *Institutes* I. vii. 2. As Calvin wrote: "If the teaching of the prophets and apostles is the foundation, this must have had an authority before the church began to exist."

26. Cochrane, ed., *Reformed Confessions*, 120.

27. *The Book of Concord*, 464.

28. Ibid., 25. sec. 8.

29. Ibid., 48.

30. Ibid., 95, sec. 5.

31. Ibid., 99, sec 9.

32. Ibid., 295, sec. 15.

33. Ibid., 465, sec. 7.

34. Schaff, *Creeds of Christendom*, I:313.

35. *Book of Concord*, 503-4, sec. 3.

36. No attempt is made here to be exhaustive of either the Reformed Confessions or the complete teachings on Scripture in the ones cited. For a fuller treatment of sixteenth-century Reformed Confessions on Scripture, see *AIB*, 116-25.

37. For the text of Zwingli's Sixty-seven Articles, see Cochrane, ed., *Reformed Confessions*, 33-44.

39. For the English text of French Confession, see Cochrane, ed., *Reformed Confessions*, 137-58.

40. For the text of the Scots Confession, see *The Book of Confessions*, 3.01-3.251, and Cochrane, ed., *Reformed Confessions*, 159-84. See also Rogers, *Presbyterian Creeds*, 79-95.

41. For the text of the Second Helvetic Confession, see *The Book of Confessions*, which is reprinted from Cochrane, ed., *Reformed Confessions*, 220-301. On the Second Helvetic Confession, see Rogers, *Presbyterian Creeds*, 116-39.

42. See *AIB*, 125.

43. For the text of the Westminster Confession, see the section reprinted in *AIB*, 468-70 from *The Confession of Faith of the Assembly of Divines at Westminster: From the Original Manuscript Written by Cornelius Burges in 1646*, ed. S. W. Carruthers and published by the Presbyterian Church of England in 1946. See also *The Book of Confessions*, 6.001-6.178. On the Westminster Confession, see Rogers, *Creeds*, 140-71.

44. For a detailed exposition of the Westminster Confession's views on Scripture, see Jack B. Rogers, *Scripture in the Westminster Confession* (Grand Rapids: Eerdmans, 1967); see also *AIB*, 200-18, and Rogers, *Presbyterian Creeds*, 161-65.

45. For the text of The Theological Declaration of Barmen, see Arthur C. Cochrane, *The Church's Confession Under Hitler* (Philadelphia: Westminster, 1962), 237-42; reprinted in *The Book of Confessions*, 8.01-8.28, and Cochrane, ed., *Reformed Confessions*, 332-36.

46. See Cochrane, ed., *Church's Confession;* Rogers, *Presbyterian Creeds*, 175-201; and Donald K. McKim, "The Declaration of Barmen After 50 Years," *The Presbyterian Outlook* 166, 2 (June 4, 1984): 6-8.

47. For the text of The Confession of 1967, see *The Book of Confessions*, 9.01-9.56.

48. On the Confession of 1967, see *AIB*, 437-40, and Rogers, *Presbyterian Creeds*, 202-30. Of further interest are two studies on Scripture received in 1982 and 1983 by the current Presbyterian Church (USA). These are *Biblical Authority and Interpretation* and *Presbyterian Understanding and Use of Holy Scripture* (Office of the General Assembly, 100 Witherspoon St., Louisville, KY 40202-1396).

49. The term *left wing* was coined by Roland Bainton in "The Left Wing of the Reformation," *The Journal of Religion* 21 (1941): 124-34, and then revised in *Studies on the Reformation* (Boston: Beacon, 1963). For

"radical Reformation," see George H. Williams, *The Radical Reformation* (Philadelphia: Westminster, 1962) and Timothy George, *Theology of the Reformers* (Nashville: Broadman, 1988), 252-55.

50. Ernst Troeltsch, *The Social Teaching of the Christian Churches,* trans. Olive Wyon, 2 vols. (Chicago: University of Chicago Press, 1981), 2:691ff, see also 742.

51. See *Spiritualist and Anabaptist Writers,* eds. George H. Williams and Angel M. Mergal, Library of Christian Classics (Philadelphia: Westminster, 1957), 20ff.

52. See Henning Graf Reventlow, *The Authority of the Bible and the Rise of the Modern World,* trans. John Bowden (Philadelphia: Fortress, 1985), 49. Reventlow cites H. Fast, ed., *Der linke Flugel der Reformations* (Bremen: C. Schunemann, 1962) for this delineation.

53. Reventlow, 50 and the extensive notes he cites.

54. Jaroslav Pelikan, *Reformation of Church and Dogma (1300-1700),* The Christian Tradition: A History of the Development of Doctrine (Chicago: University of Chicago Press, 1984), 314.

55. Harold J. Grimm, *The Reformation Era 1500-1650* (New York: Macmillan, 1965), 265.

56. Among sources on Anabaptism, see W. R. Estep, *The Anabaptist Story* (Grand Rapids: Eerdmans, 1975); Hans J. Hillerbrand, *A Fellowship of Discontent* (New York: Harper & Row, 1967); William Keeney, *The Development of Dutch Anabaptist Thought and Practice 1539-1564* (Nieuwkoop: de Graaf, 1968); William Klassen, *Covenant and Community* (Grand Rapids: Eerdmans, 1968). See also the bibliography in Grimm, *The Reformation Era 1500-1650,* 645ff.

57. See Grimm, *The Reformation Era 1500-1650,* 266.

58. Cited in Hans J. Hillerbrand, *Christendom Divided,* Theological Resources, eds. John P. Whalen and Jaroslav Pelikan (Philadelphia: Westminster, 1971), 73.

59. Ibid.

60. On these, see among others the works of Grimm, Hillerbrand; Peter J. Klassen, *Europe in the Reformation* (Englewood Cliffs, N.J.: Prentice-Hall, 1979), 116ff.; and George, *Theology of the Reformers,* chap. 6.

61. Williams, ed., *Spiritual and Anabaptist Writers,* 31.

62. For the Schleitheim Confession, see the translation by John H. Yoder in *The Legacy of Michael Sattler* (Scottdale, Pa.: Herald Press, 1973), 34-43, and also J. C. Wenger, "The Schleitheim Confession of Faith," *Mennonite Quarterly Review* 19 (1945): 243-53. See also the Introduction in John Calvin, *Treatises Against the Anabaptists and Against the Libertines,* ed. and trans. Benjamin Wirt Farley (Grand Rapids: Baker Book House, 1982). This work was Calvin's response to the Schleitheim Confession. See also Willem Balke, *Calvin and the Aanabaptist Radicals,* trans. William Heynen (Grand Rapids: Eerdmans, 1981). For Zwingli's response, see Leland Harder, "Zwingli's Reaction to the Schleitheim Confession of Faith of the Anabaptists," *The Sixteenth Century Journal* (1980): 51-66.

63. Pelikan, *Reformation,* 317.

64. Reventlow, 52, citing H. Bender, *Das tauferische Leitbild,* 44.

65. See particularly Franklin Littell, *The Anabaptist View of the Church,* 2nd ed. rev. (Boston: Starr King, 1957), 11ff.

66. Cited in Pelikan, *Reformation,* 319.

67. Grimm, *The Reformation Era 1500-1650,* 267.

68. Reventlow, *Das tauferische Leitbild,* 53.

69. Ibid., 53. See also John H. Yoder, "The Hermeneutics of the Anabaptists," in *Essays on Biblical Interpretation: Anabaptist-Mennonite Perspectives,* ed. Willard Swartley, Text-Reader Series No. 1 (Elkhart, Ind.: Institute of Mennonite Studies, 1984), 18. This is a most helpful volume with an extensive bibliography.

70. Reventlow, *Das tauferische Leitbild,* 53. See also William Klassen, "Anabaptist Hermeneutics: The Letter and the Spirit," in Swartley, ed., *Essays on Biblical Interpretation,* 77-90

71. Yoder, "Hermeneutics," 18.

72. Ibid.

73. These points are summarized from Ben C. Ollenburger, "The Hermeneutics of Obedience: Reflections on Anabaptist Hermeneutics" in Swartley, ed., *Essays on Biblical Interpretation,* 47-48.

74. These points are summarized from ibid., 48-50. See also the similar emphases in Yoder, "Hermeneutics."

75. See Farley's "Introduction" to Calvin, *Treatises Against the Anabaptists and Against the Libertines,* 28. See also Reventlow, *Das tauferische Leitbild,* 57-59. Zwingli had also written against the Anabaptists in his *Refutation of the Tricks of the Baptists* in *Ulrich Zwingli: Selected Works,* ed. Samuel Macauley Jackson (Philadelphia: University of Pennsylvania Press, 1972), 123-258.

76. Henry Poettcker, "Menno Simons' Encounter with the Bible" in Swartley, ed., *Essays on Biblical Interpretation*, 65. See also George, *Theology of the Reformers*, 272-80, on Menno Simons and his discussion of Scripture in Menno's thought.

77. Walter Klaassen, "Anabaptist Hermeneutics: Presuppositions, Principles and Practice," in ibid., 10.

78. Ibid., 10.

79. Ibid., 6.

80. Cited in Reventlow, 53.

81. Reventlow links the Anabaptists' use of Scripture to Erasmus when he writes: "Following the insights gained by Erasmus, this theology of scripture culminates in an ethic of discipleship modelled on the example and the teaching of Jesus" (54). Numerous essays in Swartley's book bear out this stress on obedience and discipleship. See, for example, C. J. Dyck, "Hermeneutics and Discipleship," 29-44.

82. See George, *Theology of the Reformers*, 274.

83. Melchior Hofmann, "Ordinance of God" from *Spiritual and Anabaptist Writers*, 203.

3. LIBERAL THEOLOGY

1. Quoted in Karl Barth, *Protestant Theology in the Nineteenth Century: Its Background & History* (Valley Forge: Judson, 1973), 425.

2. Ibid., 425.

3. On Schleiermacher, see ibid., 425-73, and his 1923/24 Göttingen lectures published as *The Theology of Schleiermacher*, ed. Dietrich Ritschl, trans. Geoffrey W. Bromiley (Grand Rapids: Eerdmans, 1982). Among the other vast literature, see Martin Redeker, *Schleiermacher: Life and Thought*, trans. John Wallhausser (Philadelphia: Fortress, 1973); Robert R. Williams, *Schleiermacher the Theologian: The Construction of the Doctrine of God* (Philadelphia: Fortress, 1978); and Brian A. Gerrish, *A Prince of the Church* (Philadelphia: Fortress, 1984).

4. This would be true of theologians like Karl Barth and Paul Tillich.

5. For this story, see among other sources William E. Hordern, *A Layman's Guide to Protestant Theology* (New York: Macmillan, 1968), 73ff.; Robert Clyde Johnson, *Authority in Protestant Theology* (Philadelphia: Westminster, 1959), Parts II and III.

6. Kenneth Cauthen, *The Impact of American Religious Liberalism* (New York: Harper & Row, 1962), 3.

7. Ibid., 5.

8. Bernard M. G. Reardon, ed., *Liberal Protestantism*, A Library of Modern Religious Thought, ed. Henry Chadwick (Stanford, Calif.: Stanford University Press, 1968), 11.

9. Hordern, *A Layman's Guide to Protestant Theology*, p. 74.

10. See Barth, *Protestant Theology*, 459; Hordern, *A Layman's Guide to Protestant Theology*, pp. 44-47; and Lloyd J. Averill, *American Theology in the Liberal Tradition* (Philadelphia: Westminster, 1967), 34-39.

11. Williams, *Schleiermacher the Theologian*, p. 2. Barth deals with Kant in *Protestant Theology*, chap. 7.

12. Friedrich Schleiermacher, *On Religion: Speeches to Its Cultured Despisers*, intro. Rudolf Otto (New York: Harper and Bros., 1958), 13. See also Averill, *American Theology in the Liberal Tradition*, p. 37.

13. Schleiermacher wrote: "The sum total of religion is to feel that, in its highest unity, all that moves us in feeling is one; to feel that aught single and particular is only possible by means of this unity; to feel, that is to say, that our being and living is a being and living in and through God" (*On Religion*, 49-50).

14. Ibid., 39.

15. Ibid., 36.

16. See Barth, *Protestant Thought*, 467.

17. Averill, *American Theology in the Liberal Tradition*, pp. 36-37.

18. See Hordern, *A Layman's Guide to Protestant Theology*, p. 46.

19. On Ritschl, see Barth, *Protestant Thought*, chap. 29; Hordern, *A Layman's Guide to Protestant Theology*, pp. 46-49; David Mueller, *An Introduction to the Theology of Albrecht Ritschl* (Philadelphia: Westminster, 1969); Reardon, *Liberal Protestantism*, pp. 20-34, and Averill, *American Theology in the Liberal Tradition*, pp. 39-43.

20. Albrecht Ritschl, *The Christian Doctrine of Justification and Reconciliation* (Edinburgh: T.& T. Clark, 1902), III:10. See also William R. Hutchison, *The Modernist Impulse in American Protestantism* (Cambridge, Mass.: Harvard University Press, 1976), 122-29 on "Ritschlianism and the Uniqueness of Christianity."

21. Hordern, *A Layman's Guide to Protestant Theology*, p. 47.

22. On Harnack, see Reardon, *Liberal Protestantism*, pp. 44-48; Averill, *American Theology in the Liberal Tradition*, pp. 45-47; Philip Hefner, *Faith and the Vitalities of History* (New York: Harper & Row, 1966); G. Wayne Glick, *The Reality of Christianity: A Study of Adolf von Harnack as Historian and Theologian*, Makers of Modern Theology, ed. Jaroslav Pelikan (New York: Harper & Row, 1967); and Hutchison who points out that Harnack influenced more American liberals than had Ritschl (Hutchinson, *The Modernist Impulse in American Protestantism*, pp. 129-30).

23. Adolf von Harnack, *What Is Christianity?* trans. T. B. Saunders (New York: Harper and Bros., 1957), 8. Harnack's 1899–1900 lectures were entitled "Das Wesen des Christentums."

24. Ibid., 51.

25. The following discussion is drawn from Cauthen's excellent study, *The Impact of American Religious Liberalism*, chap. 1. Also of value is Averill, *American Theology in the Liberal Tradition*, chap. 3: "A Profile of American Theological Liberalism 1879-1917."

26. Cauthen, *The Impact of American Religious Liberalism*, 6.

27. Ibid., 9.

28. Ibid.

29. Ibid., 12.

30. See Cauthen, *The Impact of American Religious Liberalism*, 16. He points out that this reaction is seen in various philosophies such as the distinctions between the pure and practical reason (Kant), understanding and reason (Coleridge), the natural and the supernatural (Bushnell), and nature and moral personality (Ritschl).

31. On the period generally, see *AIB*, 407, and H. G. Reventlow, *Biblical Authority and the Rise of the Modern World*, trans. John Bowden (Philadelphia: Fortress, 1985).

32. John Herman Randall, Jr., *The Making of the Modern Mind* (Boston: Houghton Mifflin Co., 1926), 391.

33. Cauthen, *The Impact of American Religious Liberalism*, 22.

34. Ibid., 23. Cauthen points out that "this application of evolutionary ideas to the study of the Hebrew religion by the Wellhausen school of thought came to dominate biblical studies in the latter part of the nineteenth century."

35. Harry Emerson Fosdick, *The Living of These Days* (New York: Harper and Bros., 1956), vii.

36. Cauthen, *The Impact of American Religious Liberalism*, 27.

37. Harry Emerson Fosdick, *The Modern Use of the Bible* (New York: Macmillan, 1961), Lecture IV. Cauthen cites Henry P. Van Dusen, *The Vitality of the Christian Tradition*, ed. George F. Thomas (New York: Harper and Bros., 1944), 168-69, as the source of the distinctions among liberals. Also helpful is Averill's chap. 4, "The Varieties of Liberalism: Three Significant Variables," in which he makes methodological, ethical, and institutional distinctions.

38. Cauthen, *The Impact of American Religious Liberalism*, 30. Cauthen's work analyzes the thought of representatives of both varieties of liberal theology. See also the selections in *American Protestant Thought: The Liberal Era*, ed. William R. Hutchison (New York: Harper & Row, 1968).

39. Cauthen, *The Impact of American Religious Liberalism*, 45. See also Avery Dulles, *Models of Revelation* (New York: Doubleday, 1983), chap. 5.

40. Cauthen, *The Impact of American Religious Liberalism*, 45. He makes this comment in his study of William Adams Brown.

41. L. Harold DeWolf, *The Case for Theology in Liberal Perspective* (Philadelphia: Westminster, 1959), 17. Walter Rauschenbusch wrote that for a Christian "the only sure guide in speaking of God is the mind of Christ. That is our logic and metaphysic," *A Theology for the Social Gospel* (New York: Macmillan, 1917), 264.

42. DeWolf, *Case*, 18.

43. Ibid., 18.

44. C. H. Dodd, *The Authority of the Bible*, rev. ed. (London: Collins, 1967), 27. Dodd's whole approach exemplifies the emphases of liberalism. In this early writing (originally published in 1929), he saw the writers of Scripture as "religious geniuses."

45. DeWolf, *Case*, 17.

46. Ibid., 46.

47. Ibid., 47.

48. See Paul J. Achtemeier, *The Inspiration of Scripture: Problems and Proposals* (Philadelphia: Westminster, 1980), 42. He cites examples of some of these drawn from liberal theologians. See also DeWolf, *Case*, 47-48.

49. DeWolf, *Case*, 48.

50. See Achtemeier, *The Inspiration of Scripture*, p. 43.

51. L. Harold DeWolf, *A Theology of the Living Church*, rev. ed. (New York: Harper and Bros., 1960), 75.

52. DeWolf, *Case*, 48.

53. DeWolf, *A Theology*, 76.

54. See Achtemeier, *The Inspiration of Scripture*, p. 44.

55. See Bruce Vawter, *Biblical Inspiration* (Philadelphia: Westminster, 1972), 89, 126.

56. Donald E. Miller, *The Case for Liberal Christianity* (San Francisco: Harper & Row, 1981), 36.

57. Ibid., 74.

58. Ibid., 75.

59. *Spectrum of Protestant Beliefs*, ed. Robert Campbell (Milwaukee: Bruce Publishing Co., 1968), 34.

60. Miller, *The Case for Liberal Christianity*, p. 75.

61. DeWolf, *Case*, 56- 57.

62. Fosdick, *The Modern Use of the Bible*, 97-130.

63. Campbell, ed., *Spectrum*, 34.

64. See Cauthen, *The Impact of American Religious Liberalism*, 66, see also 217-18. Rauschenbusch said: "Theology needs periodic rejuvenation. Its greatest danger is not mutilation but senility" (*A Theology for the Social Gospel*, 12).

4. FUNDAMENTALIST THEOLOGY

1. *The Fundamentalist Phenomenon*, ed. Jerry Falwell with Ed Dobson and Ed Hindson (New York: Doubleday, 1981), 1. The statement was written by Dobson and Hindson, Falwell's pastoral associates at the Liberty Baptist Church in Lynchburg, Virignia.

2. George M. Marsden, *Fundamentalism and American Culture: The Shaping of Twentieth-Century Evangelicalism 1870–1925* (New York: Oxford University Press, 1980), 6. Hereafter cited as *Fundamentalism*.

3. *The Fundamentalist Phenomenon*, 1.

4. Martin E. Marty, "Fundamentalism as a Social Phenomenon," in *Evangelicalism and Modern America*, ed. George Marsden (Grand Rapids: Eerdmans, 1984), 56.

5. Martin E. Marty, "Fundamentalism Reborn," *Saturday Review*, May 1980, 38, as cited in *The Fundamentalist Phenomenon*, 1.

6. Richard N. Ostling, "Evangelical Publishing and Broadcasting," in *Evangelicalism and Modern America*, 48.

7. *The Fundamentalist Phenomenon*, 1-2.

8. Stewart G. Cole, *The History of Fundamentalism* (New York: Richard R. Smith, Inc., 1931), xi.

9. H. Richard Niebuhr, "Fundamentalism," *Encyclopedia of Social Sciences*, VI (New York: 1937), 526-27. Marsden notes that Niebuhr originally came to this interpretation in his *The Social Sources of Denominationalism* (Cleveland: World, 1929) but that "later in life he repudiated such exclusively socio-logical explanations" (*Fundamentalism*, 283).

10. Norman F. Furniss, *The Fundamentalist Controversy, 1918–1931* (New Haven, Conn.: Yale University Press, 1954); Ray Ginger, *Six Days or Forever? Tennessee v. John Thomas Scopes* (Boston: Beacon, 1958). See also Timothy P. Weber, "The Two-Edged Sword: The Fundamentalist Use of the Bible," in *The Bible in America*, eds. Nathan O. Hatch and Mark A. Noll (New York: Oxford University Press, 1982), pp. 101ff.

11. Richard Hofstadter, *Anti-Intellectualism in American Life* (New York: Random House, 1962), 121. See also Marsden, *Fundamentalism*, ch. XXIII: "Fundamentalism as a Social Phenomenon."

12. Paul Carter, "The Fundamentalist Defense of the Faith," *Change and Continuity in Twentieth-Century America: The 1920s*, eds. John Braeman, Robert Bremner, David Brody (Columbus: Ohio State University Press, 1968), 179-214.

13. Ernest R. Sandeen, *The Roots of Fundamentalism* (Chicago: University of Chicago Press, 1970).

14. Marsden, *Fundamentalism*, 4.

15. Weber, "The Two-Edged Sword," 102.

16. Marsden, *Fundamentalism*, 6. On the emergence of fundamentalism see also Marsden's, "The Rise of Fundamentalism, 1870–1930," in *Understanding Fundamentalism and Evangelicalism* (Grand Rapids: Eerdmans, 1991), chap. 1. Hereafter cited as *Understanding*.

17. On Darwinism, see Marsden, *Fundamentalism*, 18-21; "Rise," 135-44; and John D. Woodbridge, Mark A. Noll, and Nathan O. Hatch, *The Gospel in America: Themes in the Story of America's Evangelicals* (Grand Rapids: Zondervan, 1979), 49ff.; hereafter cited as *Gospel.*

18. See George M. Marsden, *The Evangelical Mind and the New School Presbyterian Experience* (New Haven, Conn.: Yale University Press, 1970).

19. Woodbridge et al. *Gospel*, 50-51.

20. Marsden, *Fundamentalism*, 21-22; "Rise," 44-46.

21. On Liberal theology, see chap. 4.

22. Woodbridge et al. *Gospel*, 52.

23. Ibid., 54.

24. *The Fundamentals: A Testimony to the Truth*, eds. R. A. Torrey et al. (Grand Rapids: Baker Book House, 1980).

25. See William R. Hutchison, *The Modernist Impulse in American Protestantism* (Cambridge, Mass.: Harvard University Press, 1976), 198; and Woodbridge et al. *Gospel*, 58.

26. On Dispensationalism, see Marsden, *Evangelical Mind*, passim., and Woodbridge et al., *Gospel*, 70-73.

27. See Marsden, *Fundamentalism*, 119-20.

28. Ibid., chap. 16.

29. On the variations of these points, see Marsden, *Fundamentalism*, 262 n. 30; and Sandeen, *Roots*, xiv-xv. In 1910 the General Assembly of the Presbyterian Church adopted five points that all ordination candidates had to affirm as "essential and necessary doctrines." These were the inerrancy of Scripture, the virgin birth of Christ, Christ's death as a sacrifice to satisfy divine justice and reconcile humankind to God, Christ's bodily resurrection and ascension to heaven and intercession, and Christ's mighty miracles. See Lefferts A. Loetscher, *The Broadening Church: A Study of Theological Issues in the Presbyterian Church Since 1869* (Philadelphia: University of Pennsylvania Press, 1954), 98. See also *The Fundamentalist Phenomenon*, 7.

30. See J. Gresham Machen, *Christianity and Liberalism* (New York: Macmillan, 1923). On Machen, see C. Allyn Russell, *Voices of American Fundamentalism: Seven Biographical Studies* (Philadelphia: Westminster, 1976), chap. 6: "J. Gresham Machen: Scholarly Fundamentalist."

31. On this controversy, see Marsden, *Fundamentalism*, chap. 19; Russell, *Voices of American Fundamentalism*, chap. 8: "Clarence E. MacCartney: Preacher-Fundamentalist"; and Bradley J. Longfield, *The Presbyterian Controversy: Fundamentalists, Modernists, and Moderates* (New York: Oxford University Press, 1991), chap. 5.

32. See Marsden, *Fundamentalism*, chap. 21; *Understanding*, 59-60, 147-49.

33. Ibid., 191.

34. On the history, see Louis Gasper, *The Fundamentalist Movement 1930–1956* (Grand Rapids: Baker Book House, 1981). See also *The Fundamentalist Phenomenon*, chaps. 5–6; Marsden, *Understanding*, chap. 2.

35. Marsden, *Fundamentalism*, 195.

36. See Donald G. Bloesch, *The Future of Evangelical Christianity: A Call for Unity Amid Diversity* (New York: Doubleday, 1983), 28-29, for a most helpful listing of fundamentalist organizations, institutions, and leaders.

37. On this, see chap. 5.

38. A. A. Hodge and B. B. Warfield, "Inspiration," *Presbyterian Review* (1881): 245. See also *AIB*, chap. 6.

39. Hodge and Warfield, "Inspiration," 234, see also 243.

40. See Harold Lindsell, *The Battle for the Bible* (Grand Rapids: Zondervan, 1976), 210. Lindsell's sequel along the same line is *The Bible in the Balance* (Grand Rapids: Zondervan, 1978). Harold J. Ockenga wrote: "By 1942, evangelical was equated with orthodox, as was evidenced by the naming of the interdenominational cooperative movement 'The National Association of Evangelicals.' Evangelicalism became a synonym for fundamentalism." See "From Fundamentalism, Through New Evangelicalism, to Evangelicalism" in *Common Roots*, ed. Kenneth Kantzer (Nashville: Thomas Nelson, 1978), 38.

41. On Neo-evangelicalism, see chap. 7.

42. See Bloesch, *Future*, 25. The authors of *The Fundamentalist Phenomenon* write that "the predominant characteristic of Fundamentalism in the last thirty years has been its strong commitment to separatism" (145).

43. George M. Marsden, "From Fundamentalism to Evangelicalism: A Historical Analysis," in *The Evangelicals*, eds. David F. Wells and John D. Woodbridge (Nashville: Abingdon, 1975), 128. George W.

Dollar, *A History of Fundamentalism in America* (Greenville, S.C.: Bob Jones University Press, 1973) distinguishes "militant" from "moderate" fundamentalists, 283-84. Richard Quebedeaux, *The Young Evangelicals: Revolution in Orthodoxy* (New York: Harper & Row, 1974), 18-28, distinguishes "separatist" and "open" fundamentalists.

44. See Bloesch, *Future,* 25.

45. Ibid., 26-27.

46. Bloesch cites the Philadelphia Conference on Reformed Theology as an heir to the scholastic stream, though "the sponsors of the conference have moved from a rigid fundamentalist posture and are better classified as neo-fundamentalist or neoevangelical" (*Future*, 27). See also Kenneth S. Kantzer, "Unity and Diversity in Evangelical Faith," in *The Evangelicals,* 38-67, for a description of varieties of evangelicalism in the fundamentalist tradition.

47. Dispensationalism spread through American Fundamentalism by the *Scofield Reference Bible* (1909). See James Barr, *Fundamentalism* (Philadelphia: Westminster, 1977), 191-207; and Marsden, "Rise," 39-41.

48. See chap. 5.

49. Charles C. Ryrie, *What You Should Know About Inerrancy* (Chicago: Moody, 1981), 17.

50. Ibid., 15.

51. Ibid.

52. "The Chicago Statement" is found in *Inerrancy,* ed. Norrman L. Geisler (Grand Rapids: Zondervan, 1979) and in *Evangelicals and Inerrancy,* ed. Ronald Youngblood (Nashville: Thomas Nelson, 1984), 230-39; hereafter cited as *EI.* The quotation is from Article VI in *EI,* 232. The emphasis on the original, autographic text is furthered in Article X, which reads: "We affirm that inspiration, strictly speaking, applies only to the autographic text of Scripture, which in the providence of God can be ascertained from available manuscripts with great accuracy. We further affirm that copies and translations of Scripture are the word of God to the extent that they faithfully represent the original" (*EI,* 233).

53. Ryrie, *What You Should Know About Inerrancy,* 16.

54. "Chicago Statement," Article VI in *EI,* 232.

55. Ryrie, *What You Should Know About Inerrancy,* 16.

56. "Chicago Statement," Article XI in *EI,* 233.

57. Ibid., Article VI in *EI,* 237.

58. Ibid., Article VII in *EI,* 232.

59. John R. Rice, *The Word of the Lord* (January 10, 1975), 41, cited in Ryrie, *What You Should Know About Inerrancy,* 35. Another contemporary fundamentalist, Bob Jones, Jr., wrote that "God Himself chose the very word that should be put down to convey exactly what He meant to convey. This precludes any possibility of human personality intruding upon and interfering with what God had to say." But he goes on to say: "We do not mean to imply by this that God merely dictated the Word to those who wrote It—that He made out of them a typewriter upon which His fingers played. God does not intrude upon human personality in that way." See *Spectrum of Protestant Beliefs,* ed. Robert Campbell (Milwaukee: Bruce Publishing Co., 1968), 30.

60. John R. Rice, *Our God-Breathed Book—The Bible* (Murfreesboro, Tenn.: Sword of the Lord, 1969), 286.

61. Ibid., 287. Lindsell affirms that he does not know "any scholar who belives in biblical inerrancy who holds that the Scriptures were received by dictation" (*Battle,* 33).

62. Ryrie, *What You Should Know About Inerrancy,* 16.

63. Ibid., 30.

64. "Chicago Statement," in *EI,* 237.

65. Ibid., 233. This latter statement concerning the teaching of Scripture on creation and the flood represents a continuation of fundamentalism's fight against evolutionism. See above note 32.

66. "Chicago Statement," Article XI in *EI,* 233.

67. Clark H. Pinnock, *Biblical Revelation—The Foundation of Christian Theology* (Chicago: Moody, 1971), 78.

68. Carl F. H. Henry in *Spectrum of Protestant Beliefs,* 32.

69. Lindsell, *Battle,* pp. 30-31. In the "Summary Statement" of the "Chicago Statement," one point is that Scripture is "of infallible divine authority in all matters upon which it touches: It is to be believed, as God's instruction, in all that it affirms," in *EI,* 213.

Article XIII elaborates the relation of inerrancy to the phenomena of Scripture: "We further deny that inerrancy is negated by Biblical phenomena such as a lack of modern technical precision, irregularities of grammar or spelling, observational descriptions of nature, the reporting of falsehoods, the use of hyperbole and round numbers, the topical arrangement of material, variant selections of material in parallel accounts, or the use of free citations," in *EI*, 234.

70. Weber, "Fundamentalist Use of the Bible," 106.

71. Ryrie, *What You Should Know About Inerrancy,* 82. See also "Chicago Statement," Article IV where it is denied that "errors and discrepanices that have not yet been resolved vitiate the truth claims of the Bible" (*EI*, 234).

72. Cited in the Presidential Address of Stanley N. Gundry to the Evangelical Theological Society in *EI*, 244.

73. Ronald Youngblood, "Preface," in *EI*, xi.

74. Avery Dulles, *Models of Revelation* (New York: Doubleday, 1983), 39.

75. Carl F. H. Henry, *God, Revelation and Authority,* vol. 2 (Waco, Tex.: Word, 1976), 87.

76. Ibid., vol. 2, 12; see also vol. 3, 455. Dulles also cites Gordon Clark: "Aside from imperative sentences and a few exclamations in the Psalms, the Bible is composed of propositions. These give information about God and his dealings with men" (*Karl Barth's Theological Method* [Nutley, N.J.: Presbyterian and Reformed Publishing Co.], 150). Francis Schaeffer: "God has spoken in a linguistic propositional form, truth concerning himself and truth concerning man, history, and the universe" (*The God Who Is There* [Chicago: Inter-Varsity, 1968], 93); and Pinnock: "Revelation is enshrined in written records and is essentially propositional in nature" (*Biblical Revlation,* 66).

77. J. I. Packer, *"Fundamentalism" and the Word of God* (Grand Rapids: Eerdmans, 1958), 91-92.

78. Ryrie, *What You Should Know About Inerrancy,* 40.

79. Ibid., 41.

5. SCHOLASTIC THEOLOGY

1. See Sydney E. Ahlstrom, *A Religious History of the American People* (New Haven, Conn.: Yale University Press, 1972), 813.

2. See ibid., 813ff. and more extensively Ernest R. Sandeen, *The Roots of Fundamentalism: British and American Millenarianism, 1800–1930* (Chicago: University of Chicago Press, 1970), chap. 5; and George M. Marsden, *Fundamentalism and American Culture: The Shaping of Twentieth-Century Evangelicalism 1870–1925* (New York: Oxford University Press, 1980), chaps. 13–14.

3. See particularly *AIB,* chaps. 5 and 6; John C. Vander Stelt, *Philosophy and Scripture: A Study in Old Princeton and Westminster Theology* (Marleton, N.J.: Mack Publishing Co., 1978); and the significant unpublished paper by John W. Stewart, "The Princeton Theologians: The Tethered Theology" (1975). This paper was expanded into Stewart's doctoral desertation, "The Tethered Theology: Biblical Criticism, Common Sense Philosophy, and the Princeton Theologians, 1812-1860." Doctoral dissertation, University of Michigan, 1990. For a variant viewpoint, see John D. Woodbridge, *Biblical Authority: A Critique of the Rogers/McKim Proposal* (Grand Rapids: Zondervan, 1982), chap. 7; John D. Woodbridge and Randall H. Balmer, "The Princetonians and Biblical Authority: An Assessment of the Ernest Sandeen Proposal," in D. A. Carson and John D. Woodbridge, eds., *Scripture and Truth* (Grand Rapids: Zondervan, 1983; reprint 1992), 251-79; D. Clair Davis, "Princeton and Inerrancy: The Nineteenth-Century Philosophical Background of Contemporary Concerns." in John D. Hannah, ed., *Inerrancy and the Church* (Chicago: Moody, 1984), 359-78; and Mark A. Noll, ed. and comp., *The Princeton Theology 1812–1851* (Grand Rapids: Baker, 1983).

4. See *AIB* and the earlier essay by Jack Rogers, "The Church Doctrine of Biblical Authority," in Jack Rogers, ed., *Biblical Authority* (Waco, Tex.: Word, 1977), 17-46, reprinted in Donald K. McKim, ed., *The Authoritative Word: Essays on the Nature of Scripture* (Grand Rapids: Eerdmans, 1983), 197-224. The Rogers/McKim view is questioned by Woodbridge and Balmer.

5. On Alexander see Lefferts A. Loetscher, *The Broadening Church: A Study of Theological Issues in the Presyterian Church Since 1869* (Philadelphia: University of Pennsylvania Press, 1954); and Loetscher's, *Facing the Enlightenment and Pietism: Archibald Alexander and the Founding of Princeton Theological Seminary* (Westport, Conn.: Greenwood, 1983); hereafter cited as *Alexander.* See also the biography by James W. Alexander, *The Life of Archibald Alexander* (New York: Charles Scribner, 1854).

6. See Noll, *The Princeton Theology 1812–1851,* 13, and his selections from Alexander's writings; *AIB,* 265-74; see also Loetscher, *Alexander.*

7. See Loetscher, *Alexander,* chaps. 1–7.

8. See *AIB,* 267, and Loetscher, *Alexander,* chap. 3: "Educational Background."

9. Loetscher, *Broadening Church,* 23.

10. See Noll, *The Princeton Theology 1812–1851,* pp. 25ff.

11. On Charles Hodge, see Archibald Alexander Hodge, *The Life of Charles Hodge* (New York: Charles Scribner's Sons, 1880). The anthology by Noll contains an excellent selective bibliography of writings by and about the Old Princeton theologians.

12. Noll, *The Princeton Theology 1812–1851*, 19, provides the statistics of those who received their primary theological training under the four Princeton professors. The 3,000 figure for Charles Hodge includes those who studied under him when he was a Professor of Oriental and Biblical Literature. The list is: (1) Alexander, 1815–1840, 1,114; (2) C. Hodge, 1841–1878, 2,082; (3) A. A. Hodge, 1879–1886, 440; (4) B. B. Warfield, 1887–1920, 2,750.

13. Ibid., 14; see also *AIB*, 275.

14. Rogers and McKim maintain that the fact that Turretin's work was the primary textbook from 1812 to 1872 is "one of the most important and least known facts of American church history" (*AIB*, xvii).

15. See Noll, *The Princeton Theology 1812–1851*, 14. On the spiritual dimensions of the work of the Princeton theologians, see W. Andrew Hoffecker, *Piety and the Princeton Theologians* (Phillipsburg, N.J.: Presbyterian and Reformed Publishing Co. 1981). Chap. 2 is on Charles Hodge.

16. Noll describes A. A. Hodge as having "the greatest capacity for precise and concise expression among the major Princetonians" (*The Princeton Theology 1812–1851*, 14).

17. On McCosh, see J. David Hoeveler, Jr., *James McCosh and the Scottish Intellectual Tradition: From Glasgow to Princeton* (Princeton, N.J.: Princeton University Press, 1981). On the Scottish philosophy, see Sydney E. Ahlstrom, "The Scottish Philosophy and American Theology," *Church History* 24 (1955): 257-22; Theodore Dwight Bozeman, *Protestants in an Age of Science: The Baconian Ideal and Antebellum American Religious Thought* (Chapel Hill: University of North Carolina Press, 1977), 3-31; and S. A. Grave, *The Scottish Philosophy of Common Sense* (Oxford: Clarendon, 1960), among other literature cited in Noll, *The Princeton Theology 1812–1851* 30ff. For the influence of this philosophy on the Princeton view of Scripture, see *AIB*.

The Scottish Common Sense Philosophy is associated with the works of Thomas Reid (1710–96), a Scots philospher who sought to answer the skepticism of David Hume (1711–1776). Reid assumed that objects in the external world were real and that the mind could encounter them directly. This assumption was based on Reid's own intuitive judgment.

18. On Warfield, see the piece by his brother Ethelbert D. Warfield, "Biographical Sketch of Benjamin Breckinridge Warfield," in Benjamin Breckinridge Warfield, *Revelation and Inspiration* (New York: Oxford University Press, 1927), v. ff.; and Samuel G. Craig, "Benjamin B. Warfield," in Benjamin Breckinridge Warfield, *Biblical and Theological Studies* (Philadelphia: Presbyterian and Reformed Publishing Co., 1952), xi-xlviii; as well as Noll, *The Princeton Theology 1812–1851*, 15ff., and *AIB*, 323-48.

19. On the controversy with Briggs, see Loetscher, *Broadening Church*, chap. 6, and *AIB*, 348-61.

20. On Machen, see Ned B. Stonehouse, *J. Gresham Machen: A Biographical Memoir* (Grand Rapids: Eerdmans, 1954); C. Allyn Russell, "J. Gresham Machen: Scholarly Fundamentalist," in his *Voices of American Fundamentalism* (Philadelphia: Westminster, 1976), chap. 6; Paul Wooley, *The Significance of J. Gresham Machen Today* (Nutley, N.J.: Presbyterian and Reformed Publishing Co., 1977); Bradley J. Longfield, *The Presbyterian Controversy: Fundamentalists, Modernists, and Moderates* (New York: Oxford University Press, 1991), chap. 2; and George M. Marsden, *Understanding Fundamentalism and Evangelicalism* (Grand Rapids: Eerdmans , 1991), chap. 7.

21. For more details see *AIB*, 366ff.

22. Edwin H. Rian, *The Presbyterian Conflict* (Grand Rapids: Eerdmans, 1940), presents an account of the conflicts from the view of those who founded Westminster Seminary.

23. Noll mentions Professor Roger Nicole, retired from Gordon-Conwell Theological Seminary, and Professor John H. Gerstner, retired from Pittsburgh Thelological Seminary (see *The Princeton Theology 1812–1851*, 18).

24. See *AIB*, 279. This was prescribed in the "Plan" of the Seminary.

25. See the description by Noll in his section "The Princetonians and Modern Controversy," *The Princeton Theology 1812–1851*, 41ff.

26. This is the position developed by Rogers and McKim in *AIB*. It also represents the basic issue in the Warfield/Briggs controversy. See *AIB*, 348-61.

27. Contemporary evangelical and Calvinist theologians who criticized the Princeton theology on these points were Thomas M. Lindsay, "The Doctrine of Scripture: The Reformers and the Princeton School," in *The Expositor*, ed. W. Robertson Nicoll, 5th series, I (London: Hodder & Stoughton, 1895), 278-93; and James Orr, *Revelation and Inspiration* (New York: Charles Scribner's Sons, 1910). For an exposition of these critiques, see *AIB*, 380-405.

28. See the works of John Woodbridge and Randall Balmer.

29. Noll, *The Princeton Theology 1812–1851*, 30.

30. See the treatments of each figure in *AIB*, chaps. 5 and 6.

31. Ibid., 269.

32. Archibald Alexander, *Evidences of the Authenticity, Inspiration and Canonical Authority of the Holy Scriptures* (Philadelphia: Presbyterian Board of Publication, 1836), 10.

33. Ibid., 12.

34. Since this was so, B. B. Warfield particularly emphasized the role of apologetics or the defense of the faith, since everyone should be able to be convinced of the existence of God. From there the next step was to "prove" that the Bible was God's Word. See *AIB*, 325ff.

35. B. B. Warfield, *The Inspiration and Authority of the Bible* (Philadelphia: Presbyterian and Reformed Publishing Co., 1970), 75. Hereafter cited as *IAB*.

36. For Charles Hodge's treatment of the work of the Holy Spirit, see his *Systematic Theology*, 3 vols. (New York: Charles Scribner's Sons, 1871), III:68; hereafter cited as *ST*.

37. Ibid., 42.

38. Ibid., 62.

39. B. B. Warfield, *Studies in Theology* (New York: Oxford University Press, 1932), 15.

40. See *AIB*, 333.

41. Warfield claimed that Calvin believed that "when the soul is renewed by the Holy Spirit to a sense for the divinity of Scripture, it is through the *indicia* of that divinity that it is brought into its proper confidence in the divinity of Scripture" (*Calvin and Augustine*, ed. Samuel G. Craig [Nutley, N.J.: Presbyterian and Reformed Publishing Co., 1974], 87).

42. Charles Hodge, *The Way of Life* (Philadelphia: American Sunday School Union, 1841), chap. 1.

43. *Selected Shorter Writings of Benjamin B. Warfield—II*, ed. John E. Meeter (Nutley, N.J.: Presbyterian and Reformed Publishing Co., 1973), 537; hereafter cited as *SWW-II*.

44. See *AIB*, 335.

45. Alexander, *Evidences*, 225.

46. Selections from "Inspiration," *Princeton Review* (October 1857), 660-698 are found in Noll, *The Princeton Theology 1812–1851*, 135-141. The section in Hodge's *Systematic Theology* is I:153-182. A letter to Marcus Dods, Free Presbytery of Glasgow (November 2, 1877) on this subject was printed in *The Presybterian* 48 (January 12, 1878), 9.

47. Hodge, *ST*, I:154.

48. Hodge, "Inspiration," 685.

49. Warfield, *IAB*, 420.

50. B. B. Warfield, "The Real Problem of Inspiration." This piece is reprinted in *IAB*, 169-226.

51. Warfield, *SWW-II*, 546. Warfield wrote: "The fundamental principle of this conception is that the whole of Scripture is the product of divine activities which enter it, however, not by superseding the activities of the human authors, but confluently with them; so that the Scriptures are the joint product of divine and human activities, both of which penetrate them at every point, working harmoniously together to the production of a writing which is not divine here and human there, but at once divine and human in every part, every word and every particular" (547; see also 629).

52. Hodge, "Inspiration," 682.

53. Ibid., 682-83.

54. Hodge, *ST*, I:170.

55. Hodge, "Inspiration," 669.

56. Hodge, *ST*, I:163.

57. Hodge, "Inspiration," 683.

58. A. A. Hodge, *Outlines of Theology* (New York: Robert Carter and Brothers, 1879), 301ff. For a fuller treatment, see *AIB*, 298ff.

59. A. A. Hodge, *Outlines* (1879), 75-76. Hodge included in his volume (656-63) a translation of the Helvetic Consensus Formula (1675), which asserted among other things that the inspiration of the "Hebrew Original of the Old Testament" was found "not only in its consonants, but in its vowels—either the vowel points themselves, or at least the power of the points." What was unknown in 1675 was that the original Hebrew Scriptures were written without vowel points. But the strong emphasis on the inspiration of the autographs of Scripture was appealing to Hodge and the Princeton theologians.

60. This significant essay has been reprinted with an introduction by Roger Nicole. See A. A. Hodge and B. B. Warfield, *Inspiration* (Grand Rapids: Baker, 1979). The piece was originally published as "Inspiration," *The Presbyterian Review* 2 (April 1881): 225-60.

61. *Presbyterian and Reformed Review* 4 (1893): 499. While A. A. Hodge and Warfield did not use the term *inerrancy* in their 1881 joint article, their commitment to the term and concept is clear, as for example in Warfield's "The Inerrancy of the Original Autographs," *The Independent* 45 (March 23, 1893): 382f., reprinted in *SWW-II*, 580-87; "The Westminster Confession and the Original Autographs," *The Presbyterian Messenger* 1, 50 (September 13, 1894): 118ff., reprinted in *SWW-II*, 588-94. Warfield believed that the inerrancy of the original autographs was taught by the Westminster Confession.

62. Warfield, *IAB*, 150. A. A. Hodge contended that "the historical faith of the Church has always been, that all the affirmations of Scripture of all kinds, whether of spiritual doctrine or duty, or of physical or historical fact, or of psychological or philosophical principle, are without any error, when the *ipsissima verba* of the original autographs are ascertained and interpreted in their natural and intended sense" (238).

63. Warfield, *SWW-II*, 584.

64. Hodge and Warfield, "Inspiration," 242.

65. Ibid., 245. Warfield's further works on Scripture can be seen from John E. Meeter and Roger Nicole, *A Bibliography of Benjamin Breckinridge Warfield 1851–1921* (Philadelphia: Presbyterian and Reformed Publishing Co. 1974).

66. For further discussions of the Old Princeton view, see Daniel P. Fuller, "Benjamin ᴅ. Warfield's View of Faith and History," *Journal of the Evangelical Theological Society* 11, 2 (Spring 1968): 75-83; George M. Marsden, "Everyone One's Own Interpreter?: The Bible, Science and Authority in Mid-Nineteenth-Century America," *The Bible in America: Essays in Cultural History,* eds. Nathan O. Hatch and Mark A. Noll (New York: Oxford, 1982), 79-100; Randall H. Balmer, "The Princetonians and Scripture: A Reconsideration," *Westminster Theological Journal* 44 (1982): 352-65; John H. Gerstner, "Warfield's Case for Biblical Inerrancy," in *God's Inerrant Word,* ed. John Warwick Montgomery (Minneapolis: Bethany Fellowship, 1974), 115-42; and other works cited in *AIB* and Noll, "Selective Bibliography."

67. While scholars differ in the exact extent to which Protestant scholasticism of the seventeenth century (e.g., Francis Turretin) determined the "scope and sweep" of the Princeton theology, it is undeniable that the Old Princeton theologians saw themselves as inheritors and perpetrators of the Protestant scholastic tradition which was marked in its most general way by a concern for a structured theology as a logical system of belief, heavily relying on Aristotelian syllogistic reasoning. The emphasis was on a rational defense of a settled deposit of doctrines. This approach can be spelled out further with specific regard to the doctrine of Scripture. See *AIB*, 185-87, for a description of characteristics of Protestant scholasticism. On the influence of Turretin on Old Princeton, see *AIB*, 279-81 and *passim,* as well as Noll, *The Princeton Theology 1812–1851,* 28-30. Noll also reprints a selection from Charles Hodge on "The Virtues of Seventeenth-Century Theologians," 114-16.

68. Richard J. Mouw, "The Bible in Twentieth-Century Protestantism: A Preliminary Taxonomy" in Hatch and Noll, *The Bible in America,* 143.

69. Ibid., 143, quoting Charles Hodge, "The Theology of the Intellect and That of Feelings," *Essays and Reviews* (New York: Robert Carter & Bros., 1857), 610.

70. David H. Kelsey, *The Uses of Scripture in Recent Theology* (Philadelphia: Fortress, 1975), 24.

71. Mouw, "The Bible in Twentieth-Century Protestantism," 143.

72. See the opening pages of Charles Hodge's *Systematic Theology,* vol. 1. It has been noted that the word *fact,* or *truth,* which are synonyous for Charles Hodge, occurs twenty-seven times in *ST,* I:1-3. See Theodore Dwight Bozeman, *Protestant in an Age of Science* (Durham, N.C.: University of North Carolina Press, 1977), 147.

73. Warfield, *IAB,* 208.

74. "The Real Problem of Inspiration," *Presbyterian and Reformed Rview* 4 (1893), 173.

75. In 1978 "The International Council on Biblical Inerrancy" was formed by some three hundred persons committed to the doctrine of inerrancy. A four thousand-word "Chicago Statement on Biblical Inerrancy" was signed by most of the participants. The group committed itself to a ten-year attempt to bring the doctrine of inerrancy into renewed prominence in Christian churches.

6. NEO-ORTHODOX THEOLOGY

1. On this, see among other sources *Revolutionary Theology in the Making: Barth-Thurneysen Correspondence 1914–1925,* trans. James D. Smart (Richmond: John Knox, 1964); *The Beginnings of Dialectic Theology,* ed. James M. Robinson, trans. Keith R. Crim and Louis De Grazia (Richmond: John Knox, 1968); and Thomas F. Torrance, *Karl Barth: An Introduction to His Early Theology 1910–1931* (London: SCM, 1962); as well as the accounts in the splendid biography by Eberhard Busch, *Karl Barth: His Life from Letters and Autobiographical Texts,* trans. John Bowden (Philadelphia: Fortress, 1976).

2. On these figures, see Busch, *Karl Barth,* and Alasdair I. C. Heron, *A Century of Protestant Theology* (Philadelphia: Westminster, 1980).

3. See Donald G. Bloesch, *The Future of Evangelical Christianity* (New York: Doubleday, 1984), 43ff., for his discussion of neo-orthodoxy. See also William E. Hordern, *A Layman's Guide to Protestant Theology,* rev. ed. (New York: Macmillan, 1968), chaps. 5–7.

4. On Niebuhr, see among other sources Theodore Minnema, "Reinhold Niebuhr," in *Creative Minds in Contemporary Theology,* ed. Philip Edgcumbe Hughes, 2nd ed. (Grand Rapid: Eerdmans, 1969), chap. 12; Hans Hofmann, "Reinhold Niebuhr," in *A Handbook of Christian Theologians,* enlarged ed., eds. Martin E. Marty and Dean G. Peerman (Nashville: Abingdon, 1984), 355-74; *Reinhold Niebuhr and the Issues of Our Time,* ed. Richard Harries (Grand Rapids: Eerdmans, 1986); Ronald H. Stone, *Reinhold Niebuhr: Prophet to Politicians* (Nashville: Abingdon, 1972); and Stone's, *Professor Reinhold Niebuhr: A Mentor to the Twentieth Century* (Louisville: Westminster/John Knox, 1992).

5. See Robinson, ed., *The Beginnings of Dialectic Theology,* 24, from the second edition of Barth's commentary. The forewords to the successive editions are in Karl Barth, *The Epistle to the Romans,* trans. Edwyn C. Hoskyns (London: Oxford University Press, 1968; rpt. of 1933 edition).

6. See T. H. L. Parker, *Karl Barth* (Grand Rapids: Eerdmans, 1970), 47-48.

7. Heron, *A Century of Protestant Theology,* 76.

8. For this emphasis of liberal theology, see chap. 3, "Liberal Theology: Scripture as Experience," as well as Busch, *Karl Barth,* chap. 3

9. Cited from Busch, *Karl Barth,* 81.

10. Cited in ibid., 85. See also Robinson, ed., *The Beginnings of Dialectic Theology,* 41.

11. The phrase "the strange new world in the Bible" is from the address of that name in Barth's *The Word of God and the Word of Man,* trans. Douglas Horton (New York: Harper & Row, 1957), 45.

12. See Barth, *Romans,* 1. This is also given in Robinson, ed., *The Beginnings of Dialectic Theology,* 61.

13. See Parker, *Karl Barth,* 36ff.; Robinson, ed., *The Beginnings of Dialectic Theology,* chap. 2; Busch, *Karl Barth,* 92-109.

14. See Karl Barth, *Church Dogmatics,* trans. G. W. Bromiley, I:2 (Edinburgh: T.& T. Clark, 1956), 494; hereafter cited as *CD.* See the debate on the historical-critical method bretween Barth and Harnack in 1923, recorded in Martin Rumscheidt, *Revelation and Theology: An Analysis of the Barth-Harnack Correspondence of 1923* (Cambridge: Cambridge University Press, 1972).

15. Barth, *CD,* I:2, 494; see also *AIB,* 425.

16. See Barth, *CD,* I:2, 481ff.; see also 103, 72, 119.

17. On this second edition, see *AIB,* 410-11; Robinson, ed., *The Beginnings of Dialectic Theology,* 24ff.; Busch, *Karl Barth,* 117-25; and Parker, *Karl Barth,* 38ff.

18. Heron, *A Century of Protestant Theology,* 76-77.

19. This is from Barth's commentary on Rom. 8:3 in *Romans,* 278.

20. See Heron, *A Century of Protestant Theology,* p. 78.

21. See Barth, *Romans,* 422. The concept of "witness" is crucial for Barth, who often referred to John the Baptist as a witness to Jesus Christ. The painting that stood above the desk on which Barth wrote his *Church Dogmatics* (now in Barbour Library at Pittsburgh Theological Seminary in Pittsburgh, Pennsylvania) was a representation of the crucifixion by Mathias Grünewald. In this painting, John the Baptist is seen standing off to the right and pointing with what Barth called his "prodigious index finger" at the crucified Christ. See *CD,* I:1, 112, 262; I:2, 125.

22. Barth, *Romans,* 93.

23. See Heron, *A Century of Protestant Theology,* 79. See also Busch, *Karl Barth,* 138-53.

24. See Busch, *Karl Barth,* 126-34. Barth's lectures on Schleiermacher from the winter semester of 1923/24 are available as Karl Barth, *The Theology of Schleiermacher,* ed. Dietrich Ritschl, trans. Geoffrey W. Bromiley (Grand Rapids: Eerdmans, 1982). His further assessment of Schleiermacher is found in Karl Barth, *Protestant Theology in the Nineteenth Century: Its Background & History* (Valley Forge: Judson, 1973), chap. 11.

25. On this, see Parker, *Karl Barth,* 69, and *AIB,* 413-14; see also Busch, *Karl Barth,* 153-64.

26. See Busch, *Karl Barth,* 205-9; Parker, *Karl Barth,* chap. 5. Barth's *Fides quaerens intellectum: Anselm's Beweis der Existenz Gottes,* translated as *Anselm: Fides quaerens intellectum: Anselm's Proof of the Existence of God in the Context of His Theological Scheme,* is reprinted in the Pittsburgh Reprint Series No. 2, ed. Dikran Y. Hadidian (Pittsburgh: Pickwick, 1975) as the translation of Ian W. Robertson (London: SCM, 1960). Arthur C. Cochrane provided a preface for the reprint edition. The importance of the Anselm work for Barth's understanding of language in general and specifically religious language in relation to his hermeneutics is highlighted in Thomas E. Provence, "The Sovereign Subject Matter: Hermeneutics in *The*

Church Dogmatics," in *A Guide to Contemporary Hermeneutics,* ed. Donald K. McKim (Grand Rapids: Eerdmans, 1986), 241-62.

27. More fully see *AIB,* 414-16.

28. Cited in Busch, *Karl Barth,* 210. Barth's commitment to theology as a science of the church is seen in the switch of names from *Christian Dogmatics* to *Church Dogmatics.* For an assessment of Barth's twentieth century influence, see *How Karl Barth Changed My Mind,* ed. Donald K. McKim (Grand Rapids: Eerdmans, 1986).

29. Barth, *CD* I:1, 295, 117ff.

30. Ibid., 132. See also I:1, 136, 141, 150; and Karl Barth, *Evangelical Theology: An Introduction,* trans. Grover Foley (London: Collins, 1969), 22-23.

31. Barth, *CD* I:1, 119ff., see also 137, 157. On Barth's doctrine of reconciliation, see Donald G. Bloesch, *Jesus Is Victor! Karl Barth's Doctrine of Salvation* (Nashville: Abingdon, 1976).

32. Barth, *CD* I:1, 88-124.

33. Ibid., 120-21. The interrelationships among the three forms constitute the unity of God. For Barth this threefold form is the singular analogy to the triunity of God. As he wrote: "In the fact that we can substitute for revelation, Scripture and proclamation the names of the divine persons Father, Son and Holy Spirit and *vice versa*" (I:1, 121).

34. Ibid., 101. *Canon* means "rod," "ruler," or "standard." For the first three hundred years of the church, it represented "that which stands fast as normative." After the fourth century, it particularly meant the list of books of Holy Scripture the church recognized as normative for its faith and practice.

35. Ibid., 107ff.

36. Ibid., 109.

37. Ibid. 110.

38. Ibid. Barth contrasted his view with that of seventeenth-century scholastic theologians who viewed the Bible as having its own divine power without regard to any effect on a reader. Thus theologian David Hollaz (1648–1713) could write that the Bible is God's Word "in the same way as the sun gives warmth even behind clouds, or as a seed of grain has force even in the unfruitful earth, or as the hand of a sleeping man is a living hand."

39. Ibid., 111.

40. Ibid. Here in reference to Grünewald's crucifixion painting Barth calls John the Baptist "the model of the biblical witness," because John "stands so notably at midpoint between the Old Testament and the New, between the prophets and the apostles" (112).

41. Ibid., 112.

42. Ibid., 113.

43. Ibid., 113-14.

44. Ibid., 115.

45. Ibid., 115, 116.

46. Ibid., 117.

47. Ibid., 118.

48. Barth, *CD* I:2, 537.

49. Ibid., 457.

50. Ibid., 485.

51. Barth, *Evangelical Theology,* 29. Barth deals with the unity of the Old and New Testament witness on 30ff.

52. Barth, *CD* I:2, 490ff.

53. A most helpful treatment of Barth's doctrine of inspiration is Howard John Loewen, "Karl Barth and the Church Doctrine of Inspiration (An Appraisal for Evangelical Theology)," 2 vols. Ph.D. diss., Fuller Theological Seminary, 1976. See 562.

54. Barth, *CD* I:2, 504ff. Loewen examines these passages extensively, "Karl Barth and the Church Doctrine of Inspiration," 124-82.

55. Barth, *CD* I:2, 505.

56. Ibid.

57. Ibid, 517.

58. Ibid., 517, 518.

59. Ibid., 520.

60. Ibid., 522-23.

61. Ibid., 523.

62. Ibid. See also 524.

63. Ibid., 525.
64. See the preface to the second edition of the *Commentary on Romans.*
65. Barth, *CD* I:2, 521.
66. Ibid., 49; see also I:1, 165-66.
67. Ibid., 501. See also I:2, 530 where Barth wrote that the Bible is "an instrument in the hand of God, i.e., it speaks to and is heard by us as the authentic witness to divine relevation and is therefore present as the Word of God." Yet, "Holy Scripture cannot stand alone as the Word of God in the Church" (I:2, 501).
68. Ibid., 501. Scripture is the Word of God in that "it too can and must—not as though it were Jesus Christ but in the same serious sense as Jesus Christ—be called the Word of God: the Word of God in the sign of the word of man, if we are going to put it accurately" (I:2, 500). See Loewen, "Karl Barth and the Church Doctrine of Inspiration," 570-71. Barth warned against trying to extract from the Bible "truths" or propositions to be propounded as "the truths of faith, salvation, and revelation." He asked whether Scripture, when it "tries to be more than witness, to be direct impartation, will it not keep from us the best, the one real thing, which God intends to tell and give us and which we ourselves need?" (I:2, 507).
69. Barth, *CD* I:1. See also I:2, 457.
70. Barth, *CD* I:2, 530.
71. Ibid., 529; see also 532.
72. Ibid., 533.
73. Ibid., 508.
74. Ibid., 509. see also, 508, 525.
75. Ibid., 509-10.
76. Ibid., 531.

7. NEO-EVANGELICAL THEOLOGY

1. See *Christianity Today,* 29, March 15, 1985, 34-36, on the life and contributions of Ockenga. On Schaeffer's life and contributions, see *Christianity Today,* 28, June 15, 1984, 60-63. Among numerous assessments of Schaeffer, see Jack Rogers, "Francis Schaeffer: The Promise and the Problem," *The Reformed Journal* 27, 5 (1977): 12-15; and 27, 6 (1977): 15-19.
2. *Christianity Today,* 29, March 15, 1985, 34. See also Ockenga's account of the need for this term in his essay, "From Fundamentalism, Through New Evangelicalism, to Evangelicalism," in *Evangelical Roots,* ed. Kenneth Kantzer (Nashville: Thomas Nelson, 1978), 35-46. I have maintained the term "Neo-evangelicalism" in this chapter, even though currently it is less prominent than the term *evangelicalism.* Yet contentions over what constitutes evangelicalism continue.
3. On these leaders, see among other sources Louis Gasper, *The Fundamentalist Movement 1930–1956* (Grand Rapids: Baker, 1981); Richard Quebedeaux, *The Young Evangelicals* (New York: Harper & Row, 1974); and John D. Woodbridge, Mark A. Noll, and Nathan O. Hatch, *The Gospel in America: Themes in the Story of America's Evangelicals* (Grand Rapids: Zondervan, 1979); hereafter cited as *Gospel.*
4. See the fine treatment by Donald G. Bloesch, *The Future of Evangelical Christianity: A Call for Unity Amid Diversity* (New York: Doubleday, 1983), chap. 2, and his *Essentials of Evangelical Theology,* 2 vols. (San Francisco: Harper & Row, 1982), vol. I, chap. 1.
5. A most helpful treatment of the controversies over Scripture within evangelicalism is found in Robert K. Johnston, *Evangelicals at an Impasse: Biblical Authority in Practice* (Atlanta: John Knox, 1979), chap. 2.
6. See "Half of U.S. Protestants are 'Born Again' Christians," *The Gallup Poll* (September 26, 1976): 1-7.
7. See Donald G. Bloesch, *The Evangelical Renaissance* (Grand Rapids: Eerdmans, 1973); Bloesch, *Future,* 9; and Quebedeaux, *Worldly Evangelicals,* chap. 1.
8. Quebedeaux, *Worldly Evangelicals,* 3.
9. See Deane William Ferm, *Contemporary American Theologies: A Critical Survey* (New York: Seabury, 1981), 96, citing *Christianity Today* of January 27, 1978.
10. See James Davison Hunter, *American Evangelicalism: Conservative Religion and the Quandary of Modernity* (New Brunswick, N.J.: Rutgers University Press, 1983), 49; see also Appendix 1.
11. Ibid., 7. As we will see, commitment to biblical inerrancy is not unanimous among all evangelicals.
12. Sydney E. Ahlstrom, "From Puritanism to Evangelicalism: A Critical Perspective," *The Evangelicals,* eds. David F. Wells and John D. Woodbridge (Nashville: Abingdon, 1975), 271.
13. Bloesch, *Future,* 15.
14. For "the legacy of Pietism" for Evangelicalism, see Bloesch, *Renaissance,* chap. 5.

15. On these see Woodbridge et al., *Gospel,* chap. 5; W. G. McLoughlin, *The American Evangelicals, 1800–1900* (New York: Harper & Row, 1968); W. G. McLoughlin, *Modern Revivalism: Charles G. Finney to Billy Graham* (New York: Ronald, 1959); and Timothy L. Smith, *Revivalism and Social Reform in Mid-Nineteenth Century America* (Nashville: Abingdon, 1957).

16. For this emphasis, see Bernard L. Ramm, *The Evangelical Heritage* (Waco, Tex.: Word, 1973), chap. 2: "Evangelical Theology Belongs to Reformation Theology." This emphasis is also struck in John H. Gerstner, "The Theological Boundaries of Evangelical Faith," in Wells and Woodbridge, *The Evangelicals,* chap. 1.

17. Bloesch, *Future,* 17. See also his *Renaissance,* chap. 3: "The Hallmarks of Evaneglicalism," and *Essentials of Evangelical Theology.*

18. See Harold Lindsell, *The Battle for the Bible* (Grand Rapids: Zondervan, 1976) and his *The Bible in the Balance: A Further Look at the Battle for the Bible* (Grand Rapids: Zondervan, 1979). On the Old Princeton theology, see chap. 5, "Scholastic Theology: Scripture as Doctrine."

19. Bloesch, *Future,* 11. See also Johnston's discussion of the varying positions on biblical authority within evangelicalism in *Impasse.* Bloesch rejects the attempt to define *evangelical* on the basis of an affirmation of the divine authority and inspiration of Scripture, because "this could include sacramentalist Roman Catholics, Moonies, Mormons, the Local Church of Witness Lee, the more tradition-bound Eastern Orthodox, and many others who would find it difficult if not impossible to accept the basic message of the Protestant Reformation" (*Future,* 13).

20. See Mark A. Noll, "Evangelicals and the Study of the Bible," in *Evangelicalsm and Modern America,* ed. George Marsden (Grand Rapids: Eerdmans, 1984), n. 39, 198-99. He lists twenty-seven books, most published since 1979, on the controversies over Scripture. Noll calls this a "partial list."

21. Johnston, *Impasse,* 3.

22. See Quebedeaux, *The Young Evangelicals* and *Worldly Evangelicals,* 7. Sydney Ahlstrom also used the term *inerrancy* as a defining mark of an "evangelical" when among his six criteria he listed: "insist upon verbal inerrancy of the received biblical text, tend to interpret revelation in strict proprositional terms, and question the value of historico-critical studies of biblical religion" (*The Evangelicals,* 270).

23. On this, see chap. 4, "Fundamentalist Theology: Scripture as Proposition."

24. See George M. Marsden, *Fundamentalism and American Culture* (New York: Oxford Univesity Press, 1980), 178.

25. Joel A. Carpenter, "From Fundamentalism to the New Evangelical Coalition," in *Evangelicalism and Modern America,* 4.

26. Ibid.

27. Ibid., 5.

28. See Carpenter's discussion of these three motifs, ibid., 5ff. See also Hunter, *American Evangelicalism,* 39.

29. Carpenter, "From Fundamentalism to the New Evangelical Coalition," 12. On the emergence and development of evangelicalism in this period, see George Marsden's essay "Evangelism Since 1930: Unity and Diversity," in his *Understanding Fundamentalism and Evangelicalism* (Grand Rapids: Eerdmans, 1991), chap. 2.

30. Quoted in Gasper, *The Fundamentalist Movement,* 23. See also Martin E. Marty, "Tensions Within Contemporary Evangelicalism: A Critical Appraisal," in Wells and Woodbridge, *The Evangelicals,* 172.

31. Carpenter, "From Fundamentalism to the New Evangelical Coalition," 12.

32. Quoted in Gasper, *The Fundamentalist Movement,* 25.

33. Hunter, *American Evangelicalism,* 41.

34. Carpenter, "From Fundamentalism to the New Evangelical Coalition," 13.

35. Quebedaeux, *The Young Evangelicals,* 43. See his discussion of the NAE, 42-44.

36. Ockenga, *Evangelical Roots,* 38.

37. Quoted in Lowell D. Streiker and Gerald S. Strober, *Religion and the New Majority: Billy Graham, Middle America, and the Politics of the 70s* (New York: Association Press, 1972), 112. Ockenga later wrote; "Doctrinally, the fundamentalists are right, and I wish to be always classified as one. In ecclesiology, I believe they are wrong and I cannot follow them" (Ockenga, *Evangelical Roots,* 40).

38. See Quebedeaux, *Worldly Evangelicals,* 22 and *passim* for his discussion these "symbols." Quebedeaux said that "in the 60s and 70s, the term *neo-evangelical* has generally been replaced by the more historic and inclusive designation, evangelical" (ibid., 9).

39. See James Barr, *Fundamentalism* (Philadelphia: Westminster, 1977).

40. See Hunter, *American Evangelicalism,* 7.

41. See Quebedeaux, *Young Evangelicals,* 18-28.

42. See Quebedeaux, *Worldly Evangelicals*, 8-9.

43. Bloesch, *Future*, 22.

44. Ibid., 24.

45. Ibid., chap. 3.

46. Bloesch, *Future*, 52. Bloesch identifies his own position as "catholic evangelical" (51) but notes also that "it can be shown that I stand partly in both neoevangelicalism and neo-orthodoxy, even though I belong mostly to catholic evangelicalism" (165 n. 67). His position on the doctrine of Scripture accords well with the approach of other "neo-evangelicals."

47. Ibid., 30.

48. Ibid. Part II of Quebedeaux's *Worldly Evangelicals* is devoted to "The Evangelical Right and Center." Part III considers "The Young Evangelical Left."

49. Bloesch categorizes those within the wings of evangelicalism on the Scripture issue: "Evangelical theologians who still move within the thought patterns of fundamentalism but try to engage in dialogue with the modern world include Francis Schaeffer, R. C. Sproul, James Boice, James Packer, Harold O. J. Brown, John Gerstner, John Warwick Montgomery and Harold Lindsell. Scholars noted for their ecumenical openness and innovative spirit but who generally remain within the framework of the Hodge-Warfield position on biblical authority and inerrancy are Carl Henry, Roger Nicole, John R. W. Stott, Morris Inch, Vernon Grounds, Ronald Nash and Kenneth Kantzer. Other scholars have questioned the emphasis on inerrancy but still see the Bible as the infallible standard for faith and practice. Among these are Clark Pinnock, F. F. Bruce, Bernard Ramm, H. M. Kuitert, Ray S. Anderson, Stephen Davis, Bruce Metzger, George Eldon Ladd, Kenneth Grider, Robert Johnston, Richard Colemen, Jack Rogers, Richard Mouw, James Daane, Ward Gasque, Paul Jewett, Lewis Smedes, M. Eugene Osterhaven and Timothy L. Smith. Not all these theologians would jettison the term 'inerrancy,' but they would reinterpret it in order to do justice to the true humanity of Scripture. [See in particular Clark H. Pinnock, *The Scripture Principle* (San Francisco: Harper & Row, 1984)]. The Lausanne Covenant, which declares that the Bible is 'without error in all that it affirms,' reflects the viewpoint of the dominant stream in neoevangelicalism today" (*Future*, 33).

50. Lindsell's contention that inerrancy should be the mark of the evangelical was countered by the essays in *Biblical Authority*, ed. Jack Rogers (Waco, Tex.: Word, 1977).

51. Johnston's four positions on Scripture for evangelicals are (1) Detailed Inerrancy, (2) Partial Infallibility, (3) Irenic Inerrancy, and (4) Complete Infallibility. (See *Impasse*, chap. 2.)

52. On these scholars see *AIB*, chap. 7.

53. See particularly Berkouwer's *Holy Scripture*, ed. and trans. Jack B. Rogers (Grand Rapids: Eerdmans, 1975). Berkouwer's esteem in the eyes of some evangelicals changed after the publication of this work. For "authors who had for years praised Berkouwer's evangelical theology felt obligated to dismiss his doctrine of Scripture because it critiqued the old Princeton slogan of 'inerrancy.' " See *AIB*, 428, citing reviews by J. I. Packer and Charles C. Ryrie.

54. See particularly Bloesch's *Essentials*; *Future*, 117-21; *Renaissance*, 55-59; *The Ground of Certainty* (Grand Rapids: Eerdmans, 1971); *A Theology of Word & Spirit: Authority & Method in Theology* (Downers Grove, Ill.: InterVarsity, 1992), chap. 3; Rogers's *Confessions of a Conservative Evangelical* (Philadelphia: Westminster, 1974); *Scripture in the Westminster Confession* (Grand Rapids: Eerdmans, 1967); with Donald K. McKim, *AIB*; and Ramm's, *The Christian View of Science and Scripture* (Grand Rapids: Eerdmans, 1954); *Special Revelation and the Word of God* (Grand Rapids: Eerdmans, 1961); *After Fundamentalism: The Future of Evangelical Theology* (San Francisco: Harper & Row, 1983).

55. See *AIB*, 23-25.

56. G. C. Berkouwer, *Man: The Image of God*, trans. Dirk W. Jellema (Grand Rapids: Eerdmans, 1962), 135.

57. G. C. Berkouwer, *General Revelation* (Grand Rapids: Eerdmans, 1955), 67. On Berkouwer's rejection of reason as the basis for the certainty of faith, see Gary D. Watts, "G.C. Berkouwer's Theological Method." Ph.D. diss., Fuller Theological Seminary, 1980, 139ff.

58. Bloesch, *Essentials*, I, 102. See also Bloesch's later statement: "Natural theology ends in idolatry because it means constructing a God out of human reason and experience" (*A Theology of Word & Spirit*, 178).

59. G. C. Berkouwer, *The Providence of God*, trans. Lewis B. Smedes (Grand Rapids: Eerdmans, 1952), 253. Of help here has been Gary Watts and Jack Rogers, "Six Theological Models of the Early 1980s: Their Theological Methods with Special Reference to Their Use of Scripture." Unpublished paper, Fuller Theological Seminary, August 1980.

60. See *AIB*, 209-21. See also Rogers, *Scripture in the Westminster Confession*.

61. Bloesch, *The Ground of Certainty*, 190. Bloesch also writes: "Reason cannot prove the validity of faith's commitment, but it can explicate faith's claims. It cannot guarantee the truth of the articles of faith, but it can serve this faith" (*A Theology of Word & Spirit*, 37).

62. Berkouwer, *Holy Scripture*, 184; see also 272, where Berkouwer writes that "in their controversy with Rome, the Reformers repeatedly emphasized that the message of salvation really came through; this was the purpose of Scripture."

63. Ibid., 14.

64. Ibid., 125. He quotes Bavinck on the "theological purpose of Scripture" to be "that we might know God unto salvation" (126).

65. Herman Bavinck, *Gereformeerde Dogmatiek*, 4 vols., 4th ed. (Kampen: J. N. Kok, 1928), I:414; hereafter cited as *GD*.

66. Bloesch, *Renaisssance*, 56.

67. John Calvin, *Institutes of the Christian Religion*, ed. John T. McNeill, trans. Ford Lewis Battles, Library of Christian Classics, 2 vols. (Philadelphia: Westminster, 1960), I.viii.1. On Calvin see *AIB*, 89-116, and Donald. K. McKim, "Calvin's View of Scripture," in *Readings in Calvin's Theology*, ed. Donald K. McKim (Grand Rapids: Baker Book House, 1984), 43-68.

68. Berkouwer, *Holy Scripture*, 148-49.

69. Ibid., 149. In introducing the essays in *The Use of the Bible in Theology: Evangelical Options*, ed., Robert K. Johnston (Atlanta: John Knox, 1985), Johnston wrote that evangelical theologians "distinguish themselves from other theologians within the Christian community by accepting as axiomatic the Bible's inherent authority." He refers to this as "evangelicalism's common theological center" (3). The book displays the diversities among evangelical theologians in doing theology in relation to the Bible.

70. Bloesch, *Essentials*, I, 76.

71. Berkouwer, *Holy Scripture*, 54-55. His chapter on "The Testimony of the Spirit" is reprinted in *The Authoritive Word: Essays on the Nature of Scripture*, ed. Donald K. McKim (Grand Rapids: Eerdmans, 1983), 155-81.

72. Berkouwer, *Holy Scripture*, 41. Berkouwer's language is reminiscent of Calvin's, who said: "We ought to seek our conviction in a higher place than human reasons, judgments, or conjectures, that is, in the secret testimony of the Spirit" and "the testimony of the Spirit is more excellent than all reason" (*Institutes*, I.vii.4.). For Berkouwer, "the *testimonium* does not supply an *a priori* certainty regarding Scripture, which afterwards is supplemented with and through its message" (*Holy Scripture*, 44).

73. Bavinck, *GD*, I, 564-65.

74. Ibid., 569.

75. See *AIB*, 106-9, 114-16.

76. Bavinck, *GD*, I, 409-10. See also Berkouwer, *Holy Scripture*, 151-57.

77. Ibid., 410..

78. Of major significance in understandig the nature of Scripture and inspiration is the concept of "accommodation." This is an insight adapted from the classical rhetoricians and shared by such theologians as Origen, Chrysostom, Augustine, and Calvin that stressed that in Scripture God condescended to the limits of human capacities in order to communicate with humanity. See the development of this theme throughout *AIB*. A most important article on accommodation in Calvin's thought is Ford Lewis Battles, "God Was Accommodating Himself to Human Capacity," *Interpretation* 31 (1977): 19-38.

79. Berkouwer, *Holy Scripture*, 181. It is argued by neo-evangelicals that this "moral" understanding of error in terms of purposeful deceit was the understanding of the central tradition of the Christian church, including Augustine and Calvin. See *AIB*.

80. See chap. 5, "Scholastic Theology: Scripture as Doctrine," and Johnston, *Impasse*, 36, who contrasts "inerrancy" and "infallibility." Bloesch writes: "Many latter day evangelical Christians have felt the need to extend the meaning of inerrancy to cover purely historical and scientific matters, even where the treatment of these in the Bible does not bear upon the message of a faith. . . . A view of error is entertained that demands literal, exact, mathematical precision, something the Bible cannot provide" (*Essentials*, I, 66). Earlier he wrote that "when evangelical theology affirms that Scripture does not err, it means that whatever Christ teaches in Scripture is completely true." In a note he added: "And we must hasten to add that this includes not only its testimony concerning God and salvation, but also its interpretation of man, life and history. But this does not imply perfect factual accuracy in all details as the extreme literalist holds" (*Renaissance*, 56).

81. Berkouwer, *Holy Scripture*, 183.

82. Ibid., 180. Berkouwer writes: "We may add the awareness that the purpose of Scripture is not to orient us concerning the composition of the cosmos in its created parts, nor to inform us scientifically about the

'composition of man.' . . . The purpose of Scripture is directly aimed at the revelation of God *in* this world and *to* man" (245).

83. Ibid., 145, 147.
84. Ibid., 333.
85. Ibid.

8. EXISTENTIAL THEOLOGY

1. See Wilhelm Pauck and Marion Pauck, *Paul Tillich: His Life and Thought* (New York: Harper & Row, 1976), 127-30; and Ronald H. Stone, *Paul Tillich's Radical Social Thought* (Atlanta: John Knox, 1980), 65.

2. Tillich's theological stature is attested to by Reinhold Niebuhr, who described him as "the Origen of our period, seeking to relate the Gospel message to the disciplines of our culture and whole history of culture" (see "Biblical Thought and Ontological Speculation in Tillich's Theology," in *The Theology of Paul Tillich*, eds. Charles W. Kegly and Robert W. Bretall [New York: Macmillan, 1952], 217). John Herman Randall, Jr., described him as "the ablest Protestant theologian of the present day" (see "The Ontology of Paul Tillich," in ibid., 161). In 1977 a survey of 554 theologians in North America revealed that Tillich ranked first as the major influence on their thought and that his three-volume *Systematic Theology* was the most widely used textbook among theologians. See John Newport, *Paul Tillich*, Makers of the Modern Theological Mind, ed. Bob E. Patterson (Waco, Tex.: Word, 1984), 16.

3. On Tillich's life, see Newport, *Paul Tillich*; Pauck and Pauck, *Paul Tillich*; and the books of Tillich's widow, Hannah Tillich, *From Place to Place* (New York: Stein and Day, 1976) and *From Time to Time* (New York: Stein and Day, 1973).

4. This is seen in the varieties of topics of interest to Tillich and on which he wrote. These included, besides theology, philosophy, and the history of Christian thought such areas as culture, art, politics, and social concerns.

5. See Paul Tillich, *Systematic Theology,* 3 vols. (Chicago: University of Chicago Press, 1951, 1957, 1963); hereafter cited as *ST*; and his *A History of Christian Thought: From Its Judaic and Hellenistic Origins to Existentialism*, ed. Carl E. Braaten (New York: Simon and Schuster, 1967).

6. Paul Tillich, *On the Boundary: An Autobiographical Sketch* (London: Collins, 1967), 13.

7. Paul Tillich, *Religiöse Verwirklichung* (Berlin: Furche, 1929), 1; see also *On the Boundary,* 13

8. Tillich's *On the Boundary* was initially published as the first chapter in his *The Interpretation of History*, trans. N. A. Rasetski and Elsa L. Talmey (New York: Charles Scribner's Sons, 1936).

9. Tillich, *ST*, II, 90.

10. See Stone, *Paul Tillich's Radical Social Thought*, 36.

11. See Newport, *Paul Tillich*, 27 and 78ff., for his description of the theological and philosphical influences on Tillich's thought. See also Arthur C. Cochrane, *The Existentialists and God* (Philadelphia: Westminster, 1966), chap. 4; and George F. McLean, "Paul Tillich's Existential Philosophy of Protestantism," in *Paul Tillich in Catholic Thought*, eds. Thomas A. O'Meara and Celestin D. Weisser (Dubuque, Iowa: The Priory Press, 1964), 42-84.

12. Tillich, *On the Boundary,* 83.

13. Newport, *Paul Tillich,* 27.

14. Tillich, *On the Boundary,* 56.

15. Ibid., 57.

16. Tillich, *ST,* I:23.

17. Ibid., I:3-8.

18. Ibid., I:12-15.

19. Ibid., I:15-18.

20. Ibid., I:18-24.

21. Ibid., I:27-28.

22. Ibid., I:28-34.

23. Ibid., I:34-40. See also George Tavard, "Christology as Symbol" in O'Meara and Weisser, *Paul Tillich in Catholic Thought,* 219-23.

24. Tillich, *ST,* I:43.

25. Ibid., I:46.

26. Ibid., I:47, 50. Gustave Weigel wrote that the "New Being" is "the pure essence of Tillich's theology." See his "Tillich's Theological Significance" in O'Meara and Weisser, *Paul Tillich in Catholic Thought,* 12.

27. Tillich, *ST,* I:51-52.

28. Ibid., I:53-54.

29. Ibid., I:57, 58.

30. Ibid., I:60, 61.

31. Ibid., I:62, 63.

32. Ibid., I:64.

33. Ibid., I:66-68.

34. See Kenan B. Osborne, *New Being: A Study of the Relationship Between Conditioned and Unconditioned Being According to Paul Tillich* (The Hague: Martinus Nijhoff, 1969), 87-89.

35. See Tillich, *ST,* I:71ff.

36. Ibid., I:75, 79-81.

37. Ibid., I:80.

38. Ibid., I:242.

39. Newport, *Paul Tillich,* 95.

40. Tillich, *ST,* I:178. See also III:406-10.

41. Ibid., I:83. Newport writes that "Tillich's whole theological or onto-theological system derives its structure and form from his understanding that ultimate reality is involved in a movement of unactualized essence into existence and then in a return to fulfilled essentialization" (*Paul Tillich,* 66). "Essentialization" is "a return to fulfilled essence" (Ibid., 69; see also 95-96).

42. Ibid., I:110.

43. Avery R. Dulles, "Paul Tillich and the Bible," in O'Meara and Weisser, *Paul Tillich in Catholic Thought,* 110.

44. Tillich, *ST,* I:110.

45. Ibid., I:112; see also 111-18. For Tillich, a miracle is "an unusual event—extraordinary either in its regularity or its irregularity—which somehow points to the ultimate source of reality and meaning" (Dulles, "Paul Tillich and the Bible," 11).

46. Newport, *Paul Tillich,* 99.

47. Tillich, *ST,* I:127.

48. Ibid., I:127.

49. David H. Kelsey, *The Uses of Scripture in Recent Theology* (Philadelphia: Fortress, 1975), 66.

50. Tillich, *ST,* I:133, 135; see also II:97-138.

51. Ibid., I:134. Tillich defines a final revelation as one that "has the power of negating itself without losing itself," I:133. This is found in the biblical picture of "Jesus as the Christ."

52. Ibid., I:137.

53. Ibid., I:146.

54. Ibid., I:147. For Tillich, "the religious word for what is called the ground of being is God" (I:156).

55. Ibid., I:147.

56. Ibid., I:157.

57. Ibid., I:157-59.

58. Ibid., I:159.

59. Ibid., I:35.

60. Ibid.

61. Ibid., I:124.

62. Ibid., I:124, 129.

63. Ibid., I:145.

64. Kelsey, *The Uses of Scripture in Recent Theology,* 66.

65. Kelsey points out that with regard to the "personal life" of Jesus: " 'personal life' we know is always marked by the conditions of 'existence,' that is to say, by alienation from self, neighbor, and God [Tillich's description of 'sin'], while 'New Being' designates unbroken unity between God and man. Yet Jesus managed to overcome the conditions of 'existence' and preserve unbroken unity with God while nonetheless truly and fully participating in our common human life" (ibid., 66; see also Tillich, *ST,* II:126, 136, 148).

66. See Kelsey, *The Uses of Scripture in Recent Theology,* 130. See also Tillich, *ST,* II:121ff.

67. Kelsey, *The Uses of Scripture in Recent Theology,* 72. For Tillich, Jesus as the Christ is "the ultimate criterion of every healing and saving process" (*ST,* II:168).

9. PROCESS THEOLOGY

1. See Jack B. Rogers, "The Search for System: Theology in the 1980's," *The Journal of Religious Thought* 37 (1980): 5-14.

2. Jack Rogers, "Bibliography: Process Theology," prepared for Theological Student's Fellowship Research. See also Illtyd Trethowan, *Process Theology and the Christian Tradition: An Essay in Post Vatican II Thinking* (Still River, Mass.: St. Bede's Publications, 1985); and Kenneth Surin, "Process Theology," in *The Modern Theologians: An Introduction to Christian Theology in the Twentieth Century,* ed. David F. Ford, 2 vols. (Cambridge, Mass.: Basil Blackwell, 1990), 2: chap. 5.

3. On Whitehead's life, see Jack B. Rogers and Forrest Baird, "The Case of Whitehead," in their *Introduction to Philosophy: A Case Study Approach* (San Francisco: Harper & Row, 1981), chap. 11.

4. Alfred North Whitehead, *Process and Reality* (New York: Macmillan, 1929). This work is quite technical in both its language and its concepts.

5. Alfred North Whitehead, *Science and the Modern World* (New York: Macmillan, 1925).

6. Alfred North Whitehead, *Religion in the Making* (New York: Macmillan, 1926). Other works on Whitehead include *A Key to Whitehead's Process and Reality,* ed. Donald W. Sherburne (New York: Macmillan, 1966); *The Philosophy of Alfred North Whitehead,* ed. Paul Arthur Schilpp, The Library of Living Philosophers, 2nd ed. (New York: Tudor, 1951); Norman Pittenger, *Alfred North Whitehead,* Makers of Contemporary Theology (Richmond: John Knox, 1969); Victor Love, *Understanding Whitehead* (Baltimore: Johns Hopkins University Press, 1962); and W. Mays, *The Philosophy of Whitehead* (New York: Crowell-Collier, 1962).

7. Alasdair I. C. Heron, *A Century of Protestant Theology* (Philadelphia: Westminster, 1980), 145. See also Robert B. Mellert, *What Is Process Theology?* (New York: Paulist Press, 1975), chap. 2; David R. Griffin, *A Process Christology* (Philadelphia: Westminster, 1973), chaps. 6 and 7; and Norman Pittenger, "Process Theology: A Whiteheadian Version," in *Religious Experience and Process Theology: The Pastoral Implications of a Major Modern Movement,* eds. Harry James Cargas and Bernard Lee (New York: Paulist Press, 1976), 3-21, for other descriptions of Whitehead's metaphysics.

8. John B. Cobb, Jr., and David Ray Griffin, *Process Theology: An Introductory Exposition* (Philadelphia: Westminster, 1976). Cobb and Griffin are two of the leading American process theologians of today.

9. Ibid., 19. Griffin had earlier written that "every actual occasion can also be called an 'occasion of experience.' . . . Every actual entity is a pulse of experience which is 'something individual for its own sake' [Whitehead, *Process and Reality,* 135]" (*Process Christology,* 168). A very lucid and helpful exposition of process thought on this theme is Marjorie Hewitt Suchocki, *God-Christ-Church* (New York: Crossroad, 1982), chap. 2.

10. Cobb and Griffin, *Process Theology,* 20. Or "As an actual occasion or moment of experience emerges, it 'feels' all the data available to it in its own universe. These are its prehensions" (Mellert, *What Is Process Theology?* 24).

11. Cobb and Griffin, *Process Theology,* 20. Mellert notes that "because an actual occasion is merely a drop of experience, we are generally conscious only of groups of actual occasions, or *nexs* (plural of nexus). A nexus is a set of actual occasions experienced as related to each other. Sometimes it is called a society of occasions." This is important because "the nexus is the way in which Whitehead explains the real connection of things in space and time" (25).

12. Ibid., 21.

13. Whitehead, *Science and the Modern World,* 88. On Whitehead's view of God, see Owen Sharkey, "The Mystery of God in Process Theology," in *God in Contemporary Thought: A Philosophical Perspective,* ed. Sebastian A. Matczak (New York: Learned Publishers, 1977), 685-93; on Hartshorne, 693-706. See also Paul R. Sponheim, *Faith and Process: The Significance of Process Thought for Christian Faith* (Minneapolis: Augsburg, 1979); David R. Griffin, *God and Religion in the Postmodern World: Essays in Postmodern Theology* (Albany: State University of New York Press, 1989); Mellert, *What Is Process Theology?* chap. 4; and the more popular presentation by Daniel Day Williams, *The Demonic and the Divine,* ed. Stacy A. Evans (Minneapolis: Fortress, 1990). See also Williams, *Essays in Process Theology,* ed. Perry LeFevre (Chicago: Exploration Press, 1985).

14. Whitehead, *Process and Reality,* 33.

15. Ibid., 34, 35. Whitehead wrote: "That 'all things flow' is the first vague generalization which the unsystematized, barely analyzed, intuition of men has produced . . . it appears as one of the first generalizations of Greek philosophy in the form of the saying of Heraclitus. . . . Without doubt, if we are to go back to that ultimate, integral experience, unwarped by the sophistications of theory, that experience whose elucidations is the final aim of philosophy, the flux of things is one ultimate generalizaiton around which we must weave our philosophical system" (43, 53, 317). See Norman L. Geisler, "Process Theology," in *Tensions in Contemporary Theology,* eds. Stanley N. Gundry and Alan F. Johnson, 2nd ed. (Grand Rapids: Baker, 1983), chap. 6; and the critiques of Whitehead by the essayists throughout *Process Theology,* ed. Ronald H. Nash (Grand Rapids: Baker, 1987).

16. Hartshorne's significant work here is *The Divine Relativity: A Social Conception of God* (New Haven: Yale University Press, 1948). In it he argued that process theology and biblical thought are compatible. The Divinity School of the University of Chicago is "the major center of theological receptivity to Whitehead's influence." See Cobb and Griffin, *Process Theology,* 176, who provide a guide to the literature on process theology, including the Chicago school. Cobb also traces the development of process thought at the University of Chicago in *Process Theology as Political Theology* (Philadelphia: Westminster, 1982), chap. 2. On "God as Dipolar" see Griffin, *Process Christology,* 181-84.

17. See Cobb and Griffin, *Process Theology,* 47-48. The "relativity" of God's knowledge and power is underscored by Griffin, who writes that "although God is the supreme power of the universe, God's creative and providential power to influence others is not unlimited. God *does not have and could not have a monopoly on power and therefore cannot unilaterally determine the events in the world.* The reason for this is that the creatures have their own inherent creative power to actualize themselves and to influence others, and this power cannot be overridden" (*God and Religion in the Postmodern World,* 65). Put another way, God is "powerless before the freedom of each individual moment" (Mellert, *What Is Process Theology?* 47).

18. Suchocki, *God-Christ-Church,* 226; see also 38. Mellert writes: "God's primordial nature, Whitehead says, is independent from his commerce with particulars. It is the abstract side of God, or God 'alone with himself' [*Process and Reality,* 39]. By virtue of his primordiality, God contains within himself the totality of possibility through his conceptual envisagement of the entire multiplicity of eternal objects. In his primordial nature God is without any temporal connotation and without any direction toward individual entities. It is the purely conceptual side of the divinity, without any actuality in itself. Rather, it is the basis of actuality, because it is the foundation for the actualization of possibilities" (*What Is Process Theology?* 45).

19. Suchocki, *God-Christ-Church,* 225. Cobb and Griffin state that Whitehead's consequent nature of God is "largely identical with what Hartshorne has called God's concrete actuality" (*Process Theology,* 48). On the differences between Whitehead and Hartshorne, see David R. Griffin, "Hartshorne's Differences from Whitehead," *Two Process Philosophers: Hartshorne's Encounter with Whitehead,* AAR Studies in Religion No. 15 (Tallahassee: AAR, 1973), 35-57; and Lewis S. Ford, "Whitehead's Differences from Hartshorne," 58-83. Mellert defines God's consequent nature as "the composite nature of all the actualities of the world, each having obtained its unique representation in the divine nature" (*What Is Process Theology?* 47).

20. Rogers and Baird, "The Case of Whitehead," 189.

21. Cobb and Griffin, *Process Theology,* 48. Norman Pittenger put the process view this way: "In Charles Hartshorne's way of saying it, God is eternally and absolutely Love-in-action and is utterly faithful to righteous and caring purposes. Yet God in the concrete and divine existence is always related to the world in such a way that there is divine self-identification with and openness to affect from the world. God is committed to the creation and, therefore, cannot be taken as statically timeless but rather as eminently 'time-full' *from* the past, *in* the present, *toward* the future. And in accomplishing the divine purpose, there is complete respect for, and a valuing and employment of, the creation's own dignity and freedom; its responsibility for decisions, and its capacity to act as a genuine cause in the total advance" (*Becoming and Belonging: The Meaning of Human Existence* [Wilton, Conn.: Moorhead Publishing, 1989], 5).

22. Ibid. In addition to love, as Pittenger writes: "We are to work with God in furthering the creative advance of the world in goodness, truth, justice, righteousness, care and love. Such is the practical Christian vocation. Therefore, our Christian attitude toward whatever is evil is a firm rejection of it and an earnest effort against it, to the end that it shall be overcome, negated, removed from the world or transformed into an occasion for good to emerge" (26). Other process theologians who have dealt with the question of evil include David Ray Griffin, *God, Power, and Evil: A Process Theodicy* (Philadelphia: Westminster, 1976); *Evil Revisited: Responses and Reconsiderations* (Albany: State University of New York Press, 1991); Marjorie Suchocki, *The End of Evil: Process Eschatology in Historical Perspective* (Albany: State University of New York Press, 1988); and Barry L. Whitney, *Evil and the Process God,* Toronto Studies in Theology, vol. 19 (New York and Toronto: Edwin Mellen Press, 1985).

23. Ibid., 30.

24. Ibid., 35, 36.

25. Ibid., 36.

26. Ibid.

27. Whitehead, *Religion in the Making,* 128.

28. Ibid., 132.

29. Cobb and Griffin, *Process Theology,* 161. "Since we believe that the prereflective content of faith refers to God and the world as well as to human existence, we prize Whitehead's for its ability to render explicit this prethematized vision of reality."

30. For a thorough listing of the literature and persons associated with process thought, see Cobb and Griffin, *Process Theology,* Appendix B. Among the contemporary major figures are Cobb, Griffin, Schubert M. Ogden, Norman Pittenger, Daniel Day Williams, Leslie Dewart, Bernard Meland, Lewis Ford, and Marjorie Suchocki.

31. Suchocki, *God-Christ-Church,* 93.

32. Ibid., 93-94. Pittenger put it in more philosophical terms: "It is God who is the supreme lure or attraction and who invites (for the most part through creaturely or 'secular' agencies) the response of the creatures as they move from their initial possibility toward their concrete actualizations. This tells us also that God is affected and influenced by what happens in the world and in human life" (*Becoming and Belonging,* 32).

33. Suchocki, *God-Christ-Church.* Griffin explains: "God affects creatures, in this view, not by determining them from without but by persuading them from within. . . . God acts in the world by presenting ideal aims to the creatures. God thereby influences all creatures but totally determines none of them. What possibilities they actualize is finally up to them. The divine power is persuasive, not coercive" ("God in the Postmodern World," in *God and Religion in the Postmodern World,* 65). Lewis S. Ford sees an emphasis on persuasion in the Old Testament and writes: "Process theism involves the persistent effort to conceive God's activity primarily in terms of persuasion. It firmly opposes those views which from its perspective imply certain kinds of coercion within divine power." He further notes that "each event requires the persuasive power of God to provide the lure or possibility or initial aim to be realized, but it also requires the creaturely power to actualize that aim by integrating together the totality of efficient causes derived from the past" (see *The Lure of God: A Biblical Background for Process Theism* [Philadelphia: Fortress, 1978], 17, 50).

34. Ibid., 95.

35. Suchocki, *God-Christ-Church.* Whitehead saw Jesus as "the revelation in act" of the idea that "the divine element in the world is to be conceived as a persuasive agency and not a coercive agency." See Griffin, *A Process Christology,* 224.

36. Ibid., 96.

37. Ibid., 101.

38. Ibid. As Daniel Day Williams put it: "The clue to Christian truth is that God's self-disclosure in Jesus Christ must come together with a critical understanding of our human experience in an intelligible unity of meaning. . . . What God's word in Christ means is truth, which we can have only through a continual reappropriation of it in the light of a critical reflection upon all our experience" (*The Demonic and the Divine,* 48).

39. Whitehead wrote that "religion collapses unless its main positions command immediacy of assent" (*Science and the Modern World,* 274).

40. David Tracy writes of Cobb: "First, Cobb insists that an integral contemporary Christian theology must assume responsibility for a critical investigation of both the Christian tradition and the modern world vision. . . . There, is, then, no substitute via any 'authorities' for careful historical investigation of either the 'vision of reality,' 'structure of existence,' or 'cognitive beliefs' of Christianity" ("John Cobb's Theological Method: Interpretation and Reflections," in *John Cobb's Theology in Process,* eds. David Ray Griffin and Thomas J. J. Altizer [Philadelphia: Westminster, 1977], 26). Cobb had earlier written: "Where then can the theologian find data for a doctrine of God such that it will overcome all rational obstacles to belief? Clearly he cannot merely point to authoritative pronouncements in Bible and creed, for it is precisely in connection with such claims to authority that much serious doubt arises. Either such claims must themselves be substantiated in terms of less doubtful criteria or else more primitive data must be found." ("Theological Data and Method," *Journal of Religion* 33 [July 1953]: 215). Particularly helpful in delineating aspects of the process view of Scripture has been Gary Watts and Jack Rogers, "Six Theological Models of the Early 1980s: Their Theological Methods with Special Reference to Their Use of Scripture." Unpublished paper, Fuller Theological Seminary, 1980.

41. Cobb and Griffin, *Process Theology,* 37.

42. Suchocki, *God-Christ-Church,* 104. As Griffin notes: "The aims given to Jesus and actualized by him during his active ministry were such that the basic vision of reality contained in his message of word and deed was the supreme expression of God's eternal character and purpose" (*A Process Christology,* 218).

43. Ibid. Whitehead had described God as "the great companion—the fellow sufferer who understands" (*Process and Reality,* 413). See also Pittenger, *Becoming and Belonging,* 26, and his other works *The*

Christian Church as Social Process (London: Epworth, 1971); *Process Thought and Christian Faith* (New York: Macmillan, 1968); *Freed to Love: A Process Interpretation of Redemption* (Wilton, Conn.: Moorhead Publishing, 1987).

44. Daniel Day Williams expressed the relation of Scripture and experience when he wrote: "If we discover that certain literal statements in the Bible cannot be brought into congruence with our understanding of nature as we experience it, then we shall have to reserve judgment and rethink the meaning of our Christian declarations until some more inclusive meaning emerges. This is not a question of importing an 'alien' natural theology into our faith as a norm above the biblical truth. It is simply our acknowledgment that the truth of God's redemptive love in Jesus Christ is a saving truth for us precisely because it illuminates and fulfills all honest searching after the realities of our existence" (*The Demonic and the Divine,* 48-49).

45. Cobb and Griffin, *Process Theology,* 40. See also Blair Reynolds, *Toward a Process Pneumatology* (Selinsgrove, Pa.: Susquehanna University Press, 1990).

46. "The divine activity desires the humanization of the world" and "works at positive growth in the world through persuasion," according to Theodore M. Snider, *The Divine Activity: An Approach to Incarnational Theology* (New York: Peter Lang, 1990), 332. As Pittenger puts it: "Basically the goal for each one of us is to become, in our belonging, as completely human as is possible for us." He laments that "Alas, it is also possible for us to opt for nonactualization of the goal and thus to fall into sheer repetition of prior states or to rest content with the *status quo* and thereby fail to advance at all toward this completeness." On the whole, "human existence is the enterprise of becoming a created finite lover, in which each person belongs to society. The aim or goal is the increase of good among all the participants" (*Becoming and Belonging,* 31, 41). The social dimensions of process thought have been increasingly spelled out by John Cobb under the general rubric of "creative transformation." See his many works, including *Christ in a Pluralistic Age* (Philadelphia: Westminster, 1975), and *Is It Too Late? A Theology of Ecology* (Beverly Hills, Calif.: Bruce, 1972).

47. Griffin indicates criteria for evaluating "proffered views of the God-world relation," which also reflect Scripture's place among other "authorities." These are (1) rootage in the key events of the biblical tradition, especially the ministry of Jesus; (2) consistency with other essential presuppositions and doctrines of Christian faith; (3) adequacy to the facts of experience; and (4) illuminating power (see *Process Christology,* 226).

10. NARRATIVE THEOLOGY

1. James William McClendon, Jr., *Biography as Theology: How Life Stories Can Remake Today's Theology* (Nashville: Abingdon, 1974), 7.

2. Lonnie D. Kliever, *The Shattered Spectrum: A Survey of Contemporary Theology* (Atlanta: John Knox, 1981), 160.

3. Gabriel Fackre, "Narrative Theology: An Overview," *Interpretation* 3 (1983): 343.

4. Kliever, *The Shattered Spectrum,* 153. He cites Joseph Campbell, *Myths to Live By* (New York: Viking, 1972), 214-15, and *The Masks of God: Creative Mythology* (New York: Viking, 1970), 608-24, for discussion of the interlocking functions of myth in primitive cultures.

5. Kliever, *The Shattered Spectrum,* 155.

6. See ibid., 155. Kliever cites Robert Scholes and Robert Kellog, *The Nature of Narrative* (London: Oxford University Press, 1966), as a source for the historical development of the narrative tradition in terms of both formal and functional analyses of story.

7. Kliever, *The Shattered Spectrum,* 155.

8. Fackre, "Narrative Theology," 341.

9. Kliever, *The Shattered Spectrum,* 156.

10. Ibid.

11. Ibid., 157. He cites here Frank Kermode, *The Sense of an Ending* (London: Oxford University Press, 1977).

12. Kliever, *The Shattered Spectrum,* 157.

13. Ibid. See also John S. Dunne, *Time and Myth* (Garden City, N.Y.: Doubleday, 1973), 113.

14. See George W. Stroup, "A Bibliographical Critique," *Theology Today* 32 (1975): 133-43, and *The Promise of Narrative Theology: Recovering the Gospel in the Church* (Atlanta: John Knox, 1981), chap. 3. See also Fackre, "Narrative Theology," and Kliever,*The Shattered Spectrum,* chap. 7.

15. Sam Keen, *To a Dancing God* (New York: Harper & Row, 1970); Harvey Cox, *The Seduction of the Spirit* (New York: Simon and Schuster, 1973); Michael Novak, *Ascent of the Mountain, Flight of the Dove* (New York: Harper & Row, 1971); Robert P. Roth, *Story and Reality* (Grand Rapids: Eerdmans, 1973);

Gabriel Fackre, *The Christian Story* (Grand Rapids: Eerdmans, 1978); Gabriel Fackre, *Ecumenical Faith in Evangelical Perspective* (Grand Rapids: Eerdmans, 1993); and John Shea, *Stories of God* (Chicago: Thomas More Press, 1978). On Novak, Cox, and Keen, see also Stanley T. Sutphin, *Options in Contemporary Theology* (Lanham, Md.: University Press of America, 1977), chap. 3.

16. Stroup, *Promise,* 72.

17. Stephen Crites, "The Narrative Quality of Experience," *Journal of the American Academy of Religion* 39 (1971): 291.

18. Ibid., 305.

19. John S. Dunne, *A Search for God in Time and Memory* (New York: Macmillan, 1969), 170.

20. Stroup, *Promise,* 77. For an extended treatment of Dunne, see Kliever, *The Shattered Spectrum,* 160-68.

21. Dunne, *Search,* xi.

22. Ibid. Stroup offers his critique of Dunne in *Promise,* 78.

23. McClendon, *Biography as Theology,* 37.

24. A fuller treatment of McClendon is found in Kliever, *The Shattered Spectrum,* 168-75.

25. Stroup cites the works of Gerhard von Rad, *Old Testament Theology,* trans. James Stalker, 2 vols. (New York: Harper & Row, 1962, 1965); Oscar Cullmann, *Christ and Time* (Philadelphia: Westminster, 1964); and G. Ernest Wright, *God Who Acts: Biblical Theology as Recital,* Studies in Biblical Theology No. 8 (London: SCM, 1952) as significant representatives of this approach. See *Promise,* 79 n. 25.

26. Amos Wilder, *The Language of the Gospel: Early Christian Rhetoric* (New York: Harper & Row, 1964), 64, 67. An important work on the literary analysis of biblical narrative is Robert Alter, *The Art of Biblical Narrative* (New York: Basic Books, 1981). See also *The Literary Guide to the Bible,* eds. Robert Alter and Frank Kermode (Cambridge, Mass.: Harvard University Press, 1990) and *Why Narrative? Readings in Narrative Theology,* eds. Stanley Hauerwas and L. Gregory Jones (Grand Rapids: Eerdmans, 1989).

27. Eric Auerbach, *Mimesis: The Representation of Reality in Western Literature,* trans. Willard R. Trash (Princeton, N.J.: Princeton University Press, 1965), 14-15.

28. Stroup, *Promise,* 81. This is the point made by Hans Frei in *The Eclipse of Biblical Narrative* (New Haven: Yale University Press, 1974). Frei's work has been of great significance to Narrative theology. See his *The Identity of Jesus Christ: The Hermeneutical Bases of Dogmatic Theology* (Philadelphia: Fortress, 1975) and the collection of essays in his honor, *Scriptural Authority and Narrative Interpretation,* ed. Garrett Green (Philadelphia: Fortress, 1987). The narrative form of Scripture stories "function[s] to invite the reader into the world of the tale." See Ronald F. Thiemann, "Radiance and Obscurity in Biblical Narrative," *Scriptural Authority,* 38, and his *Revelation and Theology: The Gospel as Narrated Promise* (Notre Dame, Ind.: University of Notre Dame Press, 1985), as well as Stroup, *Promise,* 139-44.

29. See James A. Sanders, *Torah and Canon* (Philadelphia: Fortress, 1972). See also his "Torah and Christ," *Interpretation* 29 (1975): 372-90.

30. Brevard S. Childs, *Introduction to the Old Testament as Scripture* (Philadelphia: Fortress, 1979), 72. See also Childs, "The Old Testament as Scripture of the Church," *Concordia Theological Monthly* 43 (1972): 709-22.

31. See James Barr, *Holy Scripture: Canon, Authority, Criticism* (Philadelphia: Westminster, 1983), and Child's review of it in *Interpretation* 38 (1984): 66-70. See also Donald K. McKim's review in *Journal of the American Academy of Religion* 52 (1984): 375.

32. See Sallie McFague, *Speaking in Parables* (Philadelphia: Fortress, 1975) and its sequel, *Metaphorical Theology: Models of God in Religious Language* (Philadelphia: Fortress, 1982). A detailed discussion of her work on parables is found in Kliever, *The Shattered Spectrum,* 175-81.

33. McFague, *Metaphorical Theology,* 15, see also 32ff.

34. Ibid. See also *Parables,* 39, where McFague writes: "As we have seen, metaphor is the poet's way to try and define something for which there is not dictionary meaning; it is his or her attempt to be precise and clear about something for which ordinary language has no way of talking."

35. McFague, *Metaphorical Theology,* 17-18. Jesus as a "parable of God" means Jesus both "is and is not God," writes McFague (19). She sees value in this approach in that a metaphorical theology guards against literalistic realism and idolatry. McFague writes: "In such a theology *no* finite thought, product, or creature can be identified with God and this includes Jesus of Nazareth, who as parable of God both 'is and is not' God."

36. This is the "tensive quality" of metaphors. McFague identifies the leading contemporary theorists on metaphor as I. A. Richards, Max Black, Douglas Berggren, Walter Ong, Nelson Goodman, and Paul Ricoeur. Ricoeur's work in particular has been significant for many story theologians.

37. See McFague, *Parables*, 22.

38. Dunne, *Search*, 218.

39. McFague, *Metaphorical Theology*, 40.

40. See Kliever, *The Shattered Spectrum*, 164. Of particular help here also has been Gary Watts and Jack Rogers, "Six Theological Models of the Early 1980s: Their Theological Methods with Special Reference to Their Use of Scripture." Unpublished paper. Fuller Theological Seminary, August, 1980.

41. McClendon, *Biography as Theology*, 152.

42. McFague, *Parables*, 58.

43. Ibid., 16.

44. Ibid., 79.

45. Ibid., 3. Dunne's whole point is that life should be viewed as "story."

46. Kliever, *The Shattered Spectrum*, 180.

47. Ibid.

48. McFague, *Parables*, 94.

49. See McClendon, *Biography as Theology*, 95; Fackre, *The Christian Story*, 20-21; and McFague, who writes: "The various forms of metaphorical language operative in biblical literature and in the Christian literary tradition ought to be looked at carefully as resources for theological reflection" (*Parables* 64).

50. Stanley Hauerwas with David B. Burrell, "From System to Story: An Alternative Pattern for Rationality in Ethics," in Stanley Hauerwas with Richard Bondi and David B. Burrell, *Truthfulness and Tragedy: Further Investigations in Christian Ethics* (Notre Dame, Ind.: University of Notre Dame Press, 1977), 38-39.

51. Ibid., 71. Hauerwas notes that "this does not mean that all theology must itself assume the form of narrative, but rather whatever form theological reflection may take, one of its primary tasks is reminding us of a story."

52. Ibid., 73. He goes on to argue that "story seems to be indispensable in order to express the nature of two such particulars—the self and God" (79). See also his comment that "there is no more fundamental way to talk of God than in a story. The fact that we come to know God through the recounting of the story of Israel and the life of Jesus is decisive for our truthful understanding of the kind of God we worship as well as the world in which we exist," in "The Narrative Character of Christian Convictions," *The Peaceable Kingdom: A Primer in Christian Ethics* (Notre Dame, Ind.: University of Notre Dame Press, 1983), 25.

53. Stanley M. Hauerwas, "A Tale of Two Stories," in his *Christian Existence Today: Essays on Church, World and Living In Between* (Durham, N.C.: Labyrinth Press, 1988), 40. He also writes: "These texts have been accepted as scripture because they and they alone satisfy what Reynolds Price has called our craving for a perfect story which we feel to be true. Put briefly, that story is: 'History is the will of a just God who knows us.' " See "The Moral Authority of Scripture," in *A Community of Character: Toward a Constructive Christian Social Ethic* (Notre Dame, Ind.: University of Notre Dame Press, 1981), 66.

54. Hauerwas, "Moral Authority," 63. This is different from accepting Scripture as an authority "because it sets a standard for orthodoxy." Indeed, "the very categories of orthodoxy and heresy are anachronistic when applied to scripture." Rather, Scripture is authoritative because it provides "the means for our community to find new life" (63).

55. Ibid., 66. Hauerwas defines authority as "that power of a community that allows for reasoned interpretations of the community's past and future goals" (60).

56. Ibid., 66.

57. Ibid., 67. Hauerwas writes that "narrative provides the conceptual means to suggest how the stories of Israel and Jesus are a 'morality' for the formation of Christian community and character." He sees "narrative" and "character" as "but two sides of the same coin." See "The Church in a Divided World," in *A Community of Character*, 95. See also his "Toward an Ethics of Character," in *Vision and Virtue: Essays in Christian Ethical Reflection* (Notre Dame, Ind.: Fides Publishers, 1974), 48-67; "Character, Narrative, and Growth in the Christian Life" in the same volume, 129-152; and *Character and the Christian Life* (San Antonio: Trinity University Press, 1975), where he formally defined *character* as "the qualification or determination of our self-agency, formed by our having certain intentions rather than others" (115).

58. Hauerwas, "Moral Authority," 63-64. Thus, says Hauerwas, "Scripture creates more than a world; it shapes a community which is the bearer of that world. Without that community, claims about the moral authority of scripture—or rather the very idea of scripture itself—makes no sense" (55).

59. Hauerwas, "The Church as God's New Language," in *Scriptural Authority and Narrative Interpretation*, 190. This essay is reprinted in *Christian Existence Today*, 47-65.

60. Hauerwas, *The Peaceable Kingdom*, 68. Put succinctly: "We Christians are not called on to be 'moral' but faithful to the true story, the story that we are creatures under the Lordship of a God who wants nothing more than our faithful service" (68).

61. Ibid., 70.

62. Hauerwas, "The Church as God's New Language," 193. Hauerwas also notes that "memory is a moral exercise. We must be the kind of people capable of remembering our failures and sins if we are rightly to tell the story we have been charged to keep, for a proper telling requires that we reveal our sin. To acknowledge the authority of Scripture is also to learn to acknowledge our sin and accept forgiveness. It is only through forgiveness that we are able to witness to how that story has formed our lives" (*The Peaceable Kingdom*, 69).

63. Hauerwas, "Moral Authority," 55.

64. Hauerwas, "Story and Theology," 73. See also his "The Ethicist as Theologian," *The Christian Century* 92, 15 (April 23, 1975): 408-12. This is also the grounding for Hauerwas's ethical writings, including *Vision and Virtue*. See also Hauerwas and William H. Willimon, *Resident Aliens* (Nashville: Abingdon, 1989).

65. Hauerwas, "Jesus: The Story of the Kingdom," in *A Community of Character*, 52, 45. The nature of Christian ethics, according to Hauerwas, "is determined by the fact that Christian convictions take the form of a story, or perhaps better, a set of stories that constitutes a tradition, which in turn creates and forms a community." The first task of Christian ethics is not to say "Thou shalt" or "Thou shalt not," but "to help us rightly envision the world." For "Christian ethics is specifically formed by a very definite story with determinative content." See "The Narrative Character of Christian Convictions," in *The Peaceable Kingdom*, 24, 29.

66. Hauerwas, "Jesus: The Story of the Kingdom," 51. Jesus is the kingdom or reign of God "in person" (Gr. *autobasileia*) and as such his story calls for Christian obedience to and in "a community based on Jesus' messiahship" (45, 49).

67. Stanley Hauerwas, "The Bible and America," in *Unleashing the Scripture* (Nashville: Abingdon, 1993), 39.

68. Hauerwas, *The Peaceable Kingdom*, 71.

69. Ibid., 70. Hauerwas also writes that "the text of the Scripture is not meant to be 'preserved intact' separate from the Church. God certainly uses Scripture to call the Church to faithfulness, but such a call always comes in the form of some in the Church reminding others in the Church how to live as Christians—no 'text' can be substituted for the people of God." See "Stanley Fish, the Pope, and the Bible," in *Unleashing the Scripture*, 30.

70. Hauerwas, "The Bible and America," 38. Against the views of others that individuals in isolation may find the "true meaning" of biblical texts, Hauerwas stresses the "communal presuppositions necessary for any account of the Christian use of Scripture." He points out that both Fundamentalists and biblical critics share the assumption that "the interpretation of the biblical texts is not a political process involving questions of power and authority. By privileging the individual interpreter, who is thought capable of discerning the meaning of the text apart from the consideration of the good ends of a community, fundamentalists and biblical critics make the Church incidental." See "Stanley Fish, the Pope, and the Bible," *Unleashing the Scripture*, 27-28.

11. LATIN AMERICAN LIBERATION THEOLOGY

1. See *Lift Every Voice: Constructing Christian Theologies from the Underside,* eds. Susan Brooks Thistlethwaite and Mary Potter Engel (San Francisco: HarperCollins, 1990), 284 and the introduction; Deane William Ferm, *Third World Liberation Theologies: An Introductory Survey* (Maryknoll, N.Y.: Orbis 1986); Curt Cadorette et al., eds., *Liberation Theology: An Introductory Reader* (Maryknoll, N.Y.: Orbis, 1992); Harvie M. Conn, "Theologies of Liberation: An Overview," in *Tensions in Contemporary Theology,* eds. Stanley N. Gundry and Alan F. Johnson, 2nd ed. (Grand Rapids: Baker Book House, 1983), 327. See also Conn's essay in the same book, "Theologies of Liberation: Toward a Common View," 395-434, for a discussion of various liberation theologies. An extensive annotated bibliography is found in Ronald G. Musto, *Liberation Theologies: A Research Guide* (Hamden, Conn.: Garland Publishing, 1990).

2. Lonnie D. Kliever, *The Shattered Spectrum: A Survey of Contemporary Theology* (Atlanta: John Knox 1981), 86.

3. Other forms of liberation theology are dealt with by Conn and on a smaller scale in Stanley T. Sutphin, *Options in Contemporary Theology* (Lanham, Md.: University Press of America, 1977), chap. 2. See also Kliever, *The Shattered Spectrum*, chap. 4; *The Modern Theologians: An Introduction to Christian Theology*

in the Twentieth Century, ed. David F. Ford, 2 vols. (Cambridge, Mass.: Basil Blackwell, 1989), 2:Part 4; and the introductions to Latin American Liberation Theology by Phillip Berryman, *Liberation Theology: The Essential Facts About the Revolutionary Movement in Latin America and Beyond* (New York: Pantheon Books, 1987); Leonardo Boff and Clodovis Boff, *Introducing Liberation Theology,* trans. Paul Burns (Maryknoll, N.Y.: Orbis 1987); and Robert McAfee Brown, *Liberation Theology: An Introductory Guide* (Louisville: Westminster/John Knox 1993). Also illuminating is Guillermo Cook, *The Expectation of the Poor: Latin American Basic Ecclesial Communities in Protestant Perspective* (Maryknoll, N.Y.: Orbis 1985).

4. Robert McAfee Brown, *Theology in a New Key: Responding to Liberation Themes* (Philadelphia: Westminster 1978), 52.

5. The English texts of the Medellín Conference are in *The Church in the Present-Day Transformation of Latin America in the Light of the Council Volume II. Conclusions* (Washington, D.C.: U.S. Catholic Conference, 1973). A selection from the document on peace is in Deane William Ferm, *Third World Liberation Theologies: A Reader* (Maryknoll, N.Y.: Orbis 1986), 3-11. The historical backgrounds of Latin American developments are found in Enrique Dussel, *History and the Theology of Liberation* (Maryknoll, N.Y.: Orbis, 1976). See also *Theology in the Americas,* eds. Sergio Tores and John Eagleson (Maryknoll, N.Y.: Orbis, 1976); and Francis P. Fiorenza, "Latin American Liberation Theology," *Interpretation* (1974): 441-57, for additional backgrounds.

6. Cited in Brown, *Theology in a New Key,* 53.

7. See Conn, "Overview," 344.

8. Cited in Brown, *Theology in a New Key,* 54.

9. Conn, "Overview," 344.

10. Ibid.

11. Brown, *Theology in a New Key,* 54.

12. *The Emergent Gospel: Theology from the Underside of History,* eds. Sergio Torres and Virginia Fabella (Maryknoll, N.Y.: Orbis, 1978), 182.

13. See the account of this group and documents of this conference in *Christians and Socialism,* ed. John Eagleson (Maryknoll, N.Y.: Orbis, 1975).

14. Brown, *Theology in a New Key,* 55-56.

15. Cited in ibid., 57.

16. Ibid., 57.

17. Ibid., 59.

18. Ibid.

19. Cited in José Miguez Bonino, *Doing Theology in a Revolutionary Situation,* ed. William H. Lazareth (Philadelphia: Fortress 1975), 43. See also Gustavo Gutiérrez, *A Theology of Liberation History, Politics and Salvation,* trans. and eds. Sister Caridad Inda and John Eagleson (Maryknoll, N.Y.: Orbis, 1973), 105; hereafter cited as *TL.*

20. Cited in Bonino, *Doing Theology,* 43-44.

21. Ibid., 44.

22. Conn, 359.

23. Bonino, *Doing Theology,* 74. See Rubem Alves, *A Theology of Human Hope* (Washington, D.C.: Corpus Books, 1969).

24. Cited in Bonino, *Doing Theology,* 74.

25. Ibid., 76.

26. Conn, 360.

27. Alves was critical of the view of Jürgen Moltmann, *Theology of Hope* (New York: Harper & Row, 1967), that hope is mediated only through biblical promises. This Alves calls "a new form of docetism, in which God lose his present-day dimension." See Alves, *A Theology of Human Hope,* 55-68.

28. Bonino, *Doing Theology,* 76.

29. Cited in ibid., 72 from Assmann's *Opresion-Liberacion.* The English translation of this book is found in Assmann's *Practical Theology of Liberation* (London: Search, 1975), chap. 2. See also his *Theology for a Nomad Church* (Maryknoll, N.Y.: Orbis, 1976). Rebecca Chopp writes that "Latin American liberation theology is not primarily academic discourse for academic debate; it is, rather, church theology coming out of and aimed toward its ecclesial context in basic Christian communities." See her "Latin American Liberation Theology," in *The Modern Theologians,* 2:176.

30. Cited in Bonino, *Doing Theology,* 73.

31. A shorter discussion of Gutiérrez's views is his "Freedom and Salvation: A Political Problem," in *Liberation and Change,* ed. Ronald H. Stone (Atlanta: John Knox 1977), 3-94. See also Chopp, "Latin American Liberation Theology," 182-84.

32. From *Frontiers of Theology in Latin America,* ed. Rosini Gibellini (Maryknoll, N.Y.: Orbis, 1979), x.

33. Gutiérrez, *TL,* 36.

34. Ibid., 36-37.

35. Ibid., 37; see also 175. On the centrality of justice, see Ismael García, *Justice in Latin American Theology of Liberation* (Atlanta: John Knox 1987).

36. Ibid., 177.

37. Kliever, *The Shattered Spectrum,* 87.

38. Gutiérrez, *TL,* 178.

39. Bonino, *Doing Theology,* 70.

40. Gutiérrez *TL,* 70.

41. Ibid., 153.

42. Ibid., 72. Bonino comments that "all the chapters in Guiterrez's presentation take this fundamental unity to different areas of theological thought. The couples liberation/salvation, love of the neighbor/Christology, politics/eschatology, humanity/Church, human solidarity/sacraments, cover the classical *loci* of theology indissolubly relating them to the search for socio-political liberation and the building of a new humanity" (*Doing Theology,* 71).

43. Gutiérrez, *TL,* 15.

44. Ibid., 6.

45. Ibid., 13.

46. Conn, "Overview," p. 362.

47. Stephen C. Knapp, "A Preliminary Dialogue with Gutiérrez' 'A Theology of Liberation,' " in *Evangelicals and Liberation,* ed. Carl E. Armerding (Nutley, N.J.: Presbyterian and Reformed Publishing Company, 1977), 17.

48. Gutiérrez, *TL,* 15. The implications of this for the Eucharist and human community are also explicated by Gutiérrez, see 262-79. See also his *We Drink From Our Own Wells: The Spiritual Journey of a People* (Maryknoll, N.Y.: Melbourne, 1984), and *On Job: God-Talk and the Suffering of the Innocent* (Maryknoll, N.Y.: Orbis 1987).

49. José Porfirio Miranda, *Marx and the Bible: A Critique of the Philosophy of Oppression,* trans. John Eagleson (Maryknoll, N.Y.: Orbis, 1974). See also J. Emmette Weir, "The Bible and Marx: A Discussion of the Hermeneutics of Liberation Theology," *Scottish Journal of Theology* 35 (1982): 337-50.

50. Juan Luis Segundo, *The Liberation of Theology,* trans. John Drury (Maryknoll, N.Y.: Orbis, 1976). See also Dean William Ferm, *Contemporary American Theologies: A Critical Survey* (New York: Seabury, 1981), 68; Conn, "Overview," 366-68; and Alfred T. Hennelly, "The Challenge of Juan Luis Segundo," *Theological Studies* 38 (1977): 125ff.

51. Jon Sobrino, *Christology at the Crossroads: A Latin American Approach,* trans. John Drury (Maryknoll, N.Y.: Orbis, 1978). See also Alfred T. Hennelly, "Theological Method: The Southern Exposure," *Theological Studies* 38 (1977): 722.

52. Leonardo Boff, *Jesus Christ Liberator: A Critical Christology for Our Time,* trans. Patrick Hughes (Maryknoll, N.Y.: Orbis, 1978).

53. Bonino is "considered by many to be the dean of Latin American Protestant theologians" (Conn, "Overview," 371). He is an Argentinian and teaches at the Higher Institute of Theological Studies in Buenos Aires. José Miguez Bonino, *Christians and Marxists: The Mutual Challenge of Revolution* (Grand Rapids:Eerdmans 1976). See also Conn, pp. 372-73, and Chopp, "Latin American Liberation Theology," 184-86.

54. Justo L. González, *Mañana: Christian Theology from a Hispanic Perspective* (Nashville: Abingdon 1990); *Liberation Preaching: The Pulpit and the Oppressed* (Nashville: Abingdon 1980).

55. See Gutiérrez, *TL,* 81-88, and Bonino, *Doing Theology,* 21-37, for historical analyses.

56. Gutiérrez, *TL,* 83.

57. Ibid., 84.

58. Ibid., 86.

59. See Conn, "Overview," 348.

60. Gutiérrez, *TL,* p. 87.

61. Brown, *Theology in a New Key,* 60-61.

62. Frederick Herzog, *Liberation Theology* (New York: Seabury, 1972), 258.

63. Brown, *Theology in a New Key,* 61.

64. Ibid.

65. Cited in ibid., 71. Bonino says similarly: "There is, therefore, no knowledge except in action itself, in the process of transforming the world through participation in history" (*Doing Theology,* 88).

66. Bonino, *Doing Theology,* 90.

67. Conn, "Common," 400. See also Brown, *Theology in a New Key,* 72-74. Brown's characteristics of liberation theology and its differences from classical theology are:

1. a different starting point: the poor
2. a different interlocutor: the nonperson
3. a different set of tools: the social sciences
4. a different analysis: the reality of conflict
5. a different mode of engagement: praxis
6. a different theology: the "second act."

See ibid., 60. See also the analysis by C. René Padilla, "Liberation Theology (I)," *The Reformed Journal* 33, no. 6 (1983): 21-23, and his "Liberation Thelogy (II) An Evaluation," *The Reformed Journal* 33, no. 7 (1983): 14-18.

68. Brown, *Theology in a New Key,* 79. He cites instances where the "poor" in the New Testament are "spiritualized" by bliblical commentators.

69. Bonino, *Doing Theology,* 87.

70. Gutiérrez, *TL,* 12.

71. Bonino, *Doing Theology,* 91. See also his whole chap. 5: "Hermeneutics, Truth, and Praxis," reprinted in *A Guide to Contemporary Hermeneutics,* ed. Donald K. McKim (Grand Rapids: Eerdmans, 1986), 344-57. For a discussion of Segundo's "hermeneutical circle" in this regard, see Padilla, "Liberation Theology (I)," 23, and Conn, "Overview," 367.

72. Bonino, *Doing Theology,* 91.

73. Brown, *Theology in a New Key,* 81. See also Bonino, *Doing Theology,* 101-2.

74. Gutiérrz, *TL.* Of help in seeing these uses of Scripture in liberation theology has been Gary Watts and Jack Rogers, "Six Theological Models of the Early 1980s: Their Theological Methods with Special Reference to Their Use of Scripture." Unpublished paper, Fuller Theological Seminary, 1980. See also J. A. Kirk, "The Bible in Latin American Liberation Theology," in *The Bible and Liberation,* eds. Norman K. Gottwald and Antoinette C. Wire (Berkeley, Calif.: Radical Religion, 1976).

75. Brown, *Theology in a New Key,* 88. See also John Goldingay, "The Hermeneutics of Liberation Theology," *Horizons in Bible Theology* 4–5 (1982–1983): 139ff.

76. Daniel L. Migliore, *Called to Freedom: Liberation Theology and the Future of Christian Doctrine* (Philadelphia: Westminster, 1980), 31.

77. See Gutiérrez, *TL,* 194, and Brown, *Theology in a New Key,* 90ff.

78. Gutiérrez, *TL,* 195.

79. Ibid., 162, 163.

80. Ibid., p. 167.

81. Ibid., 10.

82. Ibid., 135.

12. BLACK THEOLOGY

1. Patrick A. Kalilombe, "Black Theology," *The Modern Theologians: An Introduction to Christian Theology in the Twentieth Century,* 2 vols., ed., David F. Ford (Cambridge, Mass.: Basil Blackwell, 1989), 2:194.

2. For studies of African liberation theology, see Ferm, *Survey,* chap. 3, and Kalilombe, "Black Theology," 201-13.

3. James H. Evans, Jr., *We Have Been Believers: An African-American Systematic Theology* (Minneapolis: Fortress 1992), 2.

4. Gayraud S. Wilmore, *Black Religion and Black Radicalism: An Interpretation of the Religious History of Afro-American People,* 2nd ed. (Maryknoll, N.Y.: Orbis 1983), x.

5. Evans, *Believers,* 3, citing the work of James Cone, *Black Theology and Black Power* (New York: Seabury, 1969), and J. Deotis Roberts, *Liberation and Reconciliation: A Black Theology* (Philadelphia: Westminster 1971).

6. Kalilombe, "Black Theology," 197. Evans notes that "the most profound contribution of the black power movement to the development of black theology was its challenge to black people to show how they could be black and Christian at the same time" (4). Cone defined "Black Power" as used by its advocates in the late 1960s to mean "complete emancipation of black people from white oppression by whatever means black people deem necessary" (*Black Theology*, 6). See also his *For My People: Black Theology and the Black Church* (Maryknoll, N.Y.: Orbis 1984), 54-59.

7. See *Black Theology: A Documentary History, 1966–1979*, eds. Gayraud S. Wilmore and James H. Cone (Maryknoll, N.Y.: Orbis 1979), 4-11; and Cone, *For My People*, chap. 1: "The Origin of Black Theology."

8. See Cone's discussion of the literature of black theology and religion in *For My People*, 74-77. On Womanist theology, see chapter 14 of this book.

9. Wilmore and Cone, *Black Theology: A Documentary History, 1966–1979*, 101.

10. James H. Evans, Jr., "Black Theology," *A New Handbook of Christian Theology*, eds. Donald W. Musser and Joseph L. Price (Nashville: Abingdon 1992), 71-72.

11. See Cone, *For My People*, 63, and his study *The Spirituals and the Blues* (New York: Seabury 1972).

12. James H. Cone, *Speaking the Truth: Ecumenism, Liberation, and Black Theology* (Grand Rapids: Eerdmans 1986), 11.

13. Evans, *Believers*, 11. Cone notes that black theologians agree with Neo-orthodox theologians that God is known by God's acts in history. They go on to say that "these acts are identical with the liberation of the weak and the poor" (*For My People*, 65).

14. James H. Cone, *A Black Theology of Liberation*, 2nd ed. (Maryknoll, N.Y.: Orbis 1986), 26. He further writes, "God's revelation comes to us in and through the cultural situation of the oppressed" (28) and "I do not think that revelation is comprehensible from a black theological perspective without a prior understanding of the concrete manifestation of revelation in the black community as seen in the black experience, black history, and black culture," (29).

15. Evans, "Black Theology," 72. Evans says that, theologically speaking, "to attempt to formulate an understanding of God's revelation apart from an analysis of the unjust structures of social existence does violence to both the significance of that revelation and to the integrity of the liberation struggles carried on by the victims of society" (*Believers*, 12).

16. Evans, *Believers*, 12-13. Evans also notes that "in black theology the term 'liberation' is used to refer to salvation and more. This 'more' is necessary because of the tendency in European-American Christianity to limit the meaning of salvation to some privatistic notion of individual rescue that has no effect on one's social location in relation to God's liberation of the total person" (156, n. 2).

17. Ibid., 16.

18. See ibid., 16-18.

19. Ibid., 18.

20. Cone, *Liberation*, 37, 38.

21. Cone, *For My People*, 66-67. He continues: "In the U.S.A. this claim meant that God was on the side of oppressed blacks in their struggle for freedom and against whites who victimized them. For black clergy radicals, the best way to describe that insight was to say that 'Jesus is black.' " See also *Liberation*, chap. 6, and Evans's fine discussion "Jesus Christ: Liberator and Mediator," *Believers*, chap. 4. He notes varieties of views in the black community and the important early work by Howard Thurman, *Jesus and the Disinherited* (Nashville: Abingdon, 1949).

22. Cone, *Liberation*, 38. As Evans puts it, "The norm of Christian theological affirmations is the acme of God's self-revelation in some notion of the identity and mission or the person and work of Jesus Christ" (*Believers*, 29).

23. Cone, *Liberation*, 45.

24. Ibid. 45. In this work, Cone went on to indicate that "the black revolution in America is the revelation of God. Revelation means black power—that is, the 'complete emancipation of black people from white oppression by whatever means black people deem necessary.' " Evans goes on to develop the multidimensionality of revelation, which includes the dynamic nature of God's actions and the conviction that God is revealed in direct, personal encounters that concern "whole persons and whole communities in their particularity." Revelation is "the loving and gracious giving of Godself to the world" (*Believers*, 15).

25. Cone, *Liberation*, 30.

26. Ibid., 36.

27. A statement made both by Cone, ibid., 31, and Evans, "Black Theology," 71.

28. Evans, *Believers*, 33.

29. See Cone, *Truth*, 4. He goes on to say: "To use Scripture as the starting point of theology does not rule out other sources, such as philosophy, tradition, and our contemporary context. It simply means that Scripture will define how these sources will function in theology." Evans, in *Believers*, 33, notes that "it is necessary for the Bible to play an important, if not central, role in such theological discourse for it legitimately to be considered Christian theology."

30. Cone, *Liberation*, 31. The use of the term *witness* here indicates the influence of Karl Barth on whom Cone wrote his doctoral dissertation. See chapter 6.

31. J. Deotis Roberts, *Black Theology in Dialogue* (Philadelphia: Westminster 1987), 36.

32. Cone, *Truth*, 5-6. He notes: "If theology is derived from this divine story, then it *must* be a language about liberation. Anything else would be an ideological distortion of the gospel message."

33. Cone, *Liberation*, 31.

34. Ibid.

35. Cone, *Truth*, 10.

36. Roberts, *Black Theology*, 36.

37. Evans, *Believers*, 40. See his chap. 2: "The Bible: A Text for Outsiders."

38. See ibid., 40-45.

39. Ibid., 45-46.

40. Katie G. Cannon, "The Bible from the Perspective of the Racially and Economically Oppressed," in *Scripture: The Word Beyond the Word* (Nashville: Women's Division, General Board of Global Ministries, United Methodist Church, 1985), 38.

41. Evans, *Believers*, 46.

42. William A. Graham, *Beyond the Written Word* (Cambridge: Cambridge University Press, 1987), 5.

43. Evans, *Believers*, 50. Evans has also indicated that "a great deal of the religious self-understanding of black people is expressed in biblical language . . . it has become an integral part of black self-expression." Black folklore has interwoven biblical images into the fabric of black experience so that "now it is almost impossible to appreciate black folklore fully without attention to the Bible. The Bible is a text that is not simply the possession of the black church; rather, it is part of the language of the black community as a whole. The Bible became so important for black people in America because in it they saw their own experiences reflected. Therefore, they understood themselves to be a part of the tradition of the faithful of history for whom the Bible was the standard by which fidelity was measured" ("Black Theology," 71).

44. Evans, *Believers*, 51.

45. See Evans, "Black Theology," 73-75, for other dimensions of black theology in relation to other theological expressions.

46. See Evans, *Believers*, 51-52. He also cites Vincent L. Wimbush, "Biblical-Historical Study as Liberation: Toward an Afro-Christian Hermeneutic," *Journal of Religious Thought* 42 (Fall-Winter 1985–86); and Peter J. Paris, "The Bible and the Black Churches," in *The Bible and Social Reform*, ed. Ernest R. Sandeen (Philadelphia: Fortress 1982).

13. Asian Theology

1. Deane William Ferm, *Third World Liberation Theologies: An Introductory Survey* (Maryknoll, N.Y.: Orbis 1986), 76.

2. Kosuke Koyama, "Foreward by an Asian Theologian," in *Asian Christian Theology: Emerging Themes*, ed. Douglas J. Elwood (Philadelphia: Westminster, 1980), 14.

3. See Choan-Seng Song, *Theology from the Womb of Asia* (Maryknoll, N.Y.: Orbis 1986), 3; and his *Third-Eye Theology* (Maryknoll, N.Y.: Orbis 1979). The "third-eye" image is from a Buddhist Zen-master who spoke of the "third eye" as "the hitherto unheard-of-region shut away from us through our own ignorance. When the cloud of ignorance disappears, the infinity of heavens is manifested where we see for the first time into the nature of our own being" (cited in Song, *Third-Eye*, 11).

4. Song, *Womb*, 3. Song also writes that "it is the Asian *oikoumene*, the broader inhabited world of Asia with its histories, cultures, and religions, that is the subject of our theological concern" (*Tell Us Our Names: Story Theology from an Asian Perspective* [Maryknoll, N.Y.: Orbis 1984], 21).

5. Kosuke Koyama, "Asian Theology," in *The Modern Theologians: An Introduction to Christian Theology in the Twentieth Century*, 2 vols., ed. David F. Ford (Cambridge, Mass.: Basil Blackwell, 1989), 2:217. Koyama mentions the work of The Ecumenical Association of Third World Theolgians (EATWOT) and the six conferences they held from 1976 to 1983.

6. M. M. Thomas, *The Christian Response to the Asian Revolution* (London: SCM, 1966), preface cited by Douglas J. Elwood, "Asian Theology in the Making: An Introduction," in *Asian Christian Theology*, 24.

Elwood also notes that "when Asian Christians theologize as part of the universal church responding to its situation in Asia, there is a contribution to Christian theology which may rightly be called *Asian* theology." His introduction provides a good background of important developments.

7. Koyama, "Foreword," 13.

8. *Contextualization* has been defined as "the capacity to respond meaningfully to the gospel within the framework of one's own situation." See Theological Education Fund, *Ministry in Context: The Third Mandate Programme of the TEF, 1970–77* (London: TEF, 1972), 19, cited in Elwood, "Asian Theology," 26. See also Koyama, "Asian Theology," 217.

9. Saphir P. Athyal, "Toward an Asian Christian Theology," in *Asian Christian Theology*, 71.

10. Song, *Womb*, 60. He also writes: "Contextual theology is none other than our response to God's call to explore and experience 'God-meaning' in human sufferings and hopes that take form in cultures, histories, and religions. It has the task of pointing to 'God-meaning' in the futility and meaninglessness that conditions the lives of most persons, including Christians and theologians" (*Names*, 36).

11. The document is found in *Asian Christian Theology*, 100-109.

12. Ibid., 105.

13. See ibid., 105-6.

14. In ibid., 239-253.

15. Aloysius Pieris, "Toward an Asian Theology of Liberation: Some Religiocultural Guidelines," *Asian Christian Theology*, 246.

16. Ibid. He listed five features (drawn from the writings of Jon Sobrino) that are particularly relevant for Asian theology. These include emphasis on changing the world, the primacy of praxis over theory, the way of the cross, a spirituality of solidarity with the poor, and the emphasis on using all human potentials to anticipate the kingdom of God which still remains God's gracious gift (See. 246-47).

17. Pieris, 248.

18. For a survey of important theologians, see Ferm, *Survey*, and Koyama, "Asian Theology," as well as Richard Henry Drummond, *Toward a New Age in Christian Theology* (Maryknoll, N.Y.: Orbis 1985), *passim*.

19. Kosuke Koyama, *Waterbuffalo Theology* (Maryknoll, N.Y.: Orbis 1974), vii-viii.

20. See Kosuke Koyama, *Three Mile an Hour God* (Maryknoll, N.Y.: Orbis 1979), 6. See also his *No Handle on the Cross* (Maryknoll, N.Y.: Orbis, 1977).

21. Kosuke Koyama, *Mount Fuji and Mount Sinai: A Critique of Idols* (Maryknoll, N.Y.: Orbis 1985).

22. Koyama, *Three Mile an Hour God*, 118.

23. Choan-Seng Song, *The Compassionate God* (Maryknoll, N.Y.: Orbis 1982), 49. Put succinctly, Song writes: "God works in the histories of *all* nations. . . . There are *theo*logical forces working in all nations and peoples, creating meanings for them and bringing these meanings to interact with each other" (*Jesus and the Reign of God* [Minneapolis: Fortress, 1993], 55).

24. See Choan-Seng Song, "From Israel to Asia: A Theological Leap," in *Mission Trends No. 3*, eds. Gerald H. Anderson and Thomas F. Stransky (New York: Paulist Press, 1976), 212-22. See also Song's *Christian Mission in Reconstruction* (Maryknoll, N.Y.: Orbis 1977), 174-276; and Drummond, *Toward a New Age in Christian Theology*, 155-60.

25. Song, *Third-Eye Theology*, 116. He continues: "The histories of nations and peoples that are not under the direct impact of Christianity are not just 'natural' histories running their course in complete separation from God's redemptive love and power. In this sense, there is no 'natural' history. The history of a nation and the dynamics of its rise and fall cannot be explained entirely by natural forces or sociopolitical factors. There are redemptive elements in all nations that condemn human corruption and encourage what is noble and holy." Song also argued that "there is no reason why Christ should provide only one way of looking at the unfolding of the mystery of God's dealings with man in different spaciotemporal contexts" (See "The Divine Mission of Creation," in *Asian Christian Theology*, 188). In the context of the parable of the last judgment (Matt. 25:31-46), Song noted: "Throughout human history there are men and women who have gone about doing the king's business without being aware that they are in the king's service" (*Third-Eye Theology*, 118). These comments come from his chapter titled "The Cross and the Lotus."

26. Song, *Third-Eye Theology*, 118, 119. Song writes: "What is important, in the last analysis, is whether we are in touch with the power of redemption in what we encounter, the power that enables us to see God's anguish in human anguish and God's rejoicing in human rejoicing. This, it seems to me, is essentially what Jesus' good news is all about" (*Tell Us Our Names*, 15-16).

27. Song, "From Israel to Asia," 222.

28. See Song's *The Tears of Lady Meng: A Parable of People's Political Theology* (Maryknoll, N.Y.: Orbis 1982); *Tell Us Our Names*; and parables found throughout his other works. Song wrote: "Strictly

speaking, the church does not have its own mission. There is only one mission: the mission of God. The church exists to serve God's mission. The task of Third World theology is to help the traditional churches enlarge their vision of God's mission" (*Tell Us Our Names*, 12).

29. "Asia's Struggle for Full Humanity," *Asian Christian Theology*, 107. Song writes that "theology becomes untrue to its vocation when it is separated from this life, this world, and especially from the suffering and despairing masses" (*Tell Us Our Names*, 43-44).

30. *Asian Christian Theology*, 107.

31. Song, *Tell Us Our Names*, 39. Likewise, Song writes: "In theology we begin with where we are and what we are—that is, where God and human beings meet in space and time. We neither begin with God alone nor with humanity alone. We begin with the God-man Jesus Christ" (*Third-Eye Theology*, 79).

32. Song, *Tell Us Our Names*, 11. Also, "theology is born when we meet persons in their life and history" (32).

33. Ibid., 29.

34. Ibid., 30. Song wrote that "the totality of life is the raw material of theology. Theology deals with concrete issues that affect life in its totality and not just with abstract concepts that engage theological brains. No human problem is too humble or too insignificant for theology. Theology has to wrestle with the earth, not with heaven" (6).

35. Ibid., 30.

36. Ibid.. Song tells the story of a Zen monk who saw a peach tree in full bloom and thus realized in the contrast of the tree with his own body, which was thin and tired due to fasting and lack of sleep, that "truth does not come by making vows not to eat and sleep . . . truth is right there in front of you. . . . It discloses to you the mystery of nature: the mystery that sustains life. It reveals to you the power of the divine: the power of love that overcomes frost, snow, and wind to bring a peach tree to full bloom."

37. Ibid., 30-31.

38. Idid., 32. Song writes that "context and revelation are forever in confluence. Revelation runs into context and context runs into revelation. A context becomes a revelation, and that revelation becomes another context for another revelation" (40). Supremely, "context and revelation: the Word become flesh. This is incarnation" (42).

39. This is noted in *Lift Every Voice: Constructing Christian Theologies from the Underside*, eds. Susan Brooks Thistlethwaite and Mary Potter Engel (San Francisco: HarperCollins, 1990), 20. Song discusses the "hermeneutical circle" of Juan Luis Segundo and the black theology of James Cone in *Third-Eye Theology*, 80-83.

40. Song, *Tell Us Our Names*, x.

41. Song, *Womb*, 54.

42. Kwok Pui-lan, "Discovering the Bible in the Non-Biblical World," in *Lift Every Voice*, 276. Kwok Pui-lan is Chinese and is a writer, lecturer, mother, and theologian who teaches Religion and Society at the Chinese University of Hong Kong.

43. Song, *Womb*, p. 99.

44. Kwok Pui-lan, "Discovering the Bible," 275.

45. Ibid., 276. See also Song, *Womb*, chap. 5.

46. See Kwok Pui-lan, "Discovering the Bible," 276-77. She cites Maen Pongudom, "Creation of Man: Theological Reflections Based on Northern Thai Folktales," and Archie C. C. Lee, "Doing Theology in the Chinese Context: The David-Bathsheba Story and the Parable of Nathan," *East Asia Journal of Theology* 3, 2 (1985); Padma Gallup, "Doing Theology—An Asian Feminist Perspective," *Commission on Theological Concerns Bulletin, Christian Conference of Asia* 4 (1983); Kwok Pui-lan, "God Weeps with Our Pain," *East Asia Journal of Theology* 2, 2 (1984): 228-32; and "A Chinese Perspective," in *Theology by the People: Reflections on Doing Theology in Community*, eds. Samuel Amirtham and John S. Pobee (Geneva: World Council of Churches, 1986), 78-83.

47. See Kwok Pui-lan, "Discovering the Bible," 277 citing Cyris H. S. Moon, *A Korean Minjung Theology: An Old Testament Perspective* (Maryknoll, N.Y.: Orbis 1985).

48. Kwok Pui-lan, "Discovering the Bible," 281.

49. Song, *Tell Us Our Names*, 36.

50. "Asia's Struggle for Full Humanity," *Asian Christian Theology*, 102.

51. Song, *Womb*, 208. Song develops these insights as well from the perspectives of Jesus' resurrection and the coming reign of God. See ibid., part 4; *Third-Eye Theology*, part 3; and *The Reign of God*, where he writes that God's reign is evident in the stories of God's saving presence in Jesus, which "becomes manifest through movements of people to be free from the shackles of the past, to change the status quo of the present, and to have a role to play in the arrival of the future."

52. Kwok Pui-lan, "Discovering the Bible," 281. She sees that the "critical principle" for biblical interpretation "lies not in the Bible itself, but in the community of women and men who read the Bible and who through their dialogical imagination appropriate it for their own liberation" (280).

14. FEMINIST AND WOMANIST THEOLOGY

1. The Women's Caucus of Religious Studies, a group affiliated with the American Academy of Religion, in 1980 listed 168 members. In 1984 the group listed 336 women theologians at professional or doctoral level theological work. See Joan Turner Beifuss, "Feminist Theologians Organize, Make Gains," *National Catholic Reporter* 20 (April 13, 1984): 3. The whole issue is devoted to "Women Doing Theology."

2. Ibid. As Letty Russell writes: "strictly speaking feminist theology is *not* about women. It is about God. It is not a form of 'ego-logy' in which women just think about themselves. When women do it, they speak of feminist theology in order to express the fact that the experience from which they speak and the world out of which they perceive God's words and actions and join in those actions is that of women seeking human equality. Another way of expressing this is to say that the ecology of their theology is that of a woman living in a particular time and place" (*Human Liberation in a Feminist Perspective—A Theology* [Philadelphia: Westminster, 1974], 53).

3. Beverly W. Harrison, "Feminist Ecumenical Theory Takes Its Cues from Women's History," *National Catholic Reporter* 20 (April 13, 1984): 18.

4. Katharine Doob Sakenfeld, "Feminist Uses of Biblical Material," in *Feminist Interpretation of the Bible*, ed. Letty M. Russell (Philadelphia: Westminster, 1985), 55; hereafter cited as *FIB*.

5. Letty M. Russell, "Introduction," in *FIB*, 12. Russell also wrote that feminist theology is "written out of an experience of oppression in society. It interprets the search for salvation as a journey toward freedom, as a process of self liberation in community with others in the light of hope in God's promises" (*Human Liberation*, 21).

6. Russell, *FIB*, 12-13. See the volume Russell edited, *The Liberating Word: A Guide to Nonsexist Interpretation of the Bible* (Philadelphia: Westminster, 1976).

7. Russell, *FIB*, 14.

8. See Barbara Brown Zikmund, "Feminist Consciousness in Historical Perspective," *FIB*, 21.

9. Ibid., 22.

10. Ibid.

11. Ibid., 23.

12. Elisabeth Schüssler Fiorenza, *In Memory of Her: A Feminist Theological Reconstruction of Christian Origins* (New York: Crossroad, 1983), 13. See also Carol P. Christ, "The New Feminist Theology: A Review of the Literature," *Religious Studies Review* 3 (1977): 207.

13. See *The Original Feminist Attack on the Bible: The Woman's Bible*, ed. Elizabeth Cady Stanton, facsimile edition (New York: Arno, 1974), and *Women and Religion: A Feminist Sourcebook of Christian Thought*, eds. Elizabeth Clark and Herbert Richardson (New York: Harper & Row, 1977), 215-24 for selections from *The Woman's Bible*.

14. Christ, "The New Feminist Theology," 204.

15. Schüssler Fiorenza, *Memory*, 7.

16. Ibid., 11.

17. Ibid., 8.

18. Ibid., 11.

19. *The Woman's Bible*, 1.12, cited in Schüssler Fiorenza, *Memory*, 12.

20. Schüssler Fiorenza, *Memory*, 13.

21. Zikmund, "Feminist Consciousness in Historical Perspective," 26.

22. Ibid., 27.

23. Ibid. See also the account in *Womanspirit Rising: A Feminist Reader in Religion*, eds. Carol P. Christ and Judith Plaskow (San Francisco: Harper & Row, 1979), "Introduction: Womanspirit Rising."

24. Beifuss, "Feminist Theologians Organize," 3.

25. Zikmund, "Feminist Consciousness in Historical Perspective," 27. As Sheila Collins wrote, experience is "the crucible for doing theology" (*A Different Heaven and Earth* [Valley Forge: Judson, 1974], chap. 1).

26. The essay originally appeared in *The Journal of Religion* (April 1960), and is reprinted in *Womanspirit Rising*, 25-42.

27. In *Womanspirit Rising*, 27.

28. Mary Daly, *The Church and the Second Sex* (New York: Harper & Row, 1968).

29. Mary Daly, "The Courage to See," *The Christian Century* (September 22, 1971): 1108; cited in Deane William Ferm, *Contemporary American Theologies: A Critical Survey* (New York: Seabury, 1981), 80. On Daly see also Lonnie D. Kliever, *The Shattered Spectrum: A Survey of Contemporary Theology* (Atlanta: John Knox Press, 1981), 81-85, and Schüssler Fiorenza, *Memory,* 22-26.

30. Mary Daly, *Beyond God the Father* (Boston: Beacon, 1973).

31. For this see Daly's, *Gyn/Ecology* (Boston: Beacon, 1978).

32. See Christ and Plaskow, *Womanspirit Rising,* 8. Harrison refers to these women as "post-Christian feminists." See Harrison, "Feminist Ecumenical Theory," 18. See also Anne E. Carr, *Transforming Grace: Christian Tradition and Women's Experience* (San Francisco: Harper & Row, 1988), 96ff.

33. See section IV, "Creating New Traditions" in Christ and Plaskow, *Womanspirit Rising,* 193-287.

34. See for example, Starhawk, "Witchcraft and Women's Culture," in Christ and Plaskow, *Womanspirit Rising,* 259-68.

35. Christ and Plaskow, *Womanspirit Rising,* 10-11. See also Christ, "Why Women Need the Goddess: Phenomenological, Psychological, and Political Reflections," *Womanspirit Rising,* 273-87.

36. See Naomi R. Goldenberg, "Dreams and Fantasies as Sources of Revelation: Feminist Appropriation of Jung," Christ and Plaskow, *Womanspirit Rising,* 219-27; and her *Changing of the Gods: Feminism and the End of Traditional Religions* (Boston: Beacon, 1979). See also Patricia Wilson-Kastner, *Faith, Feminism, and the Christ* (Philadelphia: Fortress, 1983), 20-23.

37. Harrison, "Feminist Ecumenical Theory," 18.

38. On these see Christ and Plaskow, *Womanspirit Rising,* and Donald K. McKim, "Hearkening to the Voices: What Women Theologians are Saying," *The Reformed Journal* 35 (1985): 7-10.

39. See Christ and Plaskow, *Womanspirit Rising,* 7-8. The "Revolutionary/Reformist" rubric is now a standard designation in literature on feminist theology. A more sophisticated and helpful typology was offered by Mary Potter in a lecture at the University of Dubuque Theological Seminary on April 22, 1985, when she spoke of the various perspectives as Evangelical Christian, Neo-Orthodox Christian, Liberal-Revisionist Christian, Political (Liberation) Revisionist Christian, Transcendental Post-Christian, and Inductive Post-Christian.

40. Anne Carr, "Is a Christian Feminist Theology Possible?" *Theological Studies* 43 (1982): 282.

41. Ibid.

42. Ibid.

43. Harrison, "Feminist Ecumenical Theory," 18, cites this from the title of a collection of essays on feminism and nonviolence. See Pam McAllister, ed., *Reweaving the Web of Life: Feminism and Nonviolence* (Philadelphia: New Society Publications, 1982).

44. On these see McKim, "Hearkening to the Voices," 8-10, and the account by Ferm, *Contemporary American Theologies,* 83ff.

45. Beifuss, "Feminist Theologians Organize," 3.

46. Ibid. Ruether writes that "the uniqueness of feminist theology lies not in its use of the criterion of experience but rather in its use of *women's* experience, which has been almost entirely shut out of theological reflection in the past" (*Sexism and God-Talk: Toward a Feminist Theology* [Boston: Beacon, 1983], 13).

46. Beifuss, "Feminist Theologians Organize," 3. See also Pamela Dickey Young, *Feminist Theology/Christian Theology: In Search of Method* (Minneapolis: Fortress, 1990), chap. 3.

47. Rosemary Radford Ruether, "Feminist Interpretation: A Method of Correlation," in *FIB,* 116. Schüssler Fiorenza defines patriarchalism as a "social system maintaining male dominance and privilege based on female submission and marginality" ("To Comfort or to Challenge: Feminist Theological Reflections on the Pre-Conference Process," *New Woman, New Church, New Priestly Ministry,* ed. Maureen Dwyer [Rochester, N.Y.: Kirk-Wood Press, 1980], 43n). According to Sheila Collins, patriarchalism connotes "the whole complex of sentiments, the patterns of cognition and behavior, and the assumptions about human nature and the nature of the cosmos that have grown out of a culture in which men have dominated women" (*A Different Heaven and Earth,* 51).

48. Letty Russell, "Authority and the Challenge of Feminist Interpretation," *FIB,* 140-41.

49. Ruether, "Correlation," 115.

50. Ibid., 116.

51. Elisabeth Schüssler Fiorenza, "The Will to Choose or to Reject: Continuing Our Critical Work," *FIB,* 129.

52. Attention here is paid only to those "reformist" feminist theologians who wish to work with traditional Christian materials in some fashion.

53. Ruether, "Correlation," 117.

54. Margaret A. Farley, "Feminist Consciousness and the Interpretation of Scripture," *FIB*, 49. She develops the notions of equality and mutuality as presuppositions for a feminist hermeneutic of Scripture.

55. Mary Ann Tolbert, "Defining the Problem: The Bible and Feminist Hermeneutics," *Semeia* 28 (1983): 119. Tolbert later wrote: "Indeed, along with many of the so-called 'classics' of Western literature, the Bible continues to exercise over women, and other oppressed groups like homosexuals, a form of 'textual harassment,' appropriating social discrimination into textual structures and categories." See "Protestant Feminists and the Bible: On the Horns of a Dilemma," *The Pleasure of Her Text: Feminist Readings of Biblical and Historical Texts*, ed. Alice Bach (Philadelphia: Trinity Press International, 1990), 12. "Textual harassment" is a phrase from Mary Jacobus, "Is There a Woman in This Text?" *New Literary History* 14 (1982): 119.

56. Phyllis Trible, *God and the Rhetoric of Sexuality* (Philadelphia: Fortress, 1978), 7, see also 203.

57. See Tolbert, "Defining the Problem," 119.

58. Ibid., 122. Sakenfeld indicates that the starting point for all feminist theology in study of the Bible is "a stance of radical suspicion," *FIB*, 55.

59. Tolbert, "Defining the Problem," 122-23, delineates three positions as (1) prophetic tradition; (2) remnant standpoint; and (3) reconstruction of biblical history. Sakenfeld's model is (1) Looking to Texts About Women to Counteract Famous Texts Used "Against" Women; (2) Looking to the Bible Generally for a Theological Perspective Offering a Critique of Patriarchy; and (3) Looking to Texts About Women to Learn from the History and Stories of Ancient and Modern Women Living in Patriarchal Cultures, (*FIB*, 57-63).

60. Tolbert, "Defining the Problem," 119.

61. Sakenfeld, *FIB*, 57. See also Leonard Swidler, *Biblical Affirmations of Women* (Philadelphia: Westminster, 1979), for collections of biblical texts dealing with women.

62. Trible writes of "depatriarchalizing the Bible" in "Depatriarchalizing in Biblical Interpretation," *Journal of the American Academy of Religion* 41 (1973): 30-48. See her *God and the Rhetoric of Sexuality*, 4, and *Texts of Terror* (Philadelphia: Fortress, 1984). See also Schüssler Fiorenza, *Memory*, 19-21, and Carr, *Transforming Grace*, 105, on Trible's method, and Ann Loades, "Feminist Theology," *The Modern Theologians: An Introduction to Christian Theology in the Twentieth Century*, ed. David F. Ford, 2 vols. (Cambridge, Mass.: Basil Blackwell, 1989), 2:244-45.

63. Sakenfeld, *FIB*, 59.

64. Ruether, "Correlation," 117, and her chapter "Biblical Resources for Feminism: The Prophetic Principles," in *Sexism and God-Talk*. Ruether notes that "while both testaments undoubtedly contain religious sanctification of a patriarchal social order, they also contain resources for the critique of both patriarchy and the religious sanctification of patriarchy." See "Feminism and the Patriarchal Religion: Principles of Ideological Critique of the Bible," *Journal for the Study of the Old Testament* 22 (February 1982): 54. See also Schüssler Fiorenza, *Memory*, 16-19, and Carr, *Transforming Grace*, 106, on Ruether's method, and Loades, "Feminist Theology," 247-49.

65. See Ruether, "Correlation," 119ff. Ruether sees that Jesus "renews the prophetic vision whereby the Word of God does not validate the existing social and religious hierarchy but speaks on behalf of the marginalized and despised groups of society" (*Sexism and God-Talk*, 135-36). She wrote that "Jesus as liberator calls for a renunciation and dissolution of the web of status relationships by which societies have defined privilege and unprivilege. He speaks especially to outcast women, not as representatives of the 'feminine,' but because they are at the bottom of this network of oppression. His ability to be liberator does not reside in his maleness, but on the contrary, in the fact that he has renounced this system of domination and seeks to embody in his person the new humanity of service and mutual empowerment" (*To Change the World: Christology and Cultural Criticism* [New York: Crossroads, 1981], 56). See also Mary Hembrow Snyder, *The Christology of Rosemary Radford Ruether: A Critical Introduction* (Mystic, Conn.: Twenty-Third Publications, 1988), chap. 3. Ruether also noted that service should not be confused with servitude in that "service implies autonomy and power used in behalf of others." See "Feminism and Christology," An Occasional Paper of the Board of Higher Education and Ministry of The United Methodist Church, 1 (December 25, 1976): 5.

66. Russell, "Authority," 138. She also writes: "For me the Bible is Scripture because it is also script. It is an authoritative witness to what God has done and is doing in and through the lives of people and their history. It is authoritative because those who have responded to God's invitation to participate in God's action on behalf of humanity find that it becomes their own lived-out story or script through the power of God's Spirit" (*Human Liberation*, 95).

67. See Schüssler Fiorenza, *Memory*, 15-16, on Russell's method. See also the section on Russell in Stanley T. Sutphin, *Options in Contemporary Theology* (Lanham, Md.: University Press of America, 1977), 50-64.

68. Russell, "Authority," p. 138.

69. Ibid.

70. Ibid., 144. Russell wrote that "the gift of New Creation by a loving Creator should be sufficient for us to see reality in a new way, so that we see all of creation, not as a hierarchy, but as an interdependent partnership of life in which we work to bring to the world signs of wholeness and *shalom*" (*Growth in Partnership* [Philadelphia: Westminster, 1981]).

71. Ibid., 146. See also her fuller presentation in *Household of Freedom: Authority in Feminist Theology* (Philadelphia: Westminster, 1987).

72. Tolbert, "Defining the Problem," 123.

73. Schüssler Fiorenza, *Memory*, 35-36, see also 92. This approach was developed also in her " 'You Are Not to be Called Father': Early Christian History in a Feminist Perspective," *Cross Currents* 29 (1979): 301-23.

74. Schüssler Fiorenza, "Continuing Our Critical Work," 130. See also her "Toward a Feminist Biblical Hermeneutics: Biblical Interpretation and Liberation Theology," *The Challenge of Liberation Theology: A First World Response,* eds. Brian Mahan and L. Dale Richesin (Maryknoll, N.Y.: Orbis, 1981), 91-112, reprinted in *A Guide to Contemporary Hermeneutics: Major Trends in Biblical Interpretation,* ed. Donald K. McKim (Grand Rapids: Eerdmans, 1986), 358-81; and her *Bread Not Stone: Introduction to a Feminist Interpretation of Scripture* (Boston: Beacon, 1985), where she calls for a "feminist interpretive paradigm of emancipatory praxis." On Schüssler Fiorenza, see Loades, "Feminist Theology," 245-47.

75. Sharon H. Ringe, "Reading from Context to Context: Contributions of a Feminist Hermeneutic to Theologies of Liberation," *Lift Every Voice: Constructing Christian Theologies from the Underside,* eds. Susan Brooks Thistlethwaite and Mary Potter Engel (San Francisco: HarperCollins, 1990), 289.

76. Ibid., 290. Ringe notes that many feminist interpreters are "widening the definition of the system they oppose from that of 'androcentrism' (male-centeredness), where the accent is on an oppressive relationship of men to women, to 'patriarchy' " (289-90).

77. Ibid., 290.

78. Delores S. Williams, "Womanist Theology: Black Women's Voices," *Weaving the Visions: New Patterns in Feminist Spirituality,* eds. Judith Plaskow and Carol P. Christ (San Francisco: HarperCollins, 1989), 179.

79. Toinette M. Eugene, "Womanist Theology," *A New Handbook of Christian Theology,* eds. Donald W. Musser and Joseph L. Price (Nashville: Abingdon, 1992), 511. The backgrounds of black womanist theology are sketched in Katie Geneva Cannon, "The Emergence of Black Feminist Consciousness," in *FIB,* 30-40, where she deals with the struggle for human dignity, the struggle against white hypocrisy, and the struggle for justice.

80. See Alice Walker, *In Search of Our Mother's Garden* (New York: Harcourt Brace and Jovanovich, 1983), xi.

81. Cited in Williams, "Womanist Theology," 179.

82. See Jacquelyn Grant, *White Women's Christ and Black Women's Jesus: Feminist Christology and Womanist Response,* American Academy of Religion Series, ed. Susan Thistlethwaite, No. 64 (Atlanta: Scholars Press, 1989), 203.

83. Williams, "Womanist Theology," 182. See her exposition of "The Meaning of Womanist," 181-83.

84. Eugene, "Womanist Theology," 511. Grant writes: "The term 'womanist' refers to Black women's experiences. It accents, as Walker says, our being responsible, in charge, outrageous, courageous and audacious enough to demand the right to think theologically and to do it independently of both White and Black men and White women" (*White Women's Christ and Black Women's Jesus,* 209).

85. Eugene, "Womanist Theology," 511, who goes on to note that "Womanist theology moves beyond both by providing its own critique of racism in feminist theology and of sexism in black theology."

86. Grant, *White Women's Christ and Black Women's Jesus,* 195. Bell Hooks writes: "Racism abounds in the writings of white feminists, reinforcing white supremacy and negating the possibility that women will bond politically across ethnic and racial boundaries." See "Black Women: Shaping Feminist Theory," *Feminist Theory: From Margin to Center* (Boston: South End Press, 1984), 3.

87. Grant, *White Women's Christ and Black Women's Jesus,* 199-200.

88. Brenda Eichelberger, "Voices of Black Feminism," *Quest: A Feminist Quarterly* 3 (Spring): 16-28.

89. Williams, "Womanist Theology," 184.

90. Ibid. See also Katie G. Cannon, *Black Womanist Ethics,* American Academy of Religion Academy Series, ed. Susan Thistlethwaite, No. 60 (Atlanta: Scholars Press, 1988).

91. Williams, "Womanist Theology," 185.

92. Grant, *White Women's Christ and Black Women's Jesus*, 205, 209-10. See also Eugene, "Womanist Theology," 511.

93. Eugene, "Womanist Theology," 511-12.

94. Grant, *White Women's Christ and Black Women's Jesus*, 211.

95. Williams, "Womanist Theology," 185. She notes that Katie Cannon and other black female preachers and ethicists urge black Christian women to consider themselves as Hagar's sisters.

96. See ibid., 185-86, where she points out that when the nineteenth-century black abolitionist and feminist Sojourner Truth answered a white preacher's claim that women could not have equal rights with men because Christ was not a woman by saying: "Whar did your Christ come from? . . . From God and a woman! Man had nothin' to do wid Him!"—Womanist theology has "grounds for shaping a theology of the spirit informed by black women's political action."

97. Cannon, "Emergence," 40, who notes that this indicates "the Bible is the highest source of authority for most Black women," (39-40).

98. Ibid., 40.

99. Grant, *White Women's Christ and Black Women's Jesus*, 211-12.

100. Schüssler Fiorenza, "Continuing Our Critical Work," 135.

101. Ibid. She also writes: "A feminist theological hermeneutics having as its canon the liberation of women from oppressive patriarchal texts, structures, institutions, and values maintains that—if the Bible is not to continue as a tool for the patriarchal oppression of women—only those traditions and texts that critically break through patriarchal culture and 'plausibility structures' have the theological authority of revelation. The 'advocacy stance' of liberation theologies cannot accord revelatory authority to any oppressive and destructive biblical text or tradition. Nor did they have any such claim at any point in history. Such a critical measure must be applied to *all* biblical texts, their historical contexts, and theological interpretations, and not just to the texts on women" (*Memory*, 33).

102. Schüssler Fiorenza, *Memory*, 33.

103. Schüssler Fiorenza, "Continuing Our Critical Work," 135. Tolbert has suggested employing feminist literary criticism for a "feminist radical re-reading of scripture in the case of *some, not all,* biblical texts." The goal is "to retrieve the genuinely liberational ideology that gives to them their basic emotional power." She suggests certain reading strategies to perform this "hermeneutic of recuperation." For example, with role reversal in imagining Jesus and the twelve as women and a man anointing her head with oil (Mark 14:3-9) or substituting a female synagogue leader and a female prostitute for the Pharisee and tax-collector in Luke's parable (Luke 18:9-14). Other strategies, Tolbert suggests, "will need to be worked out as women re-read biblical texts *as women*" ("Protestant Feminists and the Bible," 19).

104. See Williams, "Womanist Theology," 182.

105. Eugene, "Womanist Theology," 512.

106. Sakenfeld, *FIB*, 62.

107. Schüssler Fiorenza, *Memory*, 34.

108. Phyllis Trible, "Postscript: Jottings on the Journey," in *FIB*, 149.

109. Ibid.

AFTERWORD

1. See Jack B. Rogers and Donald K. McKim, *The Authority and Interpretation of the Bible: An Historical Approach* (San Francisco: Harper & Row, 1979), xix; Jack B. Rogers and Donald K. McKim, "Pluralism and Policy in Presbyterian Views of Scripture," *The Confessional Mosaic: Presbyterian and Twentieth-Century Theology*, eds. Milton J. Coalter, John M. Mulder, and Louis B. Weeks (Louisville: Westminster/John Knox, 1990), 37-58; and *The Unfettered Word: Southern Baptists Confront the Authority-Inerrancy Question*, ed. Robison B. James (Waco, Tex.: Word, 1987), preface.

2. See Robert Wuthnow, *The Restructuring of American Religion: Society and Faith Since World War II* (Princeton: Princeton University Press, 1988) and his *The Struggle for America's Soul: Evangelicals, Liberals, and Secularism* (Grand Rapids: Eerdmans, 1989). In this book, Wuthnow examines the "current cleavage between liberals and conservatives" in the Presbyterian Church as a "typical case" (69; see chap. 4).

3. So Wuthnow, based on data on the Baptists, Lutherans, Methodists, and Catholics. See *Restructuring*, 219.

4. *Conservative, Moderate, Liberal: The Biblical Authority Debate*, ed. Charles R. Blaisdell (St. Louis: CBP Press, 1990). When asked what the conference had accomplished, a presenter said: "We all got together for two days and didn't kill each other!" (viii). A 1987 conference for Southern Baptists at Ridgecrest, North

Carolina, considered the "authority-inerrancy" question for that denomination and drew over a thousand people.

5. David H. Kelsey, *The Uses of Scripture in Recent Theology* (Philadelphia: Fortress, 1975).

6. Ibid., 15.

7. Ibid.

8. Ibid., 16.

9. See ibid., 16-30. Kelsey sees proponents of the "biblical theology" movement as belonging to the "Concepts as Content" section. See 24ff. and note 24.

10. Ibid., 7.

11. Kelsey writes toward the end of his work: "Both 'scripture' and 'authority' are best understood in functional terms" (Ibid., 207). Written before their fuller development, Kelsey's work does not deal with emergent liberation or feminist theologies.

12. Avery Dulles, *Models of Revelation* (Garden City, N.Y.: Doubleday, 1983), 27.

13. See ibid., 131ff.

14. Ibid., 26. This was also Dulles's method in *Models of the Church* (New York: Doubleday, 1974).

15. See particularly his chap. 8: "The Models Compared."

16. Dulles, *Models of Revelation*, 27.

17. See ibid., 36ff. Dulles poiints to varieties of views regarding inerrancy by those within this movement and cites five positions (40).

18. Ibid., 27. Dulles cites John Baillie (1956), Kelsey (1975), and James Barr (1963) as indicating the pervasiveness of this model. Kelsey wrote that there is "a widespread consensus in Protestant theology in the past four decades that the 'revelation' to which scripture attests is a self-manifestation by God in historical events, not information about God stated in divinely communicated dictrines or concepts" (*The Uses of Scripture*, 32).

19. Dulles, *Models of Revelation*, chap. 4.

20. Ibid., 27.

21. See ibid., chap. 5.

22. Ibid., 28.

23. Ibid. Dulles does not deal with liberation theology in his book and says that liberation theologians "have not as yet elaborated a systematic theology of revelation, though they have made major contributions to the theology of faith and hermeneutics." His few references fall under the fifth model rubric, but he notes that "there is evidence that the conflictual and praxis-oriented character of this theology will cause it to become rather sharply differentiated from the disclosure-oriented evolutionary humanism characteristic of the many type-five theologians" (29-30).

24. See ibid., chap. 7. Dulles points to Teilhard de Chardin as fostering an "anthropological shift" in which revelation is related not to "classical faith-assertions" but to "humanization and psychic growth" (99). Dulles says the Roman Catholic Edward Schillebeeckx "cannot be fitted easily in the 'new awareness' model," but that "his critique of the empiricist view of experience would be generally accepted by adherents of this model" (102). See also Edward Schillebeeckx, *Christ: The Experience of Jesus as Lord*, trans. John Bowden (New York: Crossroad, 1981), 49-54.

25. Dulles, *Models of Revelation*, 201.

26. Ibid.

27. Ibid., 257. Throughout Part II of his work, Dulles considers his view along with the others in relation to other areas of revelation theology: Christ, the religions, the Bible, the church, eschatology, and the acceptance of revelation. See chaps. 10–15.

28. Robert Gnuse, *The Authority of the Bible: Theories of Inspiration, Revelation, and the Canon of Scripture* (New York: Paulist Press, 1985), 3. Gnuse says his categories have been chosen arbitrarily and generalizations made for the sake of pedagogy so the information can be presented in manageable fashion. Some theologians, he notes, show up in more than one category (e.g., Karl Barth). He says, "A fuller or more sophisticated study would blur the distinctions and speak of a more fluid spectrum of opinions" (3-4). Gnuse mentions the paradigms of Kelsey as well as a much earlier study by Markus Barth, who saw models for biblical authority being (1) the Bible as sacred literature; (2) the humanistic or philological argument (written language should be the foundation for a high religion); (3) the Bible as a norm or law; (4) the philosophical argument (the Bible as a source for a formal principle); (5) the pragmatic argument (the Bible has authority because the church grants it); and (6) the christological argument (the Bible testifies to Christ). See Markus Barth, "Sola Scriptura," *Scripture and Ecumenism*, ed. Leonard Swidler, Duquesne Studies, Theological Studies, vol. 3 (Pittsburgh: Duquesne University, 1965), 86-92.

29. Leading figures for this view are the Roman Catholics Pierre Benoit, Karl Rahner, and John McKenzie. An important work is Louis Alonso Schökel, *The Inspired Word: Scripture in the Light of Language and Literature,* trans. Francis Martin (New York: Herder and Herder, 1972).

30. The German term *heilsgeschichte,* or "salvation history," is operative here. Gnuse notes that the view has fallen into disrepute among some biblical theologians for "its inability to explain all that occurs in the text" (*The Authority of the Bible,* 74). This includes the varying genres of Scripture.

31. See ibid., chap. 11. Gnuse notes that while christological models are "affirmed by everyone in theory, for they encapsulate the most important part of the Christian faith and emphasize the centrality of the Christ event in some form," in actuality, only a few exegetes and theologians consistently apply the model. See ibid., 94.

32. Gnuse continues the list to include Harnack and Fosdick, because they were "calling for the limitation of the Bible's authority in either direct or indirect fashion as one tried to discern and elevate the grand ideals toward which the Bible pointed" (Ibid., 99).

33. See ibid., 100. He cites Edward Farley, *Ecclesial Man: A Social Phenomenology of Faith and Reality* (Philadelphia: Fortress, 1975), 3-272.

34. Gnuse, *The Authority of the Bible,* 5. He is comparing his work to Kelsey's.

35. William C. Placher, "The Nature of Biblical Authority: Issues and Models from Recent Theology," in Blaisdell, ed., *Conservative, Moderate, Liberal,* 1-19. Placher notes that this essay "somewhat overlaps" his "Contemporary Confession and Biblical Authority" in *To Confess the Faith Today,* ed. Jack L. Stotts and Jane Dempsey Douglass (Louisville: Westminster/John Knox, 1990), 64-81.

36. The Indianapolis conference featured three speakers labeled as "conservative," "moderate," and "liberal," each of whom was responded to by speakers of the other two positions.

37. Placher, "The Nature of Biblical Authority," 6; "Contemporary Confession and Biblical Authority," 66. He notes that his analysis "owes much" to Kelsey, though it diverges from and "certainly simplified his conclusions" (78 n.3). See also Kelsey's analysis as it is presented in Edward Farley and Peter C. Hodgson, "Scripture and Tradition," *Christian Theology: An Introduction to Its Traditions and Tasks,* rev. and enlarged ed. (Philadelphia: Fortress, 1985), 77-81.

38. For Pinnock's views, see his essay, "How I Use the Bible in Doing Theology" in *The Use of the Bible in Theology: Evangelical Options* (Atlanta: John Knox, 1985), 18-34; and his *The Scripture Principle* (San Francisco: Harper & Row, 1984).

39. One could add here the work of feminist theologians such as Elisabeth Schüssler Fiorenza, who calls for a "Feminist interpretive paradigm of emancipatory praxis" in "The Function of Scripture in the Liberation Struggle," *Bread Not Stone: The Challenge of Feminist Biblical Interpretation* (Boston: Beacon, 1984), chap. 3. See also her "Toward a Feminist Biblical Hermeneutics: Biblical Interpretationand Liberation Theology," *A Guide to Contemporary Hermeneutics,* ed. Donald K. McKim (Grand Rapids: Eerdmans, 1986), 358-81; and Anne E. Carr, *Transforming Grace: Christian Tradition and Women's Experience* (San Francisco: Harper & Row, 1988), 105ff.

40. Frei's major works here are *The Eclipse of Biblical Narrative* (New Haven: Yale University Press, 1974) and *The Identity of Jesus Christ* (Philadelphia: Fortress, 1975). Lindbeck has written *The Nature of Doctrine* (Philadelphia: Westminster, 1984). The approach of Lindbeck and Frei, along with other Yale colleagues, often called "The New Yale School," is frequently referred to as "Postliberal Theology." See Placher's essay, "Postliberal Theology" in *The Modern Theologians: An Introduction to Christian Theology in the Twentieth Century,* 2 vols., ed. David F. Ford (London" Basil Blackwell, 1989), 2:115-28. Frei especially is an architect of "Narrative theology" (see chap. 10 above) for which Placher describes Scripture as functioning like "a kind of extended anecdote that tells us about God" ("The Nature of Biblical Authority," 12) or "a vivid personal anecdote" ("Contemporary Confession and Biblical Authority," 69). Frei's contributions are assessed and furthered in a volume in his honor: *Scriptural Authority and Narrative Interpretation,* ed. Garrett Green (Philadelphia: Fortress, 1987).

41. Placher, "The Nature of Biblical Authority," 13ff. In "Contemporary Confession and Biblical Authority," an essay focused on "A Brief Statement of Faith," a new confessional document for the Presbyterian Church (USA), Placher indicates that each of the three models has antecedents in the Reformed tradition (70-74).

42. For discussions of some approaches and trends, see *A Guide to Contemporary Hermeneutics,* ed. Donald K. McKim (Grand Rapids: Eerdmans, 1986); see also Donald K. McKim, "Hermeneutics Today," *The Reformed Journal* 37, 3 (March 1987): 10-15.

43. "Presbyterian Understanding and Use of Holy Scripture," 195th General Assembly of the Presbyterian Church (USA), 1983.

INDEX